Only a Few Bones

ALSO BY JOHN PHILIP COLLETTA

They Came in Ships:
*A Guide to Finding Your Immigrant
Ancestor's Arrival Record*

Finding Italian Roots:
The Complete Guide for Americans

Only a Few Bones

*A True Account of
the Rolling Fork Tragedy
and Its Aftermath*

John Philip Colletta, Ph.D.

Direct Descent
Washington, D.C.

Published by
Direct Descent
1245 Walter St., SE
Washington, DC 20003
www.genealogyjohn.com

Library of Congress Card Number: 00-190978

ISBN 0-9701327-0-0

Cover and text design by
Ann Silberlicht

Author photograph (back cover) by
Terrence E. Barr

First printing 2000
10 9 8 7 6 5 4 3 2

Printed and bound by
Thomson-Shore, Inc., Dexter, Michigan

To the memory of my grandmother,
Frances Josephine Noeth Ring
(1891–1978)

Bright and busy by nature, and by volition good and kind,
like a dependable kitchen garden, summer after summer, she gave,
yet her bounty was never exhausted,
and everyone who chanced upon her steady paths
remembers still, and fondly, and oh so thankfully,
yet another of her many humble wonders.

"On the 14th a new examination was made,
and the bricks and ashes removed,
when the remains of Joseph Ring were found,
although horribly burnt and only a few bones left."

Noah B. Parker, J.P.
Vicksburg Daily Times
March 19, 1873
Page 3

CONTENTS

LIST OF ILLUSTRATIONS, MAPS AND CHARTS

MARCH 4, 1873, 11:30 P.M.

I can see it now, the Ring & Co. store, blazing like a funeral pyre in the swampy desolation of the Yazoo-Mississippi Delta. Through the enormous flames lapping the walls and clawing across the roof, I see the outline of the two-and-a-half story building as though I were standing there, right in front of it, that Tuesday night, March 4, 1873. The heat sears my face and the smoke stings my eyes, though behind me the air is cool and filled with drizzle. It rolls down the back of my neck and chills me to the bone. The monstrous roar, the crackling and popping, spitting and smashing pierces my ears and throbs in my head and I wince from the pain.

For 30 years I have been standing here, shivering in the steamy blackness of Rolling Fork Landing, mesmerized. The broad cypress roof collapses into the second story. The second floor crumbles into the first. The gigantic chimney crashes to the soggy ground with a thud, and a geyser of sparks and ashes and thick smoke billows triumphantly skyward. I have been straining to identify, somewhere within the din, a pitiful tiny scream.

Perhaps the people inside *are* screaming. Even if there were some witness standing as close as I—and there is no one within 50 yards of the place—the victims' cries could never be heard above the clamor of the inferno. Yet I keep listening for the wail of a man or woman or child.

Blinking uncontrollably, I keep peering into the flames to see whether Joe Ring comes rushing out to the safety of the Sunflower River.

For three decades I have been planted here, appalled, and the fire keeps raging, and the huge cypress timbers keep snapping and collapsing, and the bricks of the chimney keep tumbling in thumps that vibrate the ground beneath my feet, and the pillar of smoke and sparks keeps dissipating into the mist, and still I am not satisfied.

I first heard the story of "the Rolling Fork tragedy"—a sketchy and garbled version of it, at any rate—from my grandmother when I was a boy. I had no idea that it would take possession of me. I did not even believe it. All I wanted was a family tree. It was 1963, a summer's day, and Grandma Ring had come on the bus from her home in Buffalo to ours in the suburbs. As she unfolded her cotton fabric on our dining room table, I assumed a chair nearby, a fresh Composition Notebook on my lap, a sharpened pencil in my hand. I was 14 years old.

With a sweep of her palm, the matriarch flattened the creases and expelled the air bubbles. I think it must have been a floral print, something in yellows and greens, because this is how I remember all of Grandma's dresses. Then as she arranged the odd shapes of tissue on the material, I began self-consciously to pose the questions. Grandma responded willingly, ancestor by ancestor, generation to generation, branch by branch, without looking up from her work. She was pinning the pieces to the fabric. But when I asked for the name of Grandpa Ring's grandfather, her busy fingers stopped.

Grandma did not know, as I do now, that his name was Joe Ring.

After a moment of reflection, her fingers went back into motion. She did recall hearing that the man owned a plantation. In Mississippi. A *large* plantation. In Rolling Fork.

"Ha!"—It amused Grandma to remember after so many years.— "Rolling Fork!"

"The man owned many slaves. And one day they revolted. They killed him, and burned the house to the ground."

She picked up the scissors.

"Everybody in the house was killed."

She began to cut. Her voice quivered now with outrage, as though she herself had been there.

"Oh, it was terrible!"

I sat there nonplused. Not by the far-fetched story—things like that did not happen in real life—not in *my* family, anyway. Rather, it was the strength of my grandmother's belief. Gently I pressed for details. Grandma protested.

"That's all I know! Nobody ever talked about it. It was too long ago."

The scissors maneuvered with surgical precision along the pin lines. Their rhythmic slicing measured the silence, and evidently cleared Grandma's memory.

"Somebody said once that it was highway robbers. That the man had traveled to Greenville, to take care of some plantation business. He was returning to Rolling Fork with a lot of money—a payroll or something. They killed him and robbed him, and left his body on the road."

The old woman looked up and glared at me, shaking her shears menacingly.

"But that's not how *I* heard the story! It was the darkies!"

Now she was angry.

"And they burned the house to the *ground*! With the people *inside*! It was *terrible*!"

Her eyes lowered and her hands went back to cutting. She was calm again.

"So the man's wife," she continued thoughtfully, "Barbara"—she knew *that* name because they had met once in 1912—"Barbara came back up to her family in Buffalo. She came up the Mississippi River on a steamboat, she and the boys. She had four boys. But the boat sank— the boilers were always blowing up in those things!—and the baby slipped out of the poor woman's arms and drowned. One of the other boys disappeared, too. Only in the morning they found that one. Floating on a mattress in the river. Alive."

The scissors never wavered. Grandma never looked up. A fine net flattened her grayish-brown hair. She had been a radiant young seamstress once. She clicked her tongue and shook her head.

"When I think of it! The poor woman."

Determined to fill my Composition Notebook with information more credible than this outlandish tale, I returned forthwith to questions about branches of the family Grandma knew first-hand. Nevertheless, the notion had already lodged in my head that one day I might try to find out what *really* happened to my great great grandfather.

Now I know. It *was* terrible. Grandma was right—about *that*, at least. Three decades of searching have verified that there was indeed a conflagration, and the people inside did perish. Only it was the Rings' country store, not their house. And they lived on a modest farm, *not* a large plantation. And they never owned slaves. Burglary *may* have figured into the true story—though certainly not highway robbery as Grandma had heard. And Barbara's riverboat did indeed go down, dumping the widow and her boys into the river. Only it was *not* the boiler, and it was *not* the Mississippi, and it was *not* just one member of the family who drowned.

Still, in the end, it would amaze me how much of what Grandma repeated to me on blind faith turned out to be factual.—But factual in a deceptive way, a smattering of misshapen pieces of the truth, jumbled and insufficient. Stitched together, they would never add up to a whole garment. So Grandma never knew, as I know now, how truly terrible it was.

She never knew that Joe and Barbara Ring went South *after* the Civil War, not before. Naturally, then, her narrative included no mention of Reconstruction, or carpetbaggers, as it did "the darkies." She had no clue that this mass murder—if indeed it *was* murder—was just one more obscure incident, violent and brutal, in a time and place unparalleled in American history for violence and brutality.

I turned 21 before I ventured south of the Mason-Dixon Line. I had already criss-crossed the city of Buffalo from library to historical society, from one Catholic parish to another, from cemetery to Erie County courthouse, culling every fact about Joe and Barbara Ring I could find. But their life in Buffalo shed no light on the circumstances of Joe's demise in Mississippi. So as soon as I could—it was 1971—I shifted the field of my investigation. Five more trips to the Delta would follow over the years, as well as excursions to federal, state and local repositories in other states, too. But it was on that first trip south that I discovered George F. Ring.

There was no George F. Ring in Grandma's account. Evidently she had never heard of him. Yet without him she would have had no story to tell. George would turn out to be the instigator of it all. Without him, Joe and Barbara would never have been lured away from the humble tranquility of Buffalo's Cherry Street. They would never have found themselves co-owners of a building and stock of merchandise in the savage swamps of the Delta. Yet I stumbled upon George's name by accident, in real estate transactions involving Joe Ring, and before I flew home, I had determined that the two were brothers.

Even if Grandma *had* heard of George, though, she would not (knowing Grandma) have repeated the rumor—one of many that circulated after the event—that George himself was responsible for the crime. Grandma would never have perpetuated the accusation—made by certain parties at the time—that Joe had not really perished in the fire at all.

As a boy all I wanted was to draw a family tree. I never imagined, as I transcribed the names and dates Grandma dictated while she cut out her dress, that one branch of my ancestry would lead me to this gigantic building collapsing in flame. I never imagined that I would become obsessed with unpuzzling what *really* happened, and why, and that the only way for me to behold the truth was to tailor anew the ghoulish raiment in its entirety. For that is precisely what I had to do: piece together the historical context of this family story. The events Grandma related had not happened in a void; they had transpired in a real physical place at a particular moment in time. The challenge taunting me was to reconstruct the social, political, economic, cultural and geographic conditions that prevailed in the Rolling Fork of 1873. How else could I identify suspects, and motives, and evaluate them, and determine who was innocent and who was guilty?

The task might not have taken 30 years had I not been hampered by preconceived notions of "The South." Time and again the facts I uncovered failed to fit with what I had learned in school about Mississippi, about Reconstruction and carpetbaggers, and emancipated slaves. On the contrary, my findings, at every turn, exploded stereotypes and contradicted traditional scholarship and common knowledge about "The South." Repeatedly I had to shake my head clear and start again.

Who could have imagined that Mississippi was a land of promise for Blacks after the Civil War? But it was, in the Delta. Who would have guessed that a majority of the merchants were foreign-born, and that most of those were German-speaking, and Jewish? But they were, in the Delta. Who ever heard of landowners leasing convicts from the state, or importing coolies from China, to work their fields? But it happened, after the war, in the Delta. The Yazoo-Mississippi Delta—what unexpected realities lay veiled within that compounded Indian name!

It was the last American frontier east of the Mississippi River. It engendered a new society, heterogeneous and inflexibly stratified. It was the only place where the antebellum plantation system persisted long after the Civil War. The Yazoo-Mississippi Delta, it would turn out, was a part of the South, true enough; but the South was certainly *not* the Delta. Learning the truth about my great great grandfather would require that I abandon all presumption, and examine from a purged perspective the myriad factors that collided to produce the horror of March 4, 1873.[1]

Searching document by document, year after year, I would find George, Joe and Barbara no less troublesome to discern, and no less entrancing once they took shape, than the facts of the incident itself. George F. Ring was the classic American success story: the poor immigrant who comes to America, uses his wits, drive and muscle to amass a fortune, and enjoys a self-satisfied life of comfort and prestige. Joe Ring, on the other hand, was the "unsuccess story" rarely told: the immigrant whose attempts to achieve the American dream fall short, one after the other, and lead only to a pathetic end. And Barbara, Barbara was the first-generation American: imbued from infancy with the age-old values and customs of her parents' European homeland, yet coming of age in an America more powerful and materialistic, more self-righteous and susceptible to corruption, than any middle class society the world had ever seen. Three disparate personalities interlocked and swirling together for as long as fate would allow—or God ordain—in the still eye of a national tornado: Reconstruction.

This book presents the harvest of my long season of gathering. It is a true account, a narrative grounded in fastidious research, of "the Rolling Fork tragedy." To tell the story most vividly, rather than simply relate historical facts, I have re-created the settings in which those facts occurred. However, this is *not* a novel. I never presume to know, and I do not attempt to describe, the thoughts of George or Joe or Barbara, or any of their contemporaries. I introduce no fictional characters, and I depict no action that is not suggested persuasively by documented circumstances. When there are gaps in the historical record, or contradictions, I note them, and evaluate them. Where supposition is introduced, I label it as such and state the grounds for it. Dialogue in quotation marks is taken from original sources; dialogue *not* in quotation marks is insinuated from factual situations. Every line of narration, every word of description that is documentable has a footnote citing its source. The rest is written to convey the whole truth of what all those queerly-shaped pieces add up to when sewn together.

For family historians, therefore, this book represents a case study of how to build historical context around an ancestral event. Depicting graphically how family history and national history converge, it may also remind academic historians that the story of one family often serves to enlighten the story of a whole nation. At the same time, this work at its core is a demonstration of the essential and valuable role that oral tradition plays in a thorough and accurate understanding of the past. Information gleaned from three different kinds of sources is united here to reconstruct the whole truth of "the Rolling Fork tragedy:" written records, oral lore and material culture.

Twelve possible explanations for the calamity are explored, each as it arises in the course of the narrative. These hypotheses emerged over the years as the event came into focus, and each one is tested here against the known players, to see whose thumb might fit the print.

At 11:30 Tuesday night, March 4, 1873, Barbara Ring is at home with her four boys, sleeping probably. "Joseph Ring . . . resided at that time with his family about two miles from Vicksburg," William Muller, a colleague, will state under oath, "a small farm of sixty acres."[2] The land rolls with lush spring vegetation and deep green woods. The house is almost new—built just last year—and stands on a dirt lane that winds out to Baldwin's Ferry Road.[3] In the cloudless sky glows a waxing crescent moon.[4] (Although drizzle is falling at Rolling Fork Landing,[5] newspapers will report that Vicksburg's weather has been "clear and pleasant throughout the day."[6])

At 11:30 Tuesday night, March 4, 1873, George Ring is in Vicksburg, presumably at home in bed beside his wife. "I was in Vicksburg when the fire occurred," he will testify in court,[7] and *that* statement, at least, no one will contest. The bedroom he and Catherine share is on the second story of their large residence at 700 Adams Street.[8]

And Joe Ring . . . At 11:30 p.m. on March 4, 1873—maybe still breathing, maybe still aware—Joe Ring is 40 miles distant at Rolling Fork Landing. "Enough was found to justify the jury summoned in returning a verdict," Justice of the Peace Noah Parker will report, "that the remains found were that of Joseph Ring."[9] The packet Joe intended to board this morning to return to Vicksburg never showed.[10] So he is spending one more night in the Ring & Co. store.

His last.

CHAPTER ONE

MARCH 6, 1873

Two days later on Thursday, March 6th, though it is evening, George is probably still at work when the familiar whistle of the *Tom Jasper* blows long-short-short, long-short-short. The sidewheel steamer is pulling in from St. Louis,[1] and it is not unusual for a "cotton factor and general commission merchant" such as George to linger in his office for a late-arriving shipment.[2] He may well lock up now and walk down to the Commons, as he has done on many other evenings, to claim merchandise.

The "Commons" is Vicksburg's landing, the muddy strip between the shore of the Mississippi and the first block of buildings.[3] Lining the Commons are saloons, hotels, rooming houses, warehouses, taverns, tobacco emporiums, and bait and tackle shops. Spengler's Lumber Mill dominates the river bank just above the landing, and an iron works squats just below. A few tethered wharfboats rock in the shallow brown waters. George's office is just off the Commons.[4]

The sun is drooping over the broad river as the *Tom Jasper* docks.[5] Commands and greetings waft through the clear, pleasant air. Passengers disembark. Stevedores unload cargo and drop it on the parched ground, raising puffs of dust. Drays drawn by horses and wagons pulled by mules maneuver for right-of-way. George would be supervising the removal of his merchandise to a wharfboat.[6]

As the sun slips into the swirling waters, the air takes on a chill.

Bonfires are lit for warmth and light. They crackle loudly. Along the lower deck of the *Tom Jasper* torches burst into flame, casting jittery patches of fire across the inky surface of the water.[7]

Suddenly a frenzied shout, distant, like the call of a man drowning, shoots from the river. George peers into the darkness. The cries continue. Then a skiff cuts into a patch of torchlight and George sees the man, shouting, rowing frantically toward shore.[8] All at once deck hands and draymen, pilots and clerks and hackmen, rafters and porters and merchants, every white and black man within earshot drops what he is doing and races toward the bouncing rowboat.

Now George hears it plainly—his name. The man is calling his name! George pushes his way to the center of the crowd. There, panting, stands Mr. Jaynes from Rolling Fork Landing.[9] He grabs George by the shoulders.

Dead, he gasps, all dead! Murdered! Burned to cinders—all of them! The whole place—burned to the ground!

He struggles for breath. His eyeballs dart from face to face.

GEORGE'S ADVERTISEMENT IN THE *DAILY VICKSBURGER*, 1874.

Jesse, Martha, little Willie, the whole family—murdered in their beds! And Goudchat,[10] the clerk, they killed him, too! Nothing left. Nothing. Just a pile of ashes.

George is dazed.

What about Joe? Where is Joe?

But Jaynes knows nothing of Joe. Then his eyes narrow.

Was a band of armed darkies did it! Killed them all! Then torched the place!

Murmuring to one another and shaking their heads, the men disperse to their tasks. Already speculation is germinating. Jaynes trudges up to 93 Washington Street, office of the *Vicksburg Daily Times.*[11] George secures his merchandise and walks home.

Catherine would be waiting with supper.[12] George tells her. But she cannot grasp it any more than he can. She puts the food away untouched. George, a man of action, is aching to leave right away for Rolling Fork Landing.[13] But it is wiser to wait for daylight. The only action he can take right now is to inform Barbara, so I cannot imagine him *not* striding back out into the night, mounting, and heading out Baldwin's Ferry Road.[14]

Sleepily his stallion shuffles through the dark. The two miles of roadway are rutted and dusty.[15] The hoofs fill the still countryside with a plodding cadence. As George rides up the lane to his brother's house, he sees light filtering through the parlor shutters. The door swings open and the silhouette of a woman appears, casting a long shadow in the yellow patch that fans out across the gallery. A large dog shoots out and races across the yard toward George, tail swishing, then veers off, muzzle to the ground. Barbara—and Joe's Labrador[16]—have mistaken the horseman for Joe.

Reaching the steps, George dismounts. The light behind Barbara prevents him from seeing her features. But the 32-year-old woman stands in the threshold as still as a doe that has caught a scent on the air.[17] A breeze sweeps from one end of the gallery to the other. There is a chill in it. Barbara crosses her arms above her stomach. She is eight months pregnant.[18]

George suggests they step indoors, but Barbara does not move. Her eyes are intent upon him. So he pulls the door shut on the bright round

THE *ROBERT E. LEE* TOOK ON HER FIRST SHIPMENT OF COTTON AT VICKSBURG, 1866.
(Courtesy Old Court House Museum, Vicksburg)

faces of his nephews and leads his sister-in-law to a wicker chair, perching himself on its companion. Now, looking into Barbara's face, he sees the apprehension there.

What words he speaks to his sister-in-law this evening no one will ever know, but the shock to Barbara can be imagined. Surely a hard dread lodges in her breast, and she assails her brother-in-law with questions about her husband he cannot possibly answer. All he can keep repeating is what he has heard from Jaynes.

I picture them sitting there on the gallery, disbelieving, the two figures motionless in the breeze that rustles the new-born leaves of the towering oaks and sycamores. They gaze out over the balustrade. In the black sky over the walnut hills glows a brilliant waxing gibbous moon.[19] George's stallion whinnies and stamps a forehoof, then goes back to sleep.

How can this be? How can Jesse and Martha and little Willie, all so young, so healthy, be dead? And Goudchat, too? All of them, so suddenly, so horribly . . . And Joe?

But maybe Joe was *not* in the store.

Maybe he's heading home right now.

He might show up at any moment!

But there is something more, though perhaps George does not say it right away. Maybe he gets up to leave. On the other hand, if he hesitates, Barbara would see the struggle in his face.

They say . . . Jaynes says . . . It looks like arson. Like maybe . . . they were killed.

Killed?

But nothing is known for sure! It's all just rumor. George will go up tomorrow to investigate.

As George remounts, Barbara lingers at the door, still holding herself, though the chill has passed with the breeze. She watches her brother-in-law's form diminish down the path. At last she pushes the door open. Remembering suddenly, she turns and calls for Lomo.[20] The retriever bounds onto the gallery and into the house. Barbara follows, shuts the door, and turns the key in the lock, twice.

Chapter Two

MARCH 7, 1873

Friday morning, March 7th, George saddles his stallion before daybreak.[1]

"I went to the scene of the fire as soon as I heard of it," he will testify. "I started the morning after I heard of the fire. . . . Went horseback."[2]

Rolling Fork Landing is 40 miles due north of Vicksburg. But the distance on horseback is close to twice that, and not an easy ride.[3] Horseback, however, is the fastest way to get there. Riding at a pace not to tire his mount, George reaches the Yazoo River within an hour. There he dismounts and leads his stallion by the bridle onto the ferry.[4]

Shadow blankets the water, though dazzling rays from the rising sun are quickening the greenery along the shores.[5] The air is warming, and lush with pungent smells. Overhead flocks of birds flutter and twitter.

Drifting across the Yazoo, George Ring, at 39, is a man in his prime. Healthy, robust, successful, he is disposed to good humor, and his deportment is easy and self-confident.[6] Though my research will uncover no image of him, I can surmise his appearance from photographs and descriptions of his nephews:[7]

The Ring men are all slightly over five and a half feet tall, stocky in build, and dark complected. They have oval faces with prominent features. Their grayish-blue eyes are keen, their dark brown hair short, flat and parted on the left. In Vicksburg in 1873 just about all men sport facial whiskers of some kind or other. George's mustache would resemble those of his nephews: an inverted v, tips brushing the corners of his mouth.

He looks down at the Yazoo. The water is high and actually has a current. Ordinarily it is sluggish, but there have been some early rains this year.[8]

George lifts his gaze toward the Delta. Much of the low-lying ground will be under water. Getting to the store will take a day and a half.[9]

As George enters the Delta, Friday's *Vicksburg Daily Times* is already attracting attention in the city:

An Atrocious Murder

We understand that a brutal murder has just been committed at the head of Rolling Fork, Isaquena county, the unfortunate victims being the partner of George F. Ring, Mr. Jesse Moore, his wife and child, also Mr. Goodchaw, formerly a resident of this city, and lately in the employ of Messrs. Shlenker & Co. Mr. Jaynes, the father-in-law of Mr. Moore, arrived here yesterday evening, having come down in a skiff, and brought this distressing news. He says that after murdering the entire household, they set fire to the building, in order to cover up their acts. It is supposed that it was done by a band of armed negroes. We hope to have full particulars in a few days.[10]

No mention of Joe. And several inaccuracies: Rolling Fork Landing is at the mouth of the creek, not the head; Jesse Moore's "child" is in reality the orphan, little Willie Jeans; and Mr. Jaynes is not Jesse's father-in-law.[11] More significantly, though, the piece appears on the *third* page. The editor of this Republican newspaper is obviously treading cautiously with this inflammatory report.[12]

Whether Barbara reads these words and catches these discrepancies, however, is doubtful. Being in confinement, she is not going into town for her usual daily marketing. Chances are George's wife Catherine is shopping for her these days. Venders' stalls are thrown up along the brick wall surrounding courthouse square every Monday through Saturday.[13] Catherine and her elder sister Anna Sprankler would be filing through the swarms of women with baskets on their arms when the cries of newsboys blast above the shuffling and bartering:

"Atrocious Murder! Massacre at Rolling Fork!"

The Hessian sisters, wrapped in black satin, erect and decorous as ever, are mortified. Their lives have always been private, their conduct discreet.[14]

"Mass murder in Issaquena County!"

Shopkeepers grumble among themselves: Nowadays arson is a commonplace! Customers bemoan ruefully to one another: Too much of this kind of thing is going on! Mothers and their teenaged daughters pause to exclaim to fellow shoppers: Women and children are no longer safe in their own homes![15]

"It is supposed that it was done by a band of armed negroes."—*There* is the terrifying part. Since long before the war, the most dreaded nightmare of the whites residing in the "black counties" of the Delta—the cotton-growing counties along the Mississippi—has been an armed Negro insurrection.[16] It would be an easy matter for the masses of blacks to wipe out the scant white population there—if they had a mind to, and firearms.[17]

So right after the war a law was passed (part of the "Black Code") providing that "No freedman, free Negro, or mulatto, not in the military service of the United States Government, and not licensed to do so by the board of police of his or her county, shall keep or carry firearms of any kind, or any ammunition, dirk, or bowie-knife."[18] Searches were made of their cabins, trunks and persons, and all pistols and shotguns and knives were seized.[19] But as soon as the carpetbaggers came into power, they repealed the "Black Code."[20]

Now more than ever the whites of the Delta are living in terror. They know how easy it would be in these lawless times for their black neighbors to purchase, barter, steal arms and ammunition, and hide them, stockpile them, for the moment of vengeance. For this reason, the white men of the Delta carry weapons as a matter of course, generally revolvers or rifles.[21]

Is this massacre at Rolling Fork, then, the prelude to a general

Negro uprising? How long will it be before the armed blacks of the Delta come marching on Vicksburg? Who will stop them? Issaquena County's sheriff is himself a former slave.[22] Warren County's sheriff, although white, is a former Union officer.[23] And Governor Powers—also an ex-Union officer and carpetbagger—can hardly be expected to request federal troops to pit against freedmen![24]

Local government officials, almost all Republicans and many of them black—the white ones are carpetbaggers and scalawags—cannot help but note with apprehension this latest act of violence. Within the walls of city hall, the mayor and his Board of Aldermen, and in the cavernous chambers of the courthouse, the judges, clerks and marshalls, and the sheriff with his Board of Supervisors, will soon be speculating among themselves.[25] Is this an isolated incident? Will the whites now mount a wrathful retaliation? All manner of outlandish conjecture ricochet through the streets of Vicksburg.[26]

Catherine and Anna abbreviate their marketing and proceed directly out to Barbara's. As their carriage comes wobbling up the path, Lomo barking and bounding at its wheels, I picture Barbara hurrying to meet it. The boys gather on the gallery, wide-eyed at seeing their mother rush out like this. And they have never seen fieldhands squatting on the gallery with rifles before, either.[27] Something is up.

Barbara asks for news of Joe.

Catherine shakes her head.

Barbara's face sags.

The sisters do not compound the pregnant woman's burden by relating what they have just experienced in town. They help Barbara serve the boys breakfast, and then dinner, and then they stay to nap, and wait. For it will be, as the paper noted, a few days before "full particulars" come downriver. Word of mouth is the only way news travels between the Delta and Vicksburg. There are no paved roads, few bridges, and most of the Delta's trails are impassable four to six months out of the year due to high water. Neither is there any wire communication.[28]

Perhaps, though, in the meantime (surely the women are praying for it), Joe will turn up at the front door.

It may be on this distracted afternoon that Barbara discovers the personal article Joe left at home. Perhaps she is lying on her bed beside

SOUTH STREET, VICKSBURG, LOOKING EASTWARD OVER THE LEVEE
FROM THE COMMONS, 1876.
(Courtesy Old Court House Museum, Vicksburg)

Peter (her youngest, almost two), and her mind will not rest. So she rises and paces. The glint of the silvery disk on the dresser catches her eye. How strange Joe did not take it with him! Barbara picks it up and presses the lever. The cover pops open. The hands are still, since the watch has not been wound in over a week.[29]

The *B. H. Hurt* pulls in this afternoon.[30] A crowd of curious citizens forms as the deck hands tell their tale.

It was late Tuesday night, about midnight, one of the hands is saying. We were lying at Choctaw Landing on the Little Sunflower River. A drizzle was falling. It was cool. There was no moon. Then we saw the flames rising above the cypress tree tops to the west. The sky was ablaze with a garish, misty, flickering glow.[31]

They knew it had to be Ring & Co.

But it wasn't until Wednesday, a second crew member continues, when we pulled into Holland's Landing, 40 miles above Choctaw, that we learned from parties who had ridden across the country that all of the inmates had been roasted in the burning building.[32]

He points toward the packet, and every head turns. The spellbound spectators watch as a box the length of a man is carried off the *B. H. Hurt* and slid onto a dray. The driver cracks his whip, and the mule lumbers up the bluffs. The dray turns onto Monroe Street, then pulls into an alley between China and Grove and halts at a door. It is the rear entrance to the office of J. Q. Arnold, city sexton.[33]

"Remains of A. Goudchat," Arnold records after examining the contents of the pine box, "supposed to have been murdered and burnt in Issaquena county."[34]

The *Vicksburg Daily Times* will add that Goudchat "was a native of the city of Paris, was 22 years of age, and has been in this country 7 years."[35] The remains are interred by the Young Men's Hebrew Benevolent Association in the cemetery of Temple Anshe Chesed immediately after Arnold concludes his business.[36] For it is close to sundown now, and the Sabbath.

CHAPTER THREE

MARCH 8, 1873

All morning and all afternoon, Saturday, March 8th, George's mount follows the high ground along Deer Creek.[1] The trail is familiar, and muddy; a heavy rain has fallen during the night.[2] Past Good Intent, then Reality, across the bridges over Big Black Bayou and Little Black Bayou, past Onward, then Lou Watson's place,[3] the solitary rider sees the Ring & Co. building vividly in his mind. With his own hands he built it.[4] He knows every board, every nail that went into it. Later, in a lengthy affidavit, he will recall its every measurement. Past David Hunt's Georgiana, then Elgin's store, then Shiloh, past the Widow Wright's place, George examines and re-examines his proud handiwork, struggling to comprehend how the frantic words of Mr. Jaynes could in any way be true.

The walls of the ground-floor, the warehouse, George built of latticework,[5] but latticework strong enough to keep out roving deer, wolves, bears and panthers.[6] All George ever stores there is cotton. He can picture the massive bales, hulking in the shadows, waiting to be shipped. A mule harness, traces and bridles, might hang from a rafter. An ox yoke or saddle or plowshare or scythe might lean against a wall. But it is mostly cotton that is hauled in and out through "two large lattice gates . . . hung on hinges"—as George himself will explain.[7]

There may be one other entrance to the ground level, however—

George's description is ambiguous on this point—a three-by-seven-foot door "made with double flooring put together with iron nails."[8] But no interior stairs, not even a trapdoor and ladder, connect the warehouse to the upper floors. What point would there be for any thief or assassin to break into the warehouse?

But God! what fuel for a fire . . . Fanned by a gentle breeze wafting through all that latticework.

George located what he calls the "main storeroom"[9] on the front of the second story. To enter it customers walk up a broad flight of stairs, cross a shallow gallery, and pass through two folding doors "6 by 8 feet . . . hung on large strap hinges."[10] It is impossible for customers to approach unheard; their wooden heels knocking on the cypress planks always announce their arrival.

Measuring 25 by 30 feet, the store is the largest room in the building, and the best finished. Its 14-foot-high walls are papered and lined with "55 feet of shelving."[11] There are also cabinets "with drawers, say about eighteen drawers, . . . 2 1/2 feet by 2 1/2 feet."[12] Two counters, each 25 feet long, extend from either side of the double doors all the way to the rear of the storeroom.[13] Between each counter and the wall is just enough of a corridor for the clerk to move in, reaching things down from the shelves, extracting things from the drawers. A set of scales and a cash register, both brass, glisten on one of the counters. On the plank floor, along the counters, burlap sacks and wooden crates stand up-ended and opened to vaunt their contents.

Common china, castors, padlocks, silverware, tinware and ironware, handsaws and hardware, hatchets, bolts of fabric, needles, buttons and spools of thread, ready-made clothing and boots and shoes for men and women, boys and girls, hats, hammers, kegs of nails and screws, dirk knives and pocket knives, rakes, hoes, water buckets and chamber pots, everything Deltans need fills the store. George also stocks calomel and castor oil, camphor, liniment, quinine, turpentine, a selection of chewing and smoking tobaccos, quills and ink, writing paper and envelopes, beer and whiskey, and stick candy.

And drums of highly-flammable kerosene, for lamps.

And sulphur matches, for igniting fires.

And axes.[14]

Which could be used to hack five people to death.

In one corner of the storeroom is "a stairway going up into the gar-ret . . . box stairs, with a closet underneath."[15] This half-story attic meas-ures 25 by 30 feet—same as the storeroom below—and is most likely unused space.

In his statements, George does not mention a pot-belly stove. But a pot-belly stove is such a common fixture in every country store that it may not warrant mentioning.[16] Its long pipe, cloaked in gray dust, would snake up and over to the mammoth chimney in the middle of the building.

George calls one room off the store the "grocery room."[17] It is plainer and smaller—14 by 20—with a lower ceiling—11-foot, not 14. Its walls are hidden behind "about 60 feet of shelving,"[18] and its counter runs 14 feet.

Tins and cardboard boxes, green, amber and clear glass bottles and jars, cans, jugs and crocks and cloth sacks closed with drawstrings stand in orderly ranks on the shelves. There are also sacks of flour and corn meal, rice, sugar and salt, barrels of molasses and vinegar, and jute bags full of coffee.[19] Just thinking about the grocery room, George smells its peculiar aroma of burlap, leather, hemp, coffee and cypress commingled.

BOYER'S STORE, ABOUT FIVE MILES NORTH OF INDIANOLA, 1884.
(from Fevers, Floods and Faith)

Besides being accessible from the storeroom, the grocery room may have a solid plank door opening directly onto the gallery. But this is that "unlocated" door of George's testimony, which might just as possibly be situated on the warehouse level. The living quarters—kitchen, parlor, two bedrooms and an office (which doubles as the clerks' bedroom)—wrap around the main storeroom and grocery room.[20] These rooms are all of generous proportions with 11-foot ceilings. They may be entered from the store, or directly from outdoors via a four-foot-wide staircase running down the rear of the building.

"There were thirteen glass windows, sash 10 by 12, fifteen light, no shutters"[21] that pierce the four sides of the second story. What George means by "sash 10 by 12" is unclear. The windows would be double-hung, and more likely three by six than "10 by 12." That they have no shutters is a peculiar feature which may have resulted from George's budget. Evidently he felt that at this height there was no risk in leaving the windows exposed. Yet it is likely that at least two of these windows are located in the facade, perhaps within an easy stretch from the gallery for a reasonably agile person.

Now, as George rides, his mind is free to note, one by one, the placement of these 13 expanses of glass. Which misjudgment on his part could have been the fatal one? Which oversight of his might have doomed his business, his young partners, his brother? George imagines the office, just as he left it only 16 days ago.[22] There stand the two clerks, leaning over the opened scrolltop desk, Johnny Joor—the regular clerk—explaining accounts to his temporary roommate, Alphonse Goudchat.

"They kept a sales book, a cash book and day book," Joor will state under oath. "The invoices were filed away in the store."[23]

George sees the two beds, the chest of drawers, maybe a night stand with crazed bowl and pitcher, an oval mirror hanging on a wire. As one of the beds is Joor's, the other is most likely where George and Joe sleep when either one of them stays at the store. However, since Goudchat has been lodging here for the past two months, where did Joe make his bed the night of March 4th?

Could Goudchat really be dead now?

And how did Joor escape alive?

And if Joor escaped, then Joe could have escaped!

And what about the books and invoices? Surely *everything* could not be, as Jaynes said, reduced to ashes.

Ring & Co.'s predecessors, Jeans & Ring and Jeans & Moore, both kept a firearm.[24] Yet no document or testimony mentions one for Ring & Co. Nevertheless, even if no revolver is kept hidden in the storeroom or stashed in the office, Jesse Moore and Johnny Joor each own a hunting rifle, and possibly a sidearm as well, for protection against bears, wolves and panthers.[25] (Alphonse Goudchat, having never resided in the country, would own no firearm.) George taxes his memory to recall where in the building these weapons may have lain that night of March 4th.

Have any of them been fired?

He can picture the bedroom shared by Jesse and Martha Moore. The bed may be a painted iron bedstead they brought back from Vicksburg when they came home husband and wife.[26] And the bureau may be theirs, too. "There was no iron safe in the store," Joor will explain. "The cash was kept in Mr. Moore's room in a bureau drawer, which he kept locked."[27]

A newspaper reporter will write, "Mr. George F. Ring says there was $4,000 in cash in the store when it burned."[28] That is a lot of cash! The thick stack of bills—which might be the "payroll or something" that family lore will claim Joe was delivering—was locked in Jesse's bureau drawer. Why did George not install a safe in the store?[29] Was that another of his cost-cutting measures? Or simply another instance of his habitual lack of attention to detail?

In the other bedroom sleeps little Willie Jeans.[30] Was it in this room that Joe slept on the fateful night, because Goudchat was using the second bed in the office? Was it here that Joe died?

George envisions the Moore family as he last saw them in the big sunny kitchen: Jesse seated at the oak table, relating to Martha some news he has heard from upriver; little Willie on the chair beside him, fidgeting; Martha removing a cast-iron kettle, steaming, from the oven in the chimney. It is a double chimney, five feet square, serving two rooms.[31] George knows well its unorthodox construction: its brickwork rests on a tall platform, not the ground. If the store is truly ashes now, then that enormous chimney has surely collapsed!

George pictures the parlor, which may be the room that shares the chimney with the kitchen. Certainly a fireplace, and the furnishings George shipped up from Vicksburg,[32] would make this room as cozy as any found in the hinterland of the Delta in 1873. While the other five doors of the second story are all unpainted "batten doors, three by seven feet, one inch thick,"[33] the two doors in the parlor are glass, and painted. The parlor is special.

Maybe it was *here* that Joe died.

Every square inch of that mighty structure is vivid to George. How could it be gone now, vanished? The farther George progresses along Deer Creek, the more tangibly the Ring & Co. building looms in his mind; the more spiritedly Goudchat, Jesse, Martha, little Willie and Joe live; the harder it is to believe that what Mr. Jaynes raved about on the Commons could possibly be true.

Finally George comes to the Charles E. Wright plantation, where he worked once.[34] He reins his mount to the east, crosses over Deer Creek, and enters the trail leading through four miles of hardwood and cypress forests to Rolling Fork Landing. At last he rides out of the lush and shady vegetation and into the sun-filled clearing. "Got there Saturday evening."[35] The brightness stings his eyes. They blink and tear. He draws rein and sits his mount. When his vision clears, he sees what lies before him: an enormous sprawling heap of debris. Everything is sooty and black. Skewed surfaces, catching the oblique rays of the lowering sun, glint like fresh pitch. Everywhere, in sunlight and shadow, lie stagnant pools of water from last night's rain. The acrid stench of wet rot invades George's nostrils.

So it is true.

CHAPTER FOUR

MARCH 8, 1873, EVENING

Slowly, slowly George leads his weary mount around the tremendous jumble of charred beams and blackened bricks. Deformed angles jutting out in places still smolder. Hollows gaping here and there still smoke. The stallion's hooves slush in the mud. The saddle squeaks. The high water in the creeks gurgles. A yellow-green lizard scurries across a twist of iron—a plowshare?—a stove leg? For a long time the immigrant pioneer studies the ruins, circling round and round, as though he were searching for something—a decade of his life, perhaps. Perhaps a brother.

"The nearest house . . . was a dwelling occupied by Mrs. Coker," George will report, "which was about fifty yards distant."[1]

Mrs. Lucy Coker resides with her husband John F. Coker and his two younger children.[2] His elder child, Martha,[3] is married to Jesse Moore, for whom Coker works, fitting and running timber.[4] He is not much older than George.[5] Very likely he is the first person George encounters this evening, maybe on the gallery of his cabin.

Coker says he was "absent at the time of the fire in Vicksburg."[6]

Lucy says she and her mother, who was with her that night, were asleep and only "noticed the fire when it was under full headway . . . about 12 o'clock."[7] The frightful roar woke them, and the children, too. By that hour the conflagration was lighting up the horizon for miles around with its lurid glare.[8] There was nothing the women and children could do but gape in horror.

The last time Mrs. Coker saw Joe, "he was standing on the gallery of the store about 9 o'clock of the night, talking to Mr. Moore. . . . Captain John King of the steamer *Bluella* left then with his boat, about 9 o'clock, and saw him when leaving."[9] That was Tuesday night.

The next morning, though, when Justice of the Peace Noah Parker conducted his investigation of the site, he found no trace of Joe's body.[10]

Coker leads George into the cool of a glade of ash trees and shows him three fresh mounds of Delta loam: his eldest, Martha; his son-in-law, Jesse; little Willie. Coker buried them on Thursday, March 6th, when he got back from Vicksburg.[11] There was not much left of them. But he purchased three coffins just the same, and gave his daughter and her family a decent burial. Also that day he put Goudchat's remains on the *B. H. Hurt.*[12]

As George peers where Coker is pointing, the horror of what took place here starts to become real. Nearby graze Jesse Moore's 10 or 12 cattle. His 30 hogs, milk cow and calf, and 2-year-old heifer also roam the landing.[13] But their owner will never be back.

George looks up and down the currents of Rolling Fork Creek and Little Sunflower River. Their banks are submerged. "The country along the river is overflown," George will explain, adding with regard to Joe, "He could not swim. I inquired as to the probability of his escape from the place."[14]

Was there a skiff he might have used?

There was "but one skiff at the landing the night before, which remained there next morning."[15] This would be Moore's flat-bottomed boat,[16] presumably the boat Jaynes rowed downriver to Vicksburg with the news.

George turns his eyes westward to the forests leading to the higher ground along Deer Creek.

"Then he could not have gone out but one way, through the country."[17]

But Coker shakes his head. No one has seen Joe since Tuesday evening.[18]

"The next nearest house to the store was a log cabin, distant about 300 yards," George will report. "This cabin was occupied by two men,

Dr. J. W. Parberry and an Irishman known as Uncle Jimmy."[19]

Parberry, a veterinarian,[20] says that he and Uncle Jimmy "did not hear anything of the fire until next morning."[21]

What! How could anyone sleep within earshot of a two-and-a-half-story 53-by-58-foot frame building collapsing in flames?

"They said that on that night, they came down Deer Creek in a skiff and reached the landing at about 11 or 12 o'clock. Went to the store and got a bottle of whiskey from Mr. Goudchat, the clerk. That they waked him up to get the whiskey. That they went to their cabin, cooked their supper, drank freely of the whiskey, and went to bed and slept very soundly."[22]

Whether George is immediately skeptical is not recorded. Even if he is, though, he just touches the rim of his hat and withdraws. Challenging Parberry's story on the spot will serve no purpose.

George's inquiry would certainly include a chat with his clerk, his buddy of many years, Johnny Joor. Joor would have headed for the landing as soon as word reached him that George had been spotted on Deer Creek. Charging out of the woods now and into the clearing, the young man's face may be all shadow beneath the broad brim of his hat. But George would recognize the horse.

It is good to see Joor alive and shake his hand! How did he manage to save himself?

Joor was not in the store the night it burned down.[23] He happened to be attending to business matters away from the landing.

Hearing Joor's familiar drawl is reassuring. But what about Joe? Was Joe away that night, too?

"When I left the store Sunday night, Joseph Ring was at the store,"[24] Joor will depose. That was two days before the fire. "I have not seen him since."[25] All Joor knows is what he heard and witnessed the morning after the fire, when he participated in the inquest held by Justice Parker.

What about the company books and papers?

"The books and all papers were destroyed."[26]

And the four thousand dollars in cash?

Joor shakes his head. Gone.

Sitting at supper—in Coker's cabin, presumably—George listens as John Coker, his wife and Johnny Joor all venture explanations based on

RICHLAND COTTON PLANTATION'S COMMISSARY AND LANDING, MISSISSIPPI, ABOUT 1868.
(Courtesy Wadsworth Atheneum, Hartford. The Amistad Foundation Collection)

their *post facto* knowledge of the disaster. It is the consensus of the neighborhood that a band of armed Negroes slaughtered the entire household and then torched the place to cover their tracks.[27] Similar incidents of murder, looting and arson have been reported in neighboring counties.[28] Gangs of unemployed freedmen are said to be roaming the countryside, carrying firearms and terrorizing whites.[29]

Here, then, is the first of the 12 hypotheses to explain "the Rolling Fork tragedy:" "Marauding ex-slaves!"[30]

But neither Coker, nor his wife, nor Joor can answer the questions George must be posing about his brother. I can see them studying their plates, or staring at the children. They are convinced that Joe was murdered, too.[31] Only maybe his body was dumped in the river, and that is why it was not found in the rubble with the others. Not easy things to tell a man searching for his brother.

George stands up. There is still enough twilight to ride over to Noah Parker's.

It must be close to sundown this Saturday, March 8th, when George knocks on Parker's door.[32] The 27-year-old grips George's hand and steps out onto the gallery.[33] I see Noah B. Parker as a lean man, six sinewy feet tall, and darker than his mule. He used to be a slave.[34] Now he is the magistrate closest to Rolling Fork Landing.[35]

He lives with a wife and daughter on Deer Creek, where he works a small farm that does not belong to him.[36] It is about four miles from the Ring & Co. store.[37] Parker came into the Delta from his native Alabama after the war,[38] one of the host of optimistic and enterprising freedmen who migrated in to take advantage of the opportunity here. He learned to read and write,[39] probably at one of the Christian missions, or a Freedmen's Bureau school. Evidently he is a proud and articulate man,[40] and a Republican organizer.[41] In 1871 the blacks of Issaquena County elected him Justice of the Peace.[42]

These particulars, plus the fact that Parker executes the duties of his office with unbiased conscientiousness, make him unpopular among the wealthy land-owning white men of the neighborhood. They are Democrats all, who just a few years ago owned and controlled the county's massive black population. They dislike, maybe even fear, "upstart" freedmen like Parker.

"Bad characters," W. D. Brown (George's attorney) will call Parker and an associate of his in three years, when senators from Washington come to investigate why the Justice of the Peace was shot, "bad characters who were, in my judgment, dangerous to the peace of the country. They were the leaders who, in my judgment, were likely to lead the innocent, inoffensive colored people in the country into a trouble . . . a terrible bloodshed involving both whites and blacks."[43]

Nevertheless, dependent on black labor and overwhelmingly outnumbered, Issaquena's sparce white population—even W. D. Brown—acquiesce to their colored civil authorities.[44]

Parker and George are not strangers to one another. Given their positions in the community, it is likely that they have known each other for years.[45] Their dealings would be pragmatic and unabashed, for neither one of them has gotten to where he is in life by being timid or obtuse. They understand each other, perhaps even share a mutual respect. However, this particular matter is a deeply personal one for George, and this may cause both men—suddenly face to face now—an unexpected rush of discomfort.

Parker first learned of the fire on Wednesday morning, March 5th, from a Negro who had been sent from Mr. Maxwell's.[46]

"As soon as the report reached my settlement, I started for the place, and proceeded to hold an investigation of the matter. No one witnessed the events that lead up to, or caused, the terrible fire. From the testimony before me, I found out that the store and warehouse were occupied that night by Jesse Moore and his wife, Willie Jeans (a boy about 10 years old), Mr. Goudchat, a clerk in the store, and Joseph Ring, who slept there that night."[47]

Mr. Ring was "seen there at 10 o'clock, for the purpose of taking a boat to Vicksburg."[48] The *B. H. Hurt* (as George is well aware) usually leaves Rolling Fork Landing around 10 o'clock on Tuesday morning. But the steamer was running behind, so Mr. Ring ended up spending another night in the store.[49]

Parker pauses to offer George his condolences.

The first thing the Justice of the Peace did was deputize a few citizens to compose a jury of inquest.[50] After swearing the oath, the jurors clambered through the mound of debris. "The bodies of four human beings were taken from the ruins.[51] The bodies were so charred by the fire that [their] actual identity could not be seen."[52]

Parker appointed William I. Chaney examining physician.[53] The tall meticulously-groomed scion of the founder of Rolling Fork knows every white and black resident of the neighborhood.[54] He studied the remains that the jurors laid out beside the ruins. All he could say, though, was that the two larger bodies appeared to be men, the third was a woman, and the smallest was evidently a child.[55]

One of the jurors was Johnny Joor.[56] Familiar with the living quarters, he described "the position occupied by each of [the residents] when asleep."[57] "From the plan of the house and the position of the different beds, and the bodies found" in the debris, the jury reached the verdict that the remains were those of Jesse Moore, Martha Moore, little Willie Jeans, and Alphonse Goudchat.[58]

What about the rumors of murder?

Parker likely glances aside and shifts his weight. "The skull of the one we took for Moore's appeared to have a scar as if a lick had mashed in one side of the skull.[59] Goudchat's head was very nearly severed from his body."[60]

George pulls back.

The other bodies were too badly burned to ascertain how they died. However, judging from Joor's description of the living quarters, "all the bodies were found after the fire where they would have slept, except Jesse Moore's and Willie Jeans's. Both appeared to lie where the door was leading into Goudchat's room, the office."[61] Maybe they "heard the assassins in the office dispatching Mr. Goudchat,"[62] got up to investigate, and were struck down at the door.

So the jury reached a verdict of "death by violence."[63]

Parker gives his former merchant-neighbor a moment to absorb all this.

George knows as well as Parker does that it is not uncommon for a wooden structure in the country to burn to the ground. Once a fire like that gets started, there is nothing anyone can do to stop it.[64]

Here, then, is the second of the 12 hypotheses to explain "the Rolling

Fork tragedy:" "Act of God!"[65]

Usually, though, the inhabitants manage to escape, even run back into the burning building a time or two to salvage what they can. It is unthinkable that five people could have slept through such a tremendous inferno without a single one of them waking and escaping.[66]

The second story was supplied with at least three outside doors—two from the store onto the gallery and one from the apartment onto the rear staircase—and perhaps a fourth besides—that "unlocated" door of George's testimony. Though smoke could have traveled quickly through the apartment, ceilings were high, and 13 large unshuttered windows provided exits all around—a leap of about 14 feet to the ground. If the residents had been alive at the time of the fire, surely some of them, if not all, would have escaped. No, it was obvious: they were murdered first. Then the culprits set fire to the building.

But what about Joe? What happened to Joe?

Parker explains that when he conducted his inquest, "the bricks and heavy timbers were still burning and red hot, so it was impossible to remove them."[67] He will make a more thorough investigation in a few days, when the ruins are cool enough to handle. Perhaps then the body of Mr. Ring will be discovered.

Why can't the investigation be done now, tomorrow, while George is still here?

Parker suspects Sheriff Scott will want to participate. He has sent word to Tallula and is waiting to hear back.[68]

George may well arch an eyebrow at this. It will be surprising indeed if Scott gets involved![69]

What about suspects? It could not have been one person acting alone. That much, at least, is evident. It is common knowledge in the neighborhood that five people—three of them men—reside in the store. No lone individual would pit himself against those odds. Whatever their motive may have been, it had to have been two or three people working together, maybe more, certainly men.

And whoever it was, they would never have undertaken such a perilous scheme unarmed. Any fool would have known that the men in the store had firearms!

Yet Mrs. Coker never mentioned hearing shots. Through the drizzle, just 50 yards from the store, Lucy Coker would have heard if guns had been fired. The reports would have wakened her, or her mother, or the children—one of them!

A steady gaze from Parker's onyx eyes indicates that he has no explanation. (There is no suggestion yet—not at this early date—that the criminals might have used axes.)

And what about the dogs, the two dogs George keeps at the store for hunting?[70] Didn't they bark? Didn't anyone hear barking?

Apparently not.

In all likelihood neither man dares speculate further. How the culprits might have broken into the store. How they might have gotten into the apartment. How they might have committed, one after the other, the assassinations. This would be more than George can handle right now, and probably further than Parker is prepared to hypothesize.

Besides, George already knows the consensus of the white residents of the landing. It would be discomforting, in the least, and perhaps impolitic, for him to debate the merits of this opinion with the dark brown magistrate towering over him. And, after all, there could be other explanations.

The case is by no means closed, Parker vows. He will get to the bottom of it. Such a heinous crime against society will not go unpunished![71]

Does George, worldly-wise pragmatist that he is, stifle a smile at this youthful naiveté?

Pulling himself into the saddle, George feels an oppressive fatigue. The emotional strain and heavy riding of the past two days have settled into his limbs. It is dark.

He and Johnny Joor will leave for Vicksburg at daybreak. But they can be back in four days, if the weather holds. Can the inquest take place then?

Parker expects Sheriff Scott will be here by then.

CHAPTER FIVE

MARCH 10, 1873

By Monday evening, March 10th, George is back in Vicksburg[1] and proceeds straight to his sister-in-law's.[2] Though neither one will leave an account of their meeting, the scene is not hard to imagine. They are reserved people; it is a salient trait of the Germanic heritage they share, a trait manifest in subsequent generations of Rings. Both brother and wife are uncomfortable with the display of emotion.[3]

George could be riding up the lane around supper time, but more probably it is later, when the household is retiring for the night. The precise moment does not matter, because as soon as George walks in Barbara has her answer. One look at his face, and no words are necessary. Catherine and Anna hustle the boys upstairs to bed.

There stands Barbara, hollow-eyed from lack of sleep and very round with child. She is average in height and has a slender frame, that is, if she shares the stature common to her Lorrainian ancestors.[4] My probing will uncover no likeness of her. However, I will find a photograph of her father and elder brother, whom Barbara would resemble. The Millers all share prominent cheekbones and a pointy chin; eyes brown, small, and bright; nose narrow and straight. Their skin has an olive tint to it, and a smattering of faint freckles crosses the bridge of their noses. Barbara's hair, wreathed atop her head or worn in a chignon, would have the deep lustrous hue of chestnuts.

Contemporaries would call her "a handsome woman."

George seats Barbara and lowers himself beside her. Unable to find words, he rubs his palms on his thighs. He cannot even look at his sister-in-law. Lomo paces excitedly at his boots, sniffing.

Barbara stares at George's profile. His face is haggard and soiled. Like his waistcoat and trousers and the hat in his lap, George's prominent features bear the dirt and strain of the last four days. Finally he raises his grayish-blue eyes.

Now her head bows.

Like an incessant drip of water, the ticking of the mantle clock marks the stillness. Little bare feet patter overhead. Beyond the shutters dusk is deepening into a vast cool darkness. "Last evening," tomorrow's newspaper will report, "heavy floating clouds gave warning of approaching rain."[5] Lomo stretches and lies down. The ticking repeats.

Eventually George asks about household accounts. He writes out four checks.—*This* the businessman will record! One is in the amount of 20 dollars so Barbara can get some cash.[6]

Both are weary.

George must get home. He will take care of everything. Barbara should rest. Let Catherine look after the boys.

Yes. Catherine and Anna have been wonderful. And Father Bohmert came out yesterday with Holy Communion.[7] It was the second Sunday in Lent. Barbara's condition no longer allows her to get to Mass.

George asks when the baby is due.

About two weeks.

CHAPTER SIX

MARCH 11, 1873

Next morning, Tuesday, March 11th,[1] George walks into a tidy little office above a shop on Washington Street, corner of Crawford.[2] William M. Chamberlin shakes his hand, and Johnny Joor's, too, when George introduces him.[3] Then the agent presents his claims adjuster, and motions for the men to have a seat.[4]

George explains what has become of Ring & Co.

"I learn that on the night of the 4th of March a fire occurred which destroyed the entire stock of goods, with the building, all books and papers, and everything in the building," he reports. "Jesse Moore with his wife, and clerk A. Goudchat, and a little boy Willie Jeans, usually stayed in the store. And according to the best of my information and belief, all were burned up in the store."[5]

Chamberlin listens attentively. He is a man of 34, a native of Virginia.[6] Whether he came to Mississippi after the war, like Noah Parker and so many other freedmen, or whether he was sold to a Mississippi planter before the war, is not known. He might even have been born free. What is known about Chamberlin is that he is an ambitious man, enterprising and capable.[7] Somewhere he learned to read and write,[8] and cipher as well.[9] By the summer of 1871, when he married,[10] the agent was already in Vicksburg representing an array of insurers.[11] By the summer of 1872, when he became a father,[12]

Chamberlin was writing policies for George F. Ring.[13]

Photographs and engravings of black professionals of the Reconstruction era depict dapper men, men fastidious about their grooming.[14] Many of them are portly—a badge of prosperity flaunted by their Caucasian counterparts, too—and all of them sport whiskers in one style or another. I see Chamberlin in that mold, with skin the color of almonds, and cheeks hung with wooly black "Burnsides." They are the latest fashion, copied from Ambrose Burnside, the Union general who wore heavy side whiskers and a mustache, but shaved his chin.

When George finishes his account, Chamberlin expresses his outrage, as well as his condolences. It is likely, however, that he already has his doubts.

Surely this visit comes as no surprise. The agent would have read "An Atrocious Murder" in Friday's *Times*. Given his professional interest in the matter, he may have walked down to the Commons to meet the *B. H. Hurt*, watch the removal of the long pine box, and listen to the

ENGRAVING OF WASHINGTON STREET, VICKSBURG, FROM *HARPER'S WEEKLY*, 1865.

tale the crew members were telling. Perhaps he questioned a few of the passengers, too. Since then he may even have ventured into The Sunflower Exchange to linger over a foam-capped mug and eavesdrop while George's colleagues gossiped about the fire. So Chamberlin knew that George had gone to Rolling Fork Landing, knew that George would come to see him just as soon as he got back.

George pulls out his policies on Ring & Co.—all five of them.

"The policies of insurance were taken out in Vicksburg [and] put away in my safe," he hastens to clarify, "never were at Rolling Fork, and therefore saved."[15]

Evidently it does not elude him, how suspicious it looks that he is able to produce these precious documents. Does he expect it to be a simple matter now, collecting the $11,000? Surely he is aware that he insures his interests much more heavily than his colleagues do theirs, when they bother to insure at all (many do not).[16] Any insurance agent, even a relatively young and inexperienced one like Chamberlin, would look askance at *five* unusually large claims submitted within *weeks* of the expiration dates on the policies—especially claims based on the mysterious and total destruction of a firm and two of its three partners!

Chamberlin informs George that he will have to submit written "proofs of loss," of course. This is routine. However, given the . . . unusual . . . circumstances of *these* claims, the companies may require more than the customary paperwork. Would Mr. Ring mind making a sworn statement?

Chamberlin sends for a notary. Moments later he is there,[17] positioned behind the plain oak desk, asking George to stand and raise his right hand. The notary intones the oath, which George echoes, then both men sit down.

"My name is George F. Ring. Age 39 years. Residence Vicksburg, Miss. I have resided in this city since 1868, from 1858 to 1868 resided in Isaquena Co., Miss. . . ."[18]

George describes the origins of his business at Rolling Fork Landing, his original partnership with Willie Jeans, and his subsequent co-partnership with Martha Moore and Joe Ring after Jeans's death.[19]

"Our average stock was, from the commencement up to the day of the fire, about $10,000. . . ."[20] The income of the business, in addition to profits on the stock of goods, was warehouse or shipping profits. We charged 25 cents on every bale of cotton shipped, and 25 cents on every package of goods received. I estimate that about one thousand bales of cotton was shipped from the time we began to the fire, and about three thousand packages."[21]

George will need a few days to reconstruct the company's inventory and financial standing. However, reading from a few penciled notes, he estimates that the firm owes about $6,000 due in New Orleans, Vicksburg and Philadelphia.[22]

"I left Rolling Fork Landing on the 20th of February last, came down on business which required my attention here. At the time, and before, I knew or heard of no ill feeling against the firm, never heard of any threats of incendiarism, nor did I apprehend anything of the kind. . . .

"I went up to Rolling Fork Landing as soon as I learned of the fire, and saw that the building was destroyed and no evidence of any goods or other things saved. . . ."[23]

While George describes his investigation, the knock and shuffle of boots along the plank sidewalks of Washington Street ascend through the raised windows. The nip of morning mellows into the warmth of noon. It is another "very pleasant" day, the papers will report.[24] Now George accounts for the five insurance policies.

Four months ago, when merchandise started to arrive in Vicksburg and accumulate on the wharfboat, George instructed Chamberlin to insure it. The agent wrote a policy with the Franklin Fire Insurance Company of Philadelphia, dated November 4, 1872, for $2,000. That is the maximum liability the Franklin will assume on a country risk.[25]

When more shipments arrived, and George wanted additional insurance, he took out a policy with the Great Western Mutual Insurance Company of New Orleans for $3,500. This policy was written on November 8th by the company's agent, J. D. Burch—whom George had promised a risk. Burch's office is across the street from Chamberlin's.[26]

When the value of the stock increased still further, George returned to Chamberlin for more coverage. Chamberlin obliged him by writing a policy with Mechanics & Traders Insurance Company of New Orleans, dated December 5th, for $2,000.[27]

Each of these policies—totaling $7,500 in coverage—insured the merchandise for a period of six months.[28]

To protect the building, George had Chamberlin write two policies with the Andes Insurance Company. One covered his own half-interest, the other covered the half-interest still owned by the three orphans of his first partner, Willie Jeans. These policies expired on February 1, 1873, when George was at Rolling Fork Landing, but he had instructed Chamberlin to keep the building insured. So the agent wrote a $1,500 policy for George's half-interest with the Franklin (the Andes having suspended business), dated February 1, 1873.[29]

The Franklin, however, declined to assume a second risk on the same building. So when George came back to Vicksburg, Chamberlin suggested he take out a policy for the orphans' half-interest with the Liverpool, London & Globe. George assented. On February 26, 1873, Chamberlin sent a messenger across the street to fetch the company's agent, William A. Harper. Harper came into Chamberlin's office, sold George a $2,000 policy, and handed him a Certificate of Insurance.[30]

The two policies on the building—amounting to $3,500—were good for one year.[31]

"My brother Joseph Ring, as far as I am able to learn, was in the store on that night. . . . There is no evidence of his body having been burned up in the building. . . . I have made diligent enquiry, and have heard nothing from him. He has lived in that portion of country for a number of years . . . and [is] well known by every citizen. If he had attempted to have escaped from the place, some person would have seen him. . . ."[32]

"From all the information I could learn while at Rolling Fork, I am satisfied that my brother was murdered and his body disposed of, perhaps sunk in the river. I am supported in this opinion by the neighborhood around the store."[33]

George stops here. He would never be so artless as to tell the almond-toned Virginian—whose gaze has not strayed from George's countenance—that the opinion of the neighborhood is that the crime was committed by a marauding band of armed freedmen. Chamberlin, however, does not need to be told.

The deposition comes to 16 pages. The notary dates and signs it on the bottom left. George steps up to the desk and pens his customary

"Geo. F. Ring" on the bottom right.

Presently Joor stands up, raises his right hand, repeats the oath after the notary, and sits down again.

"My name is John Joor. Age 27 years. Occupation merchant. Residence Rolling Fork Ldg. Isaquena Co., Miss. Have resided in Isaquena Co. from infancy, born in the County.

"I engaged as clerk and salesman for Mssrs. Ring & Co. on or about 20 November last. I have been constantly in their employ ever since at Rolling Fork Landing. I usually slept in the office of the store with Mr. Goudchat.

"On Sunday night before the fire I went to Mr. McQuillen's and stayed all night. This was about 2 1/2 miles from the store. On Monday I went up Deer Creek on business, partly for myself and partly for the store, and returned to Mr. McQuillen's on Monday night.

"On the morning of Tuesday, I remained at the house of Mr. McQuillen; in the evening I rode up to the head of Rolling Fork [Creek], a small village about 2 1/2 miles from Mr. McQuillen's, and returned to his home and stayed all night. This Tuesday night was the night of the fire.

"On Wednesday morning, the Irishman Uncle Jimmy (referred to as the companion of Dr. Parberry) came to Mr. McQuillen's and told me of the fire. . . .

"When I got the information I was at breakfast table. Uncle Jimmy sent for me. I went out. He told me. I returned to the dining room and told Mr. McQuillen and Dr. Waddell of the burning. Got my horse and rode up to Mr. Maxwell about one mile and told him. We went to the store together after first sending a Negro to Noah Parker, a Justice of the Peace.

"When myself and Maxwell got to the store we found Mr. McQuillen, Dr. Waddell, Dr. Parberry, Uncle Jimmy the Irishman, and a few Negroes. . . . I . . . saw that everything was destroyed. As far as I know or could see there was nothing saved, no goods, books, or papers. . . . In a few hours a Jury of Inquest was empaneled, and I was on it. . . ."[34]

After reporting the findings of Justice Parker's inquest, Joor concludes.

"When I left the store Sunday night Joseph Ring was at the store. I have not seen him [or] heard of him since the fire. . . . I have no knowledge or well grounded suspicion of the cause of the fire."[35]

The statement fills four pages. After signing on the left, the notary turns the page to Joor, who approaches the desk and signs "Jno. S. Joor" on the right.

The screech of a departing steamboat's whistle—short-short-long, short-short-long—blasts down at the Commons. Chamberlin lifts his ample bulk to his feet. The other men follow suit.

The agent extends his hand to George, but his gaze may turn aside now, perhaps meeting the eyes of his claims adjuster in a glance whose conspiratorial import they alone understand. Even so, George would not suspect, not yet, that this cordial tawny man of distinguished demeanor will harden into his worst enemy.

CHAPTER SEVEN

MARCH 14, 1873

When George and Joor ride into the clearing at Rolling Fork Landing on Friday morning, March 14th,[1] the sun is reaching the treeline east of the Sunflower River. Its oblique rays, tangled in the branches of the willows and cottonwoods, spread a dappled veil across the landing.[2]

Noah Parker arrives. A few local white men ride in together. Several black men approach on foot. John Coker steps out of his cabin. As the men assemble before the jumble of burnt ruins, the dappled veil draws back, exposing the clearing to the warm sunbeams. Sheriff Scott, it turns out, will not be in attendance after all.

The tall, sinewy Justice of the Peace selects some of the men to compose a jury of inquest.[3] After administering the oath, he dispatches them into the ashen wreckage.

They clamber through the debris, stumbling and groping among the chunks of blackened lumber and scraps of deformed metal and broken glass. From time to time the searchers join forces to lift a heavy beam. They rummage through piles of charred furniture, mutilated merchandise, shreads of clothing and shards of pottery until the hands of the white and black jurors alike take on the same raven hue and smoky smell. But they uncover only a handful of identifiable items, nothing salvageable,[4] and no body.

Then one of the jurors calls out. He has found something. He found it!

The men push and climb their way through the wreckage, converging on the shouting voice. George gets there and braces himself for the shock. All crowd around and stare down the extended arm of the searcher, along the pointing finger, into the litter of bricks. At first they cannot make them out.

Where?

There!

Then they see them. Bones.

For a long time they stand transfixed, staring, until Justice Parker breaks the trance. He declares that these can only be the remains of a fifth person who perished in the building. "The large brick chimney," he will write, "had fallen in the direction where his bed had stood."[5]

Does George curse himself now for the peculiar construction of that chimney?

Parker orders the men to retrieve the remains and lay them outside the ruins. But this victim is burned far worse than the others. The remains do not make a skeleton at all. There are only a few bones.

I can imagine George gazing at the chunks of mottled gray, black and ivory. They would look like charcoal, or half-consumed birch twigs in a stove, or strange rocks. No face. No body. Only a handful of oddly-shaped and oddly-shaded chunks. How could George's mind make any connection between these crude artifacts and his brother?

"Joseph Ring had no watch with him, having left the same at home in Vicksburg," Parker will write, "but his pocket knife was found and identified, also the heel of his boot with the nails in it."[6]

The young magistrate pens his report:

> We the Jury duly Summoned to hold an inquest on Some unKnown Remains supposed to be Those of Joseph Ring, upon Examination of witnesses do Render our Verdict as follows from the Evidence etc. Befour us: We beleive that the Remains found Among the Ruins an Debris of the Store of Mssrs. Ring & Co. Destroyed By fire on the Night of the 4th Instant to Be the Remains of Joseph Ring, who has Been missing Since Said ocasion, 4th of March 1873.[7]

Each juror signs his name or scratches his mark. Then Parker signs and dates the report.

Later he will dispatch a long letter to the editor of the *Vicksburg Daily Times*: "As there have been different rumors in regard to the terrible calamity at Rolling Fork, I wish to give you a true statement of the affair. On Tuesday, the fourth of this month, about half-past eleven o'clock, the large store and warehouse occupied by Ring & Co. was burnt."[8] The Justice of the Peace will proceed to detail the findings of his two inquests, then conclude: "There certainly has been a most damnable deed committed, which has cast a deep gloom and feeling of unsecurity over our country, and it must be the wish of every good citizen that the perpetrators of such a horrible crime will be ferretted out and swift justice overtake them."[9]

George, however, must doubt whether this earnest former slave, or anybody else, will ever succeed in elucidating the horrendous events of the night of March 4, 1873. He gathers up his brother's bones and returns to Vicksburg. He would not wait for the *Lizzie*, which will not pass down for another two days.[10] Rather, he would go horseback, or perhaps in a skiff. If he rides his stallion, a burlap sack strapped to the saddle would contain his brother's scant remains. If he uses a skiff, the blackened bones may be encased in a small pine box.

One way or the other, George brings Joe home to Barbara.

CHAPTER EIGHT

JOE AND BARBARA

How Joe and Barbara first met no one knows. But it is not surprising that their paths crossed. Both resided in Buffalo's teeming and vibrant neighborhood of German-speaking tradesmen.[1]

Carpenters, cobblers, saddlers and harness makers they were, tailors, jewelers, blacksmiths and tinsmiths, coopers and bakers and butchers, carriage makers and—like Barbara's grandfather and father and uncles—bricklayers.[2] They began flowing into the city from central Europe when the Erie Canal opened in 1825. They continued to come during the 1830s, '40s, and into the '50s, building Buffalo into a congenial place of opportunity for the next generation of German-speaking emigrants, which included the Ring brothers. Few facts are known about the origin of Joe and George Ring. But those few facts place them in the same urban craftsman's class as Barbara's family, the Millers.

They were born in the Kingdom of France,[3] Joe in 1832[4] and George in 1834.[5] Natives of the province of Lorraine—like the Millers—their surname and mother tongue were German.[6] Their father was Francis Ring and their mother, Magdalena Kunz.[7] Evidently the boys received some education, because both could read and write.[8] Joe served as apprentice to a master carpenter,[9] likely his father, although no record links George specifically to that trade.

The brothers did not emigrate together. George sailed from Le

Havre on the Ship *South America* and landed in New York on May 21, 1853.[10] It was a speedy but horrific crossing. The "Marine Intelligence" column of the *New York Daily Times* reported that the *South America* had voyaged "36 days [with] ballast and 445 passengers . . . Experienced heavy weather. Carried away foremast. Had 4 deaths."[11] Storms powerful enough to topple the ship's foremast would have been tremendously violent. The four persons killed must have been crew members, as no deaths were noted on the passenger list. Passengers would have been secured below decks during tempestuous weather. George had just turned 19.

For Joe, no passenger list has been found.[12] However, one public record states that he was already in the United States by April 16, 1853, one month before George.[13] Joe would have been 21 then. Except for a single reference to an "Elisabeth Schlitzer, nata Ring," one to a "John Ring," and one to a "Pauline Ring," there is no evidence that Joe and George had any relatives in America.[14]

The earliest known mention of the Ring brothers in Buffalo appears in the records of Erie County Court: on March 28, 1856, first Joe, then George, declared their intention to become citizens.[15] The City Directory of 1857 shows them working for a builder, Darius W. Waterman, who was raising houses all over Buffalo.[16] But Waterman also owned a shipyard that turned out the city's first tug boat, so Joe and George might conceivably have been marine carpenters.[17] The directory hints at their divergent temperaments: Joe is listed as "joiner," but George is "foreman."[18] Joe was contented and easygoing, George aggressive and self-assertive.[19] From this time on, it would be George who led and Joe who followed.

It was George, not Joe, who in 1858 quit his job with Waterman and set out for the Yazoo-Mississippi Delta.[20] Joe took the more conservative step of "settling down;" he proposed to Barbara. At that time Joe's aspirations would have been embodied in Barbara's father, John Miller. John Miller epitomized their society.

He was slight of build, but sturdy, with masterful hands worn rough, and kind eyes that flashed out from deep sockets.[21] A bushy brown mustache cloaked his upper lip, miniaturizing his clean-shaven chin. Taciturn and principled and industrious, John Miller was typical of thousands, of tens of thousands, as his conduct always remained squarely within the traditional expectations and norms of his compatriots. His was the faithful conservatism that allowed a generation of uprooted families to plant themselves in American soil and thrive.[22]

John Miller was 20 when his father led the entire family out of the village of Obergailbach,[23] where Miller men had been bricklayers as far back as ancient church registers record.[24] It was 1830, and John's father had held out against the tide of emigration as long as he could.[25] Through droughts, crop failures, inflated food prices, periods of famine, overpopulation, dwindling affordable land, oppressive laws, and a flair-up of smallpox, the elder Miller had persevered. But when the unceasing exodus of neighbors to America left the Miller men masters of a superfluous trade (and his sons began reaching military age), John's father capitulated. The party of emigrants, comprising three generations, numbered 15 altogether and ranged in age from 51 down to 2.[26]

They sailed from Le Havre on the Ship *Nile* just as soon as the late ice in the harbor broke.[27] Crossing the Atlantic to New York lasted seven cold weeks—an uneventful crossing, unlike George's—followed

DECLARATIONS OF INTENTION OF JOSEPH RING AND GEORGE F. RING, MARCH 28, 1856.

by two days on a paddlewheeler chugging up the Hudson River to Albany (or, to stretch remaining funds, riding on a barge of immigrants towed *behind* the paddlewheeler), then five days traversing New York state by horse-drawn barge to the end of the Erie Canal.[28] By the time the road-weary clan arrived in Buffalo, western New York state was green and balmy.

It was a splendid frontier of virgin forests and pristine rivers, populated still by Iroquois, Aurora and Seneca tribesmen. Buffalo was a village of about 2,500 inhabitants. It had no paved streets, one Protestant church but no Catholic church, two small grammar schools, two weekly broadsides but no daily newspaper, and almost all of its primitive dwellings were wooden—*not* brick. But all that was changing fast.[29]

In a continuous flow of barges, Alsatian, Lorrainian, Swiss and German families by the thousands were alighting and setting up housekeeping. Churches, schools, places of business and public buildings were multiplying, and wells were being dug—plenty of work for bricklayers. Some houses were being built of brick now, too. Commerce on Lake Erie was expanding, and Buffalonians were dredging and developing their natural harbor. The Holland Land Company—a group of Dutch investors who had obtained western New York from the shrewd entrepreneur who had bought millions of acres from the Indians in 1798—was selling lot after lot.[30]

Within 15 months, John's father paid cash for a small frame house on Washington Street.[31] The following Saturday, in Erie County Courthouse on LaFayette Square, he renounced forever all allegiance to the King of the French and declared his bona fide intention to become a citizen of the United States.[32]

By 1832, when Buffalo incorporated as a city, its population had quadrupled to about 10,500. Most of the growth was in the Germanic neighborhood, and John Miller had no difficulty choosing for his wife a woman whose heritage was identical to his own. She was Anna Maria Jax, a native of Gros Rederching, a community within walking distance of Obergailbach. Hers, like John's, was a large family of tradesmen who had emigrated in 1830.[33] John and Anna Maria shared not only a common nationality, language, religion and culture, but neighbors, acquaintances, and possibly a relative or two as well.[34] They might as well have

VIEW OF BUFFALO, N.Y.

DRAWN FROM NATURE AND DRAWN BY E. WHITEFIELD.

LITHOGRAPHIC PRINT OF BUFFALO BY E. WHITEFIELD, 1847. *(Courtesy Buffalo & Erie County Historical Society)*

been back in the forested hills of Lorraine!

They were married in 1833 in the first Roman Catholic church of western New York.[35] It was a crude but tidy cabin of huge timbers called the "Lamb of God."[36] John Nicholas Mertz, a fellow Lorrainian and western New York's first resident priest, officiated.[37]

Observing custom, John brought his bride into the home of his parents on Washington Street.[38] Their first two children, both girls, were born there.[39] Then John moved his family into a place of their own four blocks away: 11 Cherry.[40] It was a small frame dwelling of two stories with attic, faced with narrow shingles painted white. Eventually John would put brick siding on this house,[41] where a son and daughter were born,[42] and then, on June 17, 1840, Barbara.[43]

That same day she was wrapped and carried the seven short blocks to the "Lamb of God." An aunt, Barbara Miller, held her over the baptismal font, while a Jax uncle stood as godfather.[44] It was all age-old formula. The new pastor, Father Alexander Pax—another Lorrainian—crossed the infant's forehead with holy water and christened her "*in nomine Patris et Filii et Spiritu Sancti.*"[45] Two years later the ritual was re-enacted for Lena, the sister who would share in Barbara's Mississippi adventure.[46]

As the "Lamb of God" parish grew, the log cabin was completely encased in a larger brick edifice. Since parishioners performed the labor, it is likely that John Miller contributed his masonry skills. The new building was sober and sturdy and, upon its completion in 1843, consecrated to the patron of France, Saint Louis. A new pastor was appointed by the bishop. He spoke French.[47]

Controversy erupted between the French and German speakers over divergent traditions of lay participation in parish administration. Soon the German speakers invited the Redemptorist fathers of Rochester to come and found a new parish for them. The Redemptorists accepted.[48]

The December 9, 1843, issue of *Der Weltburger*—the German-language weekly—carried a notice that on the following day services for German Catholics would be held in the basement of the Irish parish, Saint Patrick's.[49] This was the origin of Saint Mary's parish, for which a temporary church was quickly built and consecrated in 1844. This gave

THE COURTHOUSE ON LaFAYETTE SQUARE, BUFFALO, SERVED NIAGARA COUNTY,
1816–1821, AND THEN ERIE COUNTY, 1821–1876.
(Courtesy Buffalo & Erie County Historical Society)

way in 1850 to a stone structure in the Gothic style familiar to Lorrainians, with a tall steeple and large stained-glass windows. It stood just four-and-a-half blocks from 11 Cherry, and it was here that John and Anna Maria's four younger children were baptized.[50]

In 1843 the Buffalo and Attica Railroad opened, forming a continuous line of rails from Albany to Buffalo. This faster and more comfortable means of reaching western New York—gateway via the Great Lakes to the heartland of America—quickly replaced stagecoach relay and canal barge. It brought more immigrants to Buffalo, which by that year was a city of 25,000.[51]

Indians vanished from the boardwalks. Commercial establishments sprang up and prospered. Streets were paved. Wooden pipes were laid underground to convey fresh water into the city. Commerce on Lake Erie continued to expand, and Buffalo's harbor was enlarged to accommodate more tall ships and sleek new steamships. A third German-speaking parish was needed.[52]

This time the bishop, John Timon, called upon the Jesuits of Williamsville.[53] He offered them a site on Washington Street next-door to John Miller's parents' property. (The lot had been divided, and a large brick house for the aging parents now stood beside the original frame dwelling, where the family of John's younger brother resided.[54]) The Jesuits accepted, and the doors of Saint Michael's opened in 1852.[55] John and Anna Maria and their nine children were among the first parishioners.[56]

The 1850 federal census shows that the Miller and Jax clans remained as close in Buffalo as they had been for generations in the villages of Obergailbach and Gros Rederching.[57] The immigrants resided with their American-born offspring in houses clustered within blocks of one another. They retained their native language, livelihoods, foods and customs. They worshipped in churches that observed age-old rites, and congregated in a rented hall to hear their own singing society, the *Liedertafel*. Contact with the Irish laborers crowded around the port, or the Yankees living in the more gracious residences west of Main Street, was rare. And they transmitted their identity and values to the next generation, Barbara's generation, in their parochial schools.

Barbara's father, like most of the German-speaking tradesmen, had

St. Louis's R. C. Church, Buffalo, 1850s.
(Courtesy Buffalo & Erie County Historical Society)

little formal education, but could read and write.[58] Her mother, typical of the tradesmen's wives, was illiterate.[59] But they enrolled both their sons and their daughters in the parish schools.[60] At first the boys were taught by a lay man, and the girls in a separate building by a lay woman.[61] But in 1848 Bishop Timon sent six Sisters of Charity to Buffalo, and several Sisters of St. Joseph arrived in 1854. Henceforth nuns would conduct the parish schools.[62] Lessons were held in the afternoon and included reading, writing, arithmetic, some world geography and catechism, all taught in German, and later English with a German accent.[63]

Barbara's education would have started in Saint Mary's and finished in Saint Michael's. Not one Miller child continued in school beyond the age of 12 or 13.[64] Boys were apprenticed to a master craftsman, often their father or uncle. Girls learned domestic skills from their mother.

By 1851 Buffalo had grown to a metropolis of approximately 46,000 people, and the horrendous overcrowding in the immigrant quarter brought the inevitable.

"There has been and still is much and fatal sickness in some parts of the Fourth Ward. . . ." ran an article in the *Buffalo Commercial Advertiser* of August 30, 1852.[65] Three days later: "There has been considerable cholera among the foreign population, and several very worthy old residents have fallen victims to the disease. . . ."[66]

An aunt of Barbara's was the first of the family to succumb,[67] leaving an ailing husband and three youngsters and an infant.[68] Four days later, an uncle died.[69] Then in early September the ailing widower died,[70] and Barbara's grandmother, at 73, took into her home on Washington Street her four orphaned grandchildren.[71] By this time, Barbara's mother had taken ill, as had her grandfather.

The editor of the *Buffalo Commercial Advertiser* down-played the epidemic, repeating that it was confined to the German-speaking neighborhood. But each day *Der Weltburger* carried news of the myriad victims. By September 4th Barbara's mother could hold on no longer. She was 40 years old.[72] The next day Grandpa Miller, the old immigrant *paterfamilias*, died.[73]

Then it ended, abruptly. The cholera itself succumbed. Normal life resumed, but perhaps with greater sobriety. Some hardships could not be escaped, not even by crossing an ocean.

PRINT OF BUFFALO, LOOKING UP MAIN STREET FROM THE HARBOR, 1853.
(Courtesy Buffalo & Erie County Historical Society)

While Barbara's father labored with his 14-year-old son at his side, keeping house and rearing the children fell to the elder daughters, aged 16 and 15. Siblings still attending school did their chores in the morning. As the older ones married, duties shifted downward. Barbara's first adult responsibility came at the age of 14, when she held a niece over the baptismal font.[74] Childhood did not last long in Barbara's society.

Real estate ledgers in the Erie County Courthouse record numerous deeds and indentures made between members of the Miller and Jax families, especially after 1853.[75] Buffalo's charter was amended that year to bring the town of Black Rock within city limits. Black Rock was on the Niagara River above Buffalo, and had always been an arch-rival for commerce. Annexing it spurred land speculation, which was already rampant and reckless.[76] However, the many Miller and Jax transactions reflect a concern for security more than a bid for wealth. It appears that land was used to settled personal accounts, as the same lots changed hands over and over again. Tradesmen with big families did not have much liquid capital to invest.

All this speculation led to inflated land values and then, in October 1857, economic panic.[77] Just five months earlier, in May, Barbara's grandmother and uncle had sold their adjoining Washington Street lots to the Rev. Lucas Caveng, S.J., pastor of Saint Michael's.[78] Bishop Timon wanted to build a Jesuit college, and paid the Millers an astounding $2,000 for each lot! Then came the Panic of 1857 and land values dropped 80 and 90 percent. Bishop Timon was left in such straits that the doors of Canisius College—erected on the Miller land and more— would not open until 1872.[79]

A sizable black community was forming in the city, as Buffalo became a major "station" on the Underground Railroad to Canada. Even within the closely circumscribed world of the Germanic quarter, Barbara knew at least two black people. They rented rooms in Conrad Kuhn's house, right next-door to 11 Cherry. Benjamin Scott, a native of Virginia who could neither read nor write, held the job of "City cryer."[80] Frances Wiggins, born in New York State, may have done domestic work or taken in laundry.[81] Their household was a tiny isle of Africa in a Teutonic ocean.

Less conspicuous neighbors were the Ring brothers. However they

may have met, Joe and Barbara were married on November 25, 1858[82]—
a cold Thursday according to the *Buffalo Commercial Advertiser*.[83] Wind
at twelve miles an hour skimmed off the lake. But the sun shone, the
sky was like crystal, and by afternoon the temperature reached 37
degrees. (It was another of the traditions carried over from the Old
Country, I suspect, marrying in the dead of winter. Almost all of
Barbara's relatives wed in months when the ground lay frozen beneath
the snow, and bricklayers had little work to do.)

Joe and Barbara exchanged vows in St. Michael's before the Rev.
Lucas Caveng, in the presence of two male witnesses and 16-year-old
Lena.[84] The sanctuary was probably filled with the bride's family, which
nonetheless represented the groom's heritage as well. It was the society of John Miller, the German-speaking tradesmen's class. So it was fitting that Joe's brother was not there, because George was already far
distanced from this society.

Barbara had no cause yet to suspect that she would ever leave this
cradle of faith and custom. City Directories of 1859 and 1860 list "Jos.
Ring, carpenter, house Cherry near Maple"—placing the newly-weds
right on the same block as Papa.[85] Furthermore, when circumstances
would pull Barbara away, twice, she would return, twice. Never would
she grow beyond her roots.

Joe's life, on the other hand, would be a series of attempts to move
beyond the confines of this rigid heritage. First, he left his homeland.
Now, an American citizen (having completed the naturalization process
in Erie County Sessions Court on April 16, 1858),[86] he would make his
next "new beginning." Only *this* one—Joe could not have foreseen it, of
course—would expose his family to the perils of civil war.

CHAPTER NINE

THE WAR, NORTH

Perhaps it was a particularly dreary winter that prompted Joe to make the move. Buffalo's long months of gray cloudcover must have been especially oppressive after Barbara's first child died. It was a girl, born January 29, 1860, and named Magdalena Barbara (for her godmother, Lena, and her mother, as custom dictated).[1] A little cross penned above the infant's name in the baptismal register indicates that she died soon afterwards.

It is hard to imagine Barbara leaving Papa and her brothers and sisters—and the sanctified patch of earth that cradled her child—willingly. More likely, she would have voiced reservations, hoping that her starry-eyed husband's big ideas would dissipate when the weather broke and he went back to work. But when the last dirty snow melted away, Joe's determination did not. I picture him charming Barbara with a smile, rather than asserting his prerogative as head of the household.

Joe Ring was a good looking man, if his physical traits may be inferred from those of his sons.[2] No photograph or description of him survives. But his boys who lived to maturity all had dark brown hair, and I picture Joe's a bit tousled like a lad's, and his waistcoat and trousers a bit mussed, too. His mustache would have been wispy, the color of strong coffee, and his gray-blue eyes ingenuous and playful. The Ring men were all of medium height—just over five and a half feet—and rounded rather than square in features and build. The facts of Joe's life indicate that he enjoyed the same flush of health and vitality as his brother George.

He was the type of man to clench between his teeth a corn-cob pipe—as at least one of his sons always did[3]—even as he gabbed or grinned, and long after the bowl had gone cold. In common with his boys and his brother, Joe seems to have radiated an unaffected affability that made it impossible not to like him. His easy-going disposition would have charmed women and inspired trust in men, and Joe would have been well aware of it, kidding and teasing everybody good-naturedly.[4]

So as soon as Buffalo's harbor was free of ice,[5] Barbara found herself on a steamer chopping its way through an eclectic assemblage of vessels, skirting the lighthouse, and braving the windy expanse of Lake Erie. Surely her face betrayed some misgiving as she watched the thin line of her native city disintegrate into sky and sea. She was the first Miller to break away since the clan had come over on the Ship *Nile* a generation ago.[6]

Great Lakes steamers looped from port to port along the southern coast of Lake Erie, calling at Angola and Dunkirk, New York; Erie, Pennsylvania; Ashtabula and Cleveland, Ohio; and westward.[7] The shore was never out of sight. If this journey did not arouse in Barbara a sense of adventure, at least the novelties of travel would have distracted her.

Trains connecting the Great Lakes to the Ohio River had started running in 1853, when the Cincinnati, Hamilton and Dayton Railroad joined with the Mad River and Lake Erie Railroad.[8] Rail service with Cleveland followed soon thereafter. Joe and Barbara would have come ashore in Cleveland and ridden the train down to Dayton, transferring there to the line that ran into the bustling metropolis Joe had selected for a fresh start.

"Gateway to the West," that was Cincinnati: six miles of riverfront along the Ohio. Arriving at the CH&D depot downtown, the Rings might have glimpsed a sampling of the 2,985 steamboats that visited the landing that year—averaging one every three hours. Cincinnati was a younger city than Buffalo, but already, with a population of 155,000, close to twice its size. (Only Boston, New York, Philadelphia, Baltimore and New Orleans outranked it.) The 1860 federal census numbered its

Germanic community at 43,931; that was better than half the total population of Buffalo (and four times Vicksburg's!). There was no more
thoroughly German city in North America. And it was booming.[9]

Joe and Barbara settled in the Germanic community forming around
St. Augustine's Church on Bank Street,[10] probably renting a two-room
flat in someone's home. That was more than a mile from downtown, and
quite a ways up in the hills along the northern rim of the city. But horse-
car service had been initiated the previous year, because the Rings were
only two of thousands of Germanic newcomers settling on these hills.
Burgeoning neighborhoods such as Mount Auburn, Walnut Hills and
Corryville would rapidly be enfolded into city limits. In all likelihood Joe
and Barbara knew other Buffalonians who had already made the move
to the German-speaking enclave of Cincinnati.[11]

Securing employment would have required little effort of a carpen-
ter/joiner such as Joe, especially if he had acquaintances in town.
Commerce on the Ohio was at an all-time high, and building steamships
for the inland rivers provided jobs for thousands. (The *Jennie Howell*,
fateful ship in Barbara's future, would be built here in 1869.[12]) Furniture
manufacturing was another major industry, because of the ready avail-
ability of a variety of woods, and construction sites were everywhere. At
the foot of Vine Street, and on the opposite side of the Ohio in
Covington, Kentucky, two enormous stone piers destined to support the
longest suspension bridge in the world were rising. The designer was a
brilliant German-American engineer, Washington Augustus Roebling.[13]

Less than a year were the Rings settled in their new home when they
may have seen and heard the president-elect. It was February 12, 1861,
and Abraham Lincoln paused in Cincinnati on the way to his inaugura-
tion in Washington.[14] That Tuesday was unseasonably warm, 54 degrees
by noon, and not a cloud in the sky. The neighborhood around the
Indianapolis & Cincinnati Railroad Depot was a panoply of waving
American flags, red, white and blue bunting, and banners painted with
patriotic slogans. The crowd of festive spectators was enormous by mid-
afternoon, when a 34 cannon salute heralded the arrival of the soon-to-
be chief of state.[15]

A military parade with three bands, followed by a procession of
formally-attired civil dignitaries, escorted Lincoln's carriage—drawn

by six white horses—to the Burnet House. Everywhere milled throngs of cheering people. They overflowed onto the thoroughfares, waved in wide-open windows, and hurrahed from balconies, fire escapes and rooftops. The lanky Kentuckian in stovepipe hat, standing a head taller than everyone else, addressed an enormous crush of citizens from the terrace of the famous hotel. Seven southern states had already seceded and formed the Confederate States of America, yet this man who would soon be inaugurated as commander-in-chief hoped still for reconciliation.[16]

His listeners shouted exhuberant support. Cincinnatians were actively anti-slavery. Their city was a headquarters of the Underground Railroad and home to a large community of free blacks. Nonetheless, their economic mainstay was commerce with the South.[17]

That evening the president-elect attended a gala reception, and in the morning he resumed his journey.[18]

Two months later, when Lincoln called for volunteers to put down the rebellion, young men of Cincinnati by the thousands flocked to recruiting stations. Units were raised in a flush of excitement. Flags, fifes and drums, and swords and sashes for the officers, were purchased by the citizenry and presented with touching ceremony. Spectators gathered at the county fair grounds—hastily converted into Camp Harrison—to watch the new troops march and drill. There were dress parades and martial music. An entire regiment of German volunteers, nicknamed the Turners, formed.[19] Joe, however, did not join their ranks.

Black volunteers would be turned away until July of 1862, when Congress authorized the enlistment of "persons of African descent." Then companies of colored troops would form up fast.[20]

Trade with the South ceased, and the city's herculean industries switched to equipping and provisioning the Union troops. Founderies converted to munitions plants. Shipyards shifted to refitting old riverboats as gunboats, then proceeded to build scores of new gunboats, troop transports and ironclads. Factories ran at full capacity turning out clothing, shoes, harness, wagons and other war materiel. Ironworks produced rifles and cannon. Packing houses processed 600,000 hogs a year. Cincinnati was flush with wartime prosperity![21]

Then the grim reality of war came home. Wounded sons, maimed

LITHOGRAPHIC PRINT OF BURNET HOUSE, CINCINNATI, BUILT IN 1852.
(Courtesy Prints & Photographs Division, Library of Congress)

brothers, and stark diamond-shaped coffins containing the mortal remains of fathers, began arriving via the rails and the river. Suddenly Cincinnatians realized what an enticing strategic target their city was. Fear of invasion now stirred beneath the surface normalcy of their daily occupations. Construction on Roebling's spectacular link to Dixie stopped.[22]

In the spring of 1862, however, the victory of the Union ironclad, *U.S.S. Monitor*, over the Confederate ironclad, *C.S.S. Virginia* (formerly *U.S.S. Merrimac*), provided a respite of reassurance for Cincinnatians,[23] and changes came to the Ring household. First, on March 22nd, Barbara delivered her second child, another girl.[24] The baby was baptized Anna Maria—her godmother, Anna Maria Beck, presumably a neighbor. But the infant was not carried to Saint Augustine's until the 30th, which may indicate that she was not in the best of health. Besides, no godfather is named in the baptismal record, suggesting that Anna's may have been an emergency baptism *"in extremis." This* little girl, however, unlike Barbara's first, lived.

But the next change was the shocking one: Lena showed up!—With a clean-shaven and well-dressed gentleman who shared the slim build and slender features of the Millers, as well as their olive complexion and chestnut hair.[25] This was Hank Weber, her husband! They had eloped.[26] Whether Papa had forbidden their marriage, or Lena simply assumed he would, cannot be ascertained today. But the cause seems evident: Hank was not Catholic.

Henry Nicholas Weber was a 20-year-old Evangelical Lutheran, the younger son of a Lorrainian tailor of Buffalo.[27] But he never learned his father's trade, and he scorned social conventions against marrying a woman of a different faith (who was also his senior, though only by days). Natural ability and self-confidence seem to have compensated for scant formal schooling. But it appears that Hank was too independent-minded to take orders for long. His employment situations were always short-lived.[28]

The Webers stayed. Once Barbara absorbed the shock, she would have derived enormous delight from her sister's company. Besides, Lena lightened every household chore, a blessing now that there was little Annie to care for. But this period of tranquility was soon brought to a close by the war.

Throughout July a Confederate colonel named John Hunt Morgan was conducting daring and devastating cavalry raids in Kentucky.[29] His exploits were unpredictable and bold, reaching into counties bordering on the Ohio. As Union officers scrambled to secure their hold on northern Kentucky, Cincinnatians worried: Was the dreaded invasion at hand?

Then in August a Confederate army under General E. Kirby Smith was detected moving through central Kentucky.[30] Apprehension escalated: What direction would the Rebel army take? Eagerly the city's inhabitants devoured the latest dispatches printed in the *Daily Commercial* and the *Volksfreund*. By September it was clear: Smith's troops were heading north!

General Lewis Wallace arrived to take charge of the city's defenses. "Martial law was proclaimed, all business suspended, all citizens were ordered to assemble for the assignment of tasks, and the principle was adopted, 'Citizens for the labor, soldiers for the battle.'"[31]

Ohio's Governor Tod rushed to the city and on September 2nd informed the military: "Fearing invasion at all points on the Ohio I have called on the loyal men in the surrounding counties to organize themselves into companies and regiments for their defense."[32]

Trainloads of country men started pulling into the city's depots. Because of the long, antiquated hunting rifles many of them carried, someone called them "Squirrel Hunters," and the name stuck.[33] They were a rag-tag home guard, but determined. They marched and drilled constantly, raising such clouds of dust that the streets had to be hosed down. The names of Joe Ring and Hank Weber, however, do not appear on their rosters.

On September 5th Wallace received this order: "The organization of all able-bodied citizens into working corps will be perfected with the aid of the city authorities and details made from day to day, as may be necessary, so as to equalize the burden and require from each man a proper amount of labor."[34] Two "able-bodied citizens" who may have been impressed into service were Joe Ring and Hank Weber.

By this time Union regiments were converging on Cincinnati. Wallace established rings of defense around the city. On Mount Adams,

Price Hill and other strategic high points he built fortifications. In one 24-hour period he flung a pontoon bridge of coal barges across the Ohio, from the foot of one of Roebling's unfinished stone piers to the other. Then he deployed troops, artillery and supply wagons across the bridge to Covington. There guns were mounted on the heights, and three miles of entrenchments were channeled into the ground around the city. Meanwhile, ranks of Union troops continued to march into Cincinnati.[35]

More civilian laborers were needed. On September 9th military authorities in the city were ordered to ". . . send 3,000 citizens . . . across the river . . . to report to General Wallace. They will remain on fatigue duty until further orders. You will, if necessary, impress citizens to the number stated."[36] Surely Joe Ring and Hank Weber, if they had managed until now to avoid getting involved, could not have evaded the authorities any longer!

In addition, Governor Tod issued another call to arms: ". . . I have called upon all the armed Minute-men of the State, requesting each to take two days' cooked rations and a blanket."[37] Citizen soldiers poured into Cincinnati by the thousands.

Two days later came word that "Kirby Smith is in front of Cincinnati with a force variously estimated from 15,000 to 30,000."[38]

The city held its breath.

But no invaders crossed the river.

Informed of the speedy and massive preparations made against him, Smith had retreated.

"The skedaddle is complete," General Wallace was informed on September 12th, "every sign of a rout."[39]

The Squirrel Hunters were released with commendation (and reimbursement for their train fare),[40] and civilians were sent home. For the first night in two weeks, Rings and Webers and neighbors slept peacefully. Cincinnati settled back into the routine of overtly normal life.

That winter Lena gave birth to a son. Born February 26, 1863, the infant was named Edward Joseph, with Joe and Barbara standing as godparents.[41] Since the baptism took place in St. Francis Seraph Roman Catholic Church, which was quite a distance from St. Augustine's, it appears that the Webers may not have resided with the Rings. Or perhaps both families had moved together from the one parish to the other.

LITHOGRAPHIC PRINT OF GENERAL LEWIS WALLACE'S PONTOON BRIDGE ACROSS THE OHIO RIVER, 1862.
(Courtesy Prints & Photographs Division, Library of Congress)

What is certain is that by the summer of 1863 the Rings, at least, were residing in downtown Cincinnati at 233 West Sixth Street. Because that was Joe's address when he was enrolled for the draft.

On March 3, 1863, President Lincoln signed the country's first mandatory conscription law.[42] All able-bodied men, white and colored, between 20 and 45 were required to enroll, and all those inducted were to serve for three years. Joe was registered on page 276 of the "Consolidated List, Class I, Second Congressional District, Ohio," dated June 25th: "233 Sixth Street, Ring Joseph, 30, white, Carpenter, Married, Germany [incorrect birthplace]," with no prior military service noted and no remarks regarding any kind of special status or exemption.[43]

The initial "call up" of draftees was made on July 11th, and editorials in the *Daily Commerical* commended the equitableness of the law and encouraged compliance.[44] However, next to long columns of "Casualties in Ohio Regiments at Gettysburg" and "The Terms of the Surrender of Vicksburg," appeared reports of "The Anti-Conscription Riots in N.Y."[45] For many Americans, involuntary military service was anathema. The law, dissenters charged, favored the wealthy and was full of opportunity for shirking.[46]

Any man who could pay a "commutation fee" of $300, or hire a substitute, was exempt. Men could also be exempted because of "hardship," such as being the sole support of aged parents, or the eldest brother in a large family of young children. Physical disability was another cause for exemption. And while the law applied to U.S. citizens and alien residents who had declared their intention to become citizens, it ignored the many thousands of robust immigrants who had never initiated the naturalization process.[47]

Neither Joe Ring, a naturalized citizen, nor Hank Weber, a natural born citizen, was ever called up, most likely because Cincinnati's draft quota was always filled by volunteers.[48] Federal, state and local organizations offered cash bounties to enlistees, and many men—single men years younger than Joe and Hank—opted for the cash.[49] Therefore, in spite of the strong opposition to mandatory conscription demonstrated elsewhere, in Cincinnati the draft was implemented without a single disturbance.[50]

Directly across the street from the house Joe and Barbara rented

stood "two German-style market houses."[51] These constituted the western half of the two-block Sixth Street Market. The eastern half was an
expanse of pavement where vendors set up their stalls. Barbara must
have paid for this shopping convenience by enduring a great deal of
tumult on market days.

Only one "Joseph Ring" appears in the Cincinnati City Directory of
1863, with 133 Race Street as his address of employment.[52] That was
seven blocks from the Rings' residence, and just around the corner
from the Burnet House. Lining Race Street were businesses employing
builders, architects, painters, cabinet makers, and carpenters and joiners like Joe.[53]

But number 133 employed none of these. It was "Harrison &
Wilson's Coffee and Spice Mills,"[54] and the occupation of this "Joseph
Ring" is given as "watchman." If this watchman was Joe—which is all
but certain—why was he employed in an unskilled job when more than
ample work in his trade was available? Was Joe, for one reason or another, not making progress toward the goal that had lured him to
Cincinnati? Were things not working out as he had hoped?

Whatever work Joe was doing, it was certainly interrupted in July,
when Cincinnati's veneer of normalcy was pierced a second time by the
war. Once again the city's residents were following the exploits of the
notorious John Hunt Morgan—a general now—in Kentucky. The press
reported the Rebel cavalry at 6,000 to 8,000 men, which sent the civilian
population into a panic. The raiders were galloping madly ahead of federal pursuers, right for the Ohio River.[55]

On July 8th they crossed into Indiana, and residents of Ohio braced
for the worst. Four days later, as feared, Morgan veered eastward,
toward Cincinnati![56]

Once again martial law was proclaimed. Once again Governor Tod
called out the militia. This time, though, since the city's defenses were
already in place, no civilians were pressed into service. Residents
stocked up on groceries and dry goods and ammunition, cleaned their
firearms, and barricaded themselves in their houses. Business establishments closed. Streets were deserted.[57]

The city froze in expectation.

But the Rebel raiders, who actually numbered only 2,460, swept right past the hills of northern Cincinnati. They proceeded to burn and pillage an erratic swatch across southern Ohio. Union troops chased in hot pursuit, and all along the route local residents and sharpshooters harried the southern invaders. Morgan was swift and evasive. But he was unable to get his men back across the Ohio River to safety.[58]

On July 17th General Ambrose Burnside, commandant of the Military Department of the Ohio, reported: "All my cavalry is after Morgan. I have one brigade of infantry and some artillery on boats to prevent his crossing, and if he does not go too high up for our boats to go, we can probably prevent his crossing."[59]

Three days later: "Our forces have been harrassing him, and up to the last advices we have captured more than half of his force, all of his artillery, destroyed all his wagon trains, and killed some 200. . . . His command is completely broken up and scattered, and constantly surrendering in small bodies."[60]

Finally, on July 26, 1863, Burnside received this message from General Shackelford: "By the blessing of Almighty God, I have succeeded in capturing General John H. Morgan, Colonel Cluke, and the balance of the command, amounting to about 400 prisoners. I will start with Morgan and staff in first train to Cincinnati, and await the general's order for transportation for the balance."[61]

The Confederates were imprisoned in Cincinnati, though some of them would succeed in escaping to fight again.[62]

Perhaps this second threat of invasion came closer to home than Barbara could bear. Or it might have been Joe who could not abide seeing his wife and daughter exposed to such peril. Either he failed to find whatever it was that had drawn him to Cincinnati, or he decided it was not worth the risk. Before the cold drizzle of November began to fall, the Rings bundled Annie, bid farewell to Lena and Hank, kissed their godson, and returned to the safety of Cherry Street.[63]

Three-and-a-half years after venturing out, Joe was back where he started. Barbara was home.

CHAPTER TEN

BUFFALO

Back in Papa's neighborhood, Joe and Barbara found a very prosperous Buffalo. Not only were the city's numerous industries capturing their fair share of government contracts, but the war had brought an indirect benefit as well: when trade on the Mississippi was cut off, commerce on the Great Lakes mushroomed. Buffalo sat well to take full advantage. The port city was a cornicopia of plenty,[1] and the vast majority of its German-speakers had succeeded in remaining astoundingly insulated from the war.[2]

With the economic boom, however, came rising costs, and salaries were not keeping pace. Labor protests and strikes had erupted, and now Joe and Barbara would witness more of the same. Making matters worse were the persistent rumors of Confederate raiders swooping down from Canada. Buffalo's harbor, with its federal arsenal and its shipyards turning out tugs for the Union Navy, was an obvious target for the Rebels. Despite Buffalonians' apprehension, though, no soldiers in gray ever did appear on the lake.[3]

More personal troubles, however, visited the Rings. An epidemic of influenza broke out in the spring of 1864, taking 2-year-old Annie on April 28th.[4] She was buried at Pine Hill Cemetery in the shadow of the monument marking the graves of her immigrant forebears. The little girl's tombstone was a rectangle of marble, rounded on one side, laid flush in the sod, no bigger than a stepping stone.[5]

Consolation came two months later on July 1st, when Barbara delivered her first son. He was carried to Saint Michael's two days later and christened Joseph Nicholas.[6] Barbara's brother Nicholas stood as godfather, as Joe's brother was still far away in Mississippi. But it was that absent uncle the boy would eventually live with, learn from, and remember fondly in stories told to his own children.[7]

Later that July on the 18th President Lincoln issued another call for recruits, and this time he was casting the net more broadly.[8] Not only was the $300 commutation clause removed, but alien males, 20 to 45, who were enjoying any of the rights and privileges of citizenship, *whether or not* they had ever declared their intention to become naturalized, were now draftable. While editorials in the *Buffalo Commercial Advertiser* expressed confidence that Erie County would raise its quota easily, the *Buffalo Volksfreund* railed against the expanded eligibility.[9] Nevertheless, the Civil War still did not intrude upon number 11 Cherry Street, because Buffalo was able to fill nearly all of its quotas with volunteers.[10]

Offering bounties worked. In addition, wealthy and patriotic industrialists paid multiple substitutes to serve in their stead. Only small deficiencies had to be made up through conscription.[11] So the German-speaking tradesmen, who had escaped the ravages of war-torn central Europe, were able to avoid getting involved in civil war in their adopted country.[12] This fight, they probably reasoned, was not theirs.

When the long war finally came to an end in the spring of 1865, Joe Ring decided to make another new beginning outside of Buffalo. Before leaving, though, he and Barbara may have beheld President Lincoln a second time. The train carrying his body back to Illinois stopped in Buffalo on April 27, 1865.[13] The mayor proclaimed that Thursday a day of mourning. Municipal offices and businesses closed. Houses and public places were draped in black. A hushed multitude gathered at the New York Central Railroad Depot hours before the train rolled in slowly at dawn.[14]

A grand procession formed. Officers on horseback and ranks of soldiers afoot, heavy artillery, canon, two military bands, and open carriages full of civil officials wound solemnly through the wide, elm-lined

FUNERAL PROCESSION FOR ABRAHAM LINCOLN, BUFFALO, APRIL 27, 1865.
(Courtesy Buffalo & Erie County Historical Society)

streets of downtown Buffalo. Drums beat a woeful dirge. Cornets moaned. The funeral car was spectacular. An ornate canopy of rich black velvet with silver fringe all around soared above the coffin. Plumes like black flame sprouted at the four corners, while a fifth crowned the apex. Beneath this exotic tent, the long mahogany coffin rested on a catafalque, which rode on a broad platform—all three swathed and valanced to the ground in black velvet heavily fringed in silver. The car was drawn by three pair of white horses, each steed cloaked in black and led by a black groom. On either side marched the honorary pall bearers and the armed guard of honor. An immense number of people, mute and rapt, heads uncovered, stood on the boardwalks, leaned out of upper-story windows, peered down from rooftops, as "the slain martyr" passed. Thousands trailed behind the cavalcade.[15]

In Saint James Hall, festooned elaborately with swags, wreaths and bows of black and white crepe, the Kentuckian's lanky form lay at a slight viewing angle beneath an improvised chandelier. Three streams of mourners shuffled past the shrine all afternoon and all evening until after dark. Then the entire cortege reformed and processed somberly all the way back to the depot, followed by throngs of Buffalonians, white and black. Late that night the funeral train rolled on.[16]

And Joe heeded a summons from his younger brother: The promise of the Delta was about to burst open like a cotton boll. Come on down.

Chapter Eleven

GEORGE

George Ring would not recognize the Delta today. It bears no resemblance to the jungle he chose for his home in 1858.[1]

It still has the shape of an elm leaf, measuring some 200 miles from its stem at Vicksburg to its tip at Memphis, some 80 miles between the Mississippi River on the west and the Yazoo River on the east. Seasonal flooding over many millennia made the land between these two rivers the flattest and richest in the South. Topsoil in places could be six feet deep. The Delta is still veined like an elm leaf, too, with numerous waterways, each flowing southerly into a larger one flowing into the Yazoo, which flows into the Mississippi—whence the name: Yazoo-Mississippi Delta. The Little Sunflower, Big Sunflower, Lower Deer Creek, Upper Deer Creek, Bogue Phalia, Steele Bayou, Black Bayou, Indian Bayou, Rolling Fork Creek, Silver Creek, the Quiver, and hundreds of other waterways compose an intricate network. Twisting and weaving their restless ways, they divide the Delta into numerous segments, yet at the same time link all the segments together.

But today George would not recognize the Delta because this unique land has been transformed by a quintessentially American saga of exploitation. George himself was a part of that saga; to exploit was exactly what he came to do. Indeed, George's classic American success story, I would come to realize as it yielded reluctantly to my probing,

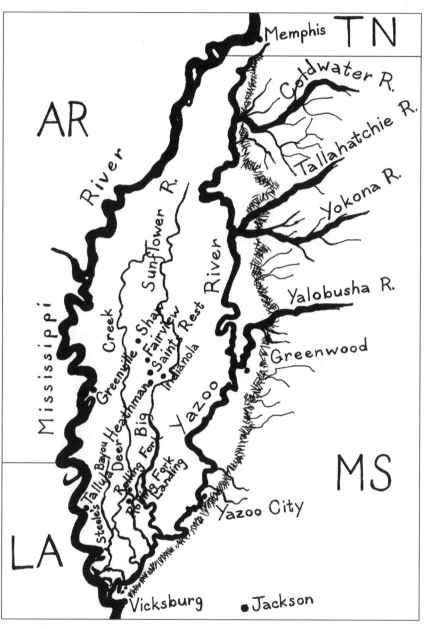

THE YAZOO-MISSISSIPPI DELTA, OFTEN CALLED THE MISSISSIPPI DELTA,
THE YAZOO DELTA, OR SIMPLY "THE DELTA."

(Map drawn by the author)

was one with the story of the Delta itself.

When George left his foreman's job in Buffalo, bid his brother Joe farewell, and headed for Mississippi, he was 24,[2] an energetic young man out to build his fortune. He had been in the United States five years then.[3] Never circumspect or meticulous, he moved with purpose and rough-and-tumble optimism. George always knew where he was headed, if not exactly how he would get there. Setbacks and reversals would never slackened his stride—not even "the Rolling Fork tragedy."

It was not by chance, therefore, that of all the places in the states and western territories, George chose the rugged frontier of the Delta. The soaring value of cotton was luring ambitious settlers into that feral frontier. Vicksburg downriver to New Orleans—called the Natchez District—had been producing cotton for years. But by the 1830s not even all those thousand-acred plantations, worked by all those thousands of slaves, could meet the spiraling world-wide demand for more cotton. Enterprising men began to look for more land.[4]

The Delta was the place!—A new and untapped corner of the United States. The Treaty of Doak's Stand, 1820, and the Treaty of Dancing Rabbit Creek, 1830, had been signed with the Choctaws, and the Treaty of Pontotoc had been signed with the Chickasaws in 1832. The fertility of the Delta topsoil was legendary, and the Delta was known to have plenty of waterways for transporting harvests to market. Florid editorials in eastern newspapers, including Buffalo's *Commercial Advertiser* and *Der Weltburger*, which George would have read, spread the word. Clearly, the Delta was where there would be development, growth and profit. The Delta was where fortunes would be made. The Delta was exactly the kind of place George Ring had crossed the Atlantic to find.

The problem was, the Delta was inhospitable.

Occupying its rich black loam were dense hardwood forests that had to be felled and uprooted before the land could be cultivated. Choking its web of waterways were thick cane brakes that had to be cut down or burned out before navigation could flow. Sprawling across thousands of Delta acres were cypress swamps that had to be drained before human habitation and overland transportation could be established. But that was not all. Bears, panthers, bobcats and wolves inhabited the Delta, as well as poisonous snakes, rats, horse flies and mosquitoes—carriers of yellow fever and malaria.[5]

More troublesome than all of this, however, was the annual flooding. The major arteries of northern Mississippi—the Coldwater, Tallahatchie, Yokona and Yalobusha—all drained into the Yazoo. During the rainy season, therefore, roughly the month of March, tremendous quantities of water flowed southward into the innumerable waterways of the Delta. Depending on local rainfall, lowlands might remain overflown into early summer. Which meant that tens of thousands of acres of land, choice bottomland, could not be tilled.[6]

Later each spring, usually May, the snow melt from the north-central United States would come hurtling down the Mississippi River, causing a second inundation that could last until late June. This deluge could push into the Delta with such force as to reverse the current of the Yazoo and its tributaries, making an enormous stagnant backwater of much of the Delta. Any land that had been plowed and harrowed, any sowing that had been done, was wiped out, and planters had to begin the cycle all over again—if enough time remained in the season to warrant the effort.[7]

The Delta could not be settled, its soil and timber and wildlife could not be tapped, until the mighty force that created and nurtured these resources, the Mississippi River, was brought under control. By the time of the Civil War, waterfront landowners had raised a modest levee along the river. Cut by the Yankees, it was repaired and strengthened after the war by the U.S. Army Corps of Engineers. However, levees along the inland rivers were another matter. Their maintenance remained in private hands, and they stayed in a perpetual state of pitiful disrepair.[8]

So the slow and arduous process of taming the Delta began in the accessible counties along the Mississippi. Issaquena was one of these, and into it, from neighboring states, came the planters with their slaves. First among them was Thomas Y. Chaney, from Louisiana.[9] He was the father of the physician who, years later, would help identify a few blackened bones as the mortal remains of Jesse Moore, Martha Moore, little Willie Jeans and Alphonse Goudchat. The elder Chaney brought his household of wife, infant son and slaves up Deer Creek as the Choctaws were vacating the region. He founded his plantation at the headwaters of Rolling Fork Creek—a site he had selected on an earlier surveying expedition—and gave it the same name he had given the creek: Rolling Fork.[10]

Other planters followed, clearing and cultivating the land along Deer Creek. They were daring pioneers. They risked their health, financial resources, and most valuable chattel—their slaves—to found fortunes in cotton. They confronted the wilderness head on, and struggled against the relentless harshness of the territory. Those who were determined enough, whose slaves were vigorous enough, became the autocratic lords of the county.[11]

Many of them would eventually choose to reside with their families in the healthier hill country of eastern Mississippi, leaving the merciless sun and steam and perils of the Delta to their overseers and bondmen.[12] But not Thomas Y. Chaney. He stayed. And his daughter Sarah would boast her entire life that she was the first white child born in Issaquena County. As she was. Within a couple of decades, a ramshackle hamlet sprouted at the gates of the Chaney place and appropriated its name: Rolling Fork.[13]

This was the land George Ring made his home: a swath roughly four miles wide between Deer Creek on the West and the Sunflower River on the East, with Rolling Fork Creek arching down from the primitive settlement of Rolling Fork to connect the two. That same year came a kindred spirit into the neighborhood, an enterprising 28-year-old from Virginia,[14] who would serve lifelong as George's model and mentor.

His name was George W. Faison. He came to grow cotton, of course, which he did. But he was quick to perceive that all the new planters settling farther and farther from Issaquena County's main avenue—Deer Creek—would need a landing closer to home for shipping their cotton to Vicksburg. So Faison bought the quarter section on the Sunflower River at the mouth of Rolling Fork Creek, and established a landing there.[15] Patching together a cabin to serve as warehouse, and probably residence, too, the Virginian opened for business.

The place came to be called, appropriately enough, Rolling Fork Landing. But that caused it to be confused with the hamlet of the same name. Some locals adopted the custom of referring to the hamlet as "the Point" to distinguish it from the landing, which they called simply

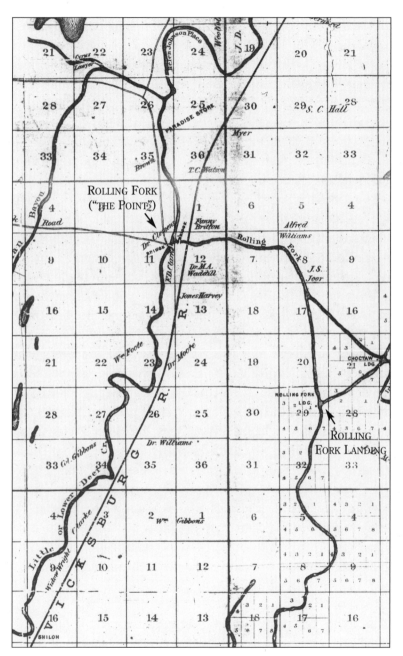

THE ROLLING FORK NEIGHBORHOOD, LAND PLATS, 1873.

"Rolling Fork."[16] But the confusion was never entirely resolved. Today not more than a handful of the residents of Rolling Fork have any idea that a landing by the same name existed once a few miles downstream.[17]

It was most likely from Faison that George learned the commercial operations of a landing, and the annual cycle of the cotton culture. From his earliest days in the Delta, he would have appreciated the vital role of the factor, the man who marketed the cotton.[18] Planters depended on the cotton factor, and the factor's profit per bale was substantial. But Faison was not the only neighbor whose association George cultivated in order to advance his ambitions.

The preeminent resident of the neighborhood was Dr. William I. Chaney, a tall and meticulously-groomed 30-year-old.[19] His wealth and position were not attributable so much to the fine classical education he had received at Princeton, or the medical degrees he held from the Universities of Pennsylvania and New York. Rather, his status derived more from the fact that his father had been the first white settler of the county, and had willed to his surgeon son several thousand acres of prime bottomland, and more than 30 slaves to cultivate them.[20]

It was the masses of slaves who constituted the overwhelming majority of the Delta's population—87 percent in 1860, though in Issaquena County it was 92 percent.[21] So when George arrived there, although the plantations had white overseers, and a number of agents were already scattered at remote landings, and a smattering of hearty yeomen farmers cultivated their own freeholds, society in the Delta was substantially two-tiered: a few wealthy masters, and their hordes of abject chattel.[22]

But that, too, like the land itself, would change with astonishing speed after the war. From two polarized classes the population would mushroom into four distinct tiers, with an increased percentage of whites in the middle.[23] George would be instrumental in effecting *that* transformation, too.

One day in June 1860 a federal census taker making his rounds in the Rolling Fork neighborhood arrived at a lone cypress cabin on the shore of Deer Creek.[24] He dismounted, retrieved from his saddlebag the blank schedules, ink, and quills, and knocked at the door. Judging from the information he gathered, it appears that the enumerator was admitted by a boy: Johnny Joor.

Johnny Joor was the son of Delta pioneers, and like so many sons of Delta pioneers, had been orphaned as a child.[25] But fate would deal more kindly with him than it did with his parents. For Joor would one day be the clerk lucky enough to be absent from the Ring & Co. store on the night of March 4, 1873. Ten years after that, he would be the sheriff intrepid enough to reopen the unsolved case.

The orphan told the census taker that he shared the cabin with George F. Ring.

The enumerator dipped his quill and wrote "J. S. Joor" on one line, followed by "G. F. Ring" on the next. Then he asked their ages.

Joor drawled that he was 14, and reckoned George to be 23. (George was 26.)

Place of birth?

Joor answered Mississippi for himself, New York for George. (Though George had indeed come down "from New York," his German accent would have pegged him as foreign-born had *he* been the one responding to the questions.)

Occupation?

Joor attended school. George was a mechanic.

George may have had training as a carpenter, since his brother did.[26] He may also have operated a cotton gin or compress, sharpened scythes and plowshares, repaired plantation equipment, or—most likely—plied all of these trades and others besides. He was employed not only by George W. Faison, but by planters along Deer Creek as well.[27] With each of them he signed a "mechanic's lien."[28] This gave George a claim against his employer's land until he received payment in full for his work.

The census taker came to the columns headed "Value of Real Estate" and "Value of Personal Estate." Joor said they had none. (Evidently the boy did not know that George, according to the 1860 Personal Property Tax Roll for Issaquena County, had $150 "loaned at interest or invested in a security."[29])

Modest start for George!

What helped him achieve his ambition in the Delta was the war. The

Civil War gave George his foothold, set him up for a bright future. It also enveloped him and his neighbors, rich and poor, white and black, in an extraordinary and improbable episode. It could only have happened in the Yazoo-Mississippi Delta.

CHAPTER TWELVE

THE WAR, SOUTH

In February 1863 Grant was at Young's Point on the Louisiana side of the Mississippi, devising a new strategy for capturing Vicksburg.[1] His plan was to penetrate the swamps of the Delta and attack the city from the north.

The Rolling Fork neighborhood had not yet been touched by the war. Cotton not sold to the North was shipped overseas (running the Union blockade of New Orleans) or stockpiled for future sale.[2] A full year after April of 1862, when the Confederate Congress had enacted a draft of all able-bodied white men, 18 to 35,[3] George Ring was still at home attending to business as usual.[4] And he was not the only one. For the draft law allowed exemptions.

"One white man on plantations of 20 negroes or more" was considered more useful to the Confederacy at home than on the battlefield. Wealthy men could buy their way out by paying a commutation fee of $300. Any draftee who could provide a substitute was also exempt from serving. Other exemptions were granted for ministers, conscientious objectors, railway employees, postmen, apothecaries, teachers, among others.[5] Perhaps what sheltered George from conscription was the fact that he was still a citizen of France.[6]

Another Issaquena County resident who did not don the gray uniform was W. D. Brown, George's attorney.[7] He had come down into the

Delta from his native Tennessee in 1858—the same year as George—bringing his law degree and his slaves.[8] He married the young mistress of a plantation on Deer Creek about a mile-and-a-half above the Chaney place (though on the west bank).[9] There they would rear three sons and three daughters.[10] When the war broke out, however, Brown was still a 28-year-old newly-wed owning 56 slaves and commanding a domain that dwarfed the landholdings of many neighbors his senior.[11]

"I happened to be a member of the legislature in this state, and I was exempted," he would explain later. "I had a family on my hands, and our country was very sparsely populated with whites, and it was not regarded as prudent to take all the white people out of the country, and to leave no one there to protect the few white families that were left."[12]

Neither did William B. McQuillen serve. His plantation lay closer than any other to Rolling Fork Landing—two-and-a-half miles up Rolling Fork Creek.[13] He was one of the pioneers of Issaquena County, having arrived as a young man from Louisiana in the late 1840s.[14] He married the daughter of a local planter,[15] and by the time George met him, he was already the proud father of a brood of small children.[16] When the war started, McQuillen, 34-year-old master of more than 30 slaves, was living as comfortable a life as the rugged frontier allowed.[17]

Still other planters of the Rolling Fork neighborhood stayed home during the war.[18] They would not risk the loss of their livelihood by leaving their cottonfields, livestock and slaves unattended. They would not compromise the safety of their wives and children by abandoning them. Even Dr. Chaney, though he held a commission in the Confederate Army, spent most of the war years on his place at Rolling Fork.[19]

As long as there were planters, there was a demand for the services of the landings. So merchants—such as George W. Faison—were unpersuaded by the Southern Cause to abandon their lucrative enterprises. Prior to 1863, therefore, the War Between the States had not disrupted the day-to-day occupations of the residents of the Rolling Fork neighborhood. Now, however, they were about to learn just how close the war could come to their front doors.

Grant's latest strategy called for ground forces to cross the Mississippi to Gwin's plantation at Eagle Bend, traverse Muddy Bayou to Steele Bayou by building a bridge, rendezvous with a fleet of ironclad warships, troop transport steamers, tugs and barges waiting in Steele Bayou to carry them up to Black Bayou, through Black Bayou to Deer Creek, and up Deer Creek to the settlement of Rolling Fork. From there the fleet would navigate down Rolling Fork Creek, past Rolling Fork Landing, down the Little Sunflower River to the Yazoo, deploy the troops on the Chickasaw Bluffs running along the eastern bank of the Yazoo, and proceed to take Vicksburg.[20]

The plan was impossible.

Progress through the narrow, crooked, overgrown bayous was unexpectedly arduous and slow. The waterways were not only at springtime flood level, but higher than usual, because the Yankees had broken through the levee on the Mississippi. Yet none of the arteries was as wide or had as much current as Grant had anticipated.[21]

For the ironclad warships and troop transport steamers to navigate the sluggish streams, working parties—which included freed slaves—had to wade waist-deep through the swamps to clear away the snags, submerged trees and canebrakes choking the channel. They also had to construct rafts to stand on to hack down the overhanging limbs, which were so dense they toppled the chimneys, mangled the cabins, and brought tumbling to the decks rats, mice, cockroaches, snakes and lizards. Even when the passages were cleared, curves and bends were so sharp that the fleet could advance only at a snail's pace. It was March 16th before the ground and naval forces in the lead finally made it to Deer Creek.[22]

General Sherman was in command of the expedition. He set up headquarters at Reality, one of the Hill plantations. He remained there with most of the ground troops to hold the place, while Admiral Porter, the next morning, took five gunboats into Deer Creek and headed northward.[23]

Planters along Deer Creek, having heard of the approach of the Yankees, had stacked their bales of cotton on the banks and set them afire rather than allow them to fall into the hands of the invaders. Fieldhands watched in amazement as the Union flotilla ran this flaming gauntlet.[24] Porter encountered only one white person, a rough, burly overseer whom the admiral later called "half bulldog, half bloodhound." The overseer did not conceal his allegiance to "Jeff Davis, first,

HARPER'S WEEKLY, APRIL 11, 1863.
(Courtesy Prints & Photographs Division, Library of Congress)

last, and all the time," but turned his back as the fleet passed by his cabin and smashed through his employer's bridge. "It don't belong to me," he told Porter.[25]

Two long, laborious and exasperating days later, the fleet was finally within 600 yards of the settlement of Rolling Fork. Where it stalled again.[26]

By this time, local citizens had rushed to inform Colonel Ferguson. Ferguson was camped with a small Confederate force on Deer Creek about 40 miles above Rolling Fork. The colonel ordered his cavalry out immediately to stop and hold the fleet until he could get his infantry and artillery there by steamer.[27]

Approaching Rolling Fork on Thursday, March 19th, the cavalry discovered that the Federal advance guard had taken up residence in Dr. Chaney's home. The Rebel horsemen surprised and routed the advance guard—the men were lying about the lawn, sleeping—and drove them back to the position of the five gunboats. There they fired from ambush at the Yankee working parties and felled trees into the channel to prevent the boats from advancing upriver.[28]

Ferguson arrived at Rolling Fork with his infantry and artillery late that afternoon. But getting his men down to the stalled Union fleet took until evening, because the road was inundated, with two bridges afloat. By early next morning, though, he had his troops in position and opened fire on the Yankees.[29]

Porter's predicament was desperate. If a message for help was to reach Sherman, it would have to be delivered by someone who knew the swamps. Porter selected a freed slave he felt could be trusted, calling him Sambo, and handed him a half dollar and a note: "Dear Sherman, Hurry up, for Heaven's sake." The black man accepted the silver coin, saying only as he left on his mission, "My name ain't Sambo, suh. My name's Tub."[30]

Meanwhile, Confederate reinforcements under General Featherston were racing toward the site from Snyder's Bluff on the Yazoo. They came up Sunflower River on steamers and disembarked at Rolling Fork Landing at about three o'clock in the afternoon of Friday, March 20th. Dr. Chaney met them there and piloted them the six miles—three-quarters of a mile through water—to the head of Rolling Fork Creek.[31]

Fighting between the Union men trapped in the ships and the Confederate forces maneuvering along the shores (out of range of the admiral's guns) continued until dark. During the night the boats began slowly to back down stream. Saturday morning, March 21st, Featherston's forces organized local slaves to fell trees into Deer Creek below the fleet to prevent its escape, continuing all the while to attack and harass the men trapped on board. Nevertheless, the Federals managed to resume their retreat, and by dark had regressed two miles down Deer Creek, where they burned every building on Dr. Moore's plantation except one small stable.[32]

Sherman and his troops, meanwhile, followed Tub as quickly as possible through short cuts in the swamps. They waded through waist-deep water in the abject blackness of the Delta night, carrying lighted candles, and arrived at Dr. Moore's devastated plantation on Sunday morning, March 22nd.[33] Skirmishes involving about 5,000 men in blue and 2,500 in gray continued all that day under heavy rain. The Federals were desperate to keep the creek behind their gunboats clear, while the Rebels were determined to trap the enemy fleet and destroy it. But the Confederates fell frustratingly short of artillery ammunition and men, and the Union fleet, with all supporting troops, continued to inch steadily back down Deer Creek.[34]

Rain continued to fall in torrents throughout the night and into Monday morning. Swelling the waterways, it allowed Sherman and Porter to reach Reality on March 24th. But skirmishes between their drenched and tattered rear guard and Confederate sharpshooters took place March 25th at Lou Watson's place, and March 26th at Charles Fore's place, just three miles up Deer Creek from Reality.[35]

Grossly overestimating the size of the Confederate force, the Union expedition continued to retreat through Black Bayou and Steele Bayou, crossed the Mississippi, and arrived back at the safety of Young's Point on March 27th.[36]

Grant abandoned his plan to capture Vicksburg from the north.[37]

Official dispatches and reports of this campaign indicate that in the spring of 1863 the neighborhood of Rolling Fork was still an ideal place to escape, and even profit from, the war. Plantations were flourishing: there was an abundance of cotton and corn, herds of cattle and sheep, and plenty of horses, mules, hogs and poultry.[38] Porter wrote to Sherman: "There is everything here the heart of a soldier could desire; everything in abundance."[39] The buyer of these goods was the Confederate army, which explains why young, strong and healthy white men like Ring, Faison, Brown and McQuillen, remaining at home, prospered.

Some residents, though, found the appearance of Porter's flotilla so close to home too unsettling, and the activities of the conscription officers too annoying, to stay put. They exited to safer havens. Faison moved his wife and son up the Sunflower River.[40] Passing through Washington County, the family penetrated the wilderness of Sunflower County, which was even more remote and primitive than Issaquena. While Faison erected a cabin, his family lived in a shantyboat.[41]

When he left, the Virginian may have turned his operations at Rolling Fork Landing over to George. Whether as country merchant, or perhaps plantation overseer, or simply by raising cotton and corn, hogs and chickens, George would certainly have had routine dealings with Rebel commissaries. But prospering in Issaquena County would become increasingly troublesome and hazardous as Grant's efforts to take Vicksburg intensified.

Aware now of the wealth of provisions and manpower available on the plantations lining Deer Creek, Grant sent General Steele into the area with clear objectives: draw as many Rebel troops as possible away from Vicksburg; confiscate all provisions destined for Vicksburg's defenders; conscript the vast numbers of black men in the region; and put all the black women and children to work on plantations under U.S. Government lessees to raise cotton and corn for the Union.[42] Steele's troops entered the Delta on April 5, 1863, at Greenville.[43]

Greenville was the seat of Washington County and the most important port on the Mississippi between Vicksburg and Memphis. Every fall an unbroken procession of steamboats docked in Greenville to take on thousands of bales of cotton destined for New Orleans.[44]

General Steele's forces slogged through seven-and-a-half miles of mud to Colonel Ferguson's camp on Deer Creek and proceeded to drive the Confederates downstream. Ferguson resisted, but he was outnumbered, and the federals pushed his men back to within 20 miles of Rolling Fork.[45] Just as Grant had hoped, the colonel asked for rein-

POSTCARD SHOWING THE LANDING AT GREENVILLE. *(Courtesy Mississippi Department of Archives and History)*

forcements, and Confederate troops steamed up the Sunflower River—
away from Vicksburg.

They disembarked at Rolling Fork Landing on April 7th, and
marched a full day overland to reach Ferguson's encampment.[46] Even
with these reinforcements, though, Ferguson had too few men to do
more than harass the flanks of the Union forces and capture stragglers.
For two weeks Federal troops ravaged the countryside on Deer Creek
above Rolling Fork, seizing stock and liberating slaves.[47]

Ferguson wrote to his superiors:

> I have burned all the bale cotton as I fell back before the
> enemy, and destroyed the bridges, to keep them as much as
> possible to our side of the creek. They have burned several
> fine steam gins that I know of, and probably all. I yesterday
> hanged a negro man, slave of William F. Smith, who, mistak-
> ing two of my men for the Abolitionists, hailed them across
> the creek, and volunteered to conduct them to the rebel
> camp, so as to surprise it; informed them of my strength and
> position, asked for a gun to kill his master, and said that he
> would knock down and rape any white woman.[48]

Steele reported:

> A great many negroes have followed the command. . . . I
> advised all the negroes that asked my advice to stay on the
> plantations where they belonged, except two engineers and a
> blacksmith. Please send me instructions as to what shall be
> done with these poor creatures. In many instances our men
> burned up everything there was to eat on the plantations, in
> spite of all my endeavors to prevent it. It is estimated by some
> of the officers that we burned 500,000 bushels of corn. There
> were 25,000 bushels burned at Thompson's, which the
> negroes said were destined for Vicksburg.[49]

A Confederate headquarters was established at Rolling Fork to repel
any further Union incursion into the region.[50] It may have been set up on
the Helen Johnson place called Mount Helena, which was built on an old
Indian mound on Deer Creek four miles above the hamlet. Mount

Helena afforded a panoramic view of the countryside. Local planters, therefore, were not put out of business by the Yankees, although their control over their black labor force was dwindling inexorably.[51] Colonel Ferguson's commanding officer, General Stephen D. Lee, wrote from his headquarters at Rolling Fork on April 12, 1863:

> The planters and negroes are much demoralized on the Mississippi, and from all I can learn large cotton crops are being planted by men who were regarded above suspicion. On some of the places the negroes are almost in a state of insurrection.[52]

Some years later W. D. Brown was asked whether the Negroes in his neighborhood had caused any disturbances during the war:

> Yes, sir. I recollect very distinctly that on one occasion a gang of colored people armed and organized and marched up Deer Creek, and they assassinated an old citizen by the name of [Joe] Clark, in his house, almost in the arms of his wife.
>
> They assassinated another man on the Hunt plantation [Georgiana], a few miles below me; killed him [Johnson] in the morning just about the time of his rising from bed.
>
> They shot a third one, an old citizen by the name of Charles Fore, and attempted to kill him, but he made his escape.
>
> They attacked another one, a little way down the creek on the same road, by the name of Sims; and on another occasion they made a similar raid and came within three-quarters of a mile of my house, but I happened, fortunately, to be absent from home, between my house and the Mississippi River, and they declared their purpose at that time to some parties at Rolling Fork to kill me.
>
> I remember those facts very distinctly, and other facts precisely of a similar character all over the country. I remember that I have remained awake many a night with my eyes open, fearful of the safety of my wife and children; and I would have preferred a thousand-fold to have been in the army, with my musket on my shoulder; and yet I have had a few old, good servants that have stood by me from the first to the last.[53]

The two raids had occurred in August 1863, Brown recalled, just a few weeks apart.[54] The only cause for them he had ever heard was "that one of those white citizens, by the name of Clark, had a few days or a few weeks before this occurrence scolded one of the boys in the crowd for leaving his gate open."[55]

Perhaps, though, the attorney also realized, but refrained from admitting, that while the Rolling Fork neighborhood had been sufficiently remote to remain in Confederate hands, it had not been isolated enough to prevent the "boys" from hearing about the Emancipation Proclamation.[56] Maybe seeing an armada of the United States Navy plowing through waters where only local packets had ever navigated before, and learning from word of mouth passed from plantation to plantation that the Yankees were forming colored regiments just a few miles up Deer Creek,[57] brought home to all the Tubs of the Rolling Fork area the reality of what this war could mean for them.

There was always a sufficient contingent of Confederate forces in the vicinity of Rolling Fork to discourage blacks from mounting an open revolt. But the men in gray were too preoccupied with the constant threat of Union attack, and too few in number, to insure law and order among the region's civilian residents.[58] George Ring would not have bedded down those nights without leaning a loaded rifle against the wall, or slipping a loaded revolver under his pillow.

Nevertheless, 100 years later, when I came to evaluate the theories that blamed the Ring & Co. carnage of March 4, 1873, on "the darkies"— as Grandma had put it—another statement of W. D. Brown's would resonate with particular relevance:

> A fact connected with these murders [of August 1863] which excited no notice at the time, but which is very noticeable now, is that these unrestrained demons did not, even though nerved to indiscriminate plunder and murder of white men, in a single case offer to injure or insult women and children.[59]

The Rolling Fork massacre included a woman and a child.

On July 4, 1863, the "Gibralter of the South" finally fell to Grant.[60] From that time through the end of the war, large portions of the Delta, especially along the Mississippi River, remained under Union control.

Yet plantations deep in the swampy interior of Issaquena County continued to be held by the Confederacy.[61] The hungry young nation was desperate for their products, and desperate, too, to replenish its thinned fighting ranks.

In January of 1864 the Confederacy's mandatory draft was widened by eliminating the $300 commutation fee provision, and by including all able-bodied white men aged 17 to 50.[62] In Mississippi, however, state legislators had just the previous month passed their own law to augment enlistment.[63] It required all male aliens, 18 to 45—George was 29 at the time—to leave the state or enlist by March 1, 1864.[64] Conscription officers redoubled their efforts to impress into service all shirkers.[65] Still, somehow, George remained a civilian at large.

By the fall of 1864 so many Mississippi men were away in military service, or had been killed or maimed, that the state legislature took action to safeguard the security of the women and children at home. It authorized the organization of a militia of the few remaining exempts. Exempts were to serve 30 days at a time, and these periods of duty were to rotate among the counties. Issaquena's turn was to come up in November. Before then, though, the war would penetrate a second time into George's back yard.[66]

More than a year after the fall of Vicksburg and the imposition of Federal control up and down the length of the Mississippi River, Confederate resistence in Washington County was unrelenting. So on August 23, 1864, a Union skipper pulled his gunboat up to the landing at Greenville and put a party of men ashore to burn the town to the ground. Only two houses escaped the blaze.[67] Plantations in the hinterland, however, persisted in supplying the Confederate army with corn, cattle, mules, sheep, hogs, poultry and horses. Although cotton was no longer getting through the blockade, even *that* was still being produced and stored for future exportation—if not sold (for dearly-prized greenbacks) to the Union men close at hand.[68]

On September 21, 1864, therefore, General Dana, commander of the Federal District of Vicksburg, ordered a mounted expedition to clear out the Rebels along Deer Creek. He sent the Third U.S. Colored Cavalry upriver, and the Fifth Illinois Cavalry downriver, to "beat up the country" and meet at William F. Smith's place at Egg Point. On September 22nd the colored cavalry attacked the commands of Rebel officers Bradford and Montgomery—about 150 men in all—set up at Mount Helena. The cavalrymen routed the Confederates from their Indian mound and pursued them for 15 miles, till they crossed the Sunflower River.[69]

The colored cavalry then returned to Mount Helena for the night. Finding a large quantity of ammunition, arms and subsistance stores hidden on the place, they burned to the ground all of its houses, tenements, out-buildings, stables and gins.[70]

Continuing up Deer Creek the next morning, the cavalrymen came upon a Rebel commissary, a captain, with an escort of 12 men, driving 300 head of cattle branded "C.S." (Confederate States). The black Union men killed eight of the escort, took the four others and the officer prisoner, and confiscated the herd of cattle. On their way to Egg Point, they also took 18 horses and 19 mules. Due to the close canebrakes, though, they arrived with only 200 of the 300 head of cattle. The Fifth Illinois Cavalry, meanwhile, had taken four prisoners and confiscated 9 horses and 13 mules.[71]

By the close of 1864, therefore, the war had finally managed to reach and impede business operations in the heart of Issaquena County. The handful of Confederate soldiers still in the area were powerless to oppose attacking Union forces, and the black field hands could no longer be restrained by their former owners. The sight of black horsemen in uniform, wielding swords above their heads, dazzled the field hands and revealed to them like a glorious band of angels that the world was no longer the same. Concerning the Deer Creek expedition and similar ones around Natchez, Dana wrote: "In all these operations 185 negro recruits were added to our colored forces."[72]

Even the few, scattered, obstinate white residents of Issaquena County now desired a return to normalcy. "I found the inhabitants anxious for peace," wrote Colonel Osband, commander of the Third U.S. Colored Cavalry, "and willing to accept it under Federal rule."[73]

And George Ring was poised to make his move once that peace arrived. Scarcely had the two Generals left Appomattox,[74] when he posted a letter to his older brother in Buffalo: The promise of the Delta was about to burst open like a cotton boll. Come on down.

CHAPTER THIRTEEN

COTTON

In the spring of 1865, as their riverboat turned to shore, Joe and Barbara could see the mass of blue uniforms bustling on the Commons.[1] Union soldiers were everywhere, checking permits and passes, monitoring transactions, initialing bills of lading and cargo manifests, patrolling. Equally visible were the hordes of black faces in the crowd. Many of the troops—it was no accident—were black. In addition, numerous freedmen stood in clusters, hands plunged deep in overalls, waiting for odd jobs, and black women and children squatted amid bulging burlap bundles, as though the next boat would be carrying them to a Promised Land upriver or down.[2] The Ring family was arriving in a city under military occupation.

When the steamboat hit the landing, Joe could plainly distinguish, placid and silent amid the turmoil and the noise, the stocky figure of his younger brother astride his stallion. For George would have come to Vicksburg to meet his northern kin and lead them into the Delta.

The Lorrainian brothers embraced. Then grinning and shaking their heads, they perused each other from brow to toe. Had it really been seven years!

Joe presented Barbara, whom George may not have met before, as well as their toddler Nicholas. Then Barbara introduced her sister Lena, Lena's husband Hank Weber, and 2-year-old Edward.

It may have been Barbara's reluctance to heed George's summons that had inspired Joe to invite her favorite sister to join them. Or perhaps Barbara herself had insisted upon it. Hank was as much in need of a stable position as Joe, and George could easily find a place for him in his plans. However it was decided, when their riverboat called at Cincinnati, the Rings had been joined by the Webers.[3]

As service up Deer Creek was not available every day, chances are good the Ring party spent at least one night, if not more, in town.[4] George would have led them to an inn, or the home of a German-speaking colleague. How strangely amusing it must have been for Barbara to watch a man whose features and gestures—probably even his voice—so resembled her husband's. But George's warm welcome would very quickly contrast with the icy reception tendered by the city: Joe and Barbara were victors among the vanquished.

The boardwalks were as busy as the Commons, and Barbara's attention would have been pulled in every direction. It was a totally new world. Before long, though, weaving through the crowds behind Joe, she would have observed that conversations were held in hushed tones, and suspended altogether while the strand of new arrivals filtered past. Her glances to the right, the left, would have caught the glare of a shopkeeper, the disdain of a pedestrian, maybe even the sneer of a black house servant. Barbara may have narrowed her vision to the back of Joe's head, and hugged Nicholas more tightly to her breast.[5]

Eventually she would learn that the suspicion and contempt she perceived this day were the shield and armor of a conquered, but unbowed, people. But Barbara could not have had—not yet—the slightest appreciation for the deep-rooted rancor she was witnessing, or the bitter ignominy borne by this Caucasian population subjected to black soldiers bearing rifles. The inexperienced daughter of a Buffalo bricklayer had no idea how totally new this world was indeed going to be![6]

When the migrant party eventually prepared to journey into the Delta, Barbara may have noticed George treating Union soldier and southern civilian, white and black alike, with unvarying politeness. Yet a business-like formality imbued his manner. It may have been now, so soon after meeting her brother-in-law, that Barbara first felt the suspicion, unsettling perhaps, that this man who so resembled her husband on the outside was an entirely dissimilar man on the inside. George was shrewd.

As the Rings and Webers headed up the Yazoo River, the perturbing tumult of the occupied city faded into the riverboat's wake. The rhythmic splashing of the paddlewheel was soothing. In the leafy canopy overhead, sharp birdcalls punctuated the wondrous calm. The terrain took on an exotic appearance. Clouds of humidity rose from the swamps and permeated the tangle of trunks and stalks and vines covering the soggy earth. The eyes of the Yankee travelers—urbanites all—would have been wide with wonder as first one, then the other, called out excitedly, pointing.

It would have been hard for George not to chuckle and mock them playfully, seasoned pioneer of the Delta that he was. But he would have taken equal delight in dispelling their ignorance. Cypress knees, Spanish moss, a flock of mallards glistening in a cane brake, an ancient Indian mound, enormous rafts of timber floating down to lumber mills in Vicksburg—I can imagine George explaining each phenomenon with the pride of a father introducing his children. The newcomers from Buffalo and Cincinnati were not, however, the only bedazzled immigrants streaming into the Delta this spring of 1865. They were but six in a flood of hundreds.[7]

Planters and merchants who had found refuge elsewhere during the war were returning to what was left of their houses and property. Confederate veterans were straggling home, too. And Northerners in droves were flowing into the Delta. They were not yet the "carpetbaggers" bent on implementing Republican policy and forging political careers, because the Reconstruction Acts would not be passed until March of 1867. Rather, at this time, they were for the most part Union veterans, and young families like the Rings and Webers, uninterested in politics or ideology, seeking only to take advantage of the economic opportunities of the post-war South. Some of the newcomers, such as Joe Ring, were foreign-born. Also among the arriving Yankees were Christian missionaries and agents of the Freedmen's Bureau, eager to insure the welfare and education of the emancipated race.[8]

But the three men who would fashion the aftermath of the Rolling Fork Landing horror of March 4, 1873, belonged to yet another immigrant group: blacks. Migrating into the Delta from other parts of Mississippi and other states of the collapsed Confederacy were large numbers of former slaves. Men came singly and in bands, some with wives, some with children, sometimes three or four families together. Because they had heard that here, not only were wages higher than in Alabama and Georgia, but the dream of owning their own farms could come true. And it could. Remarkably, for a few fleeting years, the Yazoo-Mississippi Delta was the *real* Promised Land for freed slaves.[9]

Because Delta planters needed labor. They paid taxes on their swampy and forested acres as well as their cultivated acres. Only cleared land could yield a crop; the rest was a financial burden. So landowners welcomed freedmen onto their property to perform the drudgery of clearing it and making it profitable. The labor of the freedmen not only produced a crop for the landlord, but enhanced the value of his plantation as well.[10] Indeed, during the 1870s, when the market value of cotton declined steadily, planters would have to cultivate more and more acreage just to maintain the status quo.[11] Without a continually increasing labor force, they risked losing their places altogether.

Most freedmen started out working as field hands for a flat wage, which they negotiated every January with their employer. Since their salary was set in advance, field hands had no personal stake in the size or quality of the harvest; the planter bore all the risk. But by the latter 1860s, when landowners found themselves short of cash and unable to pay wages, they would begin contracting with freedmen to work "on shares."[12]

Sharecroppers raised their own crop on a few acres of the plantation. For payment they received a percentage—generally one-third to one-half—of their harvest, the remainder going to the landowner for the use of his land. "Croppers" (as they were called) had a vested interest in the size and quality of their cotton, because their income depended on what it would bring in the market. The landlord would sell the harvest, then pay each "cropper" his share of the cash. Before paying, however, the landlord deducted all sums due him for the seed cotton and other supplies, as well as the use of his tools, equipment and mules.[13]

Over the years, some field hands and sharecroppers managed to accumulate sufficient funds to buy their own mules and equipment and work as tenant farmers. "Tenants" paid their landlord a flat annual rent—in cash or cotton—for the use of the land. This rent came out of the harvest in the fall; in the meanwhile, the landlord secured his interest by holding a lien on the tenant's growing crop. Sometimes the tenant sold his cotton himself to a local merchant, such as George W. Faison and later the Ring brothers. Often, however, it was stipulated in the lien that the landlord would handle the sale of the harvest, and also settle all of the tenant's debts with the local merchant (who had furnished the seed cotton and groceries for the season) before the tenant collected his year's income. Eventually, through years of tenancy, many black farmers saved enough money to achieve total independence: they bought their own freeholds.[14]

The dream could indeed come true in the Delta, and for many former slaves, it did. The old volumes of land deeds in the county courthouses bear witness to this.[15] But the climb up the ladder was steep and arduous, and the higher the freedmen climbed, the more debt and risk they assumed, and the less debt and risk the planters were left to shoulder. When hard times hit—and hard times aplenty lay just ahead—landowners would manage to absorb the loss by forfeiting a portion of their plantations to the state for taxes. Small farmers, on the other hand, would lose everything (often to the local furnishing merchant), and tumble back down to the bottom rung. As a consequence, the era of unprecedented opportunity for blacks in the Delta would be short-lived, and reversed entirely after Mississippi's "Redemption" in 1875.[16]

Before that happened, though, the local magistrate who would investigate the heinous crime of March 4, 1873—Noah B. Parker—and the county sheriff who would decline to assist him—Henry P. Scott—and the insurance agent who would contest George's claims in the courts—William M. Chamberlin—were all black men from other states.

In 1865, therefore, as George escorted his band of naive kin into the heart of Issaquena County, the Delta still harbingered boom times for all, white and black alike. Every newcomer brought his own goals and the determination to achieve them. Expectations soared. The mix of people was unique and untested, and transformed the Delta's pre-war population. No longer would almost every inhabitant be lord or serf; intermediate classes would form. It was a new society in gestation, the

Delta.[17] It was the chaotic, stimulating and bizarre environment in which Joe Ring was making his latest new beginning, and would suffer his final frustration.

George calls his relatives out on deck: the steamer is chugging into Deer Creek. Now the immigrants observe a changed terrain. The land along both banks is treeless and flat, and striped with long rows of dark-green plants.[18] Beyond these fields looms a wall of trees, masses of sweet gums, oaks, cottonwoods and cypress towering in such dense profusion that no gaping holes expose the bogs and bayous and swamps oozing around their trunks.[19]

For many winding miles and many languid hours this panorama persists, unchanging. Never has Barbara beheld such vast openness, such unremittingly level land, so much sky. At first the new arrivals gape in awe. But as the landscape rolls on and on without the slightest variation, their mouths shut and their brows knit in apprehension.

George's face, meanwhile, I see grow radiant, and his instruction— volunteered now—sputters out faster and faster. He points out the rare barn or stable, the occasional cotton gin, cotton press—everything constructed of wood!—every house and hut and fence and corn crib. Not a stone in the Delta![20] Finally, well into the second day of the journey, coming out of a tight bend, George bellows: they are approaching the Rolling Fork neighborhood!

Surely the urban relatives think George is poking fun at them again. On either shore, the only sign of human habitation they can make out from time to time is a small peak of weather-worn shingles, scarcely visible above the endless ranks of plants.

With a jolt the riverboat's bow hits the muddy bank. George helps his bewildered flock lug their trunks ashore.

There! George is pointing to his home, beaming with delight.

Their hearts sink, and their eyes glaze with misgiving. It is one of those isolated shanties. How does George plan to get from *this* to the budding promise he prophesied so convincingly in his letter? Doubting the wisdom of their long journey South, the immigrants watch the paddlewheeler back out into the creek. The packet chugs on doggedly upstream, abandoning the six Yankees to a soundless and expansive remoteness.

COTTON FIELDS, WASHINGTON COUNTY. (*Courtesy Prints & Photographs Division, Library of Congress*)

George points northward. The settlement of Rolling Fork is just a few miles upriver. Then he turns to the east. And just a few miles through those woods is Rolling Fork Landing.

But before the non-plussed Northerners can make any sense of this orientation, George is probably leading them with bounding strides into the long ranks of knarled green plants that stretch from the banks of Deer Creek to the wall of trees.

Cotton! All of it! Cotton!

He is jubilant, and pivots to face his stumbling followers, declaiming: Plowing began in February. March brought the rain. Planting started in early April and was completed by early May.[21] These plants are just weeks old!

It is their first lesson in "Cotton."

Is this land his?

Well, not yet. But soon enough! Soon enough George will have his own! Hell, they all will!

Barbara recoils at the profanity.[22]

George had never turned the earth himself.[23] Neither had Joe or Hank. And none of them had any intention of strapping themselves to a plow now. There were plenty of former slaves in the Rolling Fork neighborhood who knew how to handle a mule, who were admirably adept at cutting a straight furrow across a field six, seven, eight acres wide, and who needed work.[24]

But there were many other tasks to do. Goods had to be ordered in Vicksburg from time to time, and retrieved, requiring trips up and down Deer Creek. Repairs and improvements had to be made to the cabins— if, indeed, the cabins were already up. Fences had to be built to protect the crops and livestock from timber wolves, panthers and bears, which teemed in the forests and swamplands just beyond the cleared ground.[25] Joe was a carpenter by training; Hank had no trade. However, the two men would learn soon enough that in the Delta mastering *new* skills was often more important than plying *old* ones. George would show them.

Even to Barbara and Lena, the seven-year veteran of this wilderness would have had useful instruction to offer. Perhaps as helpful as

PICKING COTTON IN THE DELTA. *(Courtesy Mississippi Department of Archives and History)*

George's experience, however, was the domestic advice received from neighboring black homemakers. It may have been proffered obliquely, through George—familiar to the blacks of the community since before the war—or face-to-face with Barbara and Lena. Evidently the two city-bred sisters lacked nothing in stamina and sheer gumption.

Cypress cabins in the Delta were all of a kind: a more-or-less square foundation resting on blocks, four walls of vertical planking, with a pitched roof of weathered shingles. The two sides with gables were shorter than the two without, because an open gallery fit under the sloping roof on the front. A post at each end of the gallery supported the roof, but there was no railing. There was a window in each wall, and a door onto the gallery. Sometimes the interior was divided into two or three rooms by vertical plank partitions. Every cabin had a chimney for cooking. Almost none was whitewashed.[26]

Come June, the first blooms started to appear on the bottom of the cotton stalks. They were snow white, and mostly hidden by the wide-leafed foliage. A day or two later, their hue deepened to pink. After another day or so, they turned a stunning deep red, or purple. This colorful cycle repeated its way up each stalk, until the very tops of the plants were awash with white, pink and purple flowers.[27]

It was like nothing Joe or Barbara, Hank or Lena, had ever seen before. The vast, open, flat earth on both sides of the creek resembled a spectacular flower garden in bloom. For a precious fortnight the newcomers gazed out over the chromatic expanse, enchanted.

Then it was over. Nature's exuberant display faded, precipitously. One by one the blossoms withered and dropped off, revealing little, hard, round, green bolls, which would take weeks of sunshine to turn brown and open.[28]

By this time gargantuan weeds were pushing up as high as the plants. George sent his laborers—children and women as well as men—back into the fields to chop. "Chopping" was turning the cockleburs, lambsquarter and poke weeds into the soil with a hoe. The entire stand of cotton, George boasted to Joe and Hank, would require chopping all summer long—so well did any living thing, cultivated or wild, thrive in this rich black loam of the Delta.[29]

In early July the bolls began to unfold, those on the bottom first, then

TRANSPORTING SEED COTTON TO THE GIN. *(Courtesy Old Court House Museum, Vicksburg)*

those higher on the stalk. Each boll opened in four lobes of white fluff.[30] As the cotton grew out of each lobe, and dangled there, barely clinging, white and billowy among the ungainly branches, it may well have reminded the Buffalonians of snow. Cotton was Mississippi snow. Snow in July! What George saw, however, was more likely fields of green-backs. Already it was looking like a bumper crop.

He sent his pickers into the field in August to start gathering from the bottom of the plants. They went out again in September and October for the cotton in the middle. Finally they passed through the fields a third time in November, even into December, when the cotton on top was ripe. Their labor began as soon as the morning dew evaporated, and continued until the evening dew started to form.[31]

The black field hands tossed their pickings into long burlap sacks strapped across one shoulder and dragged behind them. When the sack got full, the picker pulled it over to George, who stood out in the field with a scale. After being weighed the contents of the sack were dumped into a deep round basket. When the basket could hold no more, a brawny laborer carried it on his head to the wagon positioned in the turnrow and emptied it. Women in the wagon took turns stomping and hurling them-selves repeatedly onto their backs to pack the cotton down.[32]

The wagon reached capacity, and George told Joe and Hank to hitch up *two* teams, as it would take four mules to pull the heavy load. Then the three men rode the harvest along the lint-covered dirt roads, past miles and miles of fields polka-dotted with dark figures in straw hats, stooped, trailing long sacks, to the steam-powered gin of a local planter.[33]

Taking a portion of the crop in payment, the gin operator had his men gin the cotton to pull all the seeds out, press the lint cotton into bales, and wrap the bales in burlap. Each bale measured about three feet square by five feet high, and weighed 400-500 pounds.[34] It took a crane to stack them back in the wagon. Every hand present, white and black, their sweaty hair and damp clothes feathered with wispish white lint, would have laughed to see how intently the Yankees followed the whole process, how fascinated they were by it all.

George made quite a few of these trips this fall of 1865. By year's end his take tallied 15 bales—a bumper crop, indeed![35]

Next year Joe would raise a crop of his own.[36]

STEAM-POWERED COTTON GIN AND COMPRESS. *(Courtesy Old Court House Museum, Vicksburg)*

CHAPTER FOURTEEN

THE STORE

THIS INDENTURE MADE & entered into this first day of
January in the year One thousand eight hundred & sixty-six
between George W. Faison of the first part, of the county of
Sunflower & State of Mississippi & George F. Ring of the
county of Issaquena, same State of the 2nd part—
    Witnesseth that the said George W. Faison for and in con-
sideration of the sum fourteen hundred dollars paid, or
secured to be paid, by the said George F. Ring, hath granted,
bargained & sold & by these presents doth grant, bargain &
sell to & unto the said George F. Ring, his heirs & assigns, a
certain [tract] or parcel of land lying on Sunflower River in
Issaquena County at & about the mouth of Rolling Fork consisting of a quarter section, more or less . . . to have & to hold
said tract or parcel of land with all the appurtenances & privileges thereunto belonging . . . .[1]

Faison did not come back to Issaquena County after the war.
Sunflower County offered greener pastures for his entrepreneurship,
and a new mother for his son. (His first wife had perished while they
were still living in the houseboat.)[2] In time this pioneering Virginian
would cultivate over 3,500 (of his 6,000) acres, dot the shores of the
Sunflower River with landings and stores, and buy two steamboats to

transport cotton.[3] He liked to eliminate the "middle man." Faison's days as role model and mentor to George had only just begun.

"Shortly after the purchase," George would tell later, "I sold to William Jeans for his wife one-half of the landing for the same price I gave. My purchase was one-half cash, balance in six months. Mrs. Jeans paid the second payment."[4]

Thus was born the firm of Jeans & Ring.

William Jeans, a native of Indiana, was a neighbor of George's.[5] He had come down into the Delta with two brothers around 1855.[6] He married a Tennessee-born woman, and they lost no time founding a family of Mississippi-born offspring.[7] When George arrived in the neighborhood, Jeans was cultivating a farm about four miles upstream from the mouth of Rolling Fork Creek. According to the Agricultural Census of 1860, Jeans owned 1,175 acres, but only 75 of those were improved. The cash value of the farm was estimated at a modest $2,500, the implements and machinery at $500. No slaves.[8]

Jeans removed his family to the safety of Illinois for the duration of the war. When hostilities ended, he brought them back to their place in the Delta, the family augmented now by his namesake, "little Willie"— the boy who would perish in the fiery disaster of March 4, 1873.[9]

"There was originally 131 acres of land, worthless except for landing privileges," George would explain. "We allowed all of it to forfeit for the taxes, except forty acres, simply to secure the landing and store site. . . . When purchased, there was no store building."[10]

There was, however, the makeshift cabin that Faison had erected to warehouse cotton—and maybe shelter his family, too.[11] Whether there was any discussion yet of building a store is not revealed in the old documents. Perhaps George had already perceived, given the post-war influx of immigrants, that the neighborhood would need, and could support, a country store. That may have been the very argument that sold Jeans on the partnership. Nevertheless, for the first couple of years George and Jeans would continue to use the landing solely as a shipping point. And they would continue to grow cotton—Jeans on his own land, George on somebody else's, maybe his partner's.

Right now, therefore, this January of 1866, the most pressing order of business for George and Jeans was to gather the labor they would need in the field. This brought them face-to-face with the Bureau of Freedmen, Refugees and Abandoned Lands.

The "Freedmen's Bureau" had been created by Congress after the war to assume certain responsibilities previously handled by the Union Army.[12] These included helping the liberated slaves establish themselves in a free market economy. There were also, however, white refugees who needed assistance, and tens of thousands of acres of abandoned farm land that required management. The Bureau in Mississippi was headquartered in Vicksburg, and by the end of 1865 there were 67 teachers and 58 agents working throughout the state.[13]

One of the functions of the Bureau was to help blacks negotiate equitable labor contracts. Freedmen were encouraged to submit all written agreements to their local agent for approval before making their mark on them.[14] Ex-slaves took advantage of the service, and planters resented bitterly this interference in their affairs. They considered the agents arrogant and overbearing, and ignorant besides, being all Union men having no appreciation for the enormous risks involved in a cotton operation.[15] The planters were more than just humiliated, however; their survival depended on getting and keeping sufficient labor to save their places. That could be a problem.

Many freedmen had abandoned the plantations and followed the federal troops into the cities.[16] Those remaining in the country were quick to realize the advantage of their position.[17] They were free to go wherever they might negotiate the best contract. As taxes on land doubled, quadrupled, octupled, and worse, in the post-war years, securing sufficient labor would grow increasingly critical for planters. Competition for the limited supply of labor would become fierce.[18] Landowners would be forced to acquiesce to contracts they considered unreasonable.— Except, for the most part, in Issaquena County.

Land in Issaquena County remained surprisingly stable after the war, despite the Delta's short-lived "Golden Age" for freed slaves.[19] Most blacks in the Rolling Fork neighborhood would still be poor and landless on the terrible night of March 4, 1873, still working the land of former masters—the Chaneys and Browns and McQuillens and Wrights and brethren.[20] The goods, services and credit freedmen needed to survive would remain in the hands of a few white men, not least of whom were the merchants. Furthermore, "Some white merchants, planters, and professionals in the plantation district found the allure of fraud difficult to resist when dealing with illiterate blacks."[21] These were the circumstances that would give rise to the theory that the Ring & Co. store—and its five inmates—were destroyed by a band of blacks who felt abused and frustrated.

Here, then, is the third of the 12 hypotheses: "Angry freedmen!"[22]

These same circumstances, however, ensured George all the hands he needed to sow and chop and pick his cotton. There was no shortage of labor in the Rolling Fork neighborhood.[23] Conditions in Vicksburg were so miserable, with no employment at all for the freed slaves, that it required little persuasion for Union Army officers and former owners to lure them back to the plantations where there was work to be done.[24]

Planting went well that spring of 1866. In May the Rings and Webers gawked like children as the long rows of cotton plants sprouted. During June they watched the scrawny stalks stretch toward the sun, then leaf out. Under their spellbound gaze, the flat fields surrounding the cabins burst suddenly into white, pink and purple flower. Then the precious bolls appeared, green at first, turning slowly to brown, and in early July, they began to erupt into snowy puffs. It would be another bumper harvest.

But then came the rain. Incessant rain. It washed the cotton out of the bolls and onto the ground. It flooded the fields. The cisterns filled, then overflowed like Niagara Falls. The creeks rose and flowed under the cabins, which stood on their blocks like frogs perched in a pond. The Rings and Webers were stranded in a steamy haze laden with fatted mosquitoes, and slimmed expectations.[25]

George resorted to the only feasible strategy for salvaging his crop: pick as much as possible as soon as possible. In late July he sent the pickers into the fields.

I can see George going out himself, too, with Joe and Hank in tow. He would have shown them how to spread their fingers like a claw, grasp the unfolded boll, and yank the cotton out of the four lobes. The tip of each lobe was pointy as a thorn; the fingers of the three men would have been scratched and raw in no time. They would have worked in the rain, too. They had no choice. It poured down all summer.

Then with August came the army worms. They consumed the bit of cotton still clinging to the plants. The crop was a near total loss.[26]

Planters devised all kinds of measures to cause delay and raise the funds necessary to keep their land and equipment from falling into the hands of bankers in New York, New Orleans and Louisville. Small farmers, however, including many disenchanted freedmen, went bankrupt and lost their freeholds to foreclosure. Many a Yankee packed up and went home.[27]

Jeans & Ring, however, appears to have wound up ahead. The 1866 Personal Property Tax Roll for Issaquena County shows that the firm's total earnings—presumably from shipping charges—amounted to $1,000.[28] Not even the $1,400 purchase price.—But something, anyway, a start.

Nor was George left destitute. He paid taxes on watches valued at $26, gold and silver coins amounting to $26, a horse and saddle valued at $40, and the 15 bales of cotton he had produced the preceding year.[29] At about 450 pounds per bale, and 32 cents per pound—the average 1866 price[30]—George's 15 bales represented $2,160 in capital. In addition, he had probably received by now two court-ordered sums from Charles E. Wright, against whom he had enforced a mechanic's lien.[31]

As for Jeans, he was far from financial embarrassment. He paid substantially more personal property tax this fall than George did.[32] The partners were not at all discouraged. On the contrary, they expanded their interests to include a herd of 30 cattle.[33]

Through the lazy winter months the sere cotton stalks rustled and clicked in the chill winds sweeping across the fields.[34] Then, come the new year, it was time once again for George and Jeans to sign up their labor. Local agents of the Freedmen's Bureau, enlightened by the debacle of 1866, may have been more flexible in the contracts they approved *this* January. During February the skeletal remnants of last year's crop were plowed under, and the land was harrowed for planting. But then March brought excessive rain. Water levels did not recede by mid-April, as they usually did, to allow for sowing. Rivers remained high and overflowing. Only a small portion of arable land could be sown. Much tillable land was still under water when the spring thaws of May flowed into the Delta, and remained submerged through the month of June.[35]

Nevertheless, a small crop did come up that summer. But in August the army worms returned. They ravaged the fields. By fall there was almost no cotton left on the stalks to pick.[36]

Once again large landowners scrambled frantically and managed to scrape by. But many yeoman farmers lost everything, and hundreds of disillusioned Yankees, including the Webers, went home.[37] I can hear Hank muttering that he had taken just about as much of the Delta as he cared to take! He packed up his belongings and scuttled his wife and son back North.[38]

Jeans & Ring, however, remained solvent. The partners now proceeded to erect the huge new building they had probably envisioned two years ago—the store, warehouse and living quarters that would burn to the ground on March 4, 1873.

"Jeans and myself built the . . . storehouse . . . in the winter of '67," George would later explain. "We paid for lumber and materials, besides our own work in the construction of said building, $5,700."[39]

The lumber, purchased in Vicksburg and shipped up to Rolling Fork Landing, cost $5,000. Nails, spikes, bricks, mortar, hinges, glass, paint, tar and other materials, also from Vicksburg, ran $700.[40]

George's statements regarding the construction do not mention his brother, despite the fact that Joe was a seasoned carpenter. Evidently Joe was not yet involved in the mercantile venture. That would come later. George does, however, refer to hired labor: "Labor was as cheap then as now."[41] He and Jeans would have employed a handful of local blacks to help erect the immense edifice—an undertaking of herculean proportions.

"The building was 53 by 58 feet from out to out," George would explain. "The building was framed, two stories high, resting on blocks two feet high. On these blocks were six sills twelve inches square, hewed cypress."[42]

The holes dug for the foundation blocks must have been deep and numerous, not only because of the swampiness of the land, but because the blocks would have to support the weight of an enormous superstructure. The laborers would have used teams of oxen to haul the huge timbers into place and stand them upright in the holes. Then they would have pounded the blocks to a uniform height and packed earth around them. To hoist the six massive sills onto the blocks, the men would have employed oxen and pulleys.

"Resting on the sills were sleepers 12 by 5 inches, hewed, and floor laid on top, one-and-a-half-inch cypress plank, nailed down, rough unplaned. . . . First floor was latticed on square hewed posts nine feet long.—Used for warehouse. . . .

"On the posts above mentioned, plates were framed, upon which were laid the sleepers for the second floor. Sleepers were 5 by 12 inches. The flooring was double, out of inch cypress plank, not tongue and grooved, rough, nailed and spiked down. . . .

"Front steps fourteen feet wide, eighteen feet long, made with two-inch cypress plank. Two side stringers, 8 by 12 inches, hewed timber, with steps morticed into them. Two middle stringers, out of two-inch cypress plank, sawed out to fit steps. Rear steps, two stringers, 8 by 12, eighteen feet long, steps four feet wide, morticed into stringers. . . .

"The sides of the second story were planked up and down, then weatherboarded. Crosswise, posts were braced, but no studding. Plank rough. The inside was not ceiled except overhead, all of which was ceiled. . . .

"Above was a half story, 25 by 30 feet, floor single, rough, laid in cypress plank one inch thick. The joists were 25 feet long, 8 by 12, hewed."[43]

The way the partners fashioned the giant chimney was very peculiar, perhaps because bricks were expensive.

"There was one double chimney, resting on a frame [of cypress timber?]. Bricks commenced two-and-a-half feet below the second floor, being then about twenty feet high. Body of about five feet square."[44]

This explains why the chimney would not remain standing through the conflagration of 1873, but would collapse onto a cot where one of the inhabitants lay sleeping, or already dead.[45]

"The main roof was held by two purloin plates, six inches square."[46] These held the rafters, which were "covered with split cypress shingles. . . . Water-tight square box gutters all around the building. The outsides whitewashed."[47]

Though George failed to mention it, the men would have covered the gallery with a shed roof supported by several posts. They would

also have hoisted to the gallery roof a plank bearing bold letters painted freehand: JEANS & RING.

But their work was still far from done. The interior spaces of the
second floor—"used for merchandise and dwelling"[48]—remained to be
finished.

"Inside of second story were 84 feet of partitions eleven feet high,
of rough one-and-a-half-inch plank, cutting off six rooms. Also 80 feet
of partition fourteen feet long, rough plank upright, separating the
storeroom."[49]

The partners put special care into the storeroom. The walls there
were 14 feet high—not the 11 feet of the rest of the second floor—and
papered.[50] The ceiling "was planed, tongue-and-grooved, and
painted"[51]—not "rough, tongue-and-grooved, not painted"[52] as in the living quarters. All of the extensive shelving and long cabinets of the storeroom they "dressed and painted on edge."[53] The men also dressed and
painted, and finished with a plain cornice, the 50 feet of counter.[54]

The ceiling of the adjoining grocery room was not as lofty as the one
in the storeroom, but George and Jeans finished it just as finely. "The
grocery room had plain counter, dressed, not painted—say, fourteen
feet long. . . ."[55]

"There were five inside batten doors, 3 by 7 feet, one inch thick. Also
two glass doors. All dressed. The glass doors only painted."[56]

There loomed the mammoth white structure, gleaming against the
dark wavy wall of trees, a stolid and incongruous presence on the shallow clearing. Standing before it, eyeing it approvingly, from the squat
blocks rising out of the earth, across the latticed first level, up the wide
staircase to the gallery, the over-sized double doors, the weather-boarded
walls of the second story punctuated with 13 windows, beyond the
gallery roof, and the JEANS & RING sign, and the tarred gutters of the
main roof, to the crowning row of red bricks in the chimney, George
beams like a first-time father.

Surely he is not blind to the homespun quality of his handiwork. It
lacks details of craftsmanship common even in the most modest of
working-class houses in Buffalo and Vicksburg. Yet compared to the
one-room cabin he has been calling home for close to 10 years, the new
abode and place of business is remarkable. And this is just the beginning.

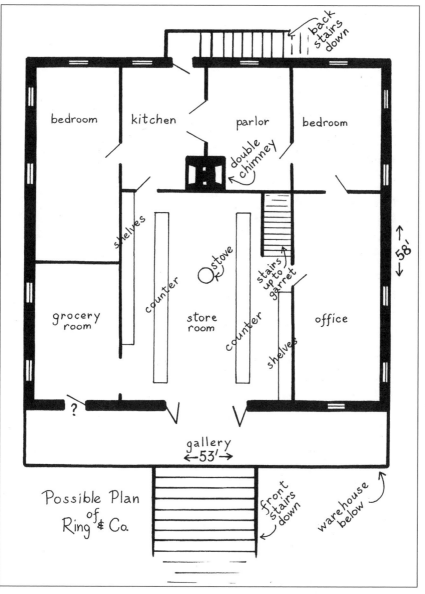

Possible Plan of Ring & Co.

POSSIBLE PLAN OF SECOND LEVEL OF RING & CO., ROLLING FORK LANDING, 1867–1873.

(Plan drawn by the author)

I can see his oval face bursting into laughter. He slaps Jeans on the back, and the two of them howl. George uncorks a jug and offers it to his partner. Jeans swings it across his shoulder to his mouth and swallows, then gives it back to George, who mimics the gesture. Then George passes the jug on to the black workers.

A silence settles. The two pioneers, the few laborers, weak from fatigue, disheveled and dirty, their lips moistened now, gaze up at the huge edifice. From chimney top to foundation blocks they admire it, while behind them the creek gurgles its way to the river, and a breeze rustles the willows along the banks.

The partners look at each other again, grin, then laugh, then howl and whistle. George accepts the jug back, sweeps it to his mouth, gulps, and passes it to Jeans, who downs another swig. Then the immigrant breaks into a rowdy German drinking song, stomping out the rhythm, and the two men enlace arms and dance clumsily together in the mud. The Negroes laugh and hoot and start clapping. George's two dogs are leaping and yelping about the swinging boots.

It is time to celebrate. And George is very good at that, too!

CHAPTER FIFTEEN

THE DELTA

Barbara, I suspect, was in no mood to celebrate. On the contrary, after two-and-a-half years of arduous subsistence on Deer Creek, she was probably ready to follow her sister back North. But on December 11, 1867, as George was erecting his great edifice, he sold Joe an interest in Rolling Fork Landing.[1] Now Joe, and therefore Barbara, were more entrenched than ever in the Delta.

Joe and Barbara would have reacted very differently to the Delta—not that either one of them left any diary or letters saying as much. But their documented actions, scrutinized in the light of their personal histories and the temperaments and personalities (presumably inherited) of their children, do allow for some speculation.[2]

Joe appears to have been well-suited to frontier life. He was relaxed and adapted effortlessly. Forsaking his homeland and braving the Atlantic Ocean are evidence enough of his desire for change. Now he was proving that he had more than the desire, he had the ability as well. The more he worked beside George, the more he seems to have absorbed the masterful ease, perhaps even some of the temerity and ambition, that characterized his younger brother.

Barbara, by contrast, must have felt sorely out of place. She appears to have drawn her sense of well-being from the inviolate tradition of her central European heritage. Total withdrawal from the environment and customs of Papa's household would have hit her hard. She seems never to have adjusted well to change.

In the beginning, Lena's company would have softened the disorientation. But the novelty of adventure would have flattened soon enough beneath the daily drudgery of survival.[3] How could Barbara and her sister not have grown homesick for the kaleidoscopic animation of their native Fourth Ward in Buffalo? They would have missed the commercial avenues lined with colorful window displays, the German bakeries and butcher shops. They would have missed the residential streets enlivened by the interaction of neighbors. They would have missed church.

Never had Barbara lived more than a short stroll from church. It was at Mass or novena or confession or vespers that she had socialized. It was at baptisms, confirmations, weddings and funerals that she had participated in her cultural inheritance. At noon, and again at six, Monday through Saturday, she was accustomed to hearing the ringing of the "*Angelus Domini*"—which meant that Joe was about to walk through the door expecting his dinner, his supper. Here in the Rolling Fork neighborhood the nearest Catholic church was St. Paul's—in Vicksburg. Forty miles distant as the crow flies. Two-and-a-half days by steamer.

Not only was there no church, there were no Catholics. Never had Barbara resided outside of a Germanic Catholic enclave. Lena's husband was perhaps the only Protestant she knew personally. In Issaquena County Barbara found herself immersed in a sea of Anglo-Saxons professing a variety of creeds she had never even heard of. But *they* had no house of worship either.[4] Surrounded by people who conducted their lives from one end of the year to the other without the liturgical observances and fellowship of a parish, how could Barbara not have felt estranged?

Perhaps the absence of a priest was not critical until January 15, 1867.[5] Barbara gave birth to her second son that day, and for a long time mother and newborn were confined to their stark shanty by the incessant rain and lingering overflow that ruined the cotton that year. And when, at long last, the rain stopped and the floodwaters receded, Barbara still could not take the baby to be baptized until he was strong enough to make the strenuous trip.

Weeks passed. Barbara fretted. She had been christened the day she was born. *All* the Millers were baptized within days of their birth.[6]

Joe, I think, would not have understood the urgency. The Ring men seem to have had a more "common sense" attitude toward religion. He might have called his wife's attention to the baby's good health.

Barbara would have reminded her husband of the two baby girls they had already lost.[7]

Joe could have said that he was quite confident his new son was in no danger of damnation.

But such nonchalance would only have irritated Barbara, not console her. It was the kind of glib remark George would make.

Finally, after 15 weeks, the infant was held over the baptismal font of St. Paul's and christened George—in honor of his enterprising uncle, no doubt, as later he would sometimes be called George F. Ring, Jr. But the enterprising uncle was not there. A total stranger, Rosalia Contella—Father Leray's housekeeper—was borrowed to serve as sole godparent.[8] This was not (I can imagine Barbara lamenting in her heart) how things were supposed to be.

It was shortly after Barbara returned from this pilgrimage that Lena went back North.[9] Gone now was the helper who shared the cooking, baking, canning, washing, ironing, housekeeping and child rearing. Gone now was the confidant, the cherished intimate, to reminisce with in the still evenings over sewing and mending. Gone was the companion for gathering mast for the hogs, picking berries for strudels.[10] Barbara was bereft of a consoling link to Papa's world.

Might she have made friends by this time? Certainly she would have had occasion to exchange a few words with a neighboring farmer's wife or daughter, maybe a pioneer woman passing upriver or down. But the white settlers were so broadly scattered that such encounters would have been rare.[11] Besides, Barbara seems to have been the type of person who would not like talking to strangers. And the neighbors who were *not* strangers were freed slaves. I suspect that too wide a gap yawned between Barbara's world and theirs for them to share anything more than a neighborly greeting.

When a field hand appeared at the door holding a couple of skinned squirrels or rabbits, he would simply touch his cap and hold out the offering.[12] When the women in headrags came by to kill and clean a

CYPRESS CABIN IN THE DELTA. *(Courtesy Prints & Photographs Division, Library of Congress)*

chicken, or sweep out the cabin, they would nod and go right to their task.[13] Barbara would report to Joe, who would see to it that such services were recompensed. I picture the black folk talking much more freely with Joe and George than with Barbara.

Often Barbara would hear the rhythmic wail of laborers in the field. The plaint of a lone male voice would be answered by a chorus of mixed voices, back and forth, back and forth.[14] Sometimes, too, she would be startled from her chores by the spritely tune of a banjo or fiddle or harmonica—mouth organ, they called it—or accordion—which they called a squeezebox.[15] Not hesitating to slip out of her apron, Barbara would gather up the baby, seize Nicholas by the hand, and hurry to a shady spot in the pecan grove.[16] I can see them sitting on a stump, clapping their hands to the beat, thankful for the musical interlude.

For in the Delta, all forms of distraction and social intercourse seemed reserved for men. It would have been George who taught his elder brother how to hunt.[17] He owned two mongrels,[18] and Joe acquired Lomo.[19] Now the two men, rifles slung across their backs, often rode off with their hounds before sun-up, and did not re-emerge from the dense, dark, leafy wall until late afternoon. Game abounded, so even a beginner like Joe never failed to return with at least a deer or turkey or possum, and in the fall, more than a couple of ducks.[20]

George would have shown him how to set traps, too, which by sunset were sure to hold a rabbit or two.[21] Of an afternoon the brothers might push a skiff into the creek and pass a few hours fishing. Such excursions invariably yielded a bountiful haul of carp and catfish.[22] Always there was a black or white local around to join in these masculine pursuits.[23]

Once in a while the white men of the neighborhood gathered for a shooting match.[24] George would nail a target to a tree trunk, and each participant paid a nickel for two shots. The marksman who hit closest to the bull's-eye won the prize, usually a ham. Interest in the match was often heightened by a friendly wager.[25]

From time to time a ring of black field hands, lanky youths to bony elders, would form behind one of the shacks. Their volley of taunts and yelps would grow to a fevered fusillade of hollering, and geysers of dust would shoot up from their midst. George and Joe would saunter over to place a bet on the cock fight or boxing match in progress.[26]

Other times the men arranged a cross-country race.[27] Then Barbara and the boys, huddled in the pecan grove, would have watched in terrified elation as the sweating, straining steeds mounted by crouching, yelling riders, galloped off toward McQuillen's place, or Jeans's place, or maybe Dr. Waddell's. Then in silence they would wait, breathless, motionless, expectant. Soon the ground would tremble. The far-off pounding would build, louder, nearer, until the horses burst into view, thundering at a terrific speed, mud flying, riders shouting. How Nicholas must have lept and cheered!

Sunday afternoons George might sit on his gallery on a bentwood chair tilted against the wall. Surveying his cotton, gnawing perhaps on a cigar, the entrepreneurial bachelor would ponder his next move. Joe, the family man, might fill his leisure with whittling kitchen utensils for Barbara, toys for the boys. Cypress wood, pinkish and fragrant, molded like butter to the sharp blade of his pocket knife—the pocket knife that would be found in the smoldering ruins of Ring & Co.[28]

Of an evening the men might gather on the gallery of George's cabin for a game of poker.[29] As the last haze of twilight retreated before the cool darkness, they would ignite a few pine knots—to smoke off mosquitoes as much as for light—and the dealing and betting would continue unabated. The grating of crickets and croaking of frogs would fill the air, while the men drained a keg of beer or jug of whiskey.[30] Card playing and hard drinking: two sins that aroused strong condemnation in more "civilized" and "church-going" communities.

That George enjoyed his liquor is documented; he drank a lot.[31] That Barbara disapproved is safe assumption.[32] She would have worried about the bad influence it had on Joe, and the bad example it set for the boys. She was probably offended by his language, too; George used curse words, sometimes even profanity.[33] Joe would have tempered his tongue long ago to his wife's sensibilities. George, however, was not the type to restrain himself. In the end, Barbara probably considered her brother-in-law a profane man. She would not have been able to warm up to him.

Nevertheless, in early 1868, when George left, it is likely that Barbara missed hearing the sound of his German. Surely Joe and

George's personality well documented

George had reverted from time to time to their native tongue. For Barbara, these instances would have been comforting reminders of her childhood home, where she had grown up speaking German to Papa.[34] But scarcely had George finished stocking his brand new store when he moved to Vicksburg.[35]

Yet Barbara stayed, because Joe stayed, in the Rolling Fork neighborhood, where the cast of characters for the stupendous disaster of March 4, 1873, had already begun to assemble.

George sells ⚭ interest to

Jesse Moore was the first to arrive. A young dry goods merchant from Pennsylvania,[36] he was settled on Rolling Fork Creek near the Jeans place by 1866.[37] Moore was eager to buy into a country business. In the spring of 1869, George sold him and Willie Jeans the interest in Rolling Fork Landing he had just bought back from Joe.[38] The Pennsylvanian was quick to clamber atop the gallery, pry off the JEANS & RING sign, and secure in its place a new shingle: JEANS & MOORE.

Nor did Moore waste any time exploiting the dense forests of the 131 acres. He acquired three yoke of oxen, a set of timber wheels, an axle, six-and-a-half log chains, two ox yokes and one ox wagon, a flat boat, and immediately started felling as much timber as he could get downriver.[39] He also sold cut and split timber to riverboat captains for fuel.[40]

A more recent arrival to the neighborhood was the log-splitter John F. Coker,[41] whom Moore hired to help with his lumbering activities. Coker brought his wife Lucy and his three children from a previous marriage: Martha, a boy, and a little girl.[42] Martha was scarcely out of childhood, yet already Jesse Moore, a bachelor, was evidently taking notice of her. *Intro of characters ⚭*

It was also about this time that the veterinarian, J. W. Parberry, started making his appearances in the vicinity of Rolling Fork.[43] His profession kept him moving up and down the rivers and creeks, treating a diseased steer on this plantation, a sick heifer on that farm, an ailing ox or mule at this landing or that settlement. With Parberry came his buddy, the Irishman known only as "Uncle Jimmy." The comrades were very mysterious. Many years of searching would not reveal where they came from originally, or where they disappeared to. Neither one seems to

involved in tragedy

have had any family. They would be the most peculiar and elusive play-ers in the terrible tragedy of March 4, 1873—as well as the most publicly-identifiable suspects.

By the spring of 1869, therefore, Joe and Barbara Ring—willingly or not—were part of a new class that was evolving in the Delta. This was the scant population of entrepreneurial whites with some education, trades and skills, who streamed in after the war.[44] They were merchants, clerks, salesmen, agents, mechanics, carpenters, blacksmiths, veteri-narians and such, and they gravitated to the landings and the hamlets that were emerging. To get a foothold, many started out by farming, either as tenants or freeholders, and felling timber and selling garden vegetables in the growing towns. They conducted business with the few wealthy landowners and the hordes of impoverished freedmen, but they socialized and married within their own class. In February 1870, for example, when Martha Coker was 16 and Jesse Moore 28, they took a packet to Vicksburg and came back husband and wife.[45]

Throughout the South, newcomers like the Moores and Cokers and Rings were identified with Republican Reconstruction. They were resented by their native-born neighbors, who reviled them as carpet-baggers.[46] But not in the Delta. In the Delta, where the frontier society was removed only one generation from Choctaw and Chickasaw days, former slaves, migrants from other states, and immigrants from abroad far outnumbered the scant native-born whites. That was part of the uniqueness of the Delta.[47]

[margin note: social/political identity of Delta]

In Issaquena County, the only inhabitants *not* associated with Republican Reconstruction were the planters—the handful of Chaneys, Browns, McQuillens and Wrights.[48] They were the Democrats subject-ed to the regime imposed by northerners and the masses of former slaves. Their rancor ran deep, but they were impotent to oust the Yankee interlopers and regain control of the black labor force.[49]—Which situation would give rise to the theory that it was local landowners who decimated the Ring & Co. building at Rolling Fork Landing.

Here, then, is the fourth of the 12 hypotheses: "Planters!"[50]

In reality, though, the Rings' relationship to their wealthy neighbors was not so clear-cut. After all, George had settled in their midst *before* the war, not after it. For years he had been conducting business with them. And Joe, though undeniably among the post-war hordes from the North, was at least George's kin. Besides, Joe did something that actually helped ingratiate him with the local planters. In any other part of the South, it would have earned him their contempt and antagonism. But not in Issaquena County.

In February of 1869 the U.S. Congress had passed a joint resolution: persons holding public office in Mississippi who could not swear that they had never supported the Confederacy were to be removed from office. The vacancies were to be filled by the Commandant of the Fourth Military District with appointees who *could* so swear. The following month Adelbert Ames, the Union general serving as Mississippi's provisional governor, was appointed Commandant of the Fourth Military District by the new president, Grant. Immediately this staunch Reconstructionist from Maine began removing from office nearly all state officials, and hundreds of county and local officials, and replacing them with men who could swear to the "iron-clad oath." Those appointees were freedmen, scalawags and northerners.[51]

In Issaquena County, the large landowners exercised what limited prerogative they could *within* the confines of this Reconstructionist regime. "Here, the difficulty of securing and maintaining black labor stability clearly overrode any inclination the whites in these districts felt to overthrow Republican rule and reduce Negroes to political impotency through violence and intimidation."[52] That is why the Ku Klux Klan never gained a foothold in the black counties of western Mississippi.[53] All the planters of the Delta could do to assuage their fears and sense of helplessness—however grudgingly—was to keep as many white men as possible in public office. And Joe Ring was white. When they learned that he was a naturalized citizen, they themselves probably enlisted his nomination.

By Special Order No. 79 of Adelbert Ames, dated April 20, 1869, Joseph Ring was appointed a member of the Board of Police, Police District No. 5, Issaquena County.[54] The Board of Police wielded substantial power. It held jurisdiction over roads, highways, ferries and bridges; called for and conducted elections; levied and collected taxes; and maintained the courthouse and jail.[55] Joe signed the "iron-clad oath" and entered into duty in May.[56] This allowed the local planters to deal, if

OATH OF OFFICE.

I, *Joseph Ring*

do solemnly swear that I have never voluntarily borne arms against the United States since I have been a citizen thereof; that I have voluntarily given no aid, countenance, counsel or encouragement to persons engaged in armed hostility thereto; that I have neither sought nor accepted, nor attempted to exercise the functions of any office whatever, under any authority, or pretended authority, in hostility to the United States; that I have not yielded a voluntary support to any pretended government, authority, power or constitution within the United States, hostile or inimical thereto. And I do further swear, or affirm, that to the best of my knowledge and ability, I will support and defend the Constitution of the United States against all enemies, foreign and domestic; that I will bear true faith and allegiance to the same; that I take this obligation freely, without any mental reservation or purpose of evasion; and that I will well and faithfully discharge the duties of the office on which I am about enter. So help me God.

Joseph Ring

Sworn and subscribed before me, at *Talula*
this *7th* day of *May*, 186*9*.

Benj. Leas
Probate Judge

JOSEPH RING'S OATH OF OFFICE, MAY 7, 1869.

not with one of their own, at least with a white man, and *not* a man who had once been listed in their plantation ledgers alongside livestock and other chattel.

Joe traveled immediately to the county courthouse in Tallula for his first session.[57] Minutes of the Board of Police contain no evidence that he performed any duty during his two-year term that might have made him a neighbor's enemy. Once he was appointed "to sell all the lumber, timber and other material of the old Bridges across Rolling Fork Creek and Deer Creek at the head of Rolling Fork. . . ."[58] Other than that, however, Joe's participation on the Board warranted no special mention. Nevertheless, the office did entail risk. According to Mississippi's Revised Statutes of 1857, "the members of the board of police are conservators of the peace within their respective counties."[59]

Bands of armed outlaws wandered through the wilderness of the Delta: veterans in tattered gray or faded blue, grown too fond of war; blacks abusing their newly-acquired liberty; convicts escaped from plantations where they were leased as labor.[60] Settlements and plantations were widespread, many inaccessible for months out of the year. Residents of landings were particularly vulnerable, as crime-committing vagrants could show up and be gone quickly.[61] It was impossible for rural sheriffs, deputy sheriffs and magistrates to enforce the laws and ensure security for the lives and property of the scattered pioneers.[62] Not surprisingly, one explanation for what happened at Rolling Fork Landing on March 4, 1873, would claim that the five inmates were killed, the store burgled, and the building torched, by a gang of bandits—pure and simple.[63]

Here, then, is the fifth of the 12 hypotheses: "Bandits!"[64]

Surely it was not the income that prompted Joe to accept this risk. "Each member of the board of police shall receive three dollars per day for each day occupied in the discharge of his duties," reads the Revised Statutes of 1857, "and five cents for each mile necessarily travelled in going to and returning from the place of holding the court."[65] In 1869 Joe received $7.10 for the May session, $17.40 for the July session, plus $10.00 for "Advertising & Selling Bridge timber."[66] In 1870, for a Special Session with the new sheriff, Henry P. Scott, he received $21.00.[67] Not substantial sums. Yet every little bit would have helped while the crops were laid by. Because Joe's responsiblities were increasing.

On June 17, 1869, Barbara delivered their third son, John.[68] Another mouth to feed. And after four years in the Delta, Joe's financial progress came nowhere close to matching his younger brother's.

"Farmer" was how the federal census taker described Joe's occupation when he came along Deer Creek in August of 1870.[69] Questioning his way column by column across the large schedule, the enumerator penned no figure at all under the heading "Value of Real Estate," and only $525 under "Value of Personal Estate." This included two mules, two horses and a carriage that Joe paid taxes on the following year, according to Issaquena County tax rolls.[70] He also owned a few pieces of household furniture, and selling his interest in Rolling Fork Landing back to George had netted him $2,500 as well.[71]

These modest assets bear witness to the hard fact that the new beginning Joe had undertaken at the behest of his brother's enticing letter had not blossomed as George's had. It never would. Joe's new beginnings never lasted very long. Circumstances always intervened to thwart them, as they did again now. In March of 1871 Willie Jeans, at the age of 42[72]—just five years Joe's senior—died.[73] Five days later his wife Elizabeth, 31, also died.[74] And there were doctors' bills.[75] So it may have been an outbreak of contagious disease that convinced Joe it was time to leave the Delta.[76]

He had ample cause for concern. Barbara was in confinement again. Indeed, so mundane a motive as the need for more living space may also have figured into Joe's decision to move. His household had outgrown their little cypress cabin. The farm he acquired as his neighbors lay dying was modest, just 61 acres.[77] But it was in Warren County,[78] a much more salubrious site, free from annual flooding and recurrent fever and perpetual peril. The land was green and undulating, spotted with dense old growth woods and traversed by a clear brook. There, just as soon as he could afford it, Joe Ring would build his family a new and ample house. On May 5th Barbara delivered their fourth son, Peter Paul,[79] and the baby, thank God!, was healthy.

Soon thereafter came another action on Joe's part that may have been prompted by the demise of Willie and Elizabeth Jeans. As an appraiser of their estate, he learned that they left their children in precarious financial straits.[80] As George would explain: "I administered on the estate of William Jeans. Sold some little personal property. His plantation was under mortgage and sold by the mortgagor. The sale paid the debt, and I collected about $5,000 of that sale. His estate is insolvent."[81] Having taken on substantial debt himself now, and having just fathered another son, Joe would not have wanted his family to suffer the fate of the Jeans orphans, should he meet with an untimely death. On July 21, 1871, his crop laid by, he purchased from the Germania Life Insurance Company of New York a $5,000 policy on his own life.[82] Within two scant years it would be redeemed.[83]

That fall Joe's cotton interests in Sunflower County yielded upwards of 40 bales, which he sold to his brother's firm of Ring & Muller for 18 cents a pound.[84] Now he could afford the new house. He hired a surveyor and a carpenter, and had a cistern built.[85] He purchased finished lumber from Spengler's Mill, and flooring, doors, shingles, nails and glass from other Vicksburg concerns.[86] In a caravan of ox-drawn wagons, the building materials lumbered their way out Baldwin's Ferry Road.[87] By early 1872 the beautiful new residence was ready for his wife and sons.

Though Barbara's yearning for the familiarity of Buffalo would not be satisfied quite yet, she was at least about to know the relief of escaping the Delta.

CHAPTER SIXTEEN

THE "VICKSBURG PLACE"

moving to Vickrburg

It is easy to imagine Barbara's heart beating fast as she stood at the guardrail of the *B. H. Hurt,* or the *Lizzie,* pulling into Vicksburg. It was early 1872. No document provides the exact date. The hour may have been morning or evening. The sky may have been bright or overcast. But whatever the specifics were, Joe Ring, once again, was hauling his family—six now—in the footsteps of his younger brother. Only *this* fresh start was by a city. Barbara would not have been able to take her eyes off it.

High atop the loftiest promontory, grandiose and elegant and shimmering white, loomed the Warren County Courthouse.[1] It was a two-storied rectangle of grand proportions, stucco, with a majestic pedimented portico gracing each side, six stately columns on the East and West, four on the North and South. Like military sentinels they stood at the head of four brick walkways leading to wide staircases that descended the terraced grounds to the four streets far below. Rising from the center of the slate roof, an octagonal clock tower with a surrounding balcony was crowned with a soaring cupola where the alarm bell hung. Day and night a watchman paced the balcony round and round, peering over the city for smoke, ready to rouse the citizens to action. It was a "Temple of Justice,"[2] reflecting not only the reverence attached to the judicial functions that transpired within its walls, but the wealth and prestige of the metropolis spread below it. Every masterful detail of its masonry, woodwork, plastering and ironwork had been fashioned by the hands of slaves.

The famous hallmark still asserts today as commanding a presence above the Mississippi as it did the day Barbara gazed at it from the deck of an approaching packet. Only now it houses the Old Court House Museum. Here, old newspapers and census schedules, funeral home account books and cemetery records, tax rolls, city directories, and other equally mundane and archaic materials contain hundreds of disparate pieces of the story of Joe Ring.[3]

Peering beyond the angled roofs of the business district, Barbara could have spied the steeple of St. Paul's towering above the bluffs.[4] She might even have heard—between the ear-splitting blasts of the steamboat's whistle—the bronze bell ringing the "*Angelus Domini*."[5] It would have filled her with joyous anticipation of Sunday Mass, the sacraments, Latin prayers, parish life!

Unlike the courthouse, though, the fortress-like church of burgundy brick familiar to the Rings no longer exists. Unsettled by a tornado in 1953,[6] it had to be torn down. In its stead rose a modern Saint Paul's, a pragmatic stone building with adjacent sacristy. Here, in a fire-proof vault, lie old sacramental registers—the ones that have survived—whose faint script, scrawled across yellowed pages, provides more pieces of Joe's story.[7]

Yet another reason why Joe chose this time to move to the city may be that Nicholas was nearing school age. There was no school in the vicinity of Rolling Fork.[8] In all likelihood, Nicholas would begin his formal education this very fall of 1872 at Vicksburg's St. Francis Xavier Academy. Sisters of Mercy taught there.[9]

The Rings filed down the landing plank. Once again, George's stout form was probably well-planted on the Commons, waiting. He would have brought an empty brougham for his brother's family, and a couple of wagons or drays for the trunks and furniture. He may even have led a crew of hired black hands to the task, allowing Joe to take Barbara and the boys directly to their new home. Lomo would have trotted alongside.

The Commons looked so different from the first time Barbara had set foot here! Gone was the crush of blue uniforms: military occupation had ended in 1870, when Mississippi was readmitted to the Union.[10]

Vanished, too, were the hosts of forlorn and huddled black families. The only black faces Barbara would have seen this time were those of the myriad laborers busy at work.[11]

The carriage slowed as the horse strained up the steep incline of Clay Street. At Levee, Barbara might have caught a glimpse of William Muller—George's partner—standing amid the open crates of fruits and vegetables balanced in front of his store under The Sunflower Exchange.[12] Or was it Jacob Schwink—George's tenant[13]—Barbara saw this day, pausing in his white apron at the louvered doors of The Sunflower Exchange? If either the grocer or the bartender called a greeting, it would have been in a pronounced German accent, if not in German.

The brougham trudged past Mulberry, Washington and Walnut Streets. This was the business district: banks, grocers, druggists, dry goods shops, saddlers and blacksmiths, hardware stores, the cotton and corn exchanges, every enterprise necessary to a thriving commercial town, including the popular Biedenharn's Candy Shop. In the second-story offices over these concerns, cotton factors, attorneys-at-law, notaries public, and insurance agents—among them, William Chamberlin—conducted their affairs.[14] Barbara would have felt much reassured to see the signs of mercantile houses bearing familiar German names.

With a population of about 13,000, Vicksburg was by far the largest city on the river between Memphis and New Orleans, and the most important cotton shipping center of Mississippi.[15] Compared to the northern metropolises Barbara had known—Buffalo and Cincinnati—Vicksburg was just a small town. But it was a vibrant, cultured, rich, sophisticated and important town, because its booming cotton industry connected it to countries around the world. Vicksburg's economy and politics, even its social life, were regulated by the ebb and flow of one industry alone: cotton.[16]

The carriage veered onto Adams Street. Barbara could have pictured the two Hessian sisters, Catherine Ring and Anna Sprankler, sitting erect and decorous, crocheting, on the long gallery of George's big house several blocks ahead. What a pleasure it would be to have the companionship of German women again!

Now the brougham is rolling along Grove Street, which runs for eight blocks to the edge of Vicksburg. There the hills stretch out in undulating ridges between brooks and streams, and Grove Street changes to Baldwin's Ferry Road.[17] The ride gets rougher. Barbara and the boys are jostled from side to side. Soon they are passing through the terrain where the Union and Confederate forces dug their opposing trenches nine years ago. Barbara has heard about the siege, but it is impossible for her to imagine the destruction and starvation and animosity. Because by 1872 the trenches of mortal combat are lost in an idyllic landscape.

Leafy green undergrowth pushes out from every crevice among the rocks and boulders. Winding veins of sparkling blue water tinkle pleasantly over stones and pebbles. Beds of yellow buttercups and other wildflowers, orange and purple, line the river banks. Towering oaks, elms and sycamores grow in profusion and soar far higher than Barbara can see from inside the carriage. The sky is laced with birds building nests, the air filled with their staccato refrain.

The carriage turns into a narrow dirt lane. Joe calls down. They are getting close.

The acreage he bought in Warren County is part of the old Barefield Plantation, which was divided into 16 lots after the war and sold off by lot.[18] Joe's is number 15, the western-most, the one closest to the city.[19] Adjoining his is number 13, owned by Anna Sprankler.[20] Joe put down $610 cash; another $610 is payable in one year with 10 percent interest; a final $610 plus interest is due in two years.[21]

In 1899 the United States will begin purchasing this site, including half of Joe's lot, for a National Military Park.[22] Numerous monuments will be erected here to commemorate the U.S. troops who assaulted, and the C.S. troops who defended, Vicksburg. But no memorial will ever be raised to the personal tragedy that Barbara Ring will endure here, in her new house, in March of 1873.

The carriage stops. Joe clambers down. Nicholas, George and John are already racing toward the house, Lomo barking and bounding at their heels. Joe takes the baby while Barbara descends. There she stands, staring, overwhelmed. The house is everything Joe promised.

It is one-and-a-half stories high, standing on blocks, sided in freshly whitewashed clapboard. The roof slopes toward the front, breaks for a dormer, then levels off over a gallery the full width of the house. Four delicately lathed pillars line the front, and a balustrade of ornately-

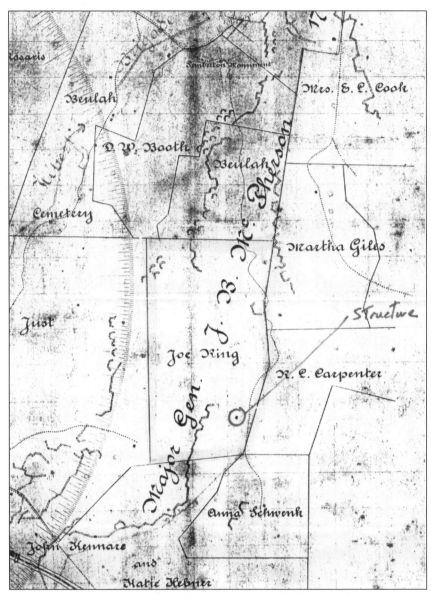

MAP SHOWING JOE RING'S "VICKSBURG PLACE," 1890S.
(Courtesy National Military Park, Vicksburg)

shaped white slats—like the rail of a riverboat—runs all around the gallery, except where three stairs lead down to the long path. Barbara may already imagine wisteria vines curling around these pillars and crawling along the edge of the roof.

This, at any rate, is how I picture it. The new house was demolished long before Grandma Ring told me the story of Joe Ring, and no visual or written representation of it survives—except for one tiny black square on a map surveyed by the U.S. Army Corps of Engineers.[23] That square is drawn in the southeast corner of the property, just outside the boundary of the National Military Park. But I have seen other middle-class houses of the period which dot to this day the Vicksburg environs, and they all tend to be variations on this theme.

Barbara steps onto the gallery and examines the tall shuttered parlor windows, the wide panelled door. Surveying the patch of dirt that will be her front yard, she may envision a dogwood or two, some crabapple trees, and azaleas, lots of bright azaleas.

Joe says he already has two sacks of grass seed.[24]

Barbara enters. The large rooms echo with the playful voices of the boys and Lomo's high-pitched yelping.

She walks through the house and throws open the back door. Scarcely visible in the distance, when Barbara peers where Joe is pointing, sway the tops of the majestic willows and birches that line the river traversing the 61 acres.[25]

How relieved Barbara must be. It looks as though Joe is finally making a fresh start that will last. Finally something permanent!

The Rings call it simply, "the Vicksburg Place."[26] In 20 years, when Vicksburg expands, the plantation will straddle the corporate line, and then it will be half-consumed by the military park. Long before then, however, Barbara and her boys will be far away. In just 15 months, in fact, they will abandon the beautiful new residence forever. Nothing of Joe's will be permanent. Nothing of Joe's will remain. Not even a recognizable corpse.

Barbara removes her bonnet. Never will this city-born and city-bred, chestnut-haired daughter of a tradesman return to the Delta.

Never.

CHAPTER SEVENTEEN

MARCH 19, 1873

On the afternoon of Wednesday, March 19th, Barbara sits in the high-ceilinged parlor of George and Catherine's elegant residence on Adams Street.[1] From the veil screening her face, to the embroidered handkerchief she holds on her pregnant lap, to the silk bows of her high shoes, the 32-year-old widow is swathed in black. Nearby lies Joe's rosewood coffin.[2]

For 10 days Barbara had endured in limbo, not knowing whether her husband was alive or dead. And then, when George came back from Rolling Fork Landing the second time and told her, even if he showed her the bones, she still could not look upon a corpse and know that it was Joe. Barbara needed to behold a casket, at least, if not a body. Besides, Joe deserved a Catholic burial.

Fisher Funeral Home was engaged to handle the interment,[3] and a notice was placed in this morning's *Vicksburg Daily Times*, inviting "friends and acquaintances of the late Joseph Ring" to attend his funeral.[4] Although if Barbara saw it, she must have cringed. It happened to be printed right beside Noah Parker's well-intentioned, but unavoidably sensational, letter to the editor about his two inquests.[5]

George probably stands out on the breezy gallery, extending a hand to business colleagues as they ascend the stairs, and tipping his hat to their wives. "The weather was changeable throughout the day," the

Vicksburg Daily Times will report tomorrow, "The sun was shining one minute and clouds obscured it the next. There was a slight fall of rain two or three times, but it did not amount to anything until about 4 in the evening, when we had a regular shower which continued through the night."[6]

The guests are no more demonstrative than the bereaved family. All observe the decorum inherent in their Germanic upbringing. Entering the parlor—where additional chairs have been carried in from the dining room—they offer their condolences to Barbara, stand or kneel briefly at the lustrous rosewood coffin, then take a seat and gaze in silence. Yet can any of them *not* be nettled by the knowledge that in the folds of the silken lining of that gorgeous casket lie only a few charred bones?

The ornate draperies of the tall windows are drawn. But that does not keep the somber room from brightening whenever the sun finds a gap in the clouds. Then it darkens again. A couple of times a random rain raps on the roof of the gallery like a distant drumroll. More guests arrive. Umbrellas are left in a stand on the veranda. The long black dresses of the ladies rustle across the threshold. The gentlemen hold their hats.

It is likely that Joe's sons are here, though perhaps not sitting among the mourners. They may be romping upstairs, their dark brown hair a bit tousled, their shirts and trousers a bit mussed, together with the two Jeans orphans who live with George and Catherine.[7] What recollection, if any, the Ring boys will retain of their father is hard to surmise. Nicholas is close to nine, an intelligent and perceptive child,[8] and in future years he will delight in regaling his own children with stories about "Uncle George." Nevertheless, Nicholas's son Louis Caffall Ring will write to me in 1985:

"He never did mention anything about the death of his Father. . . . When I was growing up I knew nothing about my Grandfather Ring."[9]

It is a surprising discovery of my 30-year investigation: No oral tradition of the murderous holocaust will pass down to Nicholas's descendants as it will—albeit distorted—in *my* branch of the family. But another discovery, a hand-written letter, reveals that a version of the story will descend in a different collateral branch.

The letter will be penned in 1958 by Hank and Lena Weber's daughter, Libbie, in response to a cousin's request for information about the family.[10] Libbie is just a pert 3-year-old living in Cincinnati on this sorrowful Wednesday afternoon, but at the age of 88 she will write down—evidently with considerable effort—what she remembers hearing:

"Joe Ring Aunt Barbara husband was kill down there he work for his brother George too he send Joe to Roling fork landing to pay the men that run the plantation and he was kill and rob'd."[11]

Here is the "highway robbery" tradition Grandma Ring will reject so emphatically in 1963 when I ask her about my ancestors:

"But that's not how *I* heard the story! It was the darkies!"

From time to time one or two of the men might slip out onto the gallery to join George. There they stand, lighting cigars perhaps, gazing out over the broad lawn, exhaling fragrant swirls. Between long silences each man, in his own native dialect, comments on the weather. Crops. Business. Joe. Then, their cigars burned down, they rejoin their wives indoors.

At three o'clock the hearse rolls up, followed by two hacks.[12] Each carriage, drawn by two shimmering black geldings, is festooned in black bunting draped from large bows with dangling streamers. An enormous oval window pierces the two lateral sides of the hearse, which is crowned with six tall black plumes. The grooms sit erect, covered in mourning livery and wearing a top hat hung in back with a short black veil.[13]

George and his male in-laws and associates don their hats and gloves. Lifting without effort Joe's reddish coffin, they bear it out the front door, across the veranda, down the steps and the long brick path and the nine steps flanked by two massive masonry newell posts, and slide it into the waiting hearse. The grooms jump down to offer an arm to mourners boarding the hacks.

I can see the widow standing on the veranda, her swollen form draped in black, her still-young face veiled. Barbara will not go to the Requiem Mass, or to the burial.[14] In her condition it would be unseemly. Besides, prudence prevents her from risking the rutted and bumpy roads, and the damp chill of a shower.

She watches the sad cortege file down Adams Street, past emerald lawns of Bermuda grass spangled with purple and blue and yellow crocuses. The azalea bushes are bright mounds of pink, scarlet, fuchsia and coral, the dogwoods have sprouted their delicate white crosses, and everywhere roses, too, are in colorful bloom.[15] When sunbeams pierce the overcast the brilliance is dazzling, but momentary.

Turning onto Crawford Street, the hearse and hacks roll out of sight, and the bronze bell of St. Paul's begins its resonant dirge. Barbara lingers on the sweeping veranda, listening. In three blocks, at Walnut Street, the procession will halt in front of the stairs that lead up to the church's entrance.[16]

The structure is unusual for a house of worship: a long narrow box of gargantuan proportions, covered with Gothic elements, but entirely of brick the color of burgundy. The four walls soar to a balustrade of brickwork that, from street level, looks like crenelation. Engaged buttresses divide the walls all around into shallow bays, five on each side and three in front and back. Each of the lateral bays frames a gigantic pointed window of colored glass. Where the buttresses intersect the balustrade, they shoot heavenward as slender pinnacles capped with stone finials—22 of them in all, all around the rim of the box. So that, since no roof is visible, St. Paul's resembles a medieval arena as much as a church.

The middle bay of the façade holds a mammoth Gothic arch embracing a row of three lancets over massive double doors. A more slender arched window stands in the bays to either side. Above the central arch, above the crenelation spiked with pinnacles, rises a square bell tower, and out of this tower a spire lifts a cross into the sky. It is this steeple with its cross that informs ship-board travelers passing up and down the river that this strange and extraordinary edifice is indeed a house of worship.[17]

Barbara can picture the pall bearers sliding the casket out of the hearse and carrying it up the staircase and into the cool sanctuary. The handful of mourners process in behind it. The grooms repair to a patch of grass beneath the sheltering bows of a huge old sycamore. The somber cadence of the solitary bell ceases.

Barbara turns and enters the house.

When the tolling begins again, the drivers spring to their feet and brush off their livery. The two great doors creak open, and the long sleek box reemerges. Then the modest cortege jerks forward, and retraces its path back up Crawford Street and onto Adams. Four blocks shy of George's house, it bends onto the Old Jackson Road. A steady rain is falling now.

ST. PAUL'S R. C. CHURCH, VICKSBURG, 1895.

By this time Barbara may be reclining in one of George's second-story bedrooms. In her mind she sees the horseman, clad in black and crouched against the weather, who has joined the procession: Father Leray.[18]

The hearse and hacks begin the strenuous ascent to Cedar Hill. The cemetery lies in the hilly forested countryside northeast of the city. The roadway is all ruts and bumps, and muddy now with puddles and flowing rivulets. The geldings strain, the carriages bounce and slide, jostling the mourners inside. The six black plumes encircling the top of the hearse are drenched and drooping, and the long black streamers, soaked, hang like lifeless pennants. All the while the rain patters on the roofs.

Outside the wrought-iron gates of Cedar Hill looms a magnolia spotted with huge waxy-white blossoms. The cortege passes and labors through the slippery mud of the narrow path. The graveyard is all slopes and hillsides. Many family plots, like the one belonging to Catherine's first husband, are 20 feet square and terraced on low red brick walls.

Here and there stand clumps of cedars. A few solitary live oaks tower over tombstones. Beneath the sprawling branches of one of these, two black men in overalls lean on muddy shovels. Nearby gapes a freshly-opened hole.[19]

The grooms draw rein. The hearse and hacks, one by one, come to a halt, and the lone horseman, too. Here, on this incline, the mourners encircle the hole under black umbrellas. The breeze puts a chilly sting in the rain. The air is redolent with earthy smells. The men remove their hats. All heads bow.

Intoning the immemorial Latin supplications, Father Leray sprinkles holy water onto the rosewood already streaming with raindrops. The hunched figures mumble "Amen," and step gingerly back to the carriages. As soon as the emptied hearse and peopled hacks and mounted pastor trudge back out past the cedars, live oaks, and the huge magnolia, the two black men in overalls start toward the hole with their shovels.

Barbara closes her eyes.

George has seen to everything, except a headstone. (Does George *ever* attend to details!) And such trauma will occupy the next few years of his life, and Barbara's, that neither one of them, nor any member of their families, nor any descendant, will ever raise a monument to mark where Joe's few charred bones were returned to the soggy earth this afternoon of spring sunshine and spring showers.

Which is why the location of Joe's grave remains unknown to this day. It is probably one of the unmarked graves in the family plot of Catherine's first husband. But the old records of Cedar Hill no longer exist to confirm or refute this.[20]

The gentle pit-pat, pit-pat, pit-pat against the tall bedroom window soothes Barbara to slumber. In 11 days she will give birth to a boy.[21]

CHAPTER EIGHTEEN

APRIL 9, 1873

By Wednesday, April 9th, when George unfolds his *Vicksburg Daily Times* and reads the report on page three, the news comes as no surprise. He heard it yesterday from one of the persons who brought it downriver. Still, seeing it in print, George would marvel at Justice of the Peace Noah Parker.

> From the officers and passengers of the Sunflower river packets, we learn that five arrests have been made of parties said to be implicated in the recent Rolingfork tragedy. Three of these are white and two colored. One of the white men is a veterinary surgeon by the name of Porberry, who is something of a celebrity in the Charbone districts, bordering on the Yazoo river. These parties, or a portion of them, occupied a house adjacent to the ill fated store, and [are] the ones referred to by us some time since as not having heard of the fire until the following morning.[1]

The "Rolling Fork tragedy"—as the press is now calling it—is the talk of the Delta. Rumors travel from plantation to plantation, landing to landing, and arrive in Vicksburg via the steamboats. Sooner or later they all reach George's ears—though perhaps not quite all. Some of what people are saying incriminates George too much to repeat in his presence.[2]

It is easy for people who do not know George and his co-partners to draw facile conclusions based on general notions about the Delta. But the disaster is not general, it is particular. It did not happen to other country stores, it happened to Ring & Co. Surely George cannot help ruminating: Why *my* store?

Maybe even the unthinkable flashes through his mind: Could the culprit have been a "friend?" Was it truly a coincidence that Johnny Joor just happened to be away from the store that night? And John Coker— was his absence from the landing that night really coincidental? Or had there been a carefully thought-out plan? Had conspirators who knew George been waiting with diabolical vigilance for the opportune moment? Had they expected to find *him* there that night?

Here, then, is the sixth of the 12 hypotheses to explain "the Rolling Fork tragedy:" "Treachery of a friend!"[3]

Musing, George's mind might even seize upon the possibility, remote yet real, that one of the five persons *inside* the store committed the atrocity. People are known to go berserk, to appear perfectly normal and then suddenly, one terrible day, to act out their psychotic delusions. The State Lunatic Asylum in Jackson is full of them.[4] One of the Ring & Co. residents, in a mad rampage, could have slaughtered the others, set fire to the store, then turned the weapon on himself, or herself.

Here, then, is the seventh of the 12 hypotheses: "A lunatic!"[5]

But then, George is not a man given to ruminating. He functions in the day-to-day world: Why *not* his store? His thoughts would tend more to the practical matters at hand: compensation for his loss (he is preparing the proofs for Chamberlin) and enforcement of the law. Will anyone apprehend and punish the perpetrators?

The sheriff of Issaquena County is Henry P. Scott, a freedman of no particular conviction or courage.[6] According to the revised Mississippi statutes of 1871, "It shall be the duty of every sheriff to keep the peace within his county, by causing all offenders against the law, in his view, to enter into bonds and recognizances, with sureties, for keeping the peace, and for appearing at the next circuit court to be holden in the same county, and by committing such offenders, in case of refusal."[7] Scott, however, enjoys the status quo.

Born in North Carolina and raised in Jackson, Mississippi, Scott moved to Vicksburg after the war.[8] He was a delegate to the 1865 Mississippi black convention there, then operated a grocery store for a few years before moving into the Delta.[9] Like Noah Parker, he was attracted by the extraordinary opportunities the place offered men of his race. He acquired land and went into farming.[10] In 1870 he was appointed sheriff by the newly-elected Reconstructionist governor, James Alcorn, and proceeded to hire two white deputies.[11] One was a native of Ohio,[12] the other was Johnny Joor.[13] Scott could not have published a less ambiguous manifesto of his desire to accommodate the planters of his jurisdiction.

Joe Ring was still a member of the Board of Police at the time, and attended a Special Session at the courthouse in Tallula with the new sheriff in December.[14] In 1871, when Scott was elected to a second two-year term on the Republican ticket, he appointed as deputy a *white Democrat!*[15] By then, however, Joe's term on the Board of Police had ended.[16]

"I regard him as rather an inefficient officer, a sort of negative character," W. D. Brown will say of the sheriff in three years, after Scott is reelected to a third term and Noah Parker is shot for making trouble. "I think the work of the office is done chiefly by deputies of some intelligence."[17]

The revised statutes allow a sheriff to appoint as many deputies as he needs, "and to remove them at his pleasure."[18] Scott has at least one at all times, often two, and six or eight during sessions of the courts.[19] By the time Ring & Co. burned down, however, Johnny Joor was no longer one of them.[20]

It appears that Sheriff Scott never makes an official move unless he has to, and then only after consulting with his deputies or—more likely—seeking the counsel of local planters.[21] He shuns any action that might jeopardize his hold on an office that brings him $3,000 a year in benefices.[22] Later he will be described as a "prosperous and well-to-do land owner."[23] Two savings accounts in the Vicksburg branch of the Freedmen's Bureau Bank bear his name.[24] Ugly and dangerous disturbances arising inland do not capture Scott's interest. He prefers the tranquility of his office in Tallula.

The seat of Issaquena County is a sprinkling of cypress shacks strewn along a muddy landing on the Mississippi River.[25] It is inaccessible from a good portion of the county, as just east of Tallula sprawls a mammoth swamp that cannot be negotiated most months of the year.[26] Consequently the river districts—Dumbarton, Skipwith and Tallula—warrant the sheriff's attention, while the Deer Creek districts—Rolling Fork and Schola—he can dismiss as remote hinterland. My search will uncover no evidence that Sheriff Scott took any action whatsoever to investigate the Rolling Fork tragedy, not even dispatching one of his white deputies in his stead.

By default, therefore, that responsibility will devolve upon the county's lower ranking officers of the law. The revised statutes mandate that two justices of the peace be elected by popular vote in each of the county's five districts.[27] Each justice's jurisdiction is co-extensive with the county,[28] though, and the statutory quota goes unachieved for long periods of time.[29] Justices of the peace may call upon constables to help them execute their duties.[30]

Public offices such as Sheriff, Deputy Sheriff, Board of Police (renamed Board of Supervisors in 1871), Justice of the Peace and Constable are sinecures held in addition to the incumbent's livelihood. They pay no salary. The officer receives a modest travel allowance and *per diem* when executing his duties, but also pockets the statutory fees required for his services, which may add up very nicely.[31] Sheriff Scott, for instance, executing his responsibility as tax collector, is legally entitled to keep five percent of the amount he collects.[32] When conflicts of interest arise, loyalty to one's livelihood—and one's personal safety—generally take precedence over devotion to the law. It is not surprising, therefore, that in documents regarding the investigation of the ugly Ring & Co. incident, only one officer's name appears. That one officer's name is Noah B. Parker.[33]

Executing the oath of his office with impartiality, the strapping Justice of the Peace risks incurring the wrath of the planters, or his own people, or both. Diligence to duty might even jeopardize his life, not to mention the well-being of his wife and daughter. Yet this ex-slave alone, this young man darker than a mule, attempts to cut through all the rumors and arrive at the facts of the Rolling Fork tragedy. He alone persists in making inquiries.

George can appreciate the delicacy of Parker's position, which is why he would marvel at reading in Wednesday's paper that five arrests have been made. It has to be Parker who made them. And that took courage.

Maybe justice will triumph after all.

CHAPTER NINETEEN

APRIL 10, 1873

On Thursday, April 10th—"a beautiful and pleasant spring day," according to the papers[1]—George mounts the stairs to William M. Chamberlin's plain little office.[2] Even though George has heard the rumors, and would know, too, about the conscientious insurance man's personal probing, he could scarcely be prepared for the blow he is about to receive. He holds out the proofs of loss he has prepared from memory, but the portly agent with wooly black Burnsides simply gestures toward a chair. There is something important Chamberlin has to tell him.

First of all, the Franklin policy on the Ring & Co. stock is invalid. George took out subsequent insurance—first with the Great Western Mutual (the policy written by J. D. Burch, whom George had promised a risk), and then with Mechanics & Traders—without giving Chamberlin notice. The Franklin policy *requires* that the insured party give notice of all additional insurance, and cause such notice to be endorsed on the policy.[3]

But when George secured the additional coverage from Burch, Chamberlin *knew* about it. And Chamberlin himself wrote the Mechanics & Traders policy![4]

"I knew of the policy in Great Western both before and after it was issued," the almond-toned agent will concede in later courtroom testimony, and "I made out the application upon which [the Mechanics &

	Brought from last page -	$9282.81
18	Inv. Geo. Dorsey (Saddler)	
	" Washington St. Vicksburg	
	" Jany 1st 1873.	6.50
19	Inv. Geo. Wm Groetsch (Wine Mcht)	
	" 112 Exchange Alley New Orleans	
	" Fr. Nov. 2/72 to Jany. 11/73	-159.00
20	Inv. Jacob Shlenker & Co. (Dry Goods)	
	" 140 Washington St. Vicksburg.	
	. Fr. Dec. 7/72 to Jany 29/73.	335.65
21	Inv. H. B. Bruser (Tin Ware &c.)	
	" # Mulberry St. Vicksburg.	
	" Dec. 7/72 to Jany 29/73	174.39
22	Inv. Chas. Rice & Co. (Furniture Mchts)	
	" 137 Washington St. Vicksburg.	
	" F. Jany 29 to Feb. 8/73	17.50
23	Inv. Louis Hoffman (Hardware &c)	
	" 136 Washington St. Vicksburg.	
	" Fr. Nov. 5th 72 to Feb. 24/73.	395.12
24	Inv. Wm Muller (Comn Mcht)	
	" Levee St. Vicksburg Miss.	
	" F. Nov. 72 to Feb. 73.	637.77
25	Inv. J. Griffin (Liquors & Wines)	
	" 11 Front St. New Orleans.	
	" December/72	45.00
26	Inv. J. Hornthal & Co. (Comn Mcht	
	" Washington St. Vicksburg.	
	" Feb. 26/73	26.84
	Forwd next page	$12080.58

PAGE FROM GEORGE'S "PROOFS OF LOSS," 1873.

Traders policy] was issued."[5] But this does not alter the fact that the Franklin policy was *not* endorsed with notice of additional insurance.

Furthermore, the Franklin policy on George's interest in the building is also invalid. Chamberlin wrote it on George's *verbal* instruction, because the Andes coverage was due to lapse while George was at Rolling Fork Landing.

"I am satisfied that no formal 'application' (in writing) was made for this policy," Chamberlin will assert.[6]

But he never told George formal application in writing was necessary!

But that is not all. When Ring & Co. burned down, a Mr. Samuel Fischel of J. Hornthal & Co. held a note secured by George's interest in the store. Which means that George's interest was a mortgage interest.[7] The Franklin does *not* insure mortgage interests.

George, however, will insist later under oath, "I was the owner of that note when the policy sued on was taken out. I still own it and it is unpaid." Besides, "I . . . asked Mr. Chamberlin . . . if I could take out a mortgage policy. Mr. Chamberlin . . . said I could insure anything."[8]

But *that* was when George approached him to write the original Andes policy, *not* the Franklin.[9] When he wrote the Franklin, Chamberlin will assert, "I do not recollect Ring's saying that his interest was a mortgage interest. . . .[10] I always in taking insurance try to get the facts as to the kind of interest to be insured, and write the policy according to the facts—as stated to me by the party—at the time. If Ring had represented his interest as a mortgage interest, I should have so related in this policy what kind of interest it was."[11]

By now the shrewd immigrant businessman must be sensing that all these details are a pretext. There is something else, something the agent is not saying. Maybe it is at this moment that it occurs to George, the one rumor his friends and colleagues were not able to bring themselves to repeat to his face:

The three co-partners of Ring & Co. were greedy Yankees who insured their business for more than it was worth, then torched it themselves! But . . . two of the three were killed. Which could have been the result of their own bungling . . . or the deliberate deed of the third. It could be that the partner who did the insuring, the partner who survived, the partner who will collect the money, is the culprit!

But that would make George the murderer of his own brother! . . . Unless—George must wonder now how he could have been so obtuse for so long—Joe is not really dead. Unless Joe, in keeping with some scheme, escaped unharmed with the payroll![12]

Here, then, is the eighth of the 12 hypotheses: "Fraud!"[13]

The revelation makes George's head reel. His gray-blue eyes lock onto the dark brown eyes of the fastidiously-groomed insurance man. Slowly he rises to his feet.

The windows are raised to the balmy April day. The creak of wagonwheels plowing the unpaved streets, the clap of wooden heels on the boardwalks, a burst of male shouting down on the Commons, all ascend into the tidy second-story room.

Now George understands. Still clutching his papers,[14] he exits without a handshake, strides down the stairs to Washington Street, and crosses to the office of William A. Harper, agent for the Liverpool, London & Globe.[15] But when he proffers the proofs of loss for the policy on Frank and Missouri Jeans's interest in the building, Harper refuses to accept them.[16]

The policy was never written. The Certificate of Insurance that George holds is "binding for 15 days unless a policy is sooner delivered or notice given that the risk is declined."[17] And Harper did, in fact, give notice to Chamberlin within the 15-day period that his company declined the risk.[18]

But Chamberlin never told George!

Pressing on directly to the office of J. D. Burch, George hears that his claim against the Great Western Mutual is also invalid.[19]

So! Chamberlin has persuaded his colleagues to join with him in denying all the claims as fraudulent.[20] Time to see a lawyer.

But not this evening. Businesses are closing. Church services are starting. It is Holy Thursday.[21] Before going home, though, George learns the news that will appear in tomorrow's *Vicksburg Daily Times*:

> We learn from Capt. Wiley, of the steamer B. H. Hurt, that Mr. Porberry and his associates, who were recently arrested upon a charge of complicity in the Rolling Fork tragedy, have been tried and exonerated from all connection with said affair.

We are pleased to hear this, but sincerely trust that the true offenders may come to grief and atone to the offended laws of God and man for the terrible crime of which they are guilty.[22]

No record of any such trial will be found.[23] Since word of the arrests and subsequent exoneration comes on packets from the Sunflower River country—the *Lizzie* and *B. H. Hurt*—and *not* from riverboats paddling down the Mississippi from Tallula—where the Issaquena County courthouse stands—it is likely that the five men were not actually "tried" for the crime, but rather simply questioned by Noah Parker.[24] George can appreciate what a frustrating exercise that would have been. With no witnesses and no tangible clues, and without the backing of his sheriff, the youthful magistrate would not have been able to come up with sufficient evidence to deliver the suspects to Tallula for trial. A final *Vicksburg Daily Times* piece appearing later in the month will refer to the proceeding as an "examination" rather than a trial:

> Some day's ago, we mentioned in our columns that five persons had been arrested, charged with being the perpetrators of this terrible tragedy—and that among the number was Dr. J. W. Parberry, a veterinary surgeon, who lives in that county—an examination was had, and as a matter of justice to Dr. Parberry, we take great pleasure in saying, that not a scintilla of evidence was produced, which could tend, in the most remote degree to implicate him in the affair. By those most thoroughly acquainted with the details of the matter, he is considered as being entirely innocent of any connection with it, and the examination, if it did nothing else, had the effect of removing all doubts on this point from the minds of even the most suspicious. It affords us pleasure to make this statement, as Dr. Parberry stands well in the community, and no charges had ever been made against him before.[25]

Nevertheless, next year, when the veterinarian is subpoenaed to appear at George's insurance trials, he will not be found in the county.[26]

CHAPTER TWENTY

APRIL 14, 1873

First thing Easter Monday, April 14th, George marches through the threshold of 143 Washington Street.[1] Behind the building's nondescript facade, the rooms are plush and florid.[2] Persian carpets sprawl across the floor. An opulent floral print covers the walls. Row upon row of leather-bound tomes twinkle behind leaded glass doors. Suspended from an ornate medalion in the ceiling is a gas chandelier whose bronze curlicues cradle cut-glass globes.

Richard S. Buck springs from behind his elaborately-carved walnut desk. Given his English ancestry, the barrister may be ruddy-complected.[3] I picture curls the color of an old penny swirling about his ears, and a walrus mustache of the same hue obscuring his upper lip.[4] He shakes George's hand, inviting him to sit down, and returns to his overstuffed armchair.

Buck is George's age[5] and, in a sense, George's peer, for he too is a self-made man. Not that he has as much money (the lawyer's assets amount to less than one-fifth of his client's, according to the 1870 census[6]), but he advanced from the modest circumstances of his birth in Union County, Kentucky, to a comfortable position in the professional society of Vicksburg.[7] He married the daughter of an old Mississippi family,[8] and is now the father of three children.[9] He also has a junior partner, Edward D. Clark.[10] The firm of Buck & Clark has been representing George in the city for almost as many years as W. D. Brown has been representing him in the country.

Buck listens to George's story, then sends for a Justice of the Peace. When the magistrate arrives, George repeats under oath the testimony he gave a month earlier in Chamberlin's office.[11] Only this time he knows the results of Noah Parker's second inquest.

George is not only convinced now that Joe was murdered, but also that his body was burned up in the store[12]—except for a few bones. In addition, he is now aware that certain parties suspect him and Joe of perpetrating the crime. George's new deposition is not only descriptive, therefore, but defensive as well.

Buck includes the disclaimers that "the said fire did not originate by any act, design, or procurement, or through any fraud or evil practice on the part of the insured, or either of them, so far as deponent [George] knows or believes,"[13] and that "deponent knows nothing of the cause or origin of said fire, but entertains the belief current in the neighborhood that it was the act of murderers and incendiaries."[14]

In addition, the attorney attaches to the testimony a copy of Noah Parker's disculpatory certification "that I [Parker] have examined personally the circumstances attending said fire; that I am acquainted with the character and circumstances of the parties injured against the same, and verily believe that they have without fraud or evil practice sustained loss by destruction of said property."[15]

Also appended to the deposition are George's proofs of loss: an account of all merchandise purchased by Ring & Co. from the time the firm was formed in October 1872 to the time of the fire; an estimate of all sales and profits from the day the store opened on November 20, 1872, to the day it burned down; and the approximate value of stock on hand the night of March 4, 1873: $12,598.47.[16]

Strutting back out onto Washington Street this April Monday, sworn proofs in hand, George probably feels rather satisfied with himself, and confident, too. Perhaps even cocky. He will deliver the stack of legal-length pages to Chamberlin's claims adjuster in the morning.[17] If the companies refuse to honor their policies, he will sue for the money in court. Though George's English still echoes with German phonetics—as it will for the rest of his life[18]—the immigrant entrepreneur has come a long way since leaving the Rolling Fork neighborhood.

CHAPTER TWENTY-ONE

CATHERINE

Whether George had moved into Vicksburg in 1868[1] to facilitate court-ing Catherine, or started courting Catherine even before leaving the Delta to ease his move into Vicksburg, no one will ever know. The writ-ten record offers no clue. Either way, though, George succeeded: he captured Catherine's fancy, and he ingratiated himself into the city's small, close-knit coterie of German-speaking merchants.[2]

Catholic, Lutheran and Jew, they had started arriving in the 1840s from Bavaria, Prussia, Hesse Darmstadt, Lorraine, Alsace, Belgium, Baden, Switzerland and the Imperial City of Bremen. Astute and hard-working, they did not amass fortunes, but garnered solid positions for themselves in the city's bourgeoisie. They were wholesalers and retail-ers, and agents for insurance companies and steamboat lines. They owned sawmills, lumber yards, clothing, liquor, dry goods and candy stores, groceries, hotels and boarding houses and dramshops. The more daring among them became commission merchants.[3]

In private life and public conduct, these men were conservative; in their commercial dealings, they were dauntless. They mortgaged their interests heavily to participate in ventures where profit or ruin depended on a single harvest and the unpredictable fluctuations of cotton exchanges on two continents. They cooperated with one another for their mutual advancement, often forming partnerships. When sudden need arose, they made one another impromptu loans of cash or collateral. Promissory notes, signed and counter-signed and counter-counter-signed, circulated among them like hard currency. This was how they prospered.[4]

The year he moved into the city, George formed a partnership with a grocer named William Muller,[5] a Prussian.[6] It was a "Grocery and Commission Business," George would say later. "I consider the firm of Ring & Muller a profitable business. We owe nothing but what we have good assets to meet it with."[7] They advertised in the *Vicksburg Daily Herald*:

RING & MULLER,
AGENTS FOR
Missouri Wine Growers,
Keep constantly on hand—
CATAWBA WINE,
CONCORD WINE,
NORTON'S VIRGINIA
in boxes and kegs, Guaranteed to be genuine and pure.[8]

George was the managing partner.[9] He and William Muller were about the same age, 33-34.[10] Muller had immigrated to the United States with his wife after the Civil War.[11] They attended St. Paul's, and had a boy and just recently a girl.[12] Muller's grocery store was located on the southwest corner of Clay and Levee Streets, under The Sunflower Exchange.[13]

The Sunflower Exchange was a saloon,[14] though it had started out as a coffee house.[15] It was here that the German-speaking merchants congregated to talk cotton, debate politics, buy and sell real estate, discuss family matters, wait patiently for a shipment of merchandise due on a late-arriving riverboat. A clatter of German dialects filled the plain room, along with the aromatic emission of pipe and cigar. During a decade of trips to Vicksburg—to order provisions, pick up supplies, trade cotton or corn or hogs at the exchanges—George would have slaked his thirst and revived his social life by stopping in The Sunflower Exchange. Surely he knew the emporium's owner, Jacob Morris.[16]

Jacob Morris was a German-speaker from Belgium.[17] He lived with his family in a modest flat over the grocery store he owned just down Clay Street from his coffee house.[18] Other German-speakers resided above *their* concerns on Clay Street, and on Washington, Mulberry, Levee and Crawford Streets, and along the Commons.[19] It would have been impossible for George, while running errands in the city, not to encounter their daughters on the covered boardwalks.

But it was not one of the daughters George would marry. Rather it was a matronly woman seven years his senior,[20] whose English—when she had to use it—betrayed her German origin and limited education.[21] She was past childbearing age and resided quietly with a 16-year-old daughter.[22] She was also, however, the owner of six properties in the heart of Vicksburg's business district, and a rambling residence in the Springfield neighborhood, all mortgage-free.[23] She was Catherine, the widow of Jacob Morris.

Jacob Morris was the epitome of the German-speaking immigrant merchants who comprised the coterie into which George was ingratiating himself. His story resembles countless other classic American success stories, including George's, until his brief career—just 18 years— was wrenched by the Civil War. Like Joe Ring, he would turn out to be one of the "unsuccess" stories of America, common enough, but seldom recalled, and almost never recounted. For all his talent and industriousness, Jacob Morris was ultimately defeated, like Joe and many others long forgotten and nameless now, by tumultuous circumstances beyond his control. After the war his life ended abruptly and tragically. How George stepped in and took Morris's place shows that the great American success stories could never have happened without the whimsical visitation of luck.

Jacob Morris had settled in Vicksburg by 1849,[24] a 33-year-old bachelor.[25] He appears in the 1850 federal census as a "merchant" owning no real property.[26] The Warren County Tax Assessment Roll of 1851 indicates that he sold a modest $300 in taxable merchandise that year.[27] But the Belgian was frugal and hard-working.[28] He became a citizen of the United States just as quickly as the law allowed, as did most of his compatriots, declaring his intention in 1852 and petitioning for naturalization in 1854.[29] This entitled him to secure real property.

Immediately, for $800 cash and an $800 promissory note, the new citizen purchased two adjoining lots on Clay Street.[30] Each was 18 feet wide and 60 feet deep. On these he erected the coffee house with the commercial space to let underneath. Seven months later, having paid off the note, Morris bought the other two lots on Clay for another $1,600.[31] Now the entire city block between Levee and the Commons belonged to him. Next to the coffee house he erected a boarding house.[32] Beside that, at the very foot of Clay Street, just yards off the Mississippi River, he built the two-story building for his grocery store and family residence.[33] These were valuable properties.

King Cotton was in his Golden Age. The Commons was alive with raftsmen, joiners, pilots and clerks, shopkeepers, roustabouts, draymen and boatmen and wharfboat guards. Many of them were young and single and needed rooms; all of them required food and drink. Jacob Morris prospered. By the spring of 1856 he was able to pay off the $1,600 note, and in 1860 he bought a third lot running the entire width of the block between Levee and the Commons—75 feet—for $600 *cash*.[34] Later that year the federal census taker recorded the value of his real estate at $20,000, and his personal estate at $3,000.[35] That was considerable wealth. In one scant decade Morris had come a long way from being a foreigner with no real property!

Typical of his Germanic confreres, Morris was older when he married, almost 34. That was on April 9, 1849.[36] His bride, Catherine Hill, was a native of Hesse Darmstadt. She was 22 then. Less typical, but not unique among Vicksburg's German-speaking merchants, it was a mixed marriage: Jacob was Jewish, Catherine, Roman Catholic.[37] Their first child and only daughter, Lizzie, was born in 1852, followed by five sons.[38] Four of the six children were baptized at St. Paul's. Three of the boys died in 1858 and 1859.[39]

In late 1860 or early 1861, years before the cast of "the Rolling Fork tragedy" began to assemble in Issaquena County, a woman fated to share in Barbara's *other* misfortune—the sinking of the riverboat—arrived in Vicksburg. She was Catherine's older sister, Anna Schwink, the future Anna Sprankler, and she came with her son and daughter.[40]

For a widow with two children to join her sister in America, especially when that sister's husband was in a position to provide both shelter and

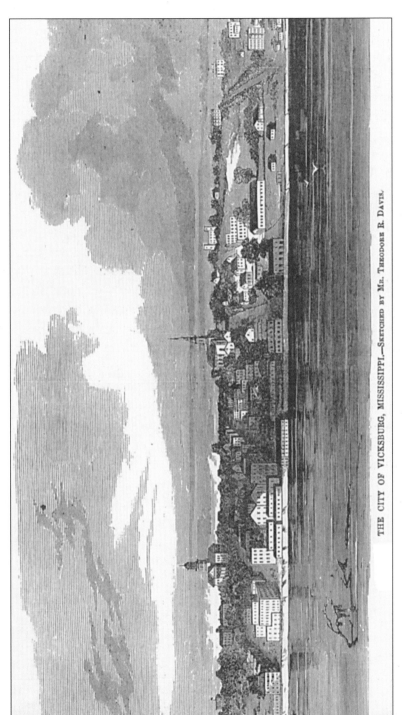

THE CITY OF VICKSBURG, MISSISSIPPI.—SKETCHED BY MR. THEODORE R. DAVIS.

ENGRAVING OF VICKSBURG FROM *HARPER'S WEEKLY*, AUGUST 2, 1862.

employment, was a commonplace of the city's immigrant population. Anna Schwink probably rented a room from Jacob Morris in his boarding house, and worked there as well, or in his grocery store. By the spring of 1861 her son, also named Jacob, though only 12, acted as godfather to one of his Morris cousins.[41] Soon thereafter the young man was probably clearing tables and washing dishes in the coffee house, which, after his uncle's death, he would operate as a saloon.[42] Anna's daughter Mary, age 10,[43] not only made a good playmate for her cousin Lizzie, 8,[44] but would some years later wed a German-born merchant whose business interests had intersected with those of Jacob Morris.[45]

For the Germanic businessmen of Vicksburg, business dealings and personal lives were all of a whole. Their activities in the workplace and at home—the two were always in close proximity, if not in the same building—reflected a unified fabric of character, experience and commitment. They were godparents to one another's children, bondsmen for marriage contracts, witnesses at weddings, executors of wills and appraisers of estates. They were one another's landlord or tenant, sponsors for naturalization, and guardians to one another's orphaned offspring. Sometimes they married a colleague's daughter.[46]

And in 1861 they opposed Mississippi's secession from the United States. War would bring commerce on the Mississippi River to a halt. No citizen of Vicksburg who prospered from the cotton industry—in one way or another that was everybody—wanted to see their avenue to world markets blockaded.[47] However, once their state did cast its lot with the Confederacy, most Vicksburgers rallied to the southern cause, among them a number of the foreign-born merchants. Jacob Morris, though, did *not* go to war.[48]

War came to him. He and his family suffered through the dreadful siege of May and June 1863.[49] Morris's buildings fell within range of the big guns of the Union flotilla on the river. For shelter from the relentless bombardment, the Morrises and Schwinks were probably forced to abandon their homes and join with neighbors in caves carved into the bluffs.[50]

After Vicksburg capitulated, the Union army occupied the city and as much of the surrounding countryside as it could hold.[51] That was when General Dana, commander of the Federal District of Vicksburg, sent the raiding parties into the Delta that came so close to George Ring's cabin in the Rolling Fork neighborhood.[52] In Vicksburg there was martial law. For the remaining two years of the war, every activity of the citizenry came under the watchful eye of Dana's troops.

One officer drew up "A List of Union Men in and around Vicksburg believed to be undoubted."[53] It named "Mores, Jacob" and other members of his coterie.[54] The Germanic businessmen were eager to resume their enterprises; the war had set them back considerably. They were happy to do business with any paying customer, Yankee or Rebel, white or black.

The city directory of 1866 shows Jacob Morris back in his grocery store, with his loved ones reinstated upstairs.[55] But the economy was in shambles. There were shortages of every necessity of daily life. No one had any money. However, northern suppliers were offering liberal credit terms to southern merchants,[56] and federal tax rolls record that "Jacob Morris & Co.," listed as "Retail Dealers," paid $10.42 in income tax that January.[57] Morris also paid an exorbitant $50 that year to secure a license as a "Wholesale liquor dealer."[58] With all the soldiers in town, there was money to be made in alcohol.[59] Perhaps it was the Belgian himself who converted The Sunflower Exchange from a coffee house to a saloon. But no mention of his boarding house appears in the city directory. Repairs may have required more capital than the cash-strapped entrepreneur could muster, or called for materials unavailable at any price.

In September cholera swept through the city,[60] snatching the breath from the last two Morris boys.[61] Then, suddenly, in the early hours of Thursday the 20th, broken in spirit by personal hardship, broken financially by the ravages of war, and broken in body by chronic heart disease, "Mr. Jacob Morris," wrote the *Vicksburg Daily Herald*, "well known as a family grocer and boarding-house keeper," died.[62] He was 51.

Catherine buried him in Cedar Hill Cemetery, in the Morris family plot, amid the graves of their sons.[63] It was a grand funeral. Five hacks followed the hearse.[64]

Jacob Morris was not the only entrepreneur of Vicksburg to lose his footing in the quake of the Civil War and collapse under its after-shocks. However, the majority of his Germanic associates managed to resume their business activities, advance their careers, and improve their families' circumstances during Reconstruction. These were the men whose circle George Ring fit into naturally. It was almost as though Morris had created an opening for George, as though the unlucky immigrant had given way to the lucky one. For Morris had done what all wise providers did: he had put his real estate in his wife's name.[65] No matter what happened to him financially, the property could not be touched by creditors. Morris's forethought would prove a blessing to Catherine, and a boon to George.

Catherine, however, was totally unprepared to take over her husband's enterprises. Never had she participated in any way in his affairs. She had no experience whatsoever in managing finances beyond her day-to-day household accounts.[66] Besides, after burying her husband and two younger sons, and with cholera still devastating the city, Catherine's mind could hardly have been on business. The Commons was no place for a grieving widow and her teen-aged daughter. Normally congested and rowdy and dangerous with the constant traffic of transients, the landing in time of epidemic was lethal. The urgent matter at hand was moving Lizzie to a safer location. On October 22, 1866, Catherine took $1,000 out of the bank and purchased the house in Springfield.[67]

Springfield covered the high ground east of the courthouse. It was a hilly area, shaded by a profusion of walnut trees—which had inspired the Spanish founders of Vicksburg to name their fortress "Nogales," or "Walnut Hills."[68] A rivulet of fresh water called Turnbull Spring Bayou glided through the neighborhood and down into Glass Bayou.[69] Well-tended houses stood on spacious green lawns dotted with azaleas, crape myrtle, and crabapple trees. Large and elegant, the white-clapboard dwellings had lace curtains at every window and an upright piano in every parlor. Their roofs were a cluster of turrets and gables and dormers. Their exteriors were wrapped in broad verandas. Carriage houses and slave quarters—leased now to freedmen and miserably overcrowded—huddled in a corner of every yard.[70] Springfield was a world apart from the bustling drays and mules and men, the blasting steamboat whistles, the shouting and brawling of the Commons. It was a quieter, healthier and more respectable place for a merchant's widow and her daughter to reside.

Catherine may have brought her sister's family into her commodious new house at 700 Adams Street, although by 1870 Anna was living five doors down the block.[71] The Hessian sisters were inseparable. Until that July night in 1873, when they would be thrown from their berths and the river would crash into their stateroom and wash over them.[72]

Complicated legal problems now pressed heavily on Catherine. Jacob Morris had died deep in debt and without a will.[73] To settle his estate—consisting entirely of personalty, since the properties were in Catherine's name—Catherine sought the counsel of her deceased husband's associates.[74] (She even managed in 1867 to acquire yet a *sixth* adjoining lot in Square I of Vicksburg!)[75] Nevertheless, sloppiness, confused names, errors in arithmetic, neglect of duties, ignorance of the law, and apologetic emendations and explanations fill Morris's probate packet in the Warren County Courthouse. Catherine needed more than the palliative companionship of a sister and the genial assistance of her deceased husband's associates. She needed a businessman to take her affairs in hand.

Enter George Ring.

They were married within the towering burgundy walls of St. Paul's on August 25, 1868[76]—at an early hour,[77] before the heat and humidity would descend over the city like a suffocating tent. Father Francis Xavier Leray, the pastor, officiated, and the rite was as much a confirmation of George's admittance into Vicksburg's German-speaking mercantile society as it was a marriage. For kneeling right beside George and Catherine at the altar rail, also being joined in holy matrimony this Tuesday morning, were Anna Schwink's 17-year-old daughter, Mary, and 29-year-old George Koch.[78]

George Koch was a dealer in tin, copper and sheet iron wares.[79] He had come downriver from Evansville, Indiana, before the war, and had fought at Shiloh and Corinth with the "Mississippi Sharp Shooters," suffering two wounds.[80] Since his discharge he had maintained a brisk commerce up and down the Mississippi with brothers/business partners in Evansville (who had served in the Union infantry).[81] Like Catherine and the Schwinks, George was a native of Hesse Darmstadt.[82] Unlike them, however, he was Evangelical Lutheran.[83]

Vicksburg's coterie of German-speaking merchants included at least as many Protestants as Catholics, perhaps more. But the city had no

GEORGE KOCH AND HIS WIFE, MARY CATHERINE SCHWINK, AROUND 1878. *(from The Johann Philipp Koch Family)*

Lutheran Church, and would not have one until 1952.[84] Mixed marriages were so common that the bishop of the Roman Catholic diocese, for expedience, conferred on Father Leray the authority to grant dispensations *vicatae religionis*.[85] The pastor would exercise that authority yet again in 1870, when he married Catherine's sister Anna Schwink to a Protestant businessman named Henry Sprankler. George Ring would sign the nuptial register of St. Paul's as witness.[86]

Still other German-speaking businessmen of Vicksburg, like Jacob Morris, were Jews. Samuel Fischel, for example, a partner in J. Hornthal & Co. who did business routinely with George, was a Jewish merchant from Bavaria.[87] A few years older than George,[88] Fischel had immigrated to Louisiana in the late 1850s with his wife. They had two children there.[89] During the war Fischel served as a Confederate cavalryman,[90] and thereafter brought his family to Vicksburg. Here a third child was born,[91] and Fischel helped to found the city's first (and only) synagogue, Anshe Chesed.[92] On the night Ring & Co. burned to the ground—as Chamberlin, the conscientious insurance man, would discover—Fischel was in possession of a note secured by George's interest in the store (making George's interest a mortgage interest). So Samuel Fischel would be summoned to testify at the insurance trials.[93]

Although the Jews of Vicksburg composed an active community with their own clubs and social events,[94] they also interacted with their Catholic and Protestant associates with no evidence of prejudice.[95] Sometimes Jewish and gentile families even intermarried. Already back in 1860, in the parlor of Jacob Morris's second-story flat on Clay Street, Mary Elizabeth Hill, a relative of Catherine's, had been wed by a probate judge to Jacob Steiner.[96] Steiner was a business associate and long-time confidant of the Morrises.[97] In 1871, Catherine's daughter Lizzie would marry a German Jew, Herman Leppich.[98] Leppich owned a saloon at 128 Washington Street,[99] and may well have purchased his liquor from Ring & Muller.

Catholic, Lutheran, Jew, the difference of creeds among the German-speaking merchants was overshadowed by their common linguistic and cultural heritage, as well as their shared immigrant experience. They were almost enlightened in their tolerance, but not quite, for it was not entirely devoid of self-interest. They were businessmen. They all benefitted. Assiduously would George Ring cultivate this multi-denominational familial/mercantile garden.

It appears that neither Joe nor Barbara traveled to Vicksburg that sultry August of 1868 to attend George and Catherine's double wedding ceremony. Four witnesses, all male, two for each marriage, signed the nuptial register, but no Joseph Ring.[100] His absence was prophetic, though, as Joe would not live to enjoy full "membership" in the city's Germanic mercantile society.

George and Catherine would prove to be well-matched. George was the businessman Catherine needed. Catherine was George's whimsical visitation of luck. It would not be long before he put his new wife's properties to work for them.

Chapter Twenty-Two

LAND

On June 15, 1869, George was probably about to return to his office after dining at home—it was a Tuesday—when he threw open the tall shutters and set on the table in front of his wife a legal-size sheet of paper covered with tight script. It was an indenture. It put one of Catherine's Levee Street properties up as collateral for short-term loans to Ring & Muller from Meyer, Deutsch & Weis of New Orleans. It assured George and his partner up to $2,000 credit "at their pleasure or as needed by them."[1]

The cotton crop of 1868 had turned out well and brought 28 cents per pound. That was two-and-a-half times the average pre-war price.[2] Consequently George, along with many of his fellow planters, was preparing to raise more cotton.[3] In addition, he would be going into factoring as well, factoring not only other planters' cotton, and cotton belonging to Ring & Muller, but his own cotton, too. Following the example of George W. Faison, George was out to eliminate "the middle man." What he needed now was land.

George flipped open the cover of the inkwell, dipped the pen, and handed it to Catherine. Who signed, as she always signed, in deliberate and unpracticed German script (I wonder how much English she actually knew): "Catharina Ring."[4]

Two days later George escorted his wife to the courthouse to have the indenture recorded. The judge took Catherine "aside from her husband," as law required, and asked whether she had signed of her own free will. She said yes. So the clerk transcribed the agreement into the deed books of Warren County.[5]

Now George began perusing the notices of sheriff's sales in the newspapers with particular interest. Maybe he even went and observed when land was auctioned off on the steps of the city's famed civic temple. Thousands of Delta acres were being sold at a fraction of their worth to satisfy unpaid taxes. Many of the forfeited acres were remote wilderness, as the owners were prudent enough to hang onto their profitable land. But many others were cleared and tillable, lying within reach of a river route. The bidder with enough cash could walk away the owner of a plantation. Getting land was easy. The trick was hanging onto it.[6]

Five months passed before he spotted the notice he was waiting for. On Monday morning, November 15th, George left his office, rounded the corner, and entered Muller's store.[7]

Lock it up!

The partners climbed the bluffs to Courthouse Square and passed through the wrought iron gates that had just recently been hung on the wall surrounding the block. Mounting the long, thrice-terraced staircase, they proceeded along the brand new brick path to the eastern portico of the courthouse.[8] Men were already gathering among the magnolia and oak saplings that had just been planted in the spring.[9]

When the sheriff stepped out onto the portico, he held a fistful of papers. Behind him trailed his deputy, followed by a man George would have recognized as the clerk who kept the deed books. The crowd of expectant bidders shuffled closer. By rote the sheriff recited the rules.[10]

Soon George was listening intently as one parcel after another came on the block, was bid on, and sold. If at first the rising sun hit the sheriff in the eyes, causing him to hold his free hand at his brow in a shading salute, it was not for long. For the sky was soon dark and the air full of rain.[11] The bidders pulled their hats to their ears and shifted uncomfortably from one leg to the other.

Then it came up. Saints Rest Plantation. George snapped to attention and jabbed Muller's arm. The partners strained to catch every word of the deputy's description: 1,695 acres on Indian Bayou in Washington

WARREN COUNTY COURTHOUSE, VICKSBURG, 1876.
(Courtesy Old Court House Museum, Vicksburg)

County, 20 miles east of Greenville.[12]

That was it! The one George had heard about from a relative of Catherine's.[13] Saints Rest was on the block because a New Yorker had failed to pay a note secured by the place. Now the holder of that note—Catherine's relative—was enforcing his prerogative to collect his money. It was prime bottomland. Much of the countryside on the other side of Indian Bayou was owned by George W. Faison.[14]

All at once a voice in the crowd shouted the initial bid. Then a second voice bid higher. Then a third. Then George called out—nervous and urgent, he may have startled himself.

The first voice raised the bid. The second raised it again. Then the third. George shouted again, louder now, probably sounding more like himself.

The sheriff's outstretched arm swung from bidder to bidder, one rigid finger extending out from the fistful of rustling papers. It pointed toward the first bidder. No response. It swung to the second. A higher bid. Then to the third. Higher still.

George kept his gaze locked on the sheriff's finger. As swiftly as it found him, he shouted his bid, then higher the next round, then higher still the next. He knew the value of the land. He knew how fabulously Faison had fared in that country.

Now the second voice did not respond. But the third did. George stood like a bird dog. The sheriff's finger found him.

One thousand forty!

The other voice shouted one thousand fifty.

The finger swung back to George.

One thousand sixty!

One thousand sixty the sheriff repeated.

His arm fell to his side.

Once! Twice! SOLD for $1,060!

George turned to Muller. The partners grinned. Ring & Muller owned a plantation!

January of 1870 found George in Washington County to sign up his labor. The Freedmen's Bureau had been dismantled by Congress,[15] and George probably considered new labor alternatives: prison convicts and Chinese immigrants.

George would have known that all of Edmund Richardson's places were worked by convicts.[16] Richardson was the richest man in the Delta, and his headquarters plantation, Refuge, was situated in Washington County. In 1868 he had obtained a contract from the state to lease Mississippi's prison population as farm hands and laborers in the burgeoning lumber industry. Convicts, most of whom were black, were cheaper than freedmen, and could be more tightly controlled. Hiring them required no bargaining, they could be disciplined, and the lessee did not need to concern himself with their long-term health.

Most planters, however, lacked both the capital and the political influence in Jackson to compete with Edmund Richardson for convict leases. Therefore, although the practice would persist to the end of the nineteenth century, convicts would never consititute more than a small fraction of the Delta's labor force.

George would also have heard about the planter in Bolivar County who was importing 16 Chinese "coolies" to work his place for five years.[17] Paying the workers' passage from Hong Kong, however—or from Cuba, where Chinese labored in tobacco and sugar fields—turned out to be very expensive. Moreover, Asians insisted on much higher wages than freedmen, and planters had to deposit substantial sums in New York banks, in advance, for the recruitment of these workers. For these reasons, none of George's neighbors in Washington County opted to experiment with Chinese labor until Frederick Metcalfe tried it in 1873.

But Metcalfe would find that mixing Chinese and black laborers engendered racial friction, and disrupted the operation of the plantation. Importing labor would never become popular among the planters, therefore, and would never bring more than a handful of Chinese to the Delta.

So George, like most Delta planters, continued to secure his field hands from the enormous pool of local freedmen.[18] He signed up laborers for set wages, as did most of his fellow landowners. That was to their advantage, so long as they had the cash. It would not be until after the Panic of 1873, when the price of cotton plummeted and planters found themselves short of cash, that they would turn their places over, section by section, to "croppers."[19]

George would also have hired a white overseer, though his name is not revealed in public records. The overseer, in turn, would have selected a black "straw boss" to act as his go-between with the field hands.[20]

Saints Rest formed the basis of George's fortune. He would climb again the many stairs to the east portico of the courthouse to bid on forfeited land.[21] Sometimes his best offer would be topped. But on occasion the bidders would be sparse, or timid, and George's frugal bid would not be bettered. So he acquired other places in Washington County (they would fall into Sunflower County along with Saints Rest when the boundary was redrawn in 1871),[22] and several modest plantations in Bolivar County.[23] Moreover, with an eye to development in Vicksburg, "on the 11th day of March AD 1870 at the Door of the Court House . . . being the highest and best bid offered," he purchased a string of swampy acres along Glass Bayou.[24]

George's cotton interests became inextricably enmeshed with his broad mercantile operations. Contracting with farmers and planters in early spring, he secured from suppliers in Philadelphia, St. Louis and New Orleans enough seed, groceries, agricultural implements, and other provisions to sustain the operations of several farms and plantations until harvest. This was called "furnishing."[25] George secured his interest in the agricultural operations he furnished by means of a "crop lien," which assured him payment in a fixed number of bales of cotton.[26] When the crop came in, George represented the planters and Ring & Muller and himself in the cotton exchanges, debating quality and grade, weighing, watching, storing, waiting, selling, shipping. Then he calculated percentages, settled with the planters, paid his suppliers, and learned how much he and his partners had profited that year.

The way George managed to pay for the "groceries and other dry goods" he ordered every spring to furnish planters, yeomen and tenant farmers was by granting liens against his properties.[27] Land was the only sure commodity upon which all financial transactions were based. It was collateral and security. It was payment rendered and payment received. It was lost for back taxes and redeemed at auction. Land was the Delta, the Delta was land. This is what George had grasped back in 1858.

Citizens came to recognize Mr. Ring's stout form and oval face when they saw him around town. He garnered the acquaintanceship of influential locals like the editor of *The Vicksburg Herald* (later called *The*

Vicksburg Times), the city's Republican press. In an issue of July 1869 the editor wrote:

> We were presented with a cluster of "Isabella" grapes, yesterday, raised by Mr. George Ring, at his residence, in this city. They are in advance of the season, and are large, fully ripe and delicious.[28]

What was more, George sought public office. Prior to the war, very few of his German-speaking colleagues had participated in the political arena. Afterwards, however, and particularly after March of 1869, when Adelbert Ames started replacing incumbents who could not swear to the iron-clad oath with loyal Union men who could, more and more foreign-born merchants filled the vacancies.[29] It was then that George solicited the office of sheriff of Issaquena County.[30] He was eligible—having been naturalized at the Circuit Court in Tallula on November 24, 1867[31]—and his letter of application bore the signatures of seven supporters, including the incumbent, all eager to see a white man fill the office. Nevertheless, Ames appointed someone else.[32] Maybe George could not swear that he had never supported the Confederacy after all![33] A dozen years would pass before he would make another bid for public office.[34]

On June 1, 1870, the federal census enumerator came to 700 Adams Street.[35] The lot was 60 feet wide and 305 feet deep.[36] The house stood quite a ways back from the dirt road, up on a knoll. It was well-shaded by a profusion of majestic elms, sprawling oaks, and somber old hickory and walnut trees, and perhaps an exotic banana tree or palm as well. The deep yard may have been embraced by crape myrtles bursting with pink, red and white flowers. A retaining wall of smooth stones lined the property along the street, except for the carriage way and, in the middle, nine steps up to the path leading to the front door. Massive masonry newell posts flanked these stairs.[37]

The fine house the enumerator entered that day is gone now. But a Sanborn Fire Insurance map provides a description of what it looked like in 1907.[38] Wooden, two-and-a-half stories high, it was an exuberance of angles and bays, broad expanses of shingle roof, and plenty of gables and dormers. On the right front stood an octagonal tower crowned with a conical tin spire. Wide eaves all around shaded the numerous and copious windows, all of which, to allow a cross-breeze, were shuttered against the sun.

Nevertheless, for the sultriest of August afternoons there were no fewer than five porches. A wide veranda swept across the facade and around one corner. Perched on its tin roof, directly above the front door, was a small porch accessible only from the upstairs. It would have had slender columns supporting a gingerbread gable. A little porch protected by a tin roof nestled in a corner of the first story. And a long, narrow porch with two levels ran along the kitchen wing on the back of the house. This one was covered with shingles.

Off the foyer—with its dark-wood staircase to the second floor—were a parlor and sitting room to the right, a dining room and study to the left, and the kitchen and pantry in the rear.[39] Upstairs were the bedchambers and a dressing room, where indoor plumbing would be installed one day. Over the kitchen and pantry ran a string of servants' rooms, and a cramped stairway wound down to the kitchen.

Ceilings were dramatically high, another device for alleviating summer heat. Elaborate gas chandeliers hung from plaster medallions. Dark hardwood molding wound its way along floors and around pannelled doors and double-paned windows.

Behind the house stretched fruit and vegetable gardens lined with arched trellises. From these, in August and September, dangled bunches of sparkling "Isabella" grapes. Beyond stood two or three outbuildings, and deep in the rear of the lot a shotgun shanty housed a black family.

Most likely the house Catherine purchased in 1866 was more modest than the one depicted on the 1907 insurance map. The two-story kitchen wing, for example, would have been a later addition, because houses in nineteenth-century Vicksburg had detached kitchens. The residence, however, was always amply large for George, who took great pleasure in hosting dinner parties that were both bountiful and raucous.[40] The value of the 36-year-old naturalized American's real and personal estate, as recorded by the census taker that June day in 1870, was six times the worth of his former partner Willie Jeans's.[41] That was substantial wealth, thanks to land. Delta land. Indeed, just as George had predicted, the promise of the Delta had burst open like a beautiful cotton boll!

Chapter Twenty-Three

RING & CO.

George sat in his office reviewing the accounts he held with Willie Jeans. It was March of 1871, and the former partner's mortal remains had just been laid in the deep rich loam of the Delta. One paper George lifted from his desk—perhaps it surprised him—to read a second time: yes, he still owned half-interest in Rolling Fork Landing. He had sold out to Jeans & Moore two years ago, but that was for $1,000 cash and a $1,500 note due February 1, 1870.[1] And that note was still unpaid![2]

It was one of the disquieting coincidences—like the *B. H. Hurt* not showing up the very day Joe Ring intended to take it home to Vicksburg—that punctuate "the Rolling Fork tragedy." So much of what happened was not premeditated treachery at all, but only mindless chance. The instrument by which George had intended to divest himself altogether of the Issaquena County venture turned out to be the fateful tie, the paper-thin yet legal tie, that bound him to Rolling Fork Landing. It would result in death for Joe and tragedy for Barbara. Because now George would bring the landing back into his network of merchandising concerns. He would form a new partnership: Ring & Co.

The sudden loss of both Willie and Elizabeth Jeans within five days of each other must have been a brutal blow to George. He had known them from his earliest days in the Delta. Laboring side-by-side, he and

Jeans had shared the exhilaration of constructing with their own hands an ambitious enterprise. The Jeanses had been family to George, as only a solitary immigrant pioneer could appreciate. Now, without hesitating, the man of action assumed the responsibilities of surviving kin. He sent W. D. Brown to Tallula to petition the Chancery Court of Issaquena County for letters of administration for the Jeans estate,[3] and guardianship of the three Jeans orphans.[4] The court granted both petitions.[5]

Immediately George posted bond of $10,000, with William Muller and Samuel Fischel acting as sureties.[6] For appraisers the court named Samuel B. Alexander (whose plantation bordered on the Jeans place, and who would be summoned to testify at George's trials after the incineration of Ring & Co.[7]), William B. McQuillen, L. C. Watson (another close neighbor[8]), John F. Coker and Joseph Ring.[9] George engaged W. D. Brown to collect all outstanding debts. But the attorney would have minimal success.[10]

"His estate was insolvent," George would testify of Jeans, "not paying over 10 cents on the dollar."[11]

George left little Willie Jeans in the Delta with Jesse and Martha Moore. Frank and Missouri Jeans, however, he brought into his own home in Vicksburg.[12] Why he settled on this disposition of the orphans is not known. But the decision had fateful consequences: little Willie would perish in the Rolling Fork disaster; Frank and Missouri would not.

Compounding the personal loss, the death of Willie Jeans dealt George a terrible financial blow. Jeans had collected monies due the defunct partnership of Jeans & Ring, but he had not settled up with George before he died.

"At the time of his death, he and his wife, on account of this copartnership, owed me at least $10,000 for accounts collected," George would testify. "The firm of Jeans & Ring wound up without a profit. We were able to pay all our outstanding debts, except what was due me. The business, so far as I was concerned, was a loss to me. I put in five thousand dollars cash, came out without a dollar."[13]

While the unpaid promissory note of 1869 confirmed George's half-interest in Rolling Fork Landing, the other half-interest fell by inheritance to Frank, little Willie and Missouri Jeans. It was George's job now as their guardian to manage that interest for them. The unabashed businessman may well have hoped to recover over time something of the $10,000 the Jeans estate owed him.[14] That would prove difficult, however, as George soon learned that Willie Jeans's second partnership, Jeans & Moore, had fared no better than Jeans & Ring.

"The firm of Jeans & Moore, my successors, lost money," George would report. "The firm was absolutely insolvent."[15]

When George had sold out his interest in the landing to Jeans & Moore, he had left all the merchandise he co-owned with Jeans in the store.

"The goods I left with Jeans to be accounted for with me for my half of them," George would explain, "he put the goods in as so much capital with him and Moore."[16] It was another fateful choice: George would lose all of it in the fire.

When Jeans succumbed, he was in the process of settling accounts with Moore to dissolve their business. They had just let the store to an independent dry goods merchant, S. A. Lloyd, on a year's lease.[17] Lloyd was a 22-year-old bachelor boarding with the family of S. B. Alexander.[18]

"Lloyd made no money," George would say later. "Did a credit business, was dissipated and neglected his business."[19]

Lloyd's lease expired in the spring of 1872,[20] and it was that fall, about the first of November, that George formed Ring & Co.[21]

"When we formed the partnership," George would explain, "Mrs. Moore was taken in to represent her husband's interest."[22] This was because Jesse Moore's finances, such as they were, were entangled in the Jeans estate. He held $740.97 worth of notes due Jeans & Moore, and gave them to W. D. Brown for collection.[23] He also held judgments that Noah B. Parker had rendered against other outstanding Jeans & Moore accounts amounting to "five hundred dollars more or less."[24] But how long it would be before he saw any cash, no one could say. Besides, he owed his own father-in-law, John F. Coker, several hundred dollars for fitting and running timber.[25] Nonetheless, the Pennsylvanian's Yankee drive was not blunted by the dubious results of his mercantile undertakings. (George must have seen much of himself in this resolute young entrepreneur!) Moore's wife Martha, now representing his interest in Ring & Co., was all of 18 years old.[26]

Joe Ring's financial position, on the other hand, looked great. In the spring he had settled Barbara and the boys on "the Vicksburg Place," and this fall he was standing for a second consecutive year in high cotton.[27] So George brought him on board as a third partner in the new firm.[28]

Ring & Co. was born. And singly, in family groups, in pairs, with none of them the wiser, the ill-fated victims of "the Rolling Fork tragedy" converged at the landing.

Jesse and Martha Moore, with little Willie in tow, set up housekeeping in the second-floor quarters of the great store.[29] Martha's father, John F. Coker, moved his family into the closest cabin.[30] Dr. J. W. Parberry and his buddy, the Irishman known only as Uncle Jimmy, took up residence in the next nearest cabin.[31] Then came Johnny Joor.

Joor was 26 now, and still a bachelor.[32] He had just served a term as deputy sheriff of Issaquena County.[33] When George offered him $75 a month plus bed and board to clerk for the new firm,[34] Joor stuffed his saddlebags with a few shirts and trousers from his room in the Tallula jailhouse and moved into the store. He made his bed in the office.[35]

The unlucky cast of the Rolling Fork catastrophe was almost complete.

Already that summer George had acquired $700 to $800 worth of goods at auction to put into the firm.[36] Then, toward the last of October, he began ordering merchandise in the name of the new copartnership from wholesalers in St. Louis, Philadelphia and Vicksburg.[37] Almost all of it was bought on time—30, 60 or 90 days.[38] George even made use of the unpaid $1,500 note from Jeans & Moore as collateral against stock from Meyer, Deutsch & Weis of New Orleans.[39] As shipments arrived, George allowed the goods to accumulate on a wharfboat at the Commons.[40]

It was at this time that concern about the security of the stock prompted George to insure it, both for himself—though his interest now was only a mortgage interest—and for the Jeans orphans—whose interest, indirectly, was George's as well, given the huge debt their parents' estate owed him. Considering the amount of insurance he procured, it is evident that George did not want to risk losing a single dollar more on the Rolling Fork Landing venture. He could not have imagined, though, that in just four months he would petition for payment of all five policies, and encounter fervid opposition to his claims.

George shipped the accumulated wares "by Steamer Lizzie to the mouth of the Sunflower, thence reshipped on Steamer Blanche to Rolling Fork Landing."[41] The stock arrived about November 15th.[42]

"We did a profitable business," George would boast. "Our sales were good. We aimed to get 33 1/3 profits. Our sales would average $75 per day, often more and sometimes less. We did not sell on Sundays. I am satisfied our average profits would reach 25 percent. Our rule was not to allow a customer to go away with the money. Our biggest trade was in groceries."[43]

Joe made occasional trips to the store, taking up merchandise and the Ring & Co. payroll, and bringing back cotton.[44] This he did whenever George, the managing partner, delegated the responsibility.[45] These trips always lasted several days, as there were only two packets providing service:

Regular Sunflower River Mail Packet
Steamer Lizzie
J.O. Stephens, Master
G.H. Smith, Clerk

Leaves Tuesday evenings at 5 o'clock, for all points on Sunflower river, as high as navigation will permit. For freight or passage, apply on board, or to Carroll, Green, & Co., agents.

Regular Sunflower River Friday Packet
Steamer B. H. Hurt
Joshua Wiley, Master
Thomas M. Hicks, Clerk

Leaves promptly at 5 o'clock every Friday evening, for all points on Sunflower river, as high as navigation will permit. Returning, she leaves Holland's landing at 8 o'clock, and Rolling Fork at 10 o'clock every Tuesday morning. For freight or passage, apply on board.[46]

The run normally took five days: two-and-a-half days up to Holland's Landing—some 40 miles above Rolling Fork Landing—and two-and-a-half days back.[47] So the whistle of the *Lizzie* would blast over Vicksburg on Sunday evenings, and the *B. H. Hurt*'s on Wednesday evenings. Often, however, the steamers fell behind schedule. An unusually large amount of cargo, or more stops than usual for passengers, or flooding, or low water in the upper bends, or a snag in the channel, would delay the steamers a day or two. It happened all the time.[48]

Barbara never knew when Joe would get home from his trips to the store.

Deed books show that George was involving Joe in business activities beyond Rolling Fork Landing, too.[49] Under the younger brother's tutelage, Joe was on his way to assuming a place within Vicksburg's circle of Germanic merchants. Patrons of The Sunflower Exchange started seeing the Ring brothers on a regular basis. Parishioners of St. Paul's watched them lead their families down the aisle and into a pew on Sunday mornings. Taken as a whole, the documentary record suggests that George and Joe Ring were affable men, and adaptable. They took things in stride. They accepted people as they were, and shrugged off the madness of Reconstruction. Like two wide-eyed country boys come to town, the Lorrainian brothers shared a sense of adventure.

"On about the 10th January 1873, Mr. Moore was attacked with rheumatism, and unable to do anything," George would explain. "We then employed Mr. A. Goudchat in his place."[50]

Alphonse Goudchat Israel was a young Frenchman,[51] formerly a clerk with Shlenker & Co. in Vicksburg.[52] He was also a Jew.

A good number of Jews entered the Delta during Reconstruction, German-speakers for the most part, from Prussia, Bavaria, Baden, Hesse and Alsace.[53] They started out as peddlers.[54] Toting their wares on their backs, they tramped the vast countryside, selling cheap goods to poor whites and blacks. In many a remote backwater, their appearance provided an entertaining respite from the travails and lonesomeness of frontier life.[55] In due time they could afford to buy a horse and wagon, then eventually a lot in a settlement, where they erected stores.

In Greenville—which had risen quickly from the Union skipper's fiery blow of 1863—nearly half of the merchants in 1870 were Jewish.[56] By 1880 their representation would increase to two out of every three.[57] (A good portion of that last third were Chinese, remnants of the post-war experiment in hiring "coolies" to work the fields.[58]) Not a few of these Jewish merchants would eventually become prosperous planters and leaders in the lumber industry.[59] The Delta Jews maintained intimate ties—and business relations—with relatives "in town." Louis Fischel, for instance, who had a store in Tallula,[60] was a brother of Samuel Fischel of J. Hornthal & Co. in Vicksburg.[61]

From its inception, therefore, the unique society that coalesced in the Delta included Jews. Moreover, historical sources suggest that they suffered no more prejudice, nor less prejudice, than any of their multifarious neighbors.[62] This was another of the unexpected features that distinguished the Delta from the rest of the Deep South. Most of the mercantile establishments that had sprouted along the Delta's waterways after the war were run by men born overseas, like the Ring brothers and Louis Fischel, or by men born out of state, like Jesse Moore.[63] Hiring a young foreign-born Jew to clerk temporarily at Rolling Fork Landing would have raised no eyebrows in the Delta in 1873.[64]

Nevertheless, for some members of the native white Protestant population, these newcomers, these foreigners, these Catholics and Jews, represented outsiders importing unwanted and pernicious change. They found it galling to watch these uninvited "meddlers," by means of their economic prowess, dominate the lives of so many defeated and impoverished Deltans.[65] The huge and arrogant headquarters of Ring & Co., some observers would suggest, had long stood as a target just begging retaliation by white southerners who despised immigrants of all kinds.

Here, then, is the ninth of the 12 hypotheses to explain the Rolling Fork disaster: "Bigots!"[66]

Indeed, in the rugged and wide-spread Delta of 1873 lone travelers of *any* hue or creed, particularly those not mounted, and most particularly those who might be carrying cash, risked misadventure. The *Vicksburg Daily Times* of January 3rd—just days before Goudchat moved out to Rolling Fork Landing—ran this notice:

To the Public.
Greenville, Miss., Dec. 17, 1872.
Editor Times & Republican:

At the last term of the circuit court held in Issaquena county, two men were tried, convicted, and sentenced to be hanged, on the 17th day of January, 1873, for the murder of a peddler, on Deer Creek, in said county, sometime last spring. The name of the murdered peddler could not at that time be ascertained; but I have since been informed that he was a man from Vicksburg, by the name of Vonderbolt. If such a man is missing, and has friends in Vicksburg or elsewhere, I shall be happy to communicate with them.

Very respectfully,
Chas. W. Clarke[67]

Vonderbolt—likely a German name, likely a Jew. The issue of January 17th informed:

The two colored men recently convicted in Issaquena of the murder of a peddlar on Deer Creek, last fall, are to be hanged to-day.[68]

Until Jesse Moore got back on his feet, Alphonse Goudchat Israel would sleep in the office of Ring & Co. with Johnny Joor.[69] Besides board, the stand-in clerk would receive $50 a month.[70]

The cast of the Rolling Fork massacre was assembled now, except for Joe. And he, blissfully unaware, would soon be gliding up.

CHAPTER TWENTY-FOUR

ROLLING FORK LANDING

"I spent most of my time at Rolling Fork Landing since I began business," George would explain. "I was the managing partner in the concern."[1] It was during this time that George would have met the woman people later called a lunatic.

No specifics of their initial encounter have been preserved in writing for posterity, but the circumstances are not difficult to conjecture. She would have appeared at the landing one day, certainly not alone, for women did not travel the wilderness without the protection of a male escort bearing arms.[2] Besides, getting tightly-packed kegs and sacks and bushels home required the brawn of a man or two. The woman would have been with her husband, and maybe other family members as well, a trip to the store being something of "an event."[3] Hearing footfalls ascending the wide stairs outside, George would have left his bookkeeping and sauntered into the storeroom.

A man was shouldering his way through the double doors as he spat into the cuspidor on the gallery.[4] He was "about 6 foot 2 1/2 inches in height," and had "large, light blue eyes . . . a pale face . . . light brown hair . . . and light moustache and beard."[5] His shirt and breeches were coarse home-spun, his vest sewn from tanned hides, and his buckskin boots had trekked a lot of backcountry miles.[6] Not only was the pioneer much bigger than George, he was better than a dozen years younger as well—maybe mid-twenties.[7] Right behind him came a buddy, roughly the same age,[8] whose frame was probably as tall and rugged and strong as the leader's. Both men carried shotguns slung across their backs, and dirk knives stashed in their belts.

By this time George recognized river folk when he saw them. His neck muscles may have tightened a bit.

The strangers nodded in George's direction, touching the floppy brim of their slouch hats. But their eyes were already inventorying the precious contents of the burlap sacks and wooden crates along the counters, and the variety of stock lining the shelves around the high walls.

George kept an eye on them.

Just then two women—one in her early twenties, the other considerably younger—stepped through the doors.[9] Their long skirts and sun bonnets were faded. Their boots betrayed as much hard use as the men's.[10] The older woman was holding a little girl by the hand.[11] Both nodded to George.

Now his shoulders relaxed.

The mother introduced herself as Jane O'Neal. Her young companion was her sister, Harriet Marsh.[12] The tall leader was Harriet's husband, George.[13] The buddy was Jane's husband, M. C.[14] They had all come into the Delta from Alabama,[15] and were presently settled about four miles from the landing.[16]

While Mrs. O'Neal spoke, George's eyes followed the two strapping men around the store. How many Marshes and O'Neals had he encountered since the war's end! A fourth tier was being added to the rigid social structure of the Delta: poor, unlettered, unskilled whites.[17]

They came looking for work and a place to raise their families. Scattered along the bayous, they ferried travelers across rivers on barges, poled rafts of goods to remote farms and settlements they alone seemed to know how to reach, and delivered messages by skiff. Some lived in shantyboats. Others squatted on somebody's forfeited back acres, making a small crop, raising hogs and perhaps a few chickens. Finding themselves in direct competition with former slaves for land and livelihood, they tended to despise blacks.[18]

Of planters, or skilled whites, or blacks, George would not have been wary. But these migrant river people had a bad reputation.

The rustic customers made their purchases. George returned to his bookkeeping. He could hear the shuffle of their well-worn heels across the gallery and down the broad staircase. In eight years Jane O'Neal would proclaim publicly that her husband and his buddy had axed Joe Ring to death and thrown his body in the creek. But folks would dismiss her as a lunatic.

As country merchant, George interacted with all four classes of Delta society. For it was at the landings that the wealthy planters, skilled whites, poor whites and freedmen intermingled.[19] All Deltans depended on getting finished goods shipped in from elsewhere, and getting their cotton shipped out. People as well as cargo circulated busily from landing to landing, up and down the waterways, like lifeblood spurting through the veins of the ancient alluvial elm leaf. Mail and newspapers arrived via the landings, too. They were the contact points with civilization beyond the Yazoo and Mississippi.[20] Consequently, the catastrophe that would reduce Ring & Co. to ashes, as well as the subsequent war of litigation George would wage to exonerate his reputation, would implicate all four tiers of Delta society.

Steamboat captains—John King of the *Bluella*, for instance—and their pilots and clerks were always ready to share with George what they had just heard upriver or down. They accepted a shot of his whiskey and lingered on the gallery, out of the sun, while the deck hands stacked a fresh load of firewood beside the steamer's boiler. Sitting on a crate up-ended, or leaning against a post, these men were grateful for the shade and a cool breeze, when one swept by. They removed their hats and wiped their brows, commented on the weather, the cotton, the corn, the high or low water in the bends, new faces seen lately in the country, politics, the latest election, before pulling back out.

Drummers, too, stopping by the landing on their seasonal circuits, brought conviviality to the landing as well as the latest models of their patented devices.[21] It would not have been unusual for these visitors to spend a night or two in the store before resuming their rounds.—

Though there is no evidence that one was sleeping there the drizzly night of March 4, 1873.

Women, when happy necessity brought them to the store, welcomed the hiatus from the solitary routine of their daily toil. While examining a bolt of calico, a pair of boots, a shipment of flowery bonnets just arrived from St. Louis, they discussed with Martha the health of their husbands and children. They shared all kinds of womanly concerns.

For the colored roustabouts, too, loading and unloading at the landing was as much a social exchange as a livelihood. From deck hands they learned of events transpiring on plantations all along the rivers. Then, drifting homeward at sunset, they scattered the news among black neighbors. In 1873 the ratio of blacks to whites in Issaquena County was seven to one.[22] But around Rolling Fork Landing it was 50 to one—50 blacks to every white.[23]

Constant was the trickle of transients through Rolling Fork Landing. There were farmers moving in or hauling out, veterans of the war searching for a place to settle, preachers of the gospel on horseback, Hebrew peddlers on foot, Chinese coolies (though never a Chinese woman or child) and sometimes, too, bands of armed outlaws. Unfamiliar faces, sometimes kind, sometimes menacing, usually unidentifiable, and quickly vanishing upriver or down, these were the faces of Rolling Fork Landing. Understandably, therefore, one of the theories for the monstrous crime of March 4, 1873, speculated that it was the vengeful act of disgruntled customers, or would-be customers.

"We sold exclusively for cash," George would remark.[24]

"We sold for cash exclusively," Joor would corroborate.[25]

This was highly unusual. Most country merchants extended liberal credit to their customers—regular customers, at least, not transients—against future harvests or salaries.[26] However, to make purchases at Ring & Co., tenant farmers and sharecroppers had to borrow cash from their landlord, and field hands had to secure cash advances from their employer. The landowners, in turn, could only make such loans by putting their property up as collateral to *their* creditors—who, often times, were the merchants! If the harvest turned out poor, the debtors risked losing their land—which is to say, their livelihood—while the creditors and cash-collecting merchants like George Ring—for the short term, at least—came out unscathed.[27]

Here, then, is the tenth of the 12 hypotheses: "Disgruntled customers!"[28]

It cannot be denied that any number of customers—transient or regular, white or black, impoverished or landed—might have felt wronged by Ring & Co., might have harbored resentment toward the firm. Furthermore, Ring & Co. paid out in cash.

"We bought cotton, paid cash for it," Joor would explain, "bought the cotton mostly from Negroes, and got a good trade from them."[29]

So any customer could have deduced that somewhere in the Ring & Co. store there had to be a considerable stash of bank notes.—Especially on those occasions, perhaps as regular as the new moon, when George or Joe came up from Vicksburg with the payroll. Such booty would have tempted sorely anyone seeking revenge on Ring & Co.

Merchants like George Ring were powerful men. Each one exercised a monopoly, because patrons could not easily take their business elsewhere.[30] The next store might be on the far side of a swamp, or eight miles upriver. On the other hand, the merchant's long-term operations, and ultimately the success or failure of his enterprise, depended on the financial health of his community. As George had learned in '66 and '67, if customers suffered a bad year, the local merchant suffered, too, in diminished business, if not uncollectible debts. The merchant-customer relationship was reciprocal.

It was in George's best interest, therefore, to accommodate his customers as much as possible. In this regard, his easy-going nature would have served him well. That same nonchalance, however, could sometimes manifest itself in a disregard for detail, negligent bookkeeping . . . leading inevitably to squabbles with customers and other merchants.[31] Which was why some people would suspect that the destruction of Ring & Co. was an act of sabotage perpetrated by a fellow mercantile operation.

Here, then, is the eleventh of the 12 hypotheses: "Rival merchants!"[32]

"Some two weeks before I left," George would state under oath, meaning about February 6, 1873, "I learned that some merchants above us six miles became dissatisfied about some business matters of the landing and threatened to thrash me out. They came down one day and threatened around as if they intended making an attack on me personally. They did not do so. Afterwards, we met and had a friendly understanding of matters."[33]

One merchant whose store stood on Deer Creek about six miles above Rolling Fork Landing was John Paradise.[34] Paradise was a Pole,[35] likely a German-speaker from East Prussia.[36] He probably stood a head taller than George's 5 1/2 feet, and weighed half again George's 140-or-so pounds.[37] Maybe it was he who had run out of patience with George and come down to settle accounts with his own two mighty fists. Indeed, Paradise would be summoned to testify at the trials after the fiery destruction of Ring & Co.[38]

Although Johnny Joor, in *his* sworn statement, named a different merchant:

"I remember on one occasion of George F. Ring and Mr. Allen having some words," Joor would say, "but afterwards [it] was settled and [they] appeared friendly."[39]

No "Mr. Allen," though, would be summoned to George's trials.

Merchants did have disagreements, and in remote and sparsely-populated backcountry like the interior of Issaquena County, arson was a notoriously effective means of "settling a score." It was certain and thorough, and could never be traced to the culprit.[40] George would maintain, however: "I never heard of ill will against my partners, or either of them."[41] And Joor would concur: "I never heard of any threats, or apprehension of incendiarism. I knew of no difficulties with the members of the firm and the neighborhood."[42]

Nevertheless, the foreign-born merchants of the Delta might well have been despised tacitly by racist poor white neighbors. Many river men like George Marsh and M. C. O'Neal loathed blacks so viscerally that they even espoused the Democratic party of the affluent landowners.[43] They could not abide seeing Caucasians treat freedmen as equals, and men like George Ring and John Paradise—whose eyes were always fixed on the bottom line—dealt impartially with the full spectrum of their diverse clientele. Black dollars, white dollars, were all the same to these capitalists. It could not be ruled out, therefore, that the Ring & Co. store and its inhabitants might have been torched by a mob of white men who despised "nigger lovers."[44]

Here, then, is the last of the 12 hypotheses: "Racists!"[45]

On Thursday, February 20, 1873, George left Rolling Fork Landing on board the *Lizzie* with three bales of cotton from the warehouse.[46] It was the last time he saw the whitewashed colossus of his own handiwork. It was the last time he saw Jesse and Martha Moore, little Willie Jeans, and Goudchat.

He pulled into Vicksburg on Sunday evening, February 23rd,[47] and met with Joe shortly thereafter. For when the *Lizzie* pulled out again on Shrove Tuesday, February 25th—precisely at 5 p.m. as advertised[48]—Joe was on board with the payroll and a lot of goods destined for Rolling Fork Landing.[49]

The following morning finds Joe riding blissfully up the Sunflower River. Leaning back on a bentwood chair, ankles crossed on the rail, corn-cob pipe between his teeth, he may be whittling a willow twig.—A toy soldier for Nicholas? A mixing spoon for Barbara?

If his thoughts turn to his family, Joe could picture them kneeling at the altar rail of St. Paul's. Sunbeams pouring through the tall lancets paint stripes of color across the regiments of pews, across the aisle, and up the marble steps of the altar. Through these projections of light passes Father Leray, side-stepping along the rail from forehead to forehead, smudging each with ashes.[50] Were Joe in Vicksburg this Ash Wednesday, he too would be kneeling there beside his wife and sons. But he is not. He is gliding unawares to his fiery end.

"*Memento, homo,*" Father Leray mumbles as his thumb forms the ashen cross on each brow, "*Quia pulvis es, et in pulverem reverteris!*" ("Remember, man, that thou art dust, and unto dust thou shalt return!")

Chapter Twenty-Five

MAY 4, 1873

Sunday, May 4th, Barbara's brown eyes peer fretfully down the long road of the Vicksburg Place.[1] The day is clear.[2] The slim woman of slender features can see for quite a distance. No one. Nearby lies the infant son born to her 11 days after his father's rainy funeral. His tiny limbs, inside a flowing and lace-fringed white gown, are jerking with "spasms."[3]

According to Barbara's financial accounts, she has already engaged the services of Dr. P. F. Whitehead, a physician and surgeon.[4] His bill for $35 probably covers several visits. However, a much larger amount is owed to Dr. Richard O'Leary, the druggist: $140.[5] That is a lot of medicine. Evidently the newborn's health has been in jeopardy for some time, perhaps since birth, for today he is five weeks old and still unbaptized. Barbara's distress, as she searches the empty road, must be terrible.

The wavy grounds around the house are past the full flush of their second spring. The dogwoods and crabapples have already flowered and are leafing out now. Even the last of the brilliant azaleas has withered, and the bushes are greening. Dangling from the wisteria vine that crawls along the gallery are constellations of perky blue stars, and in the yard the grass is tall.[6] The milk cow is roaming the place at will.[7] In the pasture a colt romps unsteadily about its mother, for Joe's gray mare has foaled this spring.[8]

But does Barbara notice the tottering pony beyond the fence? Did she notice the dogwoods and crabapples and azaleas when they were blooming? Barbara would be oblivious to the outside world. Since the birth of her sickly child, she may not even have ventured beyond the gallery. Indeed, some of the doctor bills may portend ministrations to the mother as well as the infant.

In spite of bleak preoccupation, however, Barbara cannot be unaware of the turmoil festering beyond the Vicksburg Place. George, Catherine, Anna would have spent much time with her these five weeks. Father Leray, or the pastor's assistant, Father Bohmert, may have come out on Easter Sunday with Holy Communion. Barbara could not have avoided hearing about the arrest of Dr. Parberry and four other men, about Justice Parker's interrogation of the suspects, their exoneration, and all the rumors.

No document has come to light propounding the plentiful theories in circulation that spring to explain "the Rolling Fork tragedy." But 30 years of investigation raise a broad range of hypotheses, and a rebuttal to each one:

Marauding ex-slaves!—Roving gangs of armed freedmen were dispensing retribution by killing whites indiscriminately, and pillaging and torching their property.[9]

However, although some instances of this behavior are documented, it appears that the collective white imagination, fired by fear of a Negro uprising, exaggerated grossly any report of whites harmed by blacks.

Act of God!—Fires were tragic, but natural. They happened often, and were most devastating in remote country.[10]

Yet not *one* of the five inhabitants escaped from the burning building. If any of them had been alive when the fire began, some of them, at least, if not all, would have managed to save themselves.

Angry freedmen!—While the white minority prospered, the black majority remained downtrodden.[11]

However, without the intervention of the entrepreneurial northerners, the black population would be thrown back on the whim of their former masters. It was the Yankee immigrants who provided the buffer between the interests of the planters and those of the ex-slaves. The agents of the Freedmen's Bureau had pulled out in 1868; the Union troops had left in 1870; no federal presence remained to safeguard the rights of blacks. Without white people like the Rings, and their resources, freedmen might be ousted from public office and denied the possibility of land-ownership.

Besides, if blacks were going to rampage against their oppressors, they would target the well-to-do planters, not the merchants. Wiping out Ring & Co. would serve no useful purpose to the blacks. On the contrary, it could only hurt them.

Moreover, even W. D. Brown admitted that throughout the racial strife during the war, blacks were never known to harm a white woman or child. The charred corpses of Martha Moore and little Willie Jeans refuted decisively any theory that attributed the outrage to local blacks.

Planters!—Local Democrats were eager to oust the Yankee Republicans and regain control of the black labor force.[12]

However, the planters relied too heavily on Ring & Co. to destroy it. They needed the merchants for credit and supplies. They needed the merchants to warehouse and ship their cotton. They needed the merchants to purchase the cotton of their sharecroppers and tenants. Burning Ring & Co. to the ground could only damage the aristocratic Democrats' own welfare.

Besides, one brutal act of retaliation would hardly purge the neighborhood of carpetbaggers, or eliminate the Republican strangle hold on Issaquena County.

Bandits!—The atrocity was perpetrated by a band of marauding outlaws, white or black, or both together.[13]

The appearance of such bands, though, was usually preceded by warnings that traveled ahead of them by word of mouth. Prior to the massacre, no similar incident had been reported within several days' ride of Rolling Fork Landing. Nor did anyone spot a party of armed men riding through the country afterwards.

Treachery of a friend!—Johnny Joor was behind the crime, or John Coker![14]

But all evidence contradicts this notion. Johnny Joor was George's buddy long before the disaster, and they remained friendly for the rest of their lives. When Joor married in 1878, George was his "best man."[15] That Joor happened to be away from the store the night it burned down was pure chance—one of those disturbing coincidences that mark "the

Rolling Fork tragedy." As for John Coker, even if he did for some reason hold a grudge against the Ring brothers—and the written record offers no hint of this—he would hardly have had a hand in the murder of his own daughter, Martha! Coker's absence the night of the fire was, once again, mindless coincidence.

A lunatic!—One of the five residents, in a psychopathic rampage, slew the others, set the fire, then killed himself, or herself.[16]

However, no evidence suggests that any of the five inmates had a history of mental illness. On the contrary, by all appearances, they were motivated, socially-engaged, productive and happy people. Besides, Jesse Moore was too weak and in pain from his rheumatism to execute such a crime. Martha and little Willie were too small. Joe was far from discontented. Which leaves Goudchat alone. The chances are infinitessimal.

Fraud!—Joe and George Ring torched their business for the insurance money.[17]

But if Joe had not really been burned up in the store, where was he?

Bigots!—Native-born white men despised the immigrants, Catholics and Jews who arrived after the war.[18]

However, the vast majority of people living in the Delta in 1873— unlike the rest of the South—was *not* native-born. It was a frontier society of newcomers whose diverse members, despite rigid stratification, exhibited surprising tolerance of one another—out of mutual dependence, if from no loftier impulse. Besides, many of the foreign-born merchants, George Ring included, had arrived before the war, not after it.

What was more, Jesse, Martha and little Willie were all American-born, and Protestant.[19] Martha and little Willie even belonged to families of Mississippi.

Disgruntled customers!—Any number of planters or farmers or field hands might have resented Ring & Co. for denying them the credit or cash or commodity they sought in a desperate hour.[20]

However, the disastrous financial reversals of '66 and '67 were long past. By 1873 land ownership in Issaquena County was more stable than elsewhere in the South, because so many freed slaves stayed on with former masters as wage labor or tenants. Customers might harbor complaints against Ring & Co., but no planter or yeoman or laborer was aggrieved so devastatingly as to bring down the entire store and everyone associated with it. Especially when the chief offender, the managing partner, was 40 miles away.

Rival merchants!—Neighboring businessmen were retaliating against Ring & Co. for some grievance, or simply eliminating the competition.[21]

But country merchants benefitted more by cooperating than by competing. The Delta's rugged topography and widely-scattered population imposed a limit on the volume of business any one merchandising enterprise could satisfy. Each merchant had to conduct his business within the parameters of what his neighborhood could afford, not what other merchants upriver or downriver were doing. Destroying Rolling Fork Landing would not increase substantially the revenues of any other merchant.

Besides, in the Delta in 1873 it was hardly necessary to slaughter half the population of a landing to advance a mercantile career. Any man could exercise his ambition by expanding into the tens of thousands of virgin acres farther inland.

Racists!—Since Ring & Co. treated black customers the same as white, it was destroyed by men who detested "nigger lovers."[22]

Yet such men had never before wielded their racist violence so gruesomely against fellow whites. Competing with freedmen for work and a modicum of social acceptance, poor white river men might disdain white neighbors who treated ex-slaves equitably, might ostracize them, perhaps even threaten or thrash them. But never had they murdered a white household *en masse*.

Besides, a racist fanatic would have targeted George, the managing partner of the firm, rather than everybody else in the household.

These diverse hypotheses, resulting from a 30-year inquest, are by no means mutually exclusive. On the contrary, a combination of elements from several of them may constitute an explanation no longer discernible at a distance of a century and a quarter.

Perhaps, during long hours of solitary vigil beside her baby's crib, Barbara's thoughts have wandered into this realm of woeful controversy. Day and night have alternated as usual outside, bringing a change of season to the Vicksburg Place. But indoors, time has been regulated solely by the fits and starts of the little one's struggle to grasp onto life. So it would be distant and nebulous, all this fuss about the fire, and irrelevant besides. What absorbs Barbara's attention is the ill health of her child, and the life of his immortal soul.

Finally two horsemen appear on the lane from Baldwin's Ferry Road. Yes! Father Bohmert! And a man he has mustered along the way to stand as godfather. There is no time to find a godmother.[23]

In the parlor, or maybe in one of the bedrooms upstairs, the clergyman finds a surface on which to set his small wooden case. He unlatches the cover, raises it, pulls out an embroidered silk stole, kisses it, and slips it around his neck. Then he takes out two small cream-colored candles, sets them into the two holes in the lid of the box, strikes a match, and lights them. At last, uncorking a vial of holy water, he turns to Barbara.

What is the baby to be called?

Michael Albert.

The rite takes only moments. Nicholas, George and John are probably watching, their grayish-blue eyes round with fascination. Peter would be lying there motionless, entranced by the pair of flickering flames. Maybe even Lomo stands still.

When he gets back to St. Paul's, Father Bohmert opens the Baptismal Register, dips his pen, and enters the sacramental record in Latin. Upon signing it, he notes in the margin: "*Privatim, In articulo mortis.*" ("At home, Close to death.")[24]

Tomorrow, lying inert in his long white baptismal gown fringed with lace, Michael Albert Ring will be interred.[25] And Barbara's battered heart will turn homeward.

CHAPTER TWENTY-SIX

JULY 15, 1873

Know all men by these Presents, that I, Barbara Ring, of Warren County, Mississippi, do by these presents, make constitute and appoint George F. Ring of said county and State, my agent and attorney in fact and do invest him as such with the following powers and authority, to wit:

To demand receive and receipt for a certain sum of money, in amount about Five Thousand Dollars due me from the "Germania Life Insurance Company" of the City of New York under their policy No. 29,541, on the life of my late husband Joseph Ring, now deceased—and to make execute and deliver to the said Company, in my name, all such receipts refunding Bonds and other obligations, as may be necessary to secure the payment of the said money, and as he shall in his judgment think fit;

2nd. To make leases of my lands and to receive and receipt for the rents and profits thereof;

3rd. To receive and receipt for all debts, dues or demands due or to become due to me from any source whatsoever;

4th. To loan my money, on such time and terms as he

shall think fit and to take notes and other securities therefor;

5th. Generally to manage and conduct my affairs and business for my benefit and advantage in such manner as he shall think fit; to institute and prosecute in my name all suits and other proceedings which he may deem necessary to the maintenance of my rights or the due administration of my affairs and business; to defend all such suits or actions as may be brought against me; if any to employ and pay counsel in all my affairs, whenever he may deem it necessary; to pay my debts out of my moneys or revenues, and otherwise to do for me and on my behalf all acts and things necessary to the due execution of the authority hereby conferred upon him and to the due protection and advancement of the interest hereby entrusted to his management.

In witness whereof I hereto set my hand and seal this the fifteenth day of July A.D. 1873.[1]

Barbara signs. Now, finally, no obstacle remains to her departure.

Precisely when Barbara made the decision to abandon Vicksburg, no one today can say. Whether it was during those anxious cribside reveries while Michael Albert struggled for life, or afterwards, when the days grew longer and hotter. Clearly, though, for Barbara, Vicksburg had never become "home."

For Barbara—much less flexible than the Ring brothers—the city's Germanic mercantile society must have been disconcerting. In Papa's corner of Buffalo, though German-speaking Catholics and Protestants worked together, there were sufficient Lutheran parishes to preclude any incentive for intermarriage. What was more, the German Jews of Buffalo cultivated a life apart from their Christian countrymen.[2]

Barbara could not have felt at ease with the urbane gentility of Catherine Ring and Anna Sprankler. Their tolerance would have seemed to her more like moral laxity. They were not Papa's people. Though fate did not give Barbara much time to adjust to their world, probably no amount of time would have been enough. Having grown up with many siblings, and then being devoted to her husband and children, it appears that Barbara never needed, never learned how to cultivate, friends.

Besides, Catherine and Anna were more Papa's generation than Barbara's. Catherine was 46—13 years older than Barbara—and Anna was 52. Both had been widowed and were now married a second time, and even their children were married adults. Also like Papa, the sisters were immigrants. All that Barbara had in common with Catherine Ring and Anna Sprankler, all that made her a part of their world, whether she felt comfortable there or not, was that the three of them were wives of German-speaking businessmen of Vicksburg. And now Barbara was no longer that.

It is not difficult to surmise the counsel offered by George. Certainly he understood his sister-in-law's need to see her family in this time of staggering bereavement. Indeed, the trip would do her good. But not to stay. Not to take the boys back to the German-speaking quarter of Buffalo, back to the struggle of the tradesman's class.—*That* would be like getting on a ship and sailing back to France.

George would have reminded Barbara of the advantages her sons would enjoy if allowed to "grow into" their father's enterprises. Should the boys not be allowed to inherit the budding success that had cost Joe his life? Should they not be given the chance to bring to fruition the new beginning their father had made? George may even have alluded suggestively to the fact that, having no male heir himself, he would be looking for a young man to step into his shoes one day.

The Lorrainian bricklayer's daughter, however, wanted to go home. And *not* come back. William Muller would later recall that "Joseph Ring left household furniture and . . . nearly all the furniture was taken along by his family when they left the state."[3] Barbara would hardly have taken the furniture if she intended to return.

Joe had left a considerable estate of real and personal property, and debts, and no will.

"It is quite Certain that if Joseph Ring had left a Will that I would know it," William Muller would attest some years later, "as I used to draw up most of his Papers. Besides that he was a young man, & had no idea of being taken away so soon, & so sudden, from his family. . . . I have examined the records of the Chancery Clerk's Office of Warren

County, Miss. & find that no will of Joseph Ring has been probated, or any letters of Administration on his Estate nor letters of Guardianship granted for his children."[4]

So Barbara's predicament was not unlike Catherine's when Jacob Morris died: she had never followed her husband's affairs and was entirely ignorant of the legal exigencies her new status imposed. Also like Catherine, the death of her husband was unexpected, and her grief compounded by the loss of a young son. Barbara could hardly have been expected to muster much interest in Joe's deeds and indentures, promissory notes, invoices, bank drafts, receipts and life insurance. As Catherine had done, she turned to George.[5]

Although he neglected to apply for letters of administration and guardianship, George did file Barbara's insurance claim. The company's agent, Julius Hoerner, dispatched it to New York.[6] But the directors, learning that there was no corpse, and that the alleged death had occurred under mysterious circumstances, were skeptical. They hesitated to authorize payment.[7]

George wasted no time in sending W. D. Brown to prosecute the matter in Tallula. As soon as the Circuit Court convened its May term, Brown presented Barbara's petition. The court summoned Hoerner, but he failed to appear. So the court entered a judgment by default against the Germania Life Insurance Company for the value of the policy, $5,000, plus $32 in legal fees.[8]

Now, on this scorching Tuesday ("[T]he sun came down in earnest," tomorrow's newspaper will report, "and zephyrs were not on the wing. Palmetto fans and lemon drops were very much in demand."[9]), when Barbara signs over to her brother-in-law full power of attorney, the first item on the agenda is collecting this insurance money. As it turns out, the matter will be settled in a few days, and the outcome publicized with a "Notice to the Public" in the *Vicksburg Daily Times* of July 27, 1873:

> I consider it my duty to inform the public that I have received from the Germania Life Insurance Company of New York, the insurance on the life of my late husband, Joseph Ring, with interest, amounting to five thousand and fifty-eight dollars and thirty-three cents, with the following remarks from the President of said insurance company:

Whereas Mr. G. Theisen, one of our Directors, has convinced himself personally that all the reports which have reached us about the death of Joseph Ring, are unfounded; nay, malicious, we feel it our duty not only to pay to the widow the money promptly, but to add, also, the interest for the time the money has been due.

Very respectfully,

H. Wesendonk, Pres't

I cannot otherwise but express my gratitude and thanks to the gentlemanly Agent, Mr. Julius Hoerner, and the officers of the Germania Life Insurance Company in New York, for the trouble and exertions they have been to to reach at the foundation of the rumors concerning the death of my late husband, Joseph Ring. They went so far, in order that justice might be done, as to send one of their Directors, a wealthy and prudent merchant of the city of New York, to this place. I hope and pray that the families of those persons who took so much trouble to keep me and my four fatherless children out of the insurance money may receive more charity in case misfortune should overtake them.

To the public, I can but sincerely recommend the Germania Life Insurance Company and their Agent here, Mr. Julius Hoerner. They will not alone find that the money is safely invested and the future welfare of their families secured, but will also meet in the officers men of high sense of honor and human feelings.

Barbara Ring[10]

However, by the time this notice appears, Barbara has been gone a week, and the voice sounds suspiciously more like George's than Barbara's. Is her "agent and attorney in fact" merely doing what she authorized him to do—handle her affairs as he sees fit? If this endorsement of an insurance company (by a widow with four children) happens also to include a refutation of the "malicious" "reports . . . about the death of Joseph Ring" (by a distinguished company officer), so much the better for George's defense.

Chapter Twenty-Seven

JULY 20, 1873

Very early Sunday morning, July 20th, the Rings and the Spranklers ride onto the Commons.[1] They fill at least two carriages, and a wagon loaded with trunks and suitcases follows. "The sun was overcast with heavy clouds," the *Vicksburg Daily Times* will report, "but they brought forth but little in the way of rain, as they seemed to have spent their fury in a copious and lengthy shower Saturday night."[2] So the landing on this gloomy dawn is all mud and puddles.

George supervises the transfer of the baggage to the riverboat. She is not a "floating palace" like the *Natchez* or the *Robert E. Lee*. Neither, however, is she a "floating sepulchre."[3] Her record of enrollment, made in Cincinnati where she was built in 1869, attests "that the said Ship or Vessel has three decks and no mast, and that her length is One hundred forty Seven (147) 2/10 feet, her breadth is Thirty four (34) 8/10 feet, her depth Five (5) 6/10 feet, her height Seventeen x/10 feet, and that she measures Three hundred & eighty five tons and fifteen hundreds."[4] Her hull is narrow (for speed) and shallow—the boat can navigate in three feet of water. Just last year she was lengthened 50 feet by her co-owners, one of whom, Alexander M. Halliday, is her captain.[5] This increased her tonnage to 552, making her a "large sternwheel steamer" of respectable accommodation.[6]

She is a packet, which means she transports freight as well as pas-

1873.		
Mch 10	To Cash	20 00
	" Bears (paid)	16 00
	Mrs Price	15 00
	Geo Harris	15 00
Apr 29	2½ Cords Wood (Mrs Ring)	17 50
	Insurance on house	10 00
	Note for land	706 60
June 27	L. Mass Bill	27 90
	Cash	10 00
July 25	Just Bill	34 25
	Cash for trip home	225 00
	Dr Oleary's bill	140 00
	Dr Whitehead's bill	35 00
	Post orders to Buffalo	150 00
	" " from Detroit	100 00
	4. Gollinger's bill	8 00
	Porter from Wallins	8 0.0
	Arnold for burying Chied	21 00
	Forbes & Fitzpatrick's bill	40 63
	$	5,366 79

PAGE FROM BARBARA RING'S FINANCIAL ACCOUNTS, 1874.

sengers.[7] This morning's "River Intelligence" in the *Vicksburg Daily Times* will report that the steamer:

> . . . passed up, en route for Cincinnati, with 650 tons of old boiler iron, hides and miscellaneous lumber. She had 37 cabin passengers, and added several here, among whom, the family of Mr. Ring, of the firm of Ring & Muller, who go to New York State for the summer.[8]

The cargo is stacked on the lowest deck, called the main or cargo or boiler deck, which is open to the elements and twice the height of the upper decks, where passengers and crew are housed. It is wider, too, extending beyond the hull all around (the overhang is called the "guard"). There is no rail at the bow, but bulwarks along the sides keep shifting freight from sliding into the river. Depending on the load, the main deck might hover just a foot or two above water, and amidships, where it sags the lowest, might even sink an inch or two below the surface of the river. Whether George is having Barbara's furniture carried on board now, or whether he shipped it on an earlier or later packet, is not known.

Suddenly the whistle blasts short-short-long, short-short-long, and there is an excited flurry of hasty farewells. The younger boys— George, John and little Peter—George may lift and kiss. But to Nicholas he would extend his hand, as he would to Barbara. Then George escorts Catherine up the gangplank, while Anna bids farewell to her husband Henry Sprankler.

What are the travel plans? Oral tradition will give no hint:

"So the man's wife, Barbara," Grandma Ring will tell me in 1963 when I ask about my ancestors, "Barbara came back up to her family in Buffalo. She came up the Mississippi River on a steamboat, she and the boys. She had four boys."[9]

The letter penned in 1958 by Lena Weber's daughter, Libbie, at the age of 88, will offer more. But it is full of errors:

"[T]hen Aunt Barbara had a baby a little girl Hattie when the baby was 3 months old she wanted to goe back to Buffalo to her home so George Ring wife said she would acompany her to Buffalo Aunt Barbara had 3 boys George Joe and John Mrs George Ring Mrs Spangler went with them they took the Natches . . . they where going to stop off at Cincynati to visit us."[10]

Finally, a piece in the *Evansville Daily Journal* will provide an additional clue:

> "Mrs. Ring . . . is en route to Buffalo, N.Y., to visit her father, Mr. John Miller. The other Mrs. Ring [Catherine] was en route to Cincinnati and Detroit."[11]

The plan, therefore—as well as it can be reconstructed—is for Catherine and Anna to accompany Barbara and the boys to Cincinnati, where they will all visit at the home of Hank and Lena Weber. Then the travelers will proceed on by train to Detroit,[12] where Barbara and her sons will transfer to a steamer and cross Lake Erie to Buffalo. The two Hessian sisters, however, will spend some time in Detroit—at the home of relatives probably—where George will join them just as soon as his work allows.[13]

At least one of the travelers, however, expects to stop over in Evansville, Indiana:

"Mrs. Pringle," the *Cincinnati Commercial* will print, meaning Anna Sprankler, "who was . . . going to Evansville . . . ."[14]

Anna's son-in-law George Koch has just this summer, after losing his tin plant in Vicksburg to fire, moved his family upriver to rejoin his many siblings in Evansville. Already he has built a new small shop and residence there.[15] Anna welcomes this opportunity to visit her daughter and two grandchildren.

Short-short-long, short-short-long, the whistle screams again, and George is watching the elegant vessel back out slowly into the mighty current of the Mississippi. Built entirely of wood, the riverboat is whitewashed inside and out: walls, bulwarks, rails, posts, paddlewheel, all of the fanciful gingerbread—all white as cotton. The three decks, however, which sag in unison from bow to stern like comfortable hammocks, have been left natural. The two smokestacks soar as high and black as a Delta night.[16]

She stops. The paddlewheel reverses. Steadily and smoothly, she swings upriver.

Planted in the mire of the Commons, waving farewell, George may

THE MISSISSIPPI AND OHIO RIVERS.
(Map drawn by the author)

feel a sad relief: his sister-in-law's terrible summer is over now. Now she can mend. The brother-bereft immigrant watches the great wheel churning the water round and round, the clouds of gray-black smoke gushing out of the twin chimneys. Passengers lining the steamboat's rails are waving toward shore. But no bright aurora blue penetrates the ashen and ponderous overcast that plugs the sky over Vicksburg like the lid on an iron kettle.

George and his colleague-kinsman gaze upriver. Smaller and smaller the riverboat shrinks. The churning water loses its roar. The dark trail of smoke thins. A little while later, rounding the bend, she disappears.

The *Jennie Howell.*

Newspaper reporters will call her "ill-fated."[17]

Chapter Twenty-Eight

JULY 25, 1873

At 6:00 a.m. on Friday, July 25th, Barbara and her boys, and Catherine Ring and Anna Sprankler, are roused from their slumber by the ear-splitting blasts of the *Jennie Howell*'s whistle.[1]

"CAI-RO!" the steward chants as he strides past their stateroom door. "Cairo, Illinois!"

It is their sixth day on the river, and the first to dawn without showers or threat of showers.[2] Seeing sunshine poking through the shutters, passengers dress quickly and step outside. The newborn sun is low and large and beaming. It will be the last sun ever to warm the decks of the *Jennie Howell* . . . and the countenances of three of her guests.

From the cabin deck, the Ring party cannot see the watchman crouching at the bow. But they can certainly hear his cries—"Mark four! Mark three! Mark twain!"—as the riverboat inches up to the landing. Each sounding is repeated from deckhand to deckhand to the pilot on high.[3] The mighty sternwheel stops. The *Jennie Howell* is still.

Again the steward sweeps by, this time ringing his bell, and Barbara hustles her boys back into the cabin for breakfast.

Captain Halliday operates his ship between his home city of Cincinnati and New Orleans. The run is long and slow: nine days downstream, 11 days up.[4] Advertised stops include Louisville and Paducah, Kentucky; Evansville, Indiana; Shawneetown and Cairo, Illinois;

Memphis, Tennessee; Greenville, Vicksburg and Natchez, Mississippi; and Baton Rouge, Louisiana.[5] However, Halliday also calls at any river-front plantation flying the red flag. Precise scheduling is impossible. Merchants and travelers keep abreast of the *Jennie Howell*'s progress by reading their local "River Intelligence."

"River Intelligence" runs daily in newspapers published along the inland rivers. The column reports the arrival and departure of packets, weather and river conditions, merchandise delivered, merchandise shipped, the comings and goings of members of the river community. It entertains readers with anecdotes about the captains and their crews, poking fun at beloved "characters" like Frank Buskirk, chief clerk of the *Jennie Howell*.[6] People on the rivers are all "kin" in spirit, and often in the flesh, too, such as the Kochs of Vicksburg and Evansville.[7] They share a common commerce, a common culture, and suffer alike from common disasters. Floods and gales, mudslides, murders, attacks and robberies by the armed pirates of Cave-in-Rock, boiler explosions, sink-ings, deckhands lost overboard, and every floater washed ashore—all are "communicated" in "River Intelligence."

After breakfast Barbara and her boys may go back out onto the gallery to observe the men laboring below.

The deck crew consists of about 30 roustabouts who load and unload freight. Commonly called "roosters," they are all black except for a cou-ple of older Irishmen—any deckhand over 30 is "older." Most of the cargo they tote on their backs and shoulders, or push, pull or roll along gangplanks. But to hoist heavy loads, they use two long, strong cranes affixed to the bow, one to port, one to starboard.

This morning the "roosters" unload only "40 boxes pears for Chicago."[8] That leaves "25 hogsheads sugar, 121 packages groceries for the Lower Ohio, 1000 sacks salt, 26 cases wine for Louisville, 300 tons scrap iron, 1,032 beer kegs, [and] 529 sundries for Cincinnati" remain-ing on the main deck.[9] No new freight is loaded. Fourteen travelers dis-embark with their baggage.[10]

"Business dull," the Cairo paper will report.[11]

The director of this choreography is Frank Buskirk. At every port the chief clerk checks invoices and manifests and informs Captain Halliday of the changes of cargo and passengers. Typical of men who

Newspaper

spend their lives on the rivers, Buskirk is good-natured, unhurried and unflappable. He works with diligence and pride, cognizant of the value of his skills.[12] Freight to be unloaded at one port cannot be piled behind freight scheduled for unloading at a subsequent port. Hours of manpower would be wasted at every stop. Halliday and his partner would go broke. Furthermore, cargo loaded improperly could capsize the *Jennie Howell* in a minute.

Buskirk's assistant, the second clerk, is Lewis Halliday, the captain's brother.[13] On this particular run Buskirk is also initiating a young apprentice, Billy Shaw, into the rites of managing the office.[14] It is by word of mouth that the skills of plying the inland rivers are transferred from one generation to the next.

"We have done a big business in the way of people, especially children," Buskirk tells a Cairo reporter. "All along the shore we have been picking up babies . . . the C. B. Church was compelled to leave for want of room. We started from New Orleans with half a gross of sugar-teats and they are all in use."[15]

"This, I suppose," the newspaper man will add, "includes the one I saw sticking out of Frank's vest pocket."[16]

Buskirk logs 35 cabin passengers, "all in excellent health,"[17] and one deck passenger, "a colored boy named George."[18]

Again the *Jennie Howell*'s whistle carries for miles. Within three hours of pulling into Cairo, she is ready to push back. Deckhands now glistening with sweat haul in the gangways, then drop onto their bunks. These are improvised in a corner of the main deck. For the "roosters," labor and leisure are sporadic, dictated by whether the packet is aground or under steam. Sometimes they are divided into two watches, but often they remain on call 24 hours a day, seven days a week.

The immense paddlewheel at the stern starts to rotate, pulling the *Jennie Howell* slowly away from shore. The packet's power is generated by the engine, which is fueled by the steam boiler on the main deck. This is the duty station of the engineer, and the fireman who stokes the boiler continually. Piled here is the mountain of cordwood that must be replenished twice daily at woodyards along the banks.—Another call, day or night, for the deck crew.

When the *Jennie Howell* enters the channel, her sternwheel slows to

THE *JENNIE HOWELL*, JANUARY 1873.

(*Courtesy Inland Rivers Library, Public Library of Cincinnati and Hamilton County*)

a halt. Then the enormous paddles begin to sweep in reverse, pushing the riverboat up the Ohio. By now the sun is higher, and a Cairo reporter will describe the day's weather as "clear and hot."[19]

The architecture and décor of the *Jennie Howell* must be inferred from comparable packets, because only a single photograph of her is known to exist. It was taken in January 1873, six months prior to this trip, and shows her sitting at New Orleans under 2,456 bales of cotton.[20] That was an extraordinary load, and warranted a commemorative photo. The ship was so obscured by the gargantuan cube of stacked bales, however, that she could be mistaken for a barge, were it not for the two tall smokestacks and little pilothouse sticking out on top. Cotton runs are heaviest during winter months. On the present mid-summer run, the *Jennie Howell* carries no cotton at all.

From the bow of the *Jennie Howell's* main deck, a wide staircase rises to a landing, where two narrower flights of stairs branch to the left and right, leading up to the cabin deck. The cabin houses the showpiece of every riverboat: the saloon. Long, narrow, ostentatious and airy, the saloon runs down the center of the cabin from bow to stern. It serves as dining hall and lounge for the cabin passengers, whose staterooms line its sweeping sides. The saloon's ceiling is higher than that of the staterooms, and articulated by a repetition of elaborately-carved beams painted white. These beams round the cornice in fancy latticework and descend part-way down the whitewashed walls, reminiscent of the ribcage of Jonah's great fish. A series of clerestory windows of etched glass runs between these fancy ribs above the staterooms.

As soon as Barbara hears the tinkling of the steward's bell a second time—about noon—she hurries the boys into the saloon for dinner. Waiters set meals out before passengers are seated, and bored travelers stampede to help themselves while the dishes are still hot. Latecomers face tepid left-overs.

The clerestory windows are open for ventilation this afternoon, and the daylight flooding the saloon betrays the shabbiness of the Brussels carpets, oil paintings, mirrors and brocade draperies which, on the overcast days, looked so splendid. A row of ornate chandeliers, one every few yards from one end of the saloon to the other, dramatizes the length of the great hall. Each flaunts a dozen or more whale oil lamps.

SALOON OF THE ANCHOR LINE'S *CITY OF ST. LOUIS*, 1888. *(Courtesy Prints & Photographs Division, Library of Congress)*

Beneath these chandeliers stretches a succession of round mahogany tables, and side chairs—upholstered in deep red or burgundy velvet—line the walls. Three times a day the chairs are pulled up to the tables as they are now—perhaps eight per table—and a corps of black waiters materializes to remove emptied bowls and cleared platters. The cabin crew numbers about 22 in all, and includes the chef, cooks, steward, cabin boys and chambermaids, as well as waiters.

Each tabletop is obscured beneath platters of sliced roast beef, roast pork, cooked onions, steamed rice and boiled potatoes; bowls piled high with overcooked greens, string beans, carrots and corn; a tureen of consomme; two boats of gravy, two greasy French sauces, and assorted jellies; baskets of rolls and biscuits; a salt cellar and pepper grinder; pots of tea and coffee, and pitchers of water; fruit tarts, cream tarts, rice pudding and custards that are already running.

Depending on how speedily they reach the saloon, Barbara and her boys, and Catherine and Anna, might find themselves split up at tables with strangers. Conversation is discouraged; it allows the food to get stone cold. But the Vicksburg ladies may at least meet some of the passengers with whom they are about to share the trauma of shipwreck.

One gentleman on board is Jacob Allfree. "Mr. Allfree, with his family, consisting of his wife, daughter and son," the *Evansville Daily Journal* will relate, "were returning from Arkansas to their former home near Lebanon, Kentucky."[21] The *Jenny Howell*'s sole deck passenger, the black youth named George, "was accompanying Mr. Allfree and family to Kentucky."[22]

A pair of traveling companions, Mrs. Mylard and Mrs. Stephens, are booked through to Cincinnati.[23]

There is also a Mrs. Chapman on board. She is on her way home to Evansville, Indiana.[24] Anna Sprankler, in a heavy German accent, may remark that her daughter Mary lives in Evansville with her husband George Koch and their two children.[25] Mrs. Chapman would recognize the surname right away, as *William* Koch—George's younger brother—is City Collector.[26]

The lofty saloon resonates with the tinkling of forks and knives, the clinking of china and crystal. Waiters emerge now carrying handbaskets brimming with fresh peaches, pears and blueberries. In a matter of minutes the 35 passengers are dispersing.

At one end of the saloon, a massive, ornately-sculpted mahogany table supports the water cooler. Silver, sparkling, the cooler holds gallons of fresh water and a huge cube of ice. This is a popular gathering place for after-dinner conversation. At the other end of the hall stands a mammoth, cast-iron heater on four great claws. This is the preferred spot on winter trips, when snowflakes sometimes paint the natural wood decks of the *Jennie Howell* as white as her walls.

Women retire to the ladies' parlor, located to stern in line with the staterooms. It contains sofas, rocking chairs, a sideboard, a bookcase holding a few tattered volumes, and a piano. Children's playthings litter the Brussels carpet. Men gather in the barroom, which is located to fore in line with the staterooms, across from Buskirk's office. Settling down to a game of poker, the men light cigars and call to J. B. Clouser, the barkeeper,[27] for brandies.

Meanwhile, in the galley, the chef and his cooks are just now sitting down to *their* meal. After eating, the cabin boys will scrub the oversized kettles and pans, the tureens, bowls and platters, plates, saucers, cups and water goblets, and polish the silver service and flatware. The chambermaids will launder the table cloths and napkins, hand towels, sheets and pillowcases. Though supper will be a much lighter meal, the workday of the cabin crew is far from over. When night falls, they will all hustle to make their beds in the saloon. Similar to the deck crew downstairs, the cabin crew has no permanent lodgings on the *Jennie Howell*.

After visiting the waterclosets built over the stern, then the washrooms—which provide both hot and cold water—Barbara and her boys would retire to their stateroom for a nap. Catherine and Anna, who occupy the adjoining stateroom,[28] would do likewise.

There are 10 or 12 staterooms on either side of the saloon. Each measures about eight feet square, with an upper and lower berth, and a washstand with bowl and pitcher. Passengers may exit their rooms into the saloon, or out onto the covered veranda that surrounds the cabin. Opening both inner and outer doors, while leaving the shutters latched, allows river breezes to sweep through the cabin with no loss of privacy.

The rooms of the Ring party are on the starboard side of the cabin, farthest to stern.[29] Across the saloon, on the port (sometimes called "larboard") side of the cabin, are the two staterooms occupied by the Allfree family. Mr. and Mrs. Allfree and their daughter—"aged about 14 or 15 years"[30]—share one,[31] while their son lodges next door.[32] Buskirk always assigns ladies and families the staterooms farthest to stern, because these are considered the safest. They are the most distant from the boiler. The tradeoff for the favored passengers, however, is the incessant vibration and splashing noise of the paddlewheel. On this particular run, the conscientious clerk has no way of knowing that the stern will be the deadliest place on the ship.

Above the passengers' heads is the hurricane deck, with the upper cabin in the middle. Much smaller than the passengers' cabin, the upper cabin contains the captain's quarters and lodging for his officers. Officers include the chief clerk and second clerk, two pilots and engineer. Although the ship's complement varies from one trip to the next, generally the deck crew, cabin crew and officers number about 60 persons in all.

Covering the upper cabin is the hurricane roof, or "texas," and on this, slightly to fore, stands the pilothouse, the pinnacle of the *Jennie Howell*. It measures about 14 feet by 10, and its walls are all glass from waist level up to allow unobstructed vision in every direction. Navigation is entirely by sight.

The steering wheel is eight feet in diameter, the lower half disappearing below deck. Two pilots, John Moldridge and Eugene Hanlon,[33] alternate eight-hour duty shifts. Affixed to a corner of the pilothouse roof is a slender metallic tube vital to the safe operation of the riverboat: the whistle. Forward of the pilothouse, surging out of the hurricane roof, one to port and one to starboard, tall, slender, matte black, the twin stacks rise to fancy flared crowns. When the *Jennie Howell* is under a full head of steam, billows of gray-black smoke chug out of these chimneys and trail over her like a flamboyant panache.

About 10 hours out of Cairo—roughly 7:00 p.m.—a light supper is set out in the saloon. After eating, Catherine and Anna bid Barbara and the boys, "*Guten abend!*" and disappear into their stateroom. Barbara puts the boys to bed, then undresses and lies down herself. It appears from accounts of what is about to happen, that Barbara shares the lower berth with 2-year-old Peter, while Nicholas, George and John sleep overhead in the upper berth.[34] The mantra of the river churning through the paddlewheel lulls them all to sleep.

Somewhere in the stateroom there must be two items that belonged to Joe Ring: his pocket knife, retrieved from the ashes of Ring & Co., and his watch, left at home when he went up to Rolling Fork Landing for the last time. The knife is most likely a prized possession in Nicholas's pocket now. The watch is probably in Barbara's purse, along with "$225 cash for trip home,"[35] which George handed her before she boarded. However, no mention of Joe's knife or timepiece, or Barbara's travel money, will appear in later documents. Presumably, they will all end up in the shifting silt of the Ohio.

The Ohio winds through descending rock shelves, over chutes, around boulders and sand bars, rising at times to flood level and falling at times to almost no depth at all. As a result, its channel is reconfigured continuously.[36] The Mississippi is even worse, twisting and turning back on itself like ribbon candy, with no bedrock at all to hold its course. Its powerful undercurrents redistribute sediment constantly, shaping an ever-changing channel.[37] The rivers that Captain Halliday's pilots navigate are new every trip. And always treacherous.

Darkness descends on the river. The watchman lights the *Jennie Howell*'s torches. A telegraph out of Cairo reports: "There are some few indications of an approaching rain to-night, but otherwise the weather is unchanged."[38]—That is, continued clear and hot. A galaxy of stars appears overhead. A full moon shimmers on the rippling surface of the Ohio.[39] Captain Halliday retires to his quarters, leaving Moldridge alone in the pilothouse.[40]

Nearing Curlew Point now, Moldridge is steering cautiously. Pilots coming down have warned him about the snag that has lodged here.[41] Snags are a perpetual menace. Trees, uprooted from eroding banks and washed downriver, get pounded into the riverbed by the incessant current. Visible and harmless in low water, they can sink an unsuspecting ship when the river rises.[42]

"The snag is a new, large sycamore," "River Intelligence" will communicate, "directly in the channel. . . . Pilots should look out for it, and the authorities should have it removed.[43] It is the same obstruction which sunk the *Umpire*."[44]

However, all this week, despite intermittent showers, the Ohio has fallen.[45] Moldridge should be able to spot the tree and skirt it by keeping the *Jennie Howell* as close to the Kentucky shore as he can without running her aground.[46]

CHAPTER TWENTY-NINE

JULY 26, 1873, ABOUT 2 – 4 A.M.

At about two o'clock Saturday morning, July 26th, as the *Jennie Howell* is rounding Curlew Point, the night darkens and a sprinkle of rain starts to fall.[1] Though Moldridge is experienced in steering through these bends at night, his eyes are straining now. No moonlight frames the familiar shapes along the shoreline that he relies on for guidance.[2] Captain Halliday steps to his stateroom door and opens it to take a look at the night.[3]

All at once the ship convulses and there is "a terrific noise."[4] Halliday grabs the doorjamb to keep from falling. Passengers are jostled awake in their berths. Crew members are on their feet before their eyes open. The *Jennie Howell* stops. Halliday bounds up the stairs to the hurricane roof.[5]

"He did not think the boat was high enough up to hit the snag," reporters will write later, "and asked Mr. John Moldridge, who was at the wheel, what he thought they had struck. The pilot was confident it must be a snag, but could not locate it. The pilot tried to back off, but the boat would not move, and then for fear of breaking steam pipes, Captain Halliday sent word to the engineer to cool down as fast as possible. He had scarcely given the order when he felt the roof being shoved up under his feet."[6]

Presently the watchman arrives on the roof, breathless, to report.[7]

The snag is a rough one and has torn the boat badly.[8] "It entered the hull close to the stem in the port bow, and passed up through the main and hurricane decks, and through the hurricane roof, coming out close to the stairs,"[9] where it has struck Captain Halliday's foot.

While the mighty sycamore holds the *Jennie Howell*'s port bow above water, the boat careens to starboard.[10] Twenty-five hogsheads of sugar, 121 packages of groceries, 1,000 sacks of salt, 26 crates of wine, 300 tons of scrap iron, 1,032 beer kegs, 529 sundries, several steamer trunks full of passengers' belongings—and maybe Barbara's household furniture, too—plow through the bulwark and plummet into the Ohio River in a spectacular display of geysers and gurgling.[11]

Staterooms to starboard, beginning with those farthest astern, are dipping below the surface of the river.[12] Water comes gushing into the cabin, and Barbara's is one of the first rooms to flood.[13] Shocked awake by the jolt and din, she would realize instantly that the deck is listing. Her first instinct would be to grab Peter and get out of the berth. The gravity of the moment may not hit her, however, until she feels her bare feet land in cool water ankle deep.

In the darkness she calls for the boys, her free hand searching the upper berth. Nicholas and George leap into the rapidly rising water, splash, splash.[14] Already it reaches their little waists.

John!

The angle of the deck is steepening.

John!

The growing torrent sweeps Barbara off balance.

Passengers scream as they feel the quake and hear splashing and crashing.[15] In the saloon the mahogany tables and chairs tumble against the starboard wall, smashing into stateroom doors. Chandelier globes crash and shatter, along with liquor bottles and brandy snifters loosed from shelves in the barroom. In the ladies' parlor, the sideboard topples onto the piano, which scrapes along the Brussels carpet and bashes into the cabin wall. Silverware, china and crystal overturn in the galley cabinets and collide with pots and skillets and cooking utensils. The silver water cooler dislodges from its ornately-sculpted stand and rumbles across the slanting deck. The great claws of the cast-iron heater groan as the deck tilts more and more. Finally, the heater's massive weight uproots them in a series of blasting snaps, and the behemoth topples.

Barefoot, in nightclothes, hardly awake, the passengers spring instinctively from their berths. Sloshing around the deck in the dark, they grope for loved ones. Above the roar of rushing water, tiny voices cry out, parents bellow the names of children. In less than three minutes the boat has careened to such an angle that her starboard staterooms are all in the water. To keep from drowning, every soul on board has to struggle up the steep cabin deck to the up-turned port veranda.[16]

Clinging to one another and dodging buoyant debris, clad in nothing but soaked undergarments and nightgowns, passengers and men and women of the cabin crew wade through the rising tide.[17] Husbands pull wives by the hand, fathers and mothers carry children, brothers help sisters, waiters and cabin boys lend an arm to chambermaids. But the three wives of Vicksburg businessmen have no male escort to assist them. Nor, in all likelihood, has any one of them ever learned how to swim.[18]

Four-year-old John Ring is still sleeping soundly in his upper berth.[19] The stateroom is submerged, but air is trapped near the ceiling. In the water, grasping Peter, Barbara flails her free arm and kicks and kicks, but to no avail. Her lungs are beginning to ache. Or maybe her gaping mouth does find air, only to be choked again by the river. She is helpless to save her children.

The men on the lower deck rush over the guards to the cabin and the roof, and stretch out a muscular arm to anyone in need below.[20] "Captain Halliday, his brother, the watchman, and several others," news wires will explain, "clung to the upper cabin guard, and, crawling along, opened state-room doors and pulled out all [the passengers] they could, and then let ropes down into the cabin and got out the rest."[21] Somehow the door to Barbara's sunken room gets opened.

"The clerk, Mr. Frank Buskirk, was asleep in his room on the side that went down, and rushing out [in his drawers[22]] crawled up the cabin floor to the upper guard, and through some mishap fell over it, and landed in a pile of scrap iron, where he found a lady [in a nightgown[23]] who had fallen over just before him."[24]

Neither is injured, though. The engineer comes along and rescues both by setting them on a floating stanchion.[25]

Jacob Allfree will later recount that he:

> . . . was in poor health, and his wife was sitting up with him,
> his daughter . . . occupying the upper berth, while the son was
> in another state-room. Immediately after the first crash, Mrs.
> Allfree opened the door, and saw the water rushing into the
> cabin. She closed the door, and seating herself in despair,
> expected to perish with her husband and daughter. Her hus-
> band preserved his presence of mind, and sought, and with
> some difficulty opened the outer door and the shutters, and
> reached the guard, their state-room being upon the larboard
> side of the boat. His wife had her dress on, and he was partly
> clothed, but the daughter had only her night clothes on . . . .[26]

There they encounter their son, and together the Allfrees make their
way forward, pulling hand over hand along the port rail, toward the up-
lifted bow.

"The aroused and thoroughly frightened passengers barely [had]
enough time to reach the larboard guard, which, with a portion of the
hurricane and texas, alone remained out of water."[27]

For Barbara these frantic minutes are all chaos and panic and an
instinctive fight for survival. In 1958 Lena Weber's daughter, Libbie, at
the age of 88, will write down what she recalled hearing as a child:

"[W]hen they got to shoney town and even's vill the boat sank. . . .
Aunt Barbara had the baby . . . in her arm and went down for the 3d time
she said God told her to open her arms and let the baby go and save
yourself so she did."[28]

But then in 1963 Grandma Ring will tell me what *she* remembered
being told:

"But the boat sank—the boilers were always blowing up in those
things!—and the baby slipped out of the poor woman's arms and
drowned."[29]

One way or the other, Peter is gone.

Barbara is horrified.

Five minutes after hitting the sycamore, the *Jennie Howell* lies in the
Ohio River on her starboard side, "with her bow fast on the snag and
stern in deep water."[30] The officers, aided by deck hands and cabin crew,

maneuver with dispatch and calm to ensure that everyone makes it to the port guard.[31] They respond to cries of distress. They search for persons known to be missing. They count and recount heads. But in the rain, in the dark, there is terrible confusion.[32]

By this time, though, Barbara may be reunited with Nicholas and George. There is still hope. But where are Catherine and Anna? Where is John? Where is Peter? Surely Barbara is calling for them. Gripping the rail, she would be searching frantically along the row of stupefied survivors. They number about 96 altogether, ship's complement and passengers, all sopping wet and shivering.[33] Barbara may be able to distinguish the huddled forms of the Allfree family, and perhaps she recognizes Mrs. Mylard and Mrs. Stephens, and Mrs. Chapman. But the moon is smothered, and a sprinkle continues to fall. Are Catherine and Anna here somewhere, hanging on? Is somebody holding onto John and Peter?

But in the pandemonium, who hears the mother's cries?

The splashing of a paddlewheel sounds in the distance. Everyone freezes, breathless. All eyes transfix upriver. In a moment a torch flickers into view, approaching from around the bend.[34] A chorus erupts from the miserable crowd, ninety-some desperate voices calling at once. The on-coming steamer's whistle blows, then blows again, and the survivors know they have been spotted.

Standing on the outer bulkhead, Jacob Allfree recognizes the *Quickstep*.[35] The sidewheeler is coming down from Shawneetown.[36] Allfree takes courage now, as he thinks she will reach the wreck before it sinks much deeper.[37] Twenty minutes have elapsed since the *Jennie Howell* hit the snag.[38]

"Captain Halliday says he had given Frank [Buskirk] up for lost until the torch of the *Quickstep* revealed his stalwart form roosting upon the stancheon—the most life-like picture of a shipwrecked mariner that he ever saw. Frank's eyes are very large usually, but they were unusually large just then. All he had with him were his night clothes and an umbrella."[39]

The *Quickstep* comes down swiftly, rounds to below, and comes up on the sunken side of the wreck, launching her stages upon the *Jennie Howell*'s roof.[40] Halliday's men spring into action, helping the survivors to the *Quickstep*'s gangways. Barbara, though, would not take Nicholas and George across without first informing Captain Halliday or Clerk Buskirk—or maybe even Billy Shaw, any officer at hand—that two women and two boys are still missing. So if a search for them is not already in progress, one gets under way now.

Crewmen of the *Quickstep* assist Barbara and her boys across a narrow gangway and up the forked staircase and into the saloon.[41] There, down the dim sweep of the long hall, the Rings behold a sprawl of dripping, bedraggled men, women and children. The unexpected guests slouch on chairs along the walls and recline among the tables, struggling to recover their composure and their modesty. Crewmen are distributing blankets, lighting chandeliers. Passengers in robes are coming out of staterooms, squinting, offering towels and articles of clothing.

The chief clerk of the *Quickstep*, Walter B. Pennington,[42] calculates accommodations. Available staterooms will be given to ladies and families. Single gentlemen and crew will bunk in the saloon. Barbara is escorted to the privacy of a room.[43]

Perhaps, though, the last thing in the world she can do right now is rest. On the contrary, barefooted and clutching a blanket around her shoulders, her chestnut hair all tangled and dripping, Barbara probably strides up and down the swooping length of the saloon conducting a search of her own, praying. Nicholas and George scamper to keep up, while their round bluish-gray eyes search, too. To judge from later news wires, though, they spy no relatives among the living.

Halliday and his men clamber and swim around the wreck, looking for two German women and two brown-haired boys. Maybe by this time the black deck passenger has also been reported missing. The brisk wind that brought the storm so suddenly, just as suddenly carries it away. The sky, though, remains overcast.[44] With no light except for the lanterns of the *Quickstep*, and considering the mighty current of the Ohio River, there is little hope of discovering any survivors, or even corpses.

"As soon as the people had been placed upon the Quickstep," a telegram out of Cairo will report, "the bulkhead near the office was cut away and the safe and books recovered. Luckily some one picked up a pair of pants on the hurricane roof in the pocket of which the safe key was found. How they ever got up there is a mystery."[45]

Evansville "River Intelligence" will elaborate: "We understand that Frank Buskirk . . . saved his books and the money from the safe, but escaped in his drawers, and had to borrow a pair of pants before he could go out in company. A young lady arrayed in a single garment was rescued by him, and the two were rescued by the people of the Quickstep in that meager attire."[46]

By now the upper works of the *Jennie Howell* are being carried off by the relentless push of the Ohio's stiff current. Only a small portion of the stern of her hull, and part of her gigantic paddlewheel, are visible, and these are turned nearly upside down.[47] Halliday's ship—197 feet from bow to stern, 34 feet wide, 22 feet from keel to whistle, weighing 552 tons—is ripping apart. In a little while, her cabin slides off almost entirely.[48]

The captain/co-owner orders Buskirk to accompany the survivors to Shawneetown and return with a steamer to salvage what they can.[49] Halliday, however, will remain on the wreck with a part of his crew, holding torches to warn passing steamers.[50]

The *Quickstep* picks up steam and starts shimmying upriver. Barbara feels the vibration.

No!

Pennington, or maybe Buskirk—some officer—would urge her gently back into the stateroom.

She really must get dry! The boys are liable to catch pneumonia! The chef has heated a broth.[51]

One of the earliest reports of the disaster wired from Shawneetown will state: "One body has been recovered."[52] Subsequent wires clarify, by process of elimination, that that body, found before the *Quickstep* left the *Jennie Howell*, is 2-year-old Peter.[53] It is likely, therefore, that as Barbara cruises up the Ohio River, she cradles in her tired arms an inert bundle enshrouded in a blanket.

CHAPTER THIRTY

JULY 26, 1873, DAYTIME

A turbulent rainstorm is preventing Saturday, July 26th, from dawning as Barbara approaches Shawneetown, Illinois, with her two elder sons, unharmed, and her youngest son, dead. "The storm that opened about midnight Friday, with a flurry of wind and a few drops of rain, soon passed away," the newspaper of Evansville, Indiana (35 miles northeast of Shawneetown) will report, "but new clouds gathered, and near morning another violent storm of wind with a heavier rain set in."[1] The agitated river is tossing the *Quickstep* roughly.

Over and over her whistle tears through the gusty downpour, until the distress call is picked up by the lone bell of the First Methodist Church at Third North Cross and Market Streets.[2] By the time the paddlewheeler's stages hit the landing, Shawneetown's citizens are hurrying over the levee and across the mud toward the river. Some carry an open umbrella. Others wear a hooded slicker. Flickering yellow lanterns swing at their sides.[3]

Dazed and exhausted, clutching blankets over their heads and shoulders, the survivors of the shipwrecked *Jennie Howell*, some of them still barefoot, patter onto shore.

"There were eight ladies, four children, and six or eight gentlemen passengers brought here," a Shawneetown telegram will relate, "and part of the crew."[4] Among those alighting is Frank Buskirk.[5]

Within minutes the waterfront is transformed into a purposeful cho-reography of shrouded silhouettes scurrying to and from the *Quickstep*. The stranded travelers and shipless crew members, the *Evansville Daily Journal* will report, "received kindly attention and needed assistance [from] the people of Shawneetown."[6] River folk are all too practiced at this.[7]

The first thing chief clerk Pennington of the *Quickstep* does is wire Evansville, where the *Jennie Howell* is expected later this morning:

> The steamer Jennie Howell sunk at Curlew Point, at 2 o'clock this morning. The snag entered her hull and passed through her boiler and hurricane decks, where it remains. The boat careened, and is lying on her starboard side, in about fifteen feet of water. Mrs. Pringle and two children and Mrs. Ring, from Vicksburg, were drowned.[8]

Evidently the officer is not aware that one of the missing women has been aboard the *Quickstep* all along, for the next wire to come out of Shawneetown corrects him:

"Three lives are known to be lost—one lady and two children."[9]

Catherine Ring is alive!

At what moment she and Barbara were reunited no dispatch reveals. The trip from the sunken wreck to Shawneetown would take about an hour.[10] It seems most plausible that the sisters-in-law, both distraught and seeking each other, found one another sometime during that hour. They would have shared a stateroom then, and comforted each other, and whispered reassuring words to the boys.

Subsequent communications will reiterate the corrected statistics, while continuing to misspell the names:

"Three persons are known to be lost, two children of Mrs. King, of Buffalo, New York, and a lady named Mrs. Pringle, who was from Vicksburg, going to Evansville." (Cairo)[11]

"Mrs. Springle and two children were lost." (Cincinnati)[12]

No report mentions, however, Mr. Allfree's drowned servant, the black deck passenger, George.

One frustrated reporter will complain:

All the news that I have been able to get from passing steamers concerning the disaster to the Jennie Howell was forwarded by telegraph, and is meager and unsatisfactory from the fact that none of them saw the wreck in daylight, and at the time the Quickstep lent assistance to the survivors there was so much confusion, and so little actually known of the condition of affairs, that she could not tell me much about it.[13]

Shawneetown's middling size and rustic appearance belie the port's important history.[14] Settled early in the nineteenth century, it has served as a rough-hewn gateway to the West. An endless stream of pioneers and goods have passed through its wharfs. It is county seat, land office for a vast territory, and an important financial center. On this eventful morning of 1873, Shawneetown's most recent visitors would be given shelter in the largest and grandest building on this stretch of the Ohio: the Riverside Hotel.[15]

Mimicking the latest French architecture, this four-story, 56-room, brick edifice has a dormered mansard roof and cast iron porch railings. Its showy entrance is a pair of tall doors set in a square tower that protrudes catty-corner into the intersection of Main Cross and Front Streets. Incongruous amid the cluster of low-lying roofs—like the cathedral in a medieval city—the hotel is a landmark, as its upper stories can be seen above the levee from steamers on the river. Barbara did not see it, however, when she traveled downriver with her husband and son in the spring of 1865, because the Riverside Hotel is just three years old.[16]

Presently trudging through its elegant double doors, refugees and caretakers streak wet mud across the lacquered floors and plush carpets of the lobby.

"The citizens have charge of the ladies and children," a telegram will report, "and provided clothing, as [the passengers] left the boat in their night clothes."[17] Mr. Allfree's daughter is "kindly provided with a dress by the ladies of Shawneetown."[18]

The Rings send word to George, and the news will appear in tomorrow's *Vicksburg Daily Times*:

> From a telegram received yesterday by Mr. George F. Ring, we learn that the steamer Jennie Howell sank in the Ohio

river, near Shawneetown, Illinois, on Friday night, and that among a number of passengers drowned were Mrs. Sprankler, a sister of Mrs. Ring, and mother of Mr. J. L. Schwink, of this city, and two little sons of Mrs. Joseph Ring. The latter were children of the unfortunate gentleman who was so brutally murdered, some months ago, at Rolling Fork. These, with Mrs. George F. Ring, were on their way to Evansville and Buffalo, N.Y., having left here a week ago on the ill-fated steamer. We offer every sympathy to the afflicted families in their sad bereavement.[19]

Again the storm clouds break up. But they soon reform. From 9 o'clock until noon frequent showers deluge the streets of Shawneetown.[20]

Buskirk wires Cairo, where just yesterday he saw the wrecking steamer *T. F. Eckert* salvaging sunken railroad iron. Word comes back that the *Eckert* will leave immediately and steam upriver to raise the *Jennie Howell*.[21] Then Buskirk returns to the wreck[22] on the *Arkansas Belle*.[23] Before long the chief clerk has a few roustabouts in the river, swimming around the sunken sternwheeler, diving down, searching for bodies, bringing up whatever baggage they can find, hoisting it up to him on the *Arkansas Belle*'s main deck.[24]

"Considerable baggage in a damaged condition was . . . recovered from the wreck," newspapers will report.[25] "The officers and crew," however, "lost all their clothing and effects."[26]

At noon the clouds disperse, the sky brightens, and the men gather in the *Arkansas Belle*'s saloon for a hot meal. The mercury is ranging around 84 degrees.[27] A few hours later the *Quickstep* passes down and exchanges whistle calls. She is back on her run to Cairo, which was interrupted last night by her mission of mercy.[28]

It is supper time, but still broad daylight and hot, when three whistle blasts alert the population of Shawneetown that the *Arkansas Belle* is steaming back into port. Curious citizens swarm over the levee and plod across the still-undried mud of the landing. Next time it could be *their* kin who are stranded and dependent on local river folk for assistance. Stevedores, clerks, ticket agents, captains and pilots, "River Intelligence" newsmen eager for more particulars, hackers, roustabouts, draymen and laborers and excited children, all collect at the river's edge where the steamer's bow is approaching. Barbara, too, with Catherine and Nicholas and George, are standing there, expectant, hopeful, terrified.[29]

When the landing plank settles into the mire, boys and girls bob to get a glimpse of the crewmen filing onto shore. The men's faces are drawn with fatigue, yet some of them may well be grinning. Suddenly a collective gasp sounds up front, and a wave of murmuring and shuffling ripples through the ranks of bystanders until a gap opens in front of Barbara. There stands Captain Halliday, holding in his arms a small body.

It has to be John.

Barbara braces herself to look upon her child's bloated, bloodless face. But the little body twists and two arms reach out to her.

He is alive!

"Mrs. Ring's little boy, supposed to be lost at the time of the accident, and up to the time the Quickstep left the wreck, was found shortly after floating in the state-room on a mattress asleep, and had to be wakened," a Shawneetown reporter will write. "No pen can describe the scene when the steamer Arkansas Belle brought the supposed drowned child up and delivered it over to the distressed mother alive and well. It was a heart-rending scene."[30]

Eighty-five years later, Lena Weber's daughter Libbie will pen in a letter what she remembered being told as a child:

"John was 5 years old he was floating on a mattress out in the river the captain saw him throu his binocler and send a man out to get him he said if the parents where drown he would keep the boy when he wolk up the first thing he ask where is my hat."[31]

Still more years later, on a summer's day in 1963, Grandma Ring will relate to me the episode as she recalled hearing it:

"One of the other boys disappeared, too. Only in the morning they found that one. Floating on a mattress in the river. Alive."[32]

However, Nicholas Ring's son Louis, in his 1986 reply to my request for family information, will write of the *Jennie Howell* disaster:

"My father never mentioned this to me, or to my knowledge, to my sister or brothers."[33]

How strangely tight-lipped Nicholas Ring will be about this traumatic boyhood experience of his. Only his branch of the family, the southern branch, will possess no oral tradition whatsoever of this fateful voyage.

Once again emended dispatches fan out:

"One of the children reported drowned by the Jennie Howell disaster, a boy aged four, was subsequently found safe in a state-room." (Cincinnati)[34]

"One of the children supposed to have been lost was afterward found in a state-room alive and well, but it bothers me to know, if the cabin slid off, how the child could have escaped drowning." (Cairo)[35]

"Mr. George F. Ring received a telegram from his family stating that only one child of the late Joseph Ring and Mrs. Sprinkler were drowned." (Vicksburg)[36]

Into Catherine's yearning arms, however, Captain Halliday delivers no similar miracle.

"The bodies of Mrs. Sprangler and the negro boy were not recovered, and it is believed they either leaped into the river, or were washed overboard."[37]

All during supper the elegant dining hall of the Riverside Hotel is quiet as a wake.

CHAPTER THIRTY-ONE

JULY 27, 1873

As Sunday, July 27th, dawns over Shawneetown, a number of the passengers and crew members from the *Jennie Howell* are boarding the *Arkansas Belle*.[1] They include, according to newspaper reports: "Mrs. Ring of Vicksburg, who lost a child, and her sister-in-law Mrs. Geo. F. Ring, also of Vicksburg, Jacob Allfree, wife and daughter . . . besides many others whose names we did not learn,"[2] as well as "Lewis Halliday, second clerk and brother of Captain Halliday, and J. B. Clouser, the barkeeper."[3] On the cargo deck, presumably in a small pine box, lies "the body of the child of Mrs. Ring."[4]

The *Arkansas Belle* is a modest packet in the local trade.[5] Her captain, Ben Howard, has offered the stranded travelers—"having all lost everything they possessed, except the little clothing they had on"—free passage to Evansville.[6] The trip up the Ohio takes about three to four hours.[7] It is a serpentine stretch of 70 miles, with possible stops at Uniontown, Kentucky; Mount Vernon, Indiana; and Henderson, Kentucky. It is still early morning when the *Arkansas Belle* nears Evansville.[8]

The city is more than double the size of Vicksburg, and presents an impressive panorama.[9] Block after block of commercial buildings, manufactories, warehouses and private residences sprawl around a great horseshoe bend in the river, and the avenues, 60 to 120 feet wide, many of them paved, radiate into the distance like the splayed tail of a pea-

cock. Barbara can hear the ringing of church bells from several directions; but she would glimpse the steeples only when, one at a time, they
appear momentarily between the multi-storied brick structures and tall
blackened smokestacks. For many years already Evansville has been an
important hub of commerce and shipping. No fewer than three railroad
companies maintain terminals here, and this is where the Wabash &
Erie Canal ends, too. Often the steamers are so plentiful along the landing that they have to maneuver like ducks in a pond to avoid colliding.
This morning, however, the waterfront—which is twice the length of
Vicksburg's—is eerily deserted.[10]

Standing there, watching the *Arkansas Belle* pull in, is a big man
dressed in a business suit.[11] He exudes competence far beyond his 34
years. Closely-cropped dark hair covers his round scalp, and a bushy
mustache and pointed goatee adorn his mouth and chin. His gray eyes
are expressive and intent. What a relief it is for the traumatized travelers to behold their relative's familiar and impressive Hessian form. He
is George Koch.

They would have sent him a wire from Shawneetown. So Koch
would not be surprised—though he would still be pained, particularly
for his wife—when he does not see his mother-in-law stepping ashore
with the others. Catherine and Barbara and the boys are trailed by a
husky stevedore gripping a small pine box on his shoulder. Koch points
him toward a waiting wagon; painted on the sideboard are the words,
"John G. Reising—Undertaker."[12] Then he helps the women into his
carriage, probably addressing them in German, which would reassure
them all the more. Nicholas, George and John climb soberly on board.

The somber and uncomfortable weather seems cruelly fitting. The
Evansville Daily Journal will describe this Sunday as "cloudy and warm,
with a light rain nearly all day, at times becoming quite copious. There
was scarcely any wind and the air was close and sultry. The mercury
ranged from 71 degrees to 81 degrees."[13]

Koch's carriage skirts the bend of the Ohio for about a mile, rattles
across a bridge spanning Pigeon Creek, splashes another quarter-mile
or so along a street one block from the shore, then turns up Tenth
Avenue and veers left onto West Pennsylvania Street.[14] The unassuming
house at number 1012 is narrow and very long, stretching back into a

lot that is larger than many others in the neighborhood. The yard is barren and muddy, and the trim one-and-a-half-story frame dwelling with a shingle roof is obviously brand new.[15] This is George Koch's tin shop and residence.[16]

The front door swings open, and there stands Mary. Her stature is slight and she looks delicate, with large eyes and tiny mouth.[17]

What news of her mother?

At the same time Mary Koch is welcoming her Aunt Catherine and Barbara and the boys in out of the rain, the Webers are expecting them in Cincinnati.

"[M]y Father went down to meet the boat," Lena Weber's daughter Libbie will write, "and the papers had big extra out Natches sunk and the names of all drown it said Mrs. Ring Mrs. Spangler 2 children."[18]

Evidently, if Barbara wired the Webers from Shawneetown, or if George Ring or George Koch sent a telegram, the news has not arrived in time. The initial dispatches in this morning's *Cincinnati Commercial* under the heading, "Steamer Jennie Howell Snagged and Sunk—Loss of Life," give four contradictory versions of casualties.[19] For all Hank Weber knows, Barbara might be dead.

He would try to learn more from the men on the waterfront, but in vain. Most probably he wires George, requesting a reply as soon as possible. Then he would have no choice but to take the street railway back up the hill to his home in the Corryville neighborhood and tell his wife: her favorite sister may have drowned.[20]

While the Webers wait anxiously for a telegram, many miles down the Ohio River Captain Alexander Halliday is guiding the wrecking steamer *T. F. Eckert* alongside his sunken riverboat.[21]

"He and Frank Buskirk remain with the wreck," tomorrow morning's *Evansville Daily Journal* will inform, "which lies but a short distance from that of the Umpire, sunk less than a year ago. A portion of the hull of the Jennie Howell is exposed, and the water touches the whistle at the top of the pilot house."[22]

The captain/co-owner himself will later recount:

> The Howell had a good many boxes of wine, nearly all of which was on the boiler deck forward, and was knocked into the river by the snag. As they floated down the river they were caught by the people along the shore, and the result was that nearly every person between the wreck and Caseyville were in a very high state of intoxication as the Eckert came along." [23]

Initially, optimism about saving the *Jennie Howell* is high. "Captain Ben. Howard thinks she can be easily raised," relates one "River Intelligence" man.[24] "The boat may probably be raised," a fellow reporter concurs, "but her sugar and salt will of course be a total loss."[25] Soon enough, however, Halliday himself will tell the grimmer reality:

> As soon as the Eckert arrived she began the removal of such freight as was in reach and loosened up one engine, but before it could be removed the boat began to twist and settle so fast that the Eckert had to get out of the way, and the wreck turned over, broke in two and sunk in deep water."[26]

One weathered river chronicler will sum up: "The Howell is a 'gone goose.'"[27]

All the *Eckert* manages to recover are 25 boxes, five casks of wine, and a few packages.[28] The pilot wheel and one cask of wine will be found on a flatboat near Caseyville.[29]

From the upper deck of the *T. F. Eckert*, Alexander Halliday takes a last look at the split, upside-down, sunken hull of his packet. The *Eckert*'s whistle hails a final parting salute, and the steamer heads upriver to Shawneetown. Buskirk gets off there.[30] But Halliday continues on board—joined now by his younger brother Lewis—to Cairo,[31] where the *Eckert* will resume raising sunken railroad iron.[32] The captain without a ship will send a wrecker to salvage the *Jennie Howell*'s machinery.[33]

"Captain Halliday carried only a fire risk on his boat, which was valued at not less than $25,000," the *Cincinnati Commercial* will reveal, "and the loss will consequently fall heavy on him."[34]

This evening, four miles downriver from the wreck, on the Kentucky shore near Caseyville, someone discovers a body.[35] Residents along the river south of Curlew Point, informed of the fate of the *Jennie Howell*— and snatching cases of wine[36]—have been on the lookout for floaters. H. A. Pierson, Police Judge for Caseyville,[37] is probably dozing by the stove when a knock on the door disrupts his Sunday evening leisure.

Before setting out, he sends a drayman, Burrel Johnson, to Jones & Dyer's shop to pick up a coffin and deliver it to the river.[38] He also calls on A. J. Brown to tell him he has a floater to haul to the cemetery,[39] and stops by L. B. Steel's to instruct him to dig a grave.[40] En route to the site, Pierson collects a few men to act as jurors.[41]

It is all routine, though nonetheless distasteful, and tonight particularly annoying, because the unrelenting rain has turned the paths to troughs of mire and puddles.[42] Travel is hard and sloppy and slow.

Down on the river bank, the men have no doubt when they come upon the beached floater. They pull out their handkerchiefs and tie them under their nostrils. The corpse has been in the river for almost two days. It is a woman. It takes several of the men to lift the bloated body and position it in the coffin.[43] Then they hoist the box into Brown's wagon. Struggling up the steep embankment against the rain, Brown may well be cursing the weather and his mule and the corpse all in the same breath.

Pierson rides back to town, shedding his neighbors where he found them. Then he pens his report:

State of Kentucky, Caseyville Union County Ky

An inquest held on the bank of the Ohio River a Short distance above the Town of Caseyville in Said County on the 27th day of July 1873 before me HAPierson police Judge for the Town of Caseyville County aforesaid duly commitioned and qualified according to the law upon the view of the body of an unknown white woman her name supposed to be Mrs. A. K. Sprengel There and then Lying dead and upon the oaths of Wm S Henry, M J Croker, L B Steel John E. Orr

> Richard Branham & S S Finnie good and lawful house
> Keepers of Said County who being Sworn and Charged to
> inquire on the part of the Commonwealth in what manner
> whare how and by whoom the Said unknown Woman Came
> to her death do Say upon their Oaths that they believe that
> She Came to her death by being drowned in the Ohio River
> Suposed to be drowned of the Jinnie Howel found on her per-
> son fifty dollars & Seventy five Cents Cash Trunk check No.
> 27 Marked S.F.C She had dark hair Striped dress & black
> Slippers & a breast pin & a Smal Key.[44]

So Anna had not yet undressed for the night when the river gushed into the stateroom she was sharing with Catherine, separating the two immigrant sisters forever.

> In witness whareof as well the aforesaid police Judge as the
> jurors aforesaid have to this Inquisition offered their hands &
> Seals the day and year aforesaid and at the place aforesaid.[45]

Pierson and five jurors then sign their names. Steel's signature is lacking.[46]

Ark Lodge Cemetery lies in a breezy clearing along a bluff far above the winding Ohio.[47] It takes some time for Brown's mule to negotiate the slushy ruts to the summit. Considering the gloomy weather, it must be dark when he finally arrives at the pit that Steel has opened in the soggy earth. They would have to light a pineknot or kerosene lantern to see what they are doing. The men lower the damp box into the hole and Steel covers it over as quickly as he can.[48] He is as eager as Brown to get back to the dry comfort of home.

Pierson sends a wire to Evansville,[49] then goes home to bed. In the morning he will write out five receipts: $5.00 to Jones & Dyer for one coffin; $.50 to Burrel Johnson for hauling it to the river; $1.50 to A. J. Brown for hauling the corpse to the cemetery; $9.00 to L. B. Steel for digging two graves and burying Anna; and $6.00 to himself for holding the inquest. Total expense to Union County: $22.[50]

The unassuming tin shop and residence at 1012 West Pennsylvania Street would be dark and still when late-night rapping on the front door echoes through the long string of rooms. Koch accepts the telegram.

Mary, a blunt dread in her breast, holds the oil lamp above her husband's hands. Hovering at the edge of the flickering glow, Catherine and Barbara wear nightclothes that belong to their hostess and smell of soap.

It would be a painful relief when George Koch tells them. At least now they know.

At least now they all know.

State of Kentucky,
Caseyville Union Co Ky

An inquest held on the bank of The Ohio River a short distance above the Town of Caseyville in Said County on the 27th day of July 1873 before me H A Pierson police judge for the Town of Caseyville County aforesaid duly Commissioned and qualified according to law upon the view of the body of one unknown white woman her name Supposed to be Spriegel (Mrs A K Sprankel) there and then lying dead and upon these oaths of W S Henry from M J Cocker L B Steel John E Orr Richard Branham & S S Finnie good and lawful house Keepers of Said County who being Sworn and Charged to inquire on the part of the Commonwealth in what manner where how and by whoom the Said unknown Woman came to her death do Say upon their Oaths that they believe that she Came to her death by being drowned in the Ohio River Supposed to be drowned of the Sunnel Howel found on her person fifty dollars & Seventy five Cents Cash Bank Check No 27 marked S, F, C She had dark hair Striped dress & black Slippers & a breast pin & a Small Key

In witness whareof as well the aforesaid police judge as the jurors afore said have to this Inquisition affixed there hands & Seals the day and year afore said and at the place afore said

H A Pierson, P. J. C

S S Finnie [2 5]
W S Henry [2 5]
R Branham [2 5]
John E Orr [2 5]
M J Cocker [2 5]

UNION COUNTY, KENTUCKY, CORONER'S REPORT ON ANNA SPRANKLER, JULY 27, 1873.

CHAPTER THIRTY-TWO

JULY 28, 1873

Monday, July 28th, Barbara must attend to sad preparations. How much she leaves to George Koch to do for her, though, cannot be determined; and surely Mary would have a hand in matters regarding her mother. Perhaps it is Catherine who stays at home with the children, while Koch escorts his two bereaved kinswomen from one downtown location to another.[1]

Foul weather makes their duty all the more dismal, being "more like that of April or October than July," according to the *Evansville Daily Journal*. "The day was chiefly dark and sombre, the mercury ranging from 73 to 80 degrees. There were numerous showers, some quite heavy, with a brisk wind during the day."[2]—A miserable day to be running about the city streets.

One of their first stops would be the telegraph office. Henry Sprankler has to be informed that his wife's body has been recovered.

Also on the agenda is visiting the establishment on the corner of Upper Sixth and Oak Streets: "John G. Reising—Undertaker."[3] Not only does Peter Paul have to be buried, but the remains of Anna Sprankler are to be disinterred from Ark Lodge Cemetery and shipped upriver for burial here, too.[4]

Another necessary stop is Holy Trinity Church, a substantial Gothic structure[5] flanked by a good-sized high school and a severe but commodious priest house. The three ecclesiastical buildings dominate the entire block of Upper Third Street between Division and Vine.[6] Though this is Mary's parish, her husband, being Lutheran,[7] may be a stranger to its lofty nave. Nevertheless, Roman Catholic funeral Masses must be arranged for Peter and Anna.

By now everyone in Evansville knows what has happened to the Koch family's Mississippi relations, because this morning's newspaper contains a long piece under four headers:

The Jennie Howell Disaster
Arrival of Her Passengers
Full Particulars—Only Three Lives Lost
A Marvelous Escape—A Child Sleeps on a Floating Couch.[8]

At ten-thirty, while the Koch party is dashing resolutely through the gusty downpours, the piercing whistle of the *Morning Star* signals her departure.[9] On board are Jacob Allfree and his family, embarked at last on the final leg of their disjointed voyage home.[10]

"Captain Crider, with that active humanity that has always characterized him, tendered the rescued passengers free passage . . . to Louisville," reads "The Jennie Howell Disaster" piece. "Mr. Allfree and family speak in terms of highest praise of the officers of the Quickstep and Arkansas Belle, and of the people of Shawneetown."[11]

Tomorrow's edition will add: "Mr. Allfree recovered a portion of his baggage, but it was almost utterly ruined by water. Among other things he recovered his certificate of good standing as a Royal Arch Mason."[12]

Evidently the body of the young black domestic, George, will never be recovered. For he is not mentioned again.

This evening at seven-thirty—the Kochs and their distracted house-guests would be seated around the supper table—the *Lawrence* pulls up to the landing from Shawneetown.[13] Tomorrow's edition of the *Evansville Daily Journal* will report:

> She [the *Lawrence*] had also a good passenger list, among whom were Frank Buskirk, ex-clerk of the Jennie Howell, and several of her passengers. Frank is wearing John Goff's coat,

Billy Cooper's shirt, Charley Martin's hat, and pants and shoes from the owners and attaches of Howell and Millspaugh's wharfboat, at Shawneetown. Buskirk and the passengers express the warmest thanks and most heartfelt gratitude to the officers and crews of the Quickstep and Arkansas Belle, and to the people of Shawneetown for their large hearted kindness and benevolence extended to those shipwrecked on the Howell. . . . Among the passengers of the Howell who came up on the Lawrence, were Mrs. Mylard and Mrs. Stephens, for Cincinnati, and Mrs. Chapman for this city.[14]

By the time this newsprint is read, however, the *Lawrence* is already carrying Mrs. Mylard and Mrs. Stephens on to their original destination.[15] Only the Rings have mournful family affairs holding them behind.

CHAPTER THIRTY-THREE

JULY 29, 1873

Tuesday morning, July 29th, reduced to mere specks within the immense Gothic interior of Holy Trinity, Barbara and her three surviving sons are on their knees.[1] This church is Evansville's oldest and largest German Catholic parish.[2] As Father Karl Loescher intones the Mass,[3] the Latin phrases ricochet in familiar-sounding garble throughout the hollow space. Lying at the altar rail, Peter's miniature casket almost disappears.

After the final blessing, George Koch's carriage follows Reising's hearse through the weekday traffic. The sun is resplendent, the heavy ceiling of gray clouds having finally crept eastward. "Clear and warm" is the day.[4] The brief funeral cortege rounds the U-bend of the Ohio, crosses over Pigeon Creek, turns onto West Ohio Street, and processes out St. Joseph Avenue. The congestion thins rapidly and the tandem of two coaches is soon surrounded by undulating hills of silent forests and pastures, and flat fields of sparkling green cornstalks.[5] Reaching Cynthiana Road, the coaches turn through the iron gates of St. Joseph Catholic Cemetery and clatter down the narrow brick path that descends to Section 8—the section set aside for single lots.[6]

Directly ahead looms an enormous and austere Gothic crucifix.[7] It stands in the middle of a circular mound of grass, a statue of Saint John on one side, a statue of Mary on the other. At the foot of this calvary lie the sarcophagi of the former bishop of Evansville and three of his priests, with ample room left for fellow clergy who will inevitably follow. Within a century the tombs will form two concentric rings around the lofty crucifix. Along the brick path that surrounds this ensemble, mounted on severe monoliths, are sculptural representations of the 14 Stations of the Cross. Carved of limestone, the crucifix, statues, sarcophagi and stations all show sharp and clean and new in the sunlight.[8]

Veering off the circular path, Reising's hearse and Koch's carriage bounce for several yards before halting near a solitary elm. Just beyond the blanket of shade cast by the tree's leafy bows, a miniature marble gravestone glistens in the sunshine like a jewel.[9]

The top is a half-circle that scallops out on either side like clover, then descends straight to earth. This delicate shape is echoed on the marker by a groove running a few inches from the edge, like a frame. Therein, carved in relief, with little arms outstretched, with a simple little gown fluttering over weightless legs, tiny bare feet dangling, a cherub floats contentedly heavenward. Beneath is inscribed:

PETER P.
Sohn von
J. u. B. RING
GEB.
5 MAI 1871
GEST.
26 JULI 1873[10]

Here, into a diminutive gash in the sod, Barbara and her round-faced boys watch the miniature casket sink, and disappear.[11]

CHAPTER THIRTY-FOUR

JULY 31, 1873

Two days later on Thursday, July 31st, Anna Sprankler is interred in Section 8 not far from the solitary elm that nearly shades Peter's headstone.[1] But this second burial will not be the Hessian-born woman's last. The records of St. Joseph Catholic Cemetery reveal: "Body removed Nov. 6, 1874—taken to Vicksburg, Miss."[2]

Now, after a stay of five days in Evansville, the Rings are free to continue on their way. Lena Weber's daughter Libbie will write in 1958 that "they stayed there 2 weeks to bury the dead and was able to travel again."[3] But a note in the *Vicksburg Daily Times* of August 3rd suggests that the Rings resume their travels much sooner than that:

"Mr. George F. Ring departed for Detroit, Michigan, yesterday, to join his family. We wish him a pleasant time and a safe return."[4]

Since George is headed for Detroit, rather than Evansville or Cincinnati, it appears that Catherine and Barbara and her boys do not wait for him before picking up their original itinerary. Soon after Anna's burial, they bid their Indiana kin farewell.

George and Mary Koch will lead long and full lives, raising a total of six children. Nevertheless, neither Libbie's letter, nor even oral tradition, will preserve for future descendants of the Ring family, North and South, any memory of the Kochs. Yet the role these relatives played in Barbara's stormy summer of 1873 illustrates perfectly how the German-speaking immigrant families, Catholics, Lutherans and Jews, spread out along the inland rivers, endured, persevered, and succeeded, by helping one another in time of need. Koch's metal industry will prosper and expand, and eventually his three younger sons will incorporate the business as "George Koch Sons."[5]

The Ring party arrives in Cincinnati; this time Hank Weber's trip downtown to greet his wife's kin ends happily.[6] He escorts them up to the Corryville neighborhood where he and Lena are raising Edward and Elizabeth.[7] Edward—Barbara's godson—is 10 now.[8] Elizabeth—who is called "Libbie" and who will one day write down in a long letter to a distant cousin what she remembered hearing about the murder of her Uncle Joe and the shipwreck of her Aunt Barbara—is 3.[9] Sheltered here in the caressing embrace of family, the Vicksburg relations linger, healing and regaining strength.

Then they take the train to Detroit, where George joins them. He and Catherine will stay until late September.[10] Barbara and her boys, though, transfer to a steamer heading across Lake Erie. They would reach the busy harbor of Buffalo by mid-August, with no trunks and no furniture, and that night they would sleep peacefully under Papa's roof.

Barbara is home. Again.

CHAPTER THIRTY-FIVE

VICKSBURG

"Mr. George F. Ring has returned with his family from Michigan, where they have been spending the summer," noted the *Vicksburg Daily Times* of October 3, 1873. "Judging from Mr. Ring's appearance, living was very good in that part of the country."[1]

Fit and hale, perhaps a few pounds heavier, George came home prepared to fight the insurance companies in court. Chamberlin had persuaded his fellow agents not to pay on the Ring & Co. policies, and George had not hesitated to file lawsuits against them.[2] The litigation would be acrimonious, he knew, and might drag on for years. What he did *not* know was that his personal affairs would be disrupted by race riots a congressional report would label the "Vicksburgh Troubles."[3]

George was only back a month when the November elections returned Adelbert Ames to the governor's mansion in Jackson.[4] Ames had relinquished the office back in 1870 to the popularly-elected James L. Alcorn, at which time Mississippi was re-admitted to the Union.[5] Federal occupation over, Ames retired from the military and had himself elected by the legislature to one of the state's seats in the U.S. Senate.[6] Earlier this year, however, he returned to challenge Alcorn for the governorship, and won it by popular vote. So now the ardent Reconstructionist from Maine was back in Jackson, with a black lieutenant governor, black secretary of state and black superintendent of education.[7]

The 1873 elections also filled the grandiose Warren County court-house with freedmen, and three whites.[8] Most of the new office holders had no experience in government and no knowledge of public adminis-tration. Many could neither read nor write. Among them were the black sheriff, Peter Crosby,[9] and his board of supervisors.

From the moment the ballots were tallied, Democrats contested the election.[10] Several of the Republicans-elect, including the sheriff, held questionable bonds. Furthermore, Crosby and several others were either being investigated or had already been indicted for corruption. Even well-intentioned officials could not be effectual because of the per-vasive dishonesty and incompetence of the government. Most of all, white citizens objected to the enormously increased tax burden which they, as landowners, bore. The new sheriff, Peter Crosby, by virture of his office, was also tax-collector.

City government was equally Reconstructionist.[11] The "Vicksburg Ring," as the press called it, was all Republican and all black, except for four white aldermen (one of whom, chairman of the Finance Committee, was Samuel Fischel[12]). The city council, if not downright corrupt, was at best wasteful of taxpayer money (in spite of Fischel's business savvy). White residents resolved to take matters back into their own hands.

Early in 1874 they organized a "Taxpayer's League" and nominated white candidates for the municipal elections coming up in August.[13] The slate was headed by Dr. Richard O'Leary for mayor. All over the city "white people's clubs" sprang into existence, and their members began patrolling the streets in armed gangs to intimidate black voters. The Reconstructionists responded in kind. Throughout the summer months the parading escalated, the sparring intensified, threatening bloodshed.

The lieutenant governor, and then Ames himself, tried frantically to secure two companies of federal troops to restore peace, but in vain.[14] As election day approached, Vicksburg was a tinderbox of frayed nerves. Any spark might have ignited a conflagration between the races. Yet on August 4th, without violence or bloodshed, the largest voter turnout ever recorded in the city placed the white candidates into office.

This victory emboldened the tax-paying landowners of the surrounding countryside.[15] They formed "White League" clubs aimed at ridding Warren County of "all bad and leading negroes . . . and controlling more strictly our tenants and other hands."[16] On December 2nd they rode into the city for a "Taxpayers' Meeting."[17] Perhaps 500 strong, they made no attempt to conceal the firearms they were carrying.[18]

"The Opera House was filled with white citizens and tax-payers from the City and County to-day," the *Vicksburg Daily Times* would report this Wednesday evening, "in pursuance to the call which has been posted upon our streets for some time past."[19]

They organized a committee to go to the courthouse and demand the resignation of Sheriff Crosby and his board of supervisors.[20] But the officers refused to sign the prepared resignations. When the committee returned with this report, the entire assembly marched up the lofty courthouse grounds and—still brandishing their weapons—repeated the demand. The black officers signed, and Crosby fled to the governor in Jackson.[21]

Before leaving, however, he sent a note to the Honorable George F. Brown, informing him of events.[22] Judge Brown, although white, was a fellow Republican, having been appointed by Governor Alcorn in 1870.[23] He was currently presiding in Circuit Court. Earlier this term he had heard the Ring & Co. insurance cases.[24] But the magistrate was at home when he received Crosby's note, as he had adjourned the court about noon.[25]

Judge Brown telegraphed Governor Ames that an armed mob was in possession of the courthouse and jail.[26] He was powerless to execute the laws "until such time as he could have the services of a Sheriff."[27]

Ames advised Crosby that his resignation was void, and that he had the power to call a *posse comitatus* to his aid.[28] The governor also published a "Proclamation" ordering the "unruly mob" to disperse and authorizing the captain of a Negro militia company to suppress the riot and cooperate with Crosby in his attempt to regain his office. Crosby sent runners throughout Warren County with a handbill appealing "to all good Republicans, white and black . . . to support him and fight the cause on its merits."

Sunday morning, December 6th, the handbill was read in all the black churches.[29] By evening rumor was circulating from the Walnut Hills and Springfield down to the Commons that the rural blacks were massing to march on Vicksburg the next day. Reports were exaggerated and alarming. Here it was, at last, the bloody Negro insurrection the whites had feared for so long! Visions of the gruesome massacre at Rolling Fork Landing revived in some imaginations. Envisioning slaughter, rape, arson and robbery, whites panicked.

For George and Catherine, sleep would have been fitful that night. They resided just four blocks from the courthouse, and had Frank and Missouri Jeans with them.[30] Whether George participated in the political maelstrom is impossible to say. A self-made man paying historically high taxes, he would have been upset by the very suspicion that his hard-earned dollars were being embezzled or squandered by public officials—white *or* black. Throughout the year he had been advertising in the Democratic newspaper, *The Daily Vicksburger*, and *not* in the Republican *Vicksburg Daily Times*.[31] On the other hand, he had once sought appointment to public office from Adelbert Ames.[32] It appears that George was ever the pragmatist, not an ideologue: he watched out for his own interests.

At daybreak on Monday, December 7th, the Ring household was startled from their troubled beds by the clanging of the courthouse bell.[33] But Adams Street remained eerily empty and silent. It was a false alarm.

"About 9 o'clock," according to the *Times*, the bell rang again.[34] This time the watchman in the clock tower spied large bodies of blacks approaching the city from three different directions. And they were armed with shotguns and pistols.

Doors flew open and the streets filled with excited members of the white people's clubs.[35] Gripping long-range rifles, the men mounted, galloped to the courthouse, and formed companies.

"About ten o'clock" Dr. O'Leary circulated a proclamation countermanding the incendiary proclamation of the governor:

> Whereas, Said Proclamation has excited the citizens of the county, and that I have this moment received information that armed bodies of colored men have organized and are now marching on the city, I call upon all good citizens to observe the laws of the land, and I warn all such unlawful assemblages and armed bodies of men to disperse and retire

to their homes; and for the preservation of law and order in the city, I hereby command all good citizens to hold themselves in readiness to report at any call I may make upon them for the purpose of enforcing this proclamation.[36]

At noon a second proclamation from O'Leary closed all saloons and advised: "Citizens be quiet and discreet, but firm. Your dearest interests are at stake."[37] He declared martial law and delegated command of the city to an ex-Confederate officer. Then he gathered a posse of 100 men and rode out to meet the black host.

The two bands came face to face, whites mounted, blacks on foot.[38] O'Leary asked for the leader. The two men conferred. It was agreed that the blacks would disband. They turned to head home.

Suddenly shots rang out, followed by yells, epithets, and a dusty skirmish for cover.[39] Continued gunfire left eight or nine blacks and one or two whites sprawled dead on the road. Accusations flew back and forth—who fired first? But the issue was moot. The spark had set the tinderbox aflame.

Another alarm was sounding in the city.[40] White and black gangs were clashing at the Pemberton monument, which stood at another of the eastern approaches to Vicksburg. The shotguns and pistols of the blacks were no match for the long-range rifles of the whites. The gunfight left about 10 blacks dead. Each side blamed the other for shooting first.

Later in the day the alarm bells rang yet again.[41] But the watchman in the clock tower was just edgy now. There was no black face to be seen on any street in Vicksburg.

WAR OF RACES!
The County Negroes Attempt to Capture the City!
Mayor O'Leary's Proclamation Asking for Assistance!
Fighting on All the Principle County Roads!
Fifteen Negroes Killed and Many Wounded!
One White Man Killed and One Wounded![42]

Reports in the *Times* that evening were confused, contradictory and wildly exaggerated. The number of casualties varied from one eyewitness to the next. Word-of-mouth heightened the hysteria. Bands of resolute white men rode out and, over several days, proceeded to execute blacks in the countryside.[43]

Wednesday, December 9th: "Armed men are not so numerous on our streets to-day. They have all gone to the country."[44]

Vicksburg was in chaos. Even the Honorable George F. Brown felt compelled to flee by train to Jackson.[45] No Reconstructionist, not even a white one, was safe. However, the papers also noted that the city's merchants were delighted with the unusual volume of business generated by all of the out-of-towners.[46]

Thursday, December 10th: "Our streets have once more assumed their usual busy appearance, and the indications are that the war is over."[47]

But armed white men still held the courthouse. They were planning elections to replace the black officers who had "resigned."[48]

Governor Ames called the state assembly into emergency session and convinced the legislators to petition Grant for federal troops.[49] Instead of soldiers, the president sent a proclamation ordering all "turbulent and disorderly persons" to retire peaceably to their respective homes within five days.[50]

The armed men did not retire peaceably to their respective homes.

Ames wired the president and begged him to send troops.[51]

Finally, on January 18, 1875, a squad of U.S. Army soldiers, weapons drawn, marched up the long terraced staircases of Courthouse Square, filed between the towering columns of the shimmering white Warren County Courthouse, and reinstated Sheriff Crosby and his board of supervisors.[52]

It was safe now for Judge Brown to return. From exile he had telegraphed the *Times* to explain his behavior during the crisis.[53] Rumor claimed that he had encouraged blacks to come into the city. The Republican magistrate protested that, on the contrary, he had done everything in his power to promote calm. He proceeded to convene spring term as usual and, after hearing more of the feud between George F. Ring and William M. Chamberlin, passed along to the federal court in Jackson two new suits that George filed against his insurance agent.[54]

A congressional investigation of the "Vicksburgh Troubles" followed.[55] Its majority report would fix the blame squarely on the whites, although it would concede that much misgovernment existed in

Warren County.[56]

Even while throngs of armed and angry men were marching menacingly through the city streets, Vicksburgers had continued to carry on their daily occupations. For instance, on Wednesday, November 11, 1874, the *Times* carried this:

"Mrs. A. C. Sprankle was buried this morning from St. Paul's Church."[57]

Finally, Anna received a funeral Mass.[58] George and Catherine would have accompanied Henry Sprankler to this third and final interment of his wife. It took place at Cedar Hill, in a light rain.[59]

Worse rioting in the streets, however, was still to come. Mississippi's "Redemption" was at hand.[60]

With the onset of the summer of 1875 the liveliest and most momentous political campaign in the history of Mississippi started.[61] The crusade to "redeem" the state—as Democrats were calling it—united and mobilized the native white residents as no political contest had since before the war. They were determined to regain control of the government. Reconstructionists, meanwhile, were equally determined to prevent that from happening.

Democrats left their offices and workshops, stores and fields, to take part in the canvass.[62] They attended rallies and huge open-air meetings to listen to speakers. They formed clubs of a semi-military nature and marched with rifles through the streets. They held barbeques and paraded with banners in mammoth torchlight processions. As part of their demonstrations they even fired old Civil War cannon. The sale of firearms was prodigious.

As daylight grew longer and hotter, incidents of violence between blacks and whites increased throughout the state.[63] Sheriff Crosby was shot in early June, but not mortally. When Vicksburg's Fourth of July celebration erupted into a race riot, however, several blacks were killed.

Then in September the *Vicksburg Daily Times* carried accounts of the disturbances in Yazoo City.[64] Again the provocation was political and racial, and again there were deaths—this time one white and three blacks.

Days later the paper was reporting the riot in Clinton, a Hinds County town not far from Jackson.[65] Democrats had assaulted

Republicans at a barbeque, and several men of both races were slain.

Then in October riots erupted at Friars Point in Coahoma County, a Delta county on the Mississippi River.[66] Six blacks were killed, and two whites.

Blacks appealed to the governor for protection.[67] Ames turned once again to Grant for troops. But the president responded by urging the governor to use "his own resources" to insure peace and order in his state. Washington and "the whole public" were weary of Mississippi's incessant "troubles."

Governor Ames saw no other way to ensure a safe and fair election than to form a state militia.[68] Haversacks, rations, copies of Upton's *Infantry Tactics*, and 1,000 Springfield breech-loaders were ordered. However, since it was mostly blacks who volunteered, outright war with the armed white organizations now seemed inevitable.

So the governor, with federal assistance, reached a "Peace Agreement" with the Democrats.[69] In return for their promise not to disrupt the peace, he disbanded the militia and locked the arms away in storage. A bloody race war had narrowly been averted.

On November 2nd, although the voting proceeded with surprising tranquility, it was obvious that the Democrats' campaign of intimidation to keep blacks from the polls had succeeded.[70] Native whites regained control of almost every county in the state. "Redemption" had been accomplished. Reconstruction was over.

George's insurance trials, however, already two years in the courts, were in litigation still.

CHAPTER THIRTY-SIX

THE TRIALS

Friday, November 13, 1874: the day of the showdown has finally dawned. George's suits are scheduled for trial.[1] Arriving at Courthouse Square, the plaintiff cannot help but notice a handbill posted on the brick wall: "Meeting of Taxpayers to be held in the Opera House, Dec. 2nd." Vicksburg is less than three weeks away from bloody race riots.

George struts up the many stairs to the lofty grounds, where he spots the copper curls and walrus mustache of his able counselor, Richard S. Buck. Across the lawn stands William M. Chamberlin. The meticulously-attired agent with wooly black Burnsides is in a huddle with his colleague, J. D. Burch, and Thomas A. Marshall, the insurers' attorney. Litigants, lawyers and witnesses are assembling for the day's business. Among them are the 18 men subpoenaed to testify in George's cases. J. W. Parberry and his cabinmate, Uncle Jimmy the Irishman, however, will not be showing up, as Sheriff Scott could not find the veterinarian in his county.[2]

The attorneys saunter into the grand white courthouse, leaving their clients and witnesses to linger beneath the low-hanging limbs of the magnolias and oaks that were planted five years ago.[3] Shrubbery and grass now grace the cascading grounds as well. "The weather this morning," the *Vicksburg Daily Times* will report, "was all that could be desired, it being pleasant and clear."[4]—Perfect day for lounging outdoors.

The men are animated by this break in their routine.[5] They smoke and chew and gossip heartily. There is plenty to talk about. After a nerve-racking summer, the August elections filled Vicksburg's offices with "taxpayer's party" whites. Now "White League" clubs are forming all over Warren County. Incendiary rhetoric and social tension and the threat of violence hang in the air like a rumor of yellow fever.[6] Politics, therefore, may be too incendiary a topic for this assemblage of white and black men of varied social status. Perhaps they confine their remarks to the quality and grade of this year's harvest, and speculate as to what it will bring in the market.

Presently the bailiff appears on the portico. He shouts a case number—none of George's—and a passel of men shuffles into the building. From time to time attorneys step out into the sunshine to update their clients on how the day's case load is progressing.[7]

By the time George and the insurance agents and the witnesses stagger back from dinner, they are all talked out. Squatting on the green turf, they gaze out lethargically over the jumble of roofs and chimneys of the business district to the broad Father of Waters swirling below. The mellow sun is almost in the river when the bailiff comes out to announce that George's trials are postponed until Tuesday.[8]

For three days the out-of-towners, unfettered by work and family, and oblivious to Monday's drab overcast and sprinkles, indulge in the attractions of the city.[9] It's a paid holiday!

On November 17th they re-assemble. This time, though, a driving rain forces the motley troop under the shelter of one of the monumental ionic porticoes.[10] Presently the bailiff comes and leads the men through a set of paneled doors twice their height, up a long iron staircase to a sizable landing, and, veering right, through a set of swinging louvered doors.[11]

The courtroom spans the width of the building. The walls are plaster painted an ivory color, rather stark, and soar to a ceiling 24 feet high, with an enormous gas chandelier in the middle. In the two exterior walls, a pair of paneled doors flanked by windows of many panes opens onto a balcony. These balconies extend out into the east and west porticoes, but they are very shallow; their ornate cast-iron railings do not touch the towering columns. The floor is carpeted and strewn with spit-

COURTROOM IN THE OLD WARREN COUNTY COURTHOUSE WHERE GEORGE'S SUITS WERE TRIED, PHOTOGRAPHED IN 1982.
(Courtesy Old Court House Museum, Vicksburg)

toons. Ranks of well-worn wooden benches, backless like the pews in a country church, stand on either side of a center aisle. As the 18 witnesses file into these rows, shuffling and creaking and scraping echo throughout the vast chamber.

Up front, Richard S. Buck and Thomas A. Marshall rise gravely from a long table. It stands on the other side of a decorative black iron railing that separates the public from the litigants. The attorneys extend a hand to their clients as the plaintiff and defendant pass through the swinging gate. All four sit down.

George examines the judge's bench. It is a free-standing cast-iron dias four steps high ringed with an iron railing. The whole ornate structure is painted black and sits immutably in an impressive semi-circular rotunda. To the left and right of the rotunda are two of the courtroom's four fireplaces, also two tall doors that open into large rooms occupying the corners of the building. These would be the judge's chambers and the jury's deliberation room.

Pivoting in his chair, George can see in the rear of the courtroom the narrow door that gives access to a tight staircase that spirals up to the octagonal clock tower. Up there, out in the breeze sweeping down the river, Vicksburg's watchman circumambulates the belfry. In the cupola soaring above his head hangs a huge bell. This morning it is undisturbed. But in three weeks it will bellow frantic alarms when the watchman spies bands of black men on the roads leading into the city.

George scans the faces of the jurors who are seated to one side in 12 matching straight chairs. Some of the men are white, some black. Blacks may serve on juries now, a privilege not yet accorded to women.[12] Midway between the jury and George is the witness stand, a chair on a low wooden platform that may be moved about easily.

"The Honorable George F. Brown!"

All rise.

A black robe sweeps through a door in the rotunda and circles around to mount the four steps of the bench. The magistrate's white face is familiar to the locals, and both lawyers are well acquainted with this Republican appointee's temperament. For three years they have been arguing cases before him. Judge Brown brings his gavel down with a resounding clap.

Everyone sits.

George has waited a year and a half for this moment. At long last, his constitutional right to due process is being enforced. America has been a litigious nation since the 1600s. Early on in his career this immigrant learned to imitate his neighbors and turn to the courts to enforce his every right and interest.[13]

Already back in 1865 George was on the docket of the Circuit Court in Issaquena County.[14] That fall term he brought two suits against Charles E. Wright, a landholder of the county. George sought to collect funds the planter owed him and, by enforcing a mechanic's lien he held against 200 of Wright's acres, receive punitive damages as well. The fact that the war had stripped Wright of his entire labor force of 12 slaves did not dissuade George from enforcing an agreement the planter had signed in better days.[15] Business was business. Both cases were argued in the spring term of 1866 by W. D. Brown, and both were decided in George's favor.

Four years later, right after buying Saints Rest, George sued the *Robert E. Lee.*[16] He had taken Catherine to New Orleans for Christmas, and on December 28, 1869, they boarded the famed "floating palace" to go home. George checked their trunk, and Catherine carried into their stateroom a small leather bag containing her toiletries and jewelry worth—she would claim later—$105. George retired to the gentlemen's smoking lounge. Catherine went to the ladies' parlor for tea. When they returned to their stateroom, the jewelry was gone. Despite Catherine's protests, the captain refused to compensate her for the loss. So George sued. The case was heard in Jackson in U.S. District Court for the Southern District of Mississippi in 1870. Based on a statement of facts, the court rendered summary judgment for the *Robert E. Lee.* The carrier was responsible only for baggage checked, not baggage kept by passengers.[17]

Spring term, fall term, year after year, George F. Ring, Ring & Muller, Ring & Co., Ring *et al.*, appeared as plaintiffs and defendants on court dockets.[18] Firms sued one another routinely for collection of debts and resolution of disputes, and routinely the trials lasted two, three or more terms. A business might fold, or a partnership dissolve, long before its legal affairs were decided. To expedite matters and minimize expenses, out-of-court settlements were common.[19] George, like his American colleagues, accepted litigation as a part of doing business. Sometimes he won, sometimes he lost. It was all a matter of course. Usually.

These cases, however, the insurance cases, will be different. Much more than money is at stake. So far they have proceeded like this:

Spring Term 1873:

The ruddy Kentuckian of Buck & Clark files one suit in the U.S. Circuit Court for the Southern District of Mississippi sitting in Jackson, because the Liverpool, London & Globe is a *foreign* corporation.[20] George, as guardian, seeks to collect $2,000 from the insurer for the half-interest held by his wards, Frank and Missouri Jeans, in the Ring & Co. building.

Fall Term 1873:

The Liverpool, London & Globe engages a Mr. Wharton for its defense, and denies—through its agent William A. Harper—George's claims. The case is placed on the docket for spring.

Meanwhile, Buck files four suits in the Circuit Court of Warren County, sitting in Vicksburg's grandiose courthouse. George, as sole surviving partner of Ring & Co., seeks to collect $2,000 from the Franklin,[21] $3,500 from the Great Western Mutual,[22] and $2,000 from the Mechanics & Traders,[23] for the loss of merchandise, and $1,500 from the Franklin for his own half-interest in the building.[24]

The Honorable George F. Brown summons the agents to reply.[25] Chamberlin and Burch appear with the senior partner of Marshall & Young, the firm engaged by the insurers for their defense. They claim the companies owe George nothing because: (1) neither George nor Joe (who "is not deceased, but is now living") nor Martha Moore owned any interest, absolute, contingent or qualified, in the goods or building, either when the policies were written, or on March 4, 1873, or now; (2) George had not given the Franklin notice when he purchased "additional insurance;" and (3) George and Joe Ring themselves "fraudulently burned and destroyed by fire" the goods and building.

This is what is at stake in these cases: George's reputation. And Joe's, too. Who owned what interest in Ring & Co. when, and how and when each policy was written—the formalities Chamberlin articulated so fastidiously in his office—serve only as pretext.[26] The real issue here

No. 2573.

Warren Circuit Court,

To Sept. Term, 1873

George F. Ring
Surv'g partner
vs. of
The Franklin Fire
Insurance Company.

DECLARATION.
Stock Risk

Filed and summons issued

17th September 1873

T. W. Cardozo, Clerk.

Fee Book   , page

M. Book   , page

Judgment
October 1874

Buck & Clark Atty's
for Pltff.

DOCUMENT FROM THE PACKET OF ONE OF GEORGE'S INSURANCE CASES.

is the Ring brothers. It is the Ring brothers who are on trial. For robbery, arson, murder.

Spring Term 1874:

Buck & Clark insist that the companies *do* owe George because: (1) George and Joe (who *is* deceased) and Martha Moore *did* own an interest in the stock and building; (2) George *did* give notice to Chamberlin when he purchased the additional insurance; and (3) George and Joe did *not* destroy by fire the merchandise and building.

The suits are docketed for fall.

Fall Term 1874:

The federal court in Jackson finds for George. It orders the Liverpool, London & Globe to pay Frank and Missouri Jeans the $2,000, plus $202.33 for legal fees.[27]

One down. Four to go. Now they begin.

In the vast ivory-colored upper-floor courtroom, George is called first to mount the witness stand. Seated there on the squat platform, business-like, he answers Buck's questions and identifies the policies, notes, and proofs of loss which the lawyer tenders. Each piece of evidence is read aloud to the jury, although the reverberation of every syllable in the high-ceilinged chamber garbles beyond comprehension much of the prose. When Buck retakes his seat at the long table, Marshall lifts himself confidently and approaches the stand. Calmly, on select points, he cross-examines George.

Next, Buck interrogates Chamberlin. The insurance man appears every bit as professional and restrained as his client. His responses pose no challenge to George's claims.

The plaintiff's case is made.

By now the witnesses—and jurymen, too—are suffering the effects of their weekend revels. The bailiff throws open the doors to the two balconies and raises the many-paned windows. In drifts the morning's brisk dampness, and the patter of raindrops tapping thousands of magnolia leaves and oak leaves and splattering on brick paths. "[I]t has rained almost incessantly since mid-night."[28]

Now comes Marshall's turn to argue the defense. He calls George and queries him regarding the formalities, each of which the businessman roundly contests. Then Marshall calls Chamberlin, who at long last, under oath and from the eminence of the stand, voices his contention that the fire was no accident: it was a criminal fraud perpetrated by the Ring brothers!

At once echoes of creaking and scraping fill the courtroom as the drowsy congregation rouses to attention. An exclamatory murmur rises and dissipates. Even the seasoned magistrate straightens in the folds of his raven gown. *This* is what George has been waiting for!

But Buck's cross-examination brings the almond-toned agent back to key points of fact. Chamberlin's measured responses, however, no longer conceal the vehemence of his true conviction.

The defense's case is made.

Judge Brown recesses for dinner.

When court resumes, the procession begins: 13 men of the Delta, one after the other, parade before George. They rise, amble down the carpeted aisle, pass through the decorative iron gate, cross in front of the white and black faces of the jurymen, ascend the stand with a clackity-clack of wooden heels, swear to tell the whole truth, sit, and respond to the lawyers' interrogatories.[29]

Three are well-to-do planters: William B. McQuillen, pioneering lord of the domain nearest the landing; William I. Chaney, patrician doctor who helped identify the charred remains; and S. B. Alexander, Mississippi born and bred, whose plantation borders the Jeans place.

Two are whites with skills or a profession: John F. Coker, whose wife and children watched the blaze from their cabin; and Johnny Joor, former clerk of Ring & Co., now engaged in merchandising.

Two are poor whites: Hosey McMurray[30] and E. C. Eatman,[31] unmarried men in their late twenties.

Six are former slaves:[32] Noah B. Parker, conscientious young Justice of the Peace; Alfred Williams,[33] Joseph Robertson,[34] Bob Marshall,[35] Bryant Rushing[36] and Joe Tubberville[37]—farm laborers all, and all save Parker unlettered. A couple of them work on the Chaney and McQuillen places.[38] Marshall is employed on Dr. Moore's plantation.[39] Rushing, at 66, is by far the oldest. Tubberville may be the "Tub"—"not Sambo"—who led Sherman through the swamps to the Union fleet stalled in Deer Creek.

The whole of the Delta's unique four-tiered society is represented.[40]

One by one they state their relationship to the Ring brothers and divulge what they know about the co-partnership and its destruction. Each man's voice, resounding in the hollow chamber, is familiar to George. They are all former neighbors and fellow pioneers of an inhospitable land. When dismissed, each Deltan acknowledges George as he strides back to his place on one of the benches.

Toward supper time Judge Brown adjourns for the day.

Wednesday morning, November 18th, the tedious parade resumes. "Another dull and dreary day. . . . The chain gang, consisting of five whites and three colored, were out yesterday afternoon cleaning the mud from the pavements. . . . The weather remains cloudy, with indications of rain."[41]

This time it is Vicksburgers, five of them, who traverse the cavernous room one by one and testify. Samuel Fischel, the Jewish merchant from Bavaria, George knows well, as he is a member of the city's close-knit coterie of German-speaking merchants. For a short while Fischel's firm, J. Hornthal & Co., held a note secured by George's interest in Ring & Co. (The note had been passed to J. Hornthal & Co. for collection by Meyer, Deutsch & Weis of New Orleans, who had accepted it from George as collateral.) George would also recognize the three physicians: Henry S. Fischel, a relative of Samuel's;[42] Daniel Burnet Nailor, a planter/doctor of high repute and local renown—64 years old now—whose family has resided in Warren County since Spanish colonial days;[43] and David W. Booth, city physician and—at a youthful 33—chief of staff of the Charity Hospital.[44] The final Vicksburger, however, Wesley D. Night, may be a stranger to George.[45]

Their procession of echoing testimony stretches throughout the gray morning.[46]

After dinner Buck and Marshall deliver their closing statements, and Judge Brown issues their instructions to the jury—but with emendations: as these are *civil* suits, jurors are to restrict their deliberation to the policy issues raised, and disregard all accusations of any *criminal* activity. In other words, they are to disregard entirely the claim made by the insurers, and verbalized by Chamberlin, that the Ring brothers destroyed their own business to collect the insurance money. With that, the black robe billows down the steps of the bench and disappears through a door in the semi-circular rotunda.

The variegated panel of 12 files into one of the spacious corner chambers. Attorneys, litigants and witnesses exit into the landing, descend the long iron staircase, and step out onto the portico. Lighting a cigar or pipe, or tucking a plug of tobacco inside the lower lip, the men watch the starlings poking in the rain-saturated lawn. In a short while the bailiff is beckoning them back through the tall paneled doors.

"The Honorable George F. Brown!"

He invites the foreman to stand and read the verdicts.

The jury has decided for the plaintiff, *in every case.*

The rough-and-tumble entrepreneur from Lorraine is vindicated!

Judge Brown orders Chamberlin and Burch to pay George the full amounts of the policies, plus legal fees. Then, with a smack of the gavel, he calls for the next case.[47]

The 18 witnesses scramble toward the clerk for their pay vouchers. It will take the Delta men two days of hard riding to resume their respective stations in the society of Issaquena County. "The roads leading to the city are in a very muddy condition, and keeps the farmers from bringing in cotton, etc.," the *Vicksburg Daily Times* observes.[48] The Vicksburg men will have an easier time of it, tredging home on foot. "Overcoats and rubbers are in demand this kind of weather."[49]

Before the witnesses disperse, however, George would corral as many of them as he could into The Sunflower Exchange to toast his victory. But the victor's opportunity to gloat will be short-lived. The very next day Marshall & Young are back in court claiming that Judge Brown erred when he emended their instructions, and that the jury returned a verdict contrary to the evidence. They move for a new trial.

Motion denied.

But the fight is not over yet. Only before Marshall & Young have a chance to throw their next punch, Judge Brown is compelled by the "Vicksburgh Troubles" to abandon his court and flee the city. George must wait through a winter of deadly race riots, the armed takeover of the courthouse, and the intervention of federal troops, before learning what the insurance companies will try next. Not in the least is he deterred, though. The self-assertive businessman will respond in kind to whatever they throw at him.

Spring Term 1875:

Marshall & Young tender a Bill of Exceptions, which Judge Brown signs. Whereupon they petition for a Writ of Error to appeal the decision to the Mississippi Supreme Court in Jackson.

Petition granted.

George retaliates the same day. He dispatches his trusty Kentuckian back into the lofty temple of justice to file two new suits against William M. Chamberlin, representative of the Franklin Fire Insurance Company. One seeks damages of $10,000, stating that Chamberlin:

> . . . contriving, and wickedly and maliciously intending to injure him in his good name, fame and credit, and to make it appear that he was not lawfully entitled to receive the said sums of money, and to bring the said plaintiff into public scandal, infamy and disgrace, and to cause it to be suspected by his neighbors and other good and worthy citizens that he was guilty of the crime of arson, and to subject him to the pains and penalties provided by law against the said crime, and otherwise to vex, harrass, oppress and injure the said plaintiff, did on the 17th day of November 1874, falsely, wickedly and maliciously compose and publish . . . a certain false, scandalous, malicious and defamatory libel, containing amongst other things . . . that it is not true that the property . . . was accidentally and by misfortune consumed by fire . . . but it was by the fraud of George F. Ring, and his brother Joseph Ring, fraudulently burned and destroyed by fire. . . .
>
> And also . . . on the 15th day of March 1875, in a certain discourse which the said defendant . . . had . . . in the presence of divers good and worthy citizens . . . and divers neighbors of the said plaintiff, falsely and maliciously spoke . . . the false, scandalous, malicious and defamatory words following: 'He burned up the property himself and therefore we will not pay the loss, but will carry the case to the court of last resort.' . . .
>
> And also . . . on the 15th day of March 1875, in a certain other conversation and discourse which the said defendant . . . had . . . in the presence of divers other good and worthy

citizens . . . and divers neighbors and acquaintances of the said plaintiff, falsely and maliciously spoke . . . the following other false, scandalous, malicious and defamatory words: 'It is a gigantic fraud, and the Rings are at the bottom of it.' . . .

The said plaintiff has been and is greatly injured in his good name, fame and credit, and brought into public scandal, infamy and disgrace amongst his neighbors and acquaintances and other good and worthy citizens, in so much that some of them not knowing his innocence and integrity in the premises, but believing or suspecting the said libellous and slanderous charges of the said defendant to be true, have refused and still refuse to hold or have any intercourse or acquaintance with the plaintiff, as they otherwise would do. . . .[50]

The other suit seeks damages of $2,000, stating that Chamberlin:

. . . well knowing . . . that the plaintiff was lawfully and rightfully entitled to have and receive the said sums of money, but contriving and intending to injure the plaintiff by falsely pretending that he . . . had wickedly and feloniously burned the said property . . . did . . . unjustly and vexatiously refuse to pay to the plaintiff the said sum of money. . . . And did, moreover . . . falsely, wickedly and deceitfully represent unto the 'Mechanics & Traders Insurance Company' and the 'Great Western Mutual Insurance Company' that the said plaintiff had himself wickedly and feloniously burned . . . the said property . . . and thereby persuaded, influenced and induced the said last named Insurance Companies, also, to refuse to pay the said plaintiff said sums of money. . . .

The said plaintiff was obliged to and did sue the said defendant and the said other insurance Companies, and was put to great trouble, expense and costs in his necessary suits and actions for the recovery of the said sums of money . . . which otherwise the said plaintiff should have received without any trouble, expense or costs whatever; and also to great expenses, costs and losses, otherwise than in his said suits and actions, which he would not have been put to, but for the aforesaid false, wicked and deceitful pretences and misrepresentations against him made by the said defendant. . . .[51]

Judge Brown summons Chamberlin to reply.[52] But Marshall & Young see no point in arguing two more suits in this Republican appointee's court. Since George is a citizen of Mississippi and the Franklin is a corporate citizen of Pennsylvania, the cases may be tried in federal court. So Marshall & Young move to have the cases removed to the U.S. Circuit Court for the Southern District of Mississippi in Jackson.

Motion granted.

For a year and a half longer, his resolve and confidence unshaken, George anticipates his hour of triumph.

Fall Term 1876:

It ends. Abruptly. All the venom and all the rage desist. With a dry and pro-forma notation penned into the minute book of the Mississippi Supreme Court on November 22, 1876:

> This day appeared in open Court Mr. Clarke of Counsel and suggested to the Court that the matters and things involved in this controversy have been settled and that this cause should be dismissed. And the Court being fully advised in the premises doth order and adjudge that the writ of error herein from the Judgment of the Circuit Court of Warren County rendered in this cause on the 18th day of November 1874 be and the same is hereby dismissed.[53]

Dismissed. Settled out of court. The insurance companies decided that it was wiser to accept the ruling of the lower court than to continue fighting the obstinate immigrant's lawsuits, which would evidently multiply without end. It must have been a condition of the settlement that George drop his two retaliatory cases, too, because they never made it to the federal docket.[54]

The amount George collected was never published. Chances are good, however, that it exceeded substantially the face value of the four policies, $9,000—plus Richard S. Buck's fees, of course. The self-made Kentuckian's firm would continue to profit for many years to come from George's life-long habit of engaging the courts to fight his battles.[55]

William M. Chamberlin, on the other hand, would never again benefit from George's routine practice of insuring his many interests. What was it that had turned the ambitious and capable insurance agent against his client? What had the black Virginian heard or seen? Or was it just unfounded prejudice that convinced him the German-speaking brothers were frauds? For many more years Chamberlin would sell insurance and prosper by his enterprise.[56] Whether or not he continued to represent the Franklin Fire Insurance Company of Philadelphia, however, cannot be determined from his listing in the city directories, or from the advertisement he ran in the newspaper.[57]

No matter to George. The damage was done. Business would never be the same again. Not only was his reputation suspect now, and "the Rolling Fork tragedy" as unexplained as ever, but the economy was suffering from the "Panic of 1873."

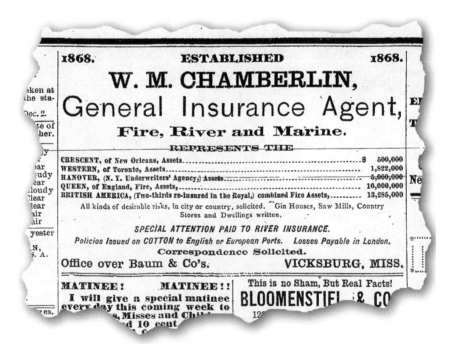

WILLIAM M. CHAMBERLIN'S ADVERTISEMENT IN
THE *VICKSBURG DAILY COMMERCIAL*, 1881.

CHAPTER THIRTY-SEVEN

BUSINESS

In the fall of 1873, when George had come home from two months of vacationing in Michigan, he was accompanied not only by Catherine, but the Webers, too.[1] It was no disrespect to Joe that George brought Hank back to take his place. It was business.[2] Business more than insurance trials, more than political race riots, preoccupied George, because of the "Panic of 1873."[3]

The financial crash hit in September. George read about it in the Detroit newspapers. Banks were closing. Sources of credit were drying up. Businesses were failing. The entire nation was affected, and it was happening fast. The price of cotton was falling, and would continue to fall until 1878, to 50 percent of what it was in 1872—about what it cost to produce it.[4] Meanwhile, George's state and county tax obligation would increase to 10 times what it was in 1866.[5] On top of that, he would pay to the Mississippi Board of Levee Commissioners four dollars annually on every acre he owned.[6] The "Great Depression" would not bottom out for five years.

The post-war boom was over.

Planters forfeited substantial acreage to debt and back taxes. Freedmen who had managed to climb up the steep and arduous ladder to land ownership lost their hard-won property now to creditors, or to the state for nonpayment of taxes. Some Vicksburg merchants went bankrupt.[7] Fortunately for George, his interests were diversified, which gave him leverage. The advertisement he ran in *The Daily Vicksburger* throughout 1874 implies that he had a more comfortable cash reserve than many of his colleagues:

> ### GEO. F. RING & CO.,
> **Cotton Factors,**
> AND
> ### GENERAL COMMISSION MERCHANTS
> **No. 5, Levee Street,**
> (Near Clay Street,)
> V I C K S B U R G, M I S S.
> All orders for purchasing will have our
> prompt attention. We also make liberal
> cash advances on consignments. Highest cash
> prices paid for hides, furs, wool, metal, etc.[8]

It is likely that George had cash on hand because he was no longer paying wages. Following the trend imposed by the new economic realities, he would have converted his plantations from wage labor to sharecropping.[9]

Saints Rest, the largest of his plantations at 1,695 acres, lay in Sunflower County now, because in 1871 the eastern boundary of Washington County had been redrawn.[10] Also in Sunflower County George owned the Cofer Place and a handful of smaller properties without names.[11] Nine miles to the North were the Ring places—known only as that, "the Ring places"—in Bolivar County. These totaled about 363 acres.[12]

Tied into these interests were Catherine's six commercial properties in Vicksburg. What was more, in keeping with his power of attorney, George was managing Joe's assets as well, including "The Vicksburg Place" in Warren County. This obligation would tie George to the financial affairs of his sister-in-law for 20 years.[13] In addition, as administrator of the Jeans estate, he was handling the modest interests of his wards, Frank and Missouri Jeans, in Issaquena County. This responsibility would last until Frank reached majority and Missouri married.[14]

Probates of deceased business partners were complex and drawn-out. Jeans's estate was doubly complicated because of his involvement in two partnerships, first with George, then with Jesse Moore—whose estate was being handled by Samuel Fischel.[15] The imbroglio of accounts would not be disentangled for years. In the end, though, George himself would profit from managing the interests Joe left.[16] He would also recoup some of the $10,000 Jeans owed him when he died.[17]

Managing an agricultural and mercantile empire spread out over four rugged counties required much arduous travel. Competent overseers notwithstanding, George would have been away from Vicksburg for weeks at a time. Frank Jeans was old enough now to ride along and learn the business of merchandising. But this left Catherine at home with Missouri Jeans, which must have concerned George, especially during the turbulent months of the "Vicksburgh Troubles."

So it is no wonder that George brought his independent-minded, jack-of-all-trades relative back down from Cincinnati to work for him again. Hank Weber's daughter Libbie would write eight decades later: "[M]y Father had charge of Comacery stores he [George] own there."[18] Each of George's plantations would have had a commissary where croppers could buy personal necessities and small luxuries against their next harvest. Managing these stores would have required George's clean-shaven and well-attired kinsman to make many trips up into the Delta. So it could have been Hank who relayed to George the story of how Noah Parker was gunned down.

When the conscientious Justice of the Peace returned to the Rolling Fork neighborhood after testifying at George's trials, he was arrested on a charge of embezzlement. He engaged a white attorney and went to trial in the spring of 1875 with a plea of not guilty. Word had it that his constable, Bowie Foreman, who was also an ex-slave, and who collected the fees, withheld large amounts.[19]

Foreman would be described by W. D. Brown as "a drunken sort of a vagabond, not worth much; considered not a character of much consideration; whisky-drinking and very unreliable."[20] But, then, Rolling Fork's lawyer/planter did not think much of Parker either, or Henry P. Scott for that matter, or any other freedman holding public office.[21]

Parker's sworn testimony that he had been too trusting of his con-

stable did not satisfy the jury. He was convicted, and his days as an elected official ended.[22] But his role in Issaquena County history was not yet
accomplished. The articulate Alabaman was sharecropping on Deer
Creek when he got caught up in what a subsequent congressional
report would call the "difficulties."[23] After it was all over, Sheriff Scott
would explain why he had kept his distance:

> The information I got led me to believe that my authority
> would not have done any good . . . I knew there was great trou-
> ble out there. I consulted with a democratic friend of mine,
> whether my life would be in danger or not, and he told me very
> positively that he did not think I could go with any authority to
> quell the disturbance out there. . . . He told me that he thought
> my life would not be safe to go there at that time.[24]

Issaquena was one of the few Mississippi counties *not* "redeemed"
by the elections of 1875. There, where Republicans outnumbered
Democrats by about 10 to one, the Reconstruction ticket prevailed
once again.[25] All county offices except two remained in the hands of
illiterate freedmen.[26] The inoffensive Henry P. Scott entered his fourth
term as sheriff.[27]

Scarcely had the ballots been counted, however, when a committee
of prominent white men of Rolling Fork placed a letter of resignation in
front of a newly re-elected member of the Board of Supervisors. They
told the black man that if he did not sign it, "they could not assure him
any protection."[28] He signed it.

Two weeks of racial "difficulties" ensued, but precisely what incident
touched them off depends on who is telling the story. W. D. Brown
placed the blame squarely on black rioters. When the senators came to
investigate, the attorney would tell them:

> On the night of the 20th of November, perhaps somewhere
> near the hour of midnight, some trouble or difficulty arose
> between a colored man and a white man, or hardly a man—
> you may call him a boy—at the town of Rolling Fork; blows
> ensued, and the colored man cursed the white man, calling
> him some very ugly names, and thereupon he struck the col-
> ored man with a knife. . . .

It was a drunken row. . . .

The boy, knowing that he was likely to be overpowered, immediately fled and concealed himself in the back room of a store. The negroes gathered a mob of about forty or fifty persons and went to the store, broke open the doors—knocked out the lights, the glass—and went into the back room and shot the boy, and brutally beat him with a large iron rod . . . and they left thinking they had killed him, but they had not.[29]

The local justice of the peace, a freedman named Harrison Smith, "issued warrants for the arrest of these negroes, and in the course of the night and quite early the following morning they had arrested them to the number of twelve or fourteen. . . ."[30] One of them was tall, lean, and darker than a mule, a former slave from Alabama, a former justice of the peace.[31] "They were lodged in an old store down there and put under a white guard. . . ."[32] Everyone expected a riot.

Brown would explain:

It was something novel in that country that white people should assume to exercise any part of the civil authority of the county. We had for years and years, in fact ever since the late war, in consideration of our small numbers, quietly acquiesced in the rule of the colored man. We felt our utter dependence upon him as the laborer of the country; we were anxious to preserve peace and would make no issue with him; and submitted to the rule of the colored man . . . until this spectacle on Sunday morning . . . of eight or ten white citizens guarding a lot of colored people as prisoners, seemed to exasperate and stir up the bad blood of a large number of these prominent negroes.[33]

A posse of "perhaps 20 to 25" white men, including W. D. Brown, gathered in town on Sunday afternoon, to quell—according to *his* account—the disturbance everyone anticipated. Late that night it came. The tense and expansive darkness of the Delta filled suddenly with the rumble of horses galloping across the wooden bridge spanning Deer Creek. The dozing white men sprang to their feet.

A band of mounted and armed blacks was hurtling toward the store.

There was a smashing of doors and sashes, a shattering of glass, a popping of gunshots, and most of the prisoners were liberated, Noah Parker among them.

That was how W. D. Brown explained the origin of the "difficulties." But Bowie Foreman's version of events blamed the whites. The former constable would inform the investigators from Washington:

> In December, when the election was over up there on Rolling Fork, there was a white man; he was in a store. I don't know what was his name. He stabbed one or two colored men with a dirk-knife across the counter, and they got a writ of arrest for him and went there for him—two men did—but [a posse of white men who had gathered in town] would not allow them to have him. They put him behind the counter, behind a big box. The two colored men, they went there and took him out, and that started the fuss between the colored men and the white men, and the white men didn't want to let him go out. . . .[34]

Whichever narration of the incident was accurate, Brown's or Foreman's, the "difficulties" had now been irrevocably touched off. Rumor spread that a black force was mustering on Deer Creek about 12 miles below Rolling Fork. The insurgents, it was said, were conspiring to attack the town, burn it down, and kill all the whites.—With firearms they were obtaining in secret from the North through Governor Ames.[35]

That was all the whites needed to hear! They were outnumbered eight to one. They would be slaughtered like hogs. Day and night the white families were anxious and sleepless.

It was then that the mysterious interloper known only as "Colonel Ball" appeared.[36] An itinerant preacher, unlettered, he took charge of organizing the white men into companies. Guards were posted around-the-clock in Rolling Fork. Spies were dispatched down Deer Creek to learn about the maneuvers and intentions of the blacks. The white men carried pistols, which filled the black population with terror. Then on Sunday, December 5th, Colonel Ball organized a dozen local planters into a posse.

W. D. Brown would later boast:

> Yes, sir, I was with that party of citizens. . . . Having a wife and

children quite dear to me, who had been sleepless for a week or ten days, and having these constant threats and rumors coming to my ears, that we were likely to be assassinated and burned up, etc, I thought it my duty to take my gun and be ready for an emergency. I think that any other citizen, under the circumstances, would have felt the same way.[37]

Riding south along Deer Creek, the posse rounded up six prominent blacks suspected of being the leaders of the supposed insurrection. They took them out to an open field between Elgin's Store and David Hunt's place called Georgiana. There they shot them, dead, all of them, including the 30-year-old one six sinewy feet tall and darker than a mule.

Someone ran the news up to his wife.

Brown would relate how the racial "difficulties" were resolved:

A day or two after the reported killing of these colored men, a number of the citizens, and I believe I am one of the class, instituted this committee, what is known as the 'Peace Meeting;' and quite a large number of the orderly, good colored people from the different parts of the county in which these disturbances took place, from Rolling Fork on down to the southern limit of the county, consented to the peace meeting and went into it.[38]

They selected representatives to discuss the unrest and devise a resolution. Nine black men and eight whites—among them "Colonel Lewis Ball," William B. McQuillen and W. D. Brown—signed a written "Agreement." The treaty named a dozen "turbulent persons," all black, all absent, who were condemned to be handed over "to the people" to answer for disturbing the peace of the community. Those men never dared set foot in Issaquena County again. Also forced to flee, though not named in the "Agreement," was Bowie Foreman.

The "difficulties" were over. A congressional inquiry followed. Many questions were asked of many residents, but no arrests would ever be made, no trial would ever be held. "Colonel Ball"—not unlike the elusive Dr. Parberry three years earlier—would vanish just as quickly and mysteriously as he had appeared. And the aloof and accommodating Henry P. Scott would go on to be elected to a seat in the state legislature.[39]

Whether George learned of Noah Parker's lynching from Hank Weber or someone else, the story could not have failed to move him. Against daunting odds, the earnest and naïve young man had done his best to solve "the Rolling Fork tragedy" and bring the evil-doers to justice. All along the way, though, the former slave's conscientiousness, leadership qualities and pride were frustrated, and ultimately, in violence, they were extinguished altogether.

For the Webers, Mississippi had fallen short once again. Maybe it was the ugly race wars, or George's bitter fight in the courts to vindicate his reputation, or the shrunken economy of the "Great Depression." Or maybe it was just too much horseback riding in wilting heat and drenching rain through swamps and jungles teeming with bears and panthers and wolves. Whatever the reason, Hank's employment situations never lasted very long. By early 1876 the slender, olive-complected and chestnut-haired man had packed up his wife and three offspring, and headed home to Cincinnati.[40] The Webers would never go South again. Not even to visit. Rather, the elopers would end up moving back to their native Buffalo, where by then the Evangelical Lutheran was an accepted member of the Miller clan. Lena would once again be close to the sister whose Mississippi adventure she had shared.[41]

By this time Rolling Fork Landing was just a loose end, an unprofitable scrap, of George F. Ring's far-flung empire. He forfeited to taxes all but 40 acres of it, keeping only the landing site.[42] In 1876 Issaquena County was divided along Steele Bayou, creating the new county of Sharkey, with the town of Rolling Fork as its seat of government.[43] So Rolling Fork Landing was a deserted and forlorn fragment of Sharkey County now. At the same time, Issaquena's county seat was relocated several miles upriver to Mayersville, as the insatiable Mississippi was gouging the mud out from under the few cypress shacks of Tallula.[44] Deprived of its life as a landing, Tallula virtually disappeared from the map and human memory.

Very quickly the swath of primitive wilderness where George had chosen 18 years ago to cast his lot, the territory that had given him his start, was changing into a new place beyond recognition. Now George's interests lay deeper in the Delta.

Nature itself seemed to be urging the land-loving Lorrainian to move permanently to where his heart was: Saints Rest. On April 26, 1876, the capricious Mississippi River cut through the DeSoto Peninsula across from Vicksburg, leaving the city stranded.[45] The economic effect for Vicksburgers was catastrophic, particularly for the merchants. To call at Vicksburg, steamboats had to leave the Mississippi's channel and churn into the stagnant backwater that used to be the river's bed. The maneuver was delicate and time-consuming, hence costly. Greenville and Memphis started getting the Delta's lucrative cotton trade. Not until 1878 would the U.S. Army Corps of Engineers begin to divert the Yazoo southward through the former bed of the Mississippi, and thereby restore Vicksburg to the status of port. But that project would take 25 years to complete, and scarcely had it gotten under way when the most devastating yellow fever epidemic in Vicksburg history invaded the metropolis.[46]

It killed Jacob Schwink, the relative/bartender whose business involvement with George Ring had grown over the years.[47] He left a widow and two children.[48]

George and Catherine moved out to Saints Rest.

And the well-to-do Delta planter with no son of his own wrote to his sister-in-law in Buffalo: Send Nicholas on down.

CHAPTER THIRTY-EIGHT

NICHOLAS

In August of 1873, sheltered once again under Papa's roof, Barbara slipped back into the German-speaking tradesman's society of Buffalo.[1] This was the world the widow chose for her sons. In the more urbane merchant society of Vicksburg, they would have been groomed by their Uncle George. Here they would absorb the rigid heritage of faith and tradition in which Barbara herself had been reared. One of the Ring boys, however, the eldest, the one most like his father, would end up back with his Mississippi uncle.

John Miller was 64 years old now, diminutive more than ever in stature, but vigorous still and plying his trade.[2] In one photograph taken on a picnic—about 1874—his ears stick out beneath the rim of a hat that is pushed back jauntily, exposing a high forehead.[3] Small kind eyes peer out above prominent cheekbones. The lower half of his face is all bushy white mustache. Age only enhanced the immigrant's stabilizing force as patriarch of an ever-expanding and ever-peregrinating American clan.

For months or years at a time, as their fortunes shifted, children of his, together with their spouses and *their* children, ebbed and flowed through Papa's houses. He owned three in a row now on the south side of Cherry: 11, 13, 15.[4] He was residing in number 15 with an unmarried son and daughter, and this is where Barbara moved into a rear flat.[5] She

John Miller (elder on the left) picnicking with the family of his son, Nicholas, perhaps in Letchworth State Park, western New York, about 1874.

(Photograph from the author's collection)

and her boys blended into the swirl of the Miller clan as though they had never been away from it.

Nicholas and George, and later John, were enrolled in Barbara's own "*Alma Mater,*" St. Michael's parish school.[6] A photograph of about 1876 shows George's class assembled outside on the stairs. Framed images of the Sacred Heart, Blessed Virgin and Saint Michael the Archangel have been carried out and hung on the brick wall behind the wide-eyed pupils. Their teacher, a nun—there were many in the city by this time, representing many different orders—stands grim-faced to one side, arms folded into her habit.

Nicholas, at 13, went on to attend Canisius College.[7] In the edifice occupying the Washington Street property that had once belonged to his ancestors, he was taught by Jesuits. But this only lasted one academic year, 1877–78, because each of the three Ring brothers was apprenticed at about the age of 14 to a master craftsman. Nicholas and George learned from an uncle who was a varnisher and cabinet maker.[8] John became an upholsterer.[9] It was the life pattern of countless generations; Barbara never strayed from the traditional norms of her society.

She kept house and lived conservatively on the income from her deceased husband's estate, which her brother-in-law managed as he saw fit.[10] There is no evidence that Barbara ever participated in any way in the handling of her assets. In 20 years the management of her finances would pass from the hands of her brother-in-law to the hands of her eldest son.[11] Additional income was provided by her boys, who started paying board just as soon as they started working.[12] In no financial need, Barbara was not obliged to remarry.

By the spring of 1878 the widow had moved her boys into their own second-story flat at number 11 Cherry Street, the house in which she had drawn her first breath.[13] That winter Nicholas was mature enough at 14 to hold a cousin over the baptismal font of St. Michael's and pass his name on to a godson.[14] Ritual and custom within the immigrant working-class neighborhood had not changed since Barbara's youth.

The surrounding city, however, had changed a great deal.[15]

On the eve of the Fourth of July in 1882, Buffalonians gathered to hear a long-winded and statistics-laden speech.[16] It opened the celebration of their city's fiftieth birthday. Their number, the orator announced,

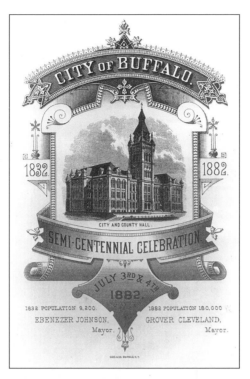

EMBLEM OF BUFFALO'S SEMI-CENTENNIAL CELEBRATION, 1882.
(Courtesy Buffalo & Erie County Historical Society)

GEORGE F. RING, JR. (LEFT OF "X") AT ST. MICHAEL'S SCHOOL, BUFFALO, ABOUT 1876.
(Photograph from the author's collection)

CANISIUS COLLEGE, BUFFALO, AROUND 1890. *(Courtesy Buffalo & Erie County Historical Society)*

had swollen to 170,000, and the astounding growth was due primarily to Germans:[17]

> These immigrants were the forerunners and the forefathers of that great German population which has contributed so largely to the prosperity and exercised such a powerful influence upon the character of our community. . . . It appears from the report of the Board of Health for 1879, that in 1878, of the children born in this city, one thousand nine hundred and seventy-five were of German descent, of all other descents two thousand and fifty-six—a difference of only eighty-one.[18]

German surnames appeared on the signs of all kinds of business establishments, and German could be heard in virtually all of the city's streets. Twenty-two breweries were producing beer. There were *two* German choral societies now, and *two* German-language newspapers. In 1876 the city had elected its first German-born mayor, and in this semi-centennial year of 1882, the German-American Bank opened its doors.[19]

Buffalo was a dynamo of commerce dominated by transportation and the grain trade—referred to simply as "The Dock." Railroad lines on the continent and steamship lines on the Great Lakes, combined with the burgeoning labor force and the constantly-increasing market, allowed the lumber, coal, cattle and meatpacking, iron and steel industries to expand rapidly. Fabulously wealthy industrialists resided in mansions along Delaware Avenue, said to be "the most fashionable street in America." Monday through Saturday the city toiled. Then on Sunday mornings the steeple bells of myriad denominations beckoned the populace to prayer and repose. Few now were the citizens who could recall, as Papa could, when Buffalo was a remote village with no paved streets, no daily newspaper, one Protestant church, one log-cabin Catholic church, and almost as many Iroquois, Aurora and Seneca faces were seen on the boardwalks as European faces.[20]

Nicholas, George and John matured into "gentle and kind" young men—as Louis Caffall Ring would describe his father in a letter of 1985.[21] They had the build of all the Ring men, standing just over five feet six inches and tending to stocky, with oval faces, dark complexions, dark brown hair, and eyes that appeared at times to be gray, other times

VIEW OF BUFFALO IN 1882. (Courtesy Buffalo & Erie County Historical Society)

blue, and still other times hazel. In addition, all three wore trim chevron-shaped mustaches which accentuated their fraternal resemblance.[22] George was the one whose easy-going temperament was reflected in the corn cob pipe that dangled from the corner of his mouth.[23]

If, every spring, when the widow and her three strapping boys knelt at the altar rail of St. Michael's to have their foreheads crossed with ashes, Barbara was reminded of the terrible Lent of 1873, she evidently betrayed no bitterness. Nicholas, in future years, would tell his children nothing at all about the death of his father;[24] and John, when asked, "If either parent has died, state cause," replied simply, "Father: Burned to death."[25] It appears that Barbara remembered Joe, not as "only a few bones," but rather as the charmer, the kidder who made her laugh in spite of herself, the man whose life she had elected freely and solemnly to share. Joe was the partner devoted to her and their children through 14 happy Easters. His repeated "new beginnings," although frustrated ultimately by circumstances beyond his control, never failed to provide comfortably for his family. Somehow the heritage of Papa's household had girded Barbara to weather the heart-thrashing tempests of the summer of 1873. Her roots had held her in good stead. And she clung to them.

And maybe Barbara was not left without some tangible memento of her husband after all. Maybe she had kept Joe's pocket watch on her person, and *not* lost it in the shifting silt of the Ohio River. Maybe Nicholas—or even Barbara herself—had guarded Joe's penknife in some deep pocket, and so treasured it still. Keepsakes or no keepsakes, Barbara delighted in the most precious legacy Joe had left her: Nicholas, George and John. So it would have been hard for her, that June of 1881—the summer just before Buffalo's semicentennial celebration—to let her eldest go.

I can see Barbara standing on the platform at the railroad station.[26] She is a mature woman of 41. Her brown eyes are fixed on the window where Nicholas's profile has just settled. George and John stand beside her, taller now than their mother. The car lurches with a screech, then lumbers ponderously forward. Barbara lifts a gloved hand. George and John shake their caps like pennants. Nicholas's handsome face appears and his palm rises, but already the pane of glass is diminishing down the

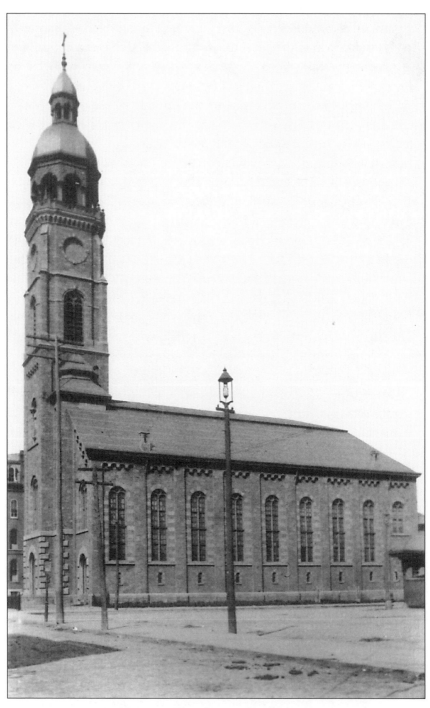

ST. MICHAEL'S R. C. CHURCH, BUFFALO, 1880S.
(Courtesy Buffalo & Erie County Historical Society)

platform. The long cars race by, each chasing the one before it. Barbara's dress flaps like a flag, the boys' trouser legs, too. She presses a palm to her quivering bonnet. Suddenly the rear porch of the caboose is fleeing from them. Then nothing is left but two endless rails of steel. High overhead the smoke is dissipating against the frosted glass canope.

The two young men wait patiently for their mother. Slowly her raised hand comes down, then the hand off her bonnet.

In a moment, Barbara is strolling home with her boys.

Her brother-in-law, who has no male heir of his own, has written from Saints Rest: Send Nicholas on down.

GEORGE F. RING, JR., AT ABOUT 15 YEARS OF AGE, ABOUT 1882,
BEFORE HE GREW A MUSTACHE AND STARTED SMOKING A CORN COB PIPE.
(Photograph from the author's collection)

CHAPTER THIRTY-NINE

SAINTS REST

Suitcase in hand, Nicholas steps down to the platform of the Greenville railroad station.[1] Waiting there to welcome him back to the Yazoo-Mississippi Delta is Uncle George.

Is George taken aback? Not only is the nephew no longer a boy, but his man's face and his man's deportment are those of his father. George would be marveling at the image of his deceased brother. Nicholas, too, is surprised. Uncle George has grown stockier, his oval face looser on the bone, and lined. At 47 his forehead is higher, too, and his dark brown hair and mustache show traces of gray.[2] But the high-strung young Labrador prancing and sniffing about the newcomer's trousers looks exactly like the young Lomo![3]

Soon uncle and nephew, suitcase and retriever, are in the buggy heading due east.

"I understood that my father was born in Buffalo and came South when he was 16 to work on his uncle George's plantation," Louis Caffall Ring would write in 1985. "This was Saint's Rest Plantation, between Heathman and Shaw."[4]

Nicholas Ring would recognize the Delta today, because he—unlike his uncle—lived to witness the complete transformation of that land.[5] Already this summer of 1881, when the native Buffalonian entered the ancient bottomland for a second time, it was noticeably changed from

JOSEPH NICHOLAS RING AT ABOUT 18 YEARS OF AGE, ABOUT 1882.
(Photograph from the author's collection)

the forbidding jungle his Uncle George had entered just one generation earlier.

Deep in the interior now the bogues and bayous and creeks were being cleared of cane brakes.[6] Systems of levees were being erected to control the annual overflow, and irrigation canals were being dug to channel the water from natural sloughs into the fields. There were more roads in the Delta now, too, although none paved yet, and bridges spanned some of the waterways whose intricate network, like the veins of an elm leaf, had been etched over millennia. It would be awhile yet before packet service succumbed to the railways; but that, too, Nicholas would witness.

Parallel lines of steel had first begun piercing the Delta in the late 1870s. But none penetrated Sunflower County quite yet. Sunflower County was the bullseye of the wilderness, lying mid-way between Greenville on the Mississippi to the west and Greenwood on the Yazoo to the east, between Memphis to the north and Vicksburg to the south. Nonetheless, the Georgia Pacific had already bought the Greenville, Columbus and Birmingham, and was now in the process of extending that fledgling line as part of a daring east-coast-to-west-coast railway project.

The engineering feat was unprecedented and stupendous. Working conditions were horrendous. Laborers had to hack their way through the tangled underbrush and carve a passage through the dense virgin timberland, felling the huge ancient cypress, sweet gum, ash, oak and sycamore trees, removing them, and uprooting the stumps. To carry the rails through the swamps, they built up beds of earth higher than flood level. Over Deer Creek, Bogue Phalia and the Sunflower River, they laid the track across sturdy timber trestles.

At night, in camp, sentries kept a lookout for bears, panthers, bobcats, wolves and other more annoying than dangerous animals, such as deer, opossums and raccoons. But spotting pestilence was not so easy; sickness and disease ravaged the workforce. Old timers recalled how the black bondmen of the Delta's earliest pioneers, herded from neighboring states to the edge of the Father of Waters, muscles straining and sleek with sweat, labored against the same terrible harshness, and the frightful toll the wilderness exacted back then, too. Nevertheless, by

September of this year, 1881, the first train would chug across Sunflower County, and in seven years the astounding Georgia Pacific line would reach Atlanta. Nicholas would see development throughout the Delta shift from waterway to railway.[7]

He would witness the rise of the lumber industry, for a camp of 20 to 30 men could always be found at the head of the advancing rails. Sawmills were constructed over streams with decent current, so felled timber no longer had to be floated downriver to Vicksburg to be milled. The deafening whine of saws carried for miles above the milder sounds of nature. As the lumber camps pushed deeper and deeper into the Delta, thousands of acres were being stripped of their towering hardwood forests, and extensive fields of cotton, unbroken from horizon to horizon, were stretching out in their wake. Timber was already rivaling cotton as the fortune-maker.[8]

Tenaciously the Delta resisted, but in vain. Section by section the vast alluvial elm leaf was being entirely transformed by implacable entrepreneurs like Nicholas Ring's Uncle George, and George's one-time employer and life-long mentor, George W. Faison.

One of the earliest pioneers to settle on the upper Sunflower River, Faison had instigated much of the development that came on the heels of the Civil War, when immigrants wandered in from every direction. As railroads opened the country and the lumber industry prospered, Faison was there to play a leading role in the incipient local government.[9] Now the ambitious Virginian was the most successful planter of Sunflower County, as well as its largest taxpayer, with 3,500 acres under cultivation, 2,500 undeveloped, dry goods stores thriving at several landings, and his own line of river packets yet to come.[10]

In the vast, virginal Yazoo-Mississippi Delta, no enterprising man with cash in his pocket or good credit to his name contented himself with a single livelihood. Planters were lawyers, doctors, legislators, and investors in steamships and railroads. Merchants were cotton factors, bankers, sheriffs and postmasters. Some merchants were planters, too. Farmers were justices of the peace, deputy sheriffs, members of the Board of Supervisors, court clerks and bailiffs.[11]

When George F. Ring decided to leave Vicksburg and make his permanent home in the Delta—it must have been late 1880 or early 1881,[12] though he may have repaired to Saints Rest as a refuge during the terrible yellow fever epidemic of 1878—he continued to follow the example of George W. Faison: he became involved in public affairs. The annals of Sunflower County show that George readily assumed the civic responsibilities incumbent upon a resident of his stature. He sat on the grand jury in 1879 and 1880.[13] In January 1882, when Saints Rest was designated a mail stop by the U.S. Postal Service, George became its first postmaster.[14] That fall he was appointed along with George W. Faison to the Board of Commissioners to supervise the construction of the courthouse.[15]

Faison and a neighbor donated a suitable acre on the south bank of Indian Bayou, and the building that went up was built entirely of well-seasoned cypress.[16] Two-stories, weatherboarded, ceilinged, shingled, and whitewashed all around, it bore an honest, home-spun aspect, not unlike George's store before the devastating fire. Only the courthouse was smaller—"thirty-six by forty-eight feet in the clear"—and bannistered porticoes graced its entrances on the north and south.[17]

Within two years a jail was erected nearby—brick, with steel-clad cells[18]—and the name of the community that aggregated around the county seat was changed from Indian Bayou to Indianola.[19] In 1883 George was appointed to the Equalization Board,[20] and in 1888 he was a member of the county's Board of Health.[21] Eighteen-ninety-one found George once again serving on the Grand Jury,[22] and three years later, in a letter published in the *Sunflower Tocsin*, the naturalized citizen—despite having spent a lifetime of almost perpetual litigation—lashed out against not only the courthouse in Indianola, but the American jury system itself:

> Editor Tocsin:
>
> If observations of a disinterested party at court in Indianola last week are [of] interest to anyone, I will state that being called to court as a witness for a defendant, and after four days sitting on a straight-back bench made of cypress strips, in what I considered a most uncomfortable and no doubt the poorest excuse for a court house in this State, if not in the United States, I was quietly informed that the plaintiff had no case in court and I wouldn't be needed.

But, sir, while there, almost a prisoner because I could
not leave as there was no one who could tell when the case
would be called, I naturally amused myself by learning what
I could.

I saw and heard many things. Some of them I thought very
funny and others very absurd. But I certainly admired the
patience and even temper of His Honor, Judge Williamson, try-
ing to do justice to all. Now for example, take a small civil case
which occupied the court nearly a whole day. His honor scrutinized the smallest detail in the interest of justice, to turn out
with a hung jury, 11 to 1. That makes me believe the
Vicksburg Herald man is right when he said a slight amend-
ment to the jury law would save thousands of dollars to the taxpayers. As one side of the case must always be wrong, could
not an intelligent people find a way to do justice with more
speed and less expense? I believe they can, if they will try.

Very truly,

Geo. F. Ring[23]

Deed books show that between 1872 and 1900 George was involved
in over 80 land deals in Sunflower County alone.[24] In 1890, where railroad lines cut through a stand of holly trees on a southwest corner of
Saints Rest, he would have a village surveyed and laid out, including a
Ring Street East and a Ring Street West. He would call it Holly Ridge,
and serve as its first mayor.[25] At the opposite end of Saints Rest, to the
northeast, George would have a hand, if not in founding, then at least in
building up, the community of Fairview.[26] But his name appears fre-
quently in the deeds of adjoining counties as well.[27]

"Col. Geo. F. Ring," one short piece in the *Vicksburg Evening Post* of
March 5, 1898, would claim, "owns about 5,000 acres in that section."[28]

His reputation spread, and people who never actually met the stout
man who spoke with a German accent knew him simply as "the
Dutchman."[29] A well-to-do planter like the ones whose wealth had dazzled him in 1858, George realized the dream of success that had urged
him across an ocean. It was the status he had worked aggressively to
attain, the role he had been preparing for all his life. And it suited him
to a tee.

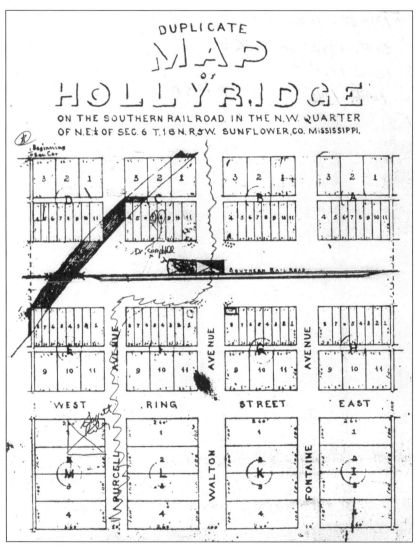

SURVEYOR LAMAR FONTAINE LAID OUT HOLLY RIDGE IN 1890;
THIS IS A CERTIFIED COPY MADE IN 1900 OF HIS ORIGINAL PLAN.
(Courtesy Mr. James C. Robertson, Saints Rest)

Before coming out from Vicksburg, George had sent Frank Jeans on ahead to Saints Rest.[30] The orphan turned 21 in 1880, so he was no longer George's ward.[31] But he would work closely with George for many years, and the two men would remain friends for the rest of their lives.[32] When George brought Catherine to Saints Rest, he moved Jeans to his largest place in Bolivar County.[33] Soon afterwards the railroad reached the place, and a village sprouted there. Called Sunrise at first, then Shawsburgh, then finally Shaw, "B. F. Jeans" was appointed its postmaster.[34] In 1884 he would marry in Greenville an immigrant from Lorraine, France, named Pauline Ring. The bride was undoubtedly a relative of George's.[35]

Missouri Jeans, on the other hand, would never leave Vicksburg. She would wed in the elegant high-ceiled parlor of 700 Adams Street the same year her brother married in the Delta—though she was only 17—thereby transferring to her husband the guardianship that had been George's.[36] Thereafter the youngest Jeans orphan would remain as aloof from George as her brother was close to him. Convinced that her parents had left a large inheritance that George had squandered, Missouri "hated the Rings and anything to do with them."[37]

I can picture George seated in the buggy, Nicholas at his side. The uncle reins the horse northward onto a dusty lane that parallels the western bank of Indian Bayou. In a few minutes he is informing his wide-eyed nephew that they have reached Saints Rest. The place borders the sluggish bayou for a little more than two miles.[38] Two unpainted cypress buildings rise up on the left. The smaller, George explains, is his seed house. The larger is his gin, steam-powered.

It is the beginning of Nicholas's education in "Cotton."

Just beyond the seed house and gin lies a patch of wooden crosses and headboards: the "colored" cemetery.

Then George points to the shop where his mechanics maintain the equipment, and beyond that to his 10 1/2 acre grove of pecan trees. A little farther up the trail, mentor and protégé are riding past a long narrow building on blocks, one story high, built of vertical, unpainted cypress plank, with a peaked roof that runs lengthwise and terminates in a ragged gable over a shallow gallery. This is Saints Rest's commissary. An oak tree pushes up threateningly close to the gallery. It has an

COTTON PLANTATION IN ISSAQUENA COUNTY WITH THE MAIN HOUSE BUILT ON A BAYOU, AS GEORGE'S WAS AT SAINTS REST IN SUNFLOWER COUNTY.
(Courtesy Prints & Photographs Division, Library of Congress)

iron hitching ring in its trunk.

A moment later George gives the reins a tug and the buggy halts in front of the house. If Nicholas expects a classical mansion like the ones he remembers seeing along the Mississippi, with stately columns across the front, he is disappointed. Plantation houses in the Delta—the few built before the war as well as the many that came afterwards— were most likely constructed on the pattern of the plantation houses of Louisiana.[39] So if George's was typical—it is no longer standing, and no picture of it has been found—what Nicholas sees is a perfectly square structure of whitewashed lumber, one-and-a-half stories high, standing on blocks.

The hip roof of cypress shingles swoops down on all four sides to cover the veranda that wraps around the entire house. All of the windows are tall and shuttered and, positioned at regular intervals around the four walls, may be used as doors when raised. Towering ungainly chimneys and squat bedroom dormers poke through the four expansive triangles of roof.

A wide hallway bisects the house and may be entered from either end. A huge dining room occupies one half, a formal parlor the other, and a plain staircase rises to the bedrooms. In the rear a covered walkway leads to the kitchen and wash house. A smoke house and smaller outbuildings dot the yard.

The abode is comfortable, though far more practical than elegant, and it appears much larger than it is because of the wrap-around veranda. Facing east, it looks out on the long wall of willows and cypress, climbing vines and cane, that grow along Indian Bayou. A stand of towering sycamore trees shelters the house from the pounding sun of August and the pelting storms of March. The site was chosen deliberately: this is the highest ground on Saints Rest.

Observing his nephew taking it all in, George must be amused. The young urbanite's face is full of wonder. How could it not remind George of his younger brother on that memorial spring day in 1865 when Joe, together with Barbara and Hank and Lena Weber, riding up Deer Creek, marvelled at all they saw?

Behind the house spread two grazing pastures. One is an acre and a half for George's three horses and 10 mules.[40] The other is 80 acres for

MULE PEN ON A PLANTATION. *(Courtesy Mississippi Department of Archives and History)*

his 15 head of cattle.[41] (The herd is small this year.[42]) George points to the three large unpainted cypress sheds beyond: barns. One holds plows and other equipment and gear, and seven "carriages or other wheeled vehicles."[43] There are also cribs to hold feed corn, and cribs to hold George's 10 swine.[44]

Now, sweeping his arm across the horizon like a general, George indicates the cabins dotting the long dirt lane beyond the pastures. They are all the same, all small, all sitting on identical plots. These are the sharecroppers' quarters, George explains. He has 20 black families on the place.[45]

Beyond the croppers' shanties, on sprawling acres Nicholas cannot see from his seat in the buggy, are the cotton fields. By 1905 the place will include about 1,210 cleared, 258 wooded, 94 slough, and 21 acres of Indian Bayou.[46] A long cypress lake marks the far western boundary of Saints Rest.[47]

The only building still standing today which Nicholas gazed upon in 1881 is nothing more than a shell, weather-worn and dilapidated: the commissary.[48] It was moved the 50-yards-or-so to its present site in the mid-twentieth century, because the mighty oak—whose ivy-clad trunk still bears the old iron hitching ring—had lifted the gallery end of the swaybacked building and it was leaning precariously. Other than this single artifact preserved for sentimental reasons by the current owners of Saints Rest, nothing of George's survives. Not a single weathered and sagging corn crib, not one split and broken fence post. Nothing. Even the old cypress crosses in the Negro burial ground have given way to modest stone monuments.[49] Only the land endures. The land is still plowed and planted every spring. Cotton is still harvested and ginned and baled every fall.

George and Nicholas descend from the buggy and follow the frisky Labrador toward the house. Catherine is standing out on the veranda. Erect and alert, she is swathed in multiple layers of billowing fabric, her arms and head covered, modest and matronly now at 54. She will enjoy good health for many years yet.[50] By the time her husband and his pro-tégé reach the steps, she has already called inside for a tray of tall drinks with ice.

In the fall George will take Nicholas down the Sunflower and Yazoo

THE OLD COMMISSARY ON SAINTS REST, 1999.
(Photograph by Mr. James C. Robertson, Saints Rest)

OAK TREE ON SAINTS REST WITH OLD IRON HITCHING RING IN ITS TRUNK, 1999.
(Photograph by Mr. James C. Robertson, Saints Rest)

Rivers with a copious load of cotton. The uncle will teach his nephew how to judge a crop's two essentials, quality and grade, and bargain for the best sale price in Vicksburg's exchanges. In due time George will delegate to Nicholas full responsibility for selling the crop.

"I think my father took care of the plantation business for his Uncle George," Nicholas's son will write in 1984. "He told me he made trips to New Orleans to sell the cotton crop, which was sent down by river boat."[51]

Introduction to the hardships of the cotton culture will come without delay to the novice. On November 28, 1881—within months of Nicholas's arrival—the *Vicksburg Daily Commercial* will report:

> The steam ginhouse and thirty bales of cotton of Mr. Geo. F. Ring on his plantation in Sunflower county, was burned Friday evening last at four o'clock. Loss on gin and cotton five thousand dollars; insured for two thousand.[52]

That catastrophe will be followed in March of 1882 with the worst flooding in Sunflower County history.[53] For months all of Saints Rest— except for the highest ground along Indian Bayou where the house stands—will lie submerged under standing water.[54]

But the Buffalonian will also be introduced to long nights of feasting and celebration such as he, while under the stern tutelage of the Jesuits, dared not imagine.

"We were right royally entertained by Captain George Ring at his elegant plantation near Fairview last Saturday evening."[55]

Notes similar to this one will appear regularly throughout the 1890s in the county newspaper, the *Sunflower Tocsin*. The "Dutchman" enjoys his comforts, and it pleases him greatly to regale his friends in a grand manner.—Which may explain how he came to be addressed not only as "Captain," but often "Colonel," too![56] It is likely from his Uncle George that Nicholas will learn to appreciate a fine cigar.[57]

The nephew will prove a worthy pupil. Already in 1885 George will bring Frank Jeans back to Saints Rest, and entrust his Bolivar places to Nicholas.[58] Uncle and nephew will get along like brothers, probably because Nicholas is not at all like George. On the contrary, Nicholas has inherited the milder and less aggressive temperament of his father, and

WEIGHING PICKED COTTON IN THE FIELD. (*Courtesy Mississippi Department of Archives and History*)

Joe's affability, too, if not his playfulness.[59] Greater sobriety has been given Nicholas in his mother's blood. He is a soft-spoken man who takes his catechism seriously, a church goer—when there is one to go to, the closest Catholic church to Saints Rest being St. Joseph's in Greenville. Which is where Nicholas will marry in 1892, with his rich planter-uncle standing as witness.[60]

George and Catherine and Nicholas rock comfortably on the gallery, sipping their tall iced drinks. The nephew talks of his mother and brothers in Buffalo. His father has been gone eight years now. "The Rolling Fork tragedy," although never solved, has faded from popular memory here in the Delta. Only rarely does some incident, such as the one reported in the *Greenville Times* on January 19, 1878, recall it to mind:

Robbery on Deer Creek

One of the boldest outrages ever perpetrated in the county occurred at Spingarn's Store on Deer Creek last Saturday night, the 12th. At about 12 o'clock at night the clerk was aroused by a knocking upon the door, and, upon opening it, a gang of negroes rushed in, seized the clerk, and while some of the crowd held him and choked him, others loaded the wagon at the door with flour, meat, sugar, coffee, etc. And the party drove off with the spoil, after coolly informing the terrified clerk that they would pay him another visit as soon as he replenished his stock. Attempts to track the wagon were rendered useless by the muddy condition of the road.[61]

The mystery of Joe Ring's demise, however, is about to be resurrected in dreadful detail.

CHAPTER FORTY

"A DREADFUL MYSTERY"

RESURRECTION OF A DREADFUL MYSTERY.
Two Well Known Citizens Charged With a Horrible
Arson and Murder that Occurred 10 Years Ago.
It was learned from parties, who came down this morning on
the steamer Sunflower, that Geo. Marsh and M.C. O'Neal were
arrested by Deputy Sheriff Judge Powell, of Sharkey county,
upon the affidavit made by said deputy sheriff, charging Marsh
and O'Neal of the murder and burning of the store-house of
Ring & Moore, located at Rolling Fork landing, on Sunflower
river, which took place in 1873, wherein Mr. Jessie Moore and
wife, and Mr. Jayns' little son, together with the clerk, were
burned alive.[1]

The "parties, who came down" with the shocking news—arriving in
Vicksburg before dawn on Monday, August 20, 1883—included George
F. Ring himself.[2] Word of bizarre new developments in the unsolved
"Rolling Fork tragedy" case had evidently reached him at Saints Rest.
So on his next trip downriver, he stopped in Rolling Fork to learn more.
The sheriff of Sharkey County at this time happened to be George's
buddy of 25 years, Johnny Joor.[3]

All that Joor could tell his one-time employer, however, was the
story M. C. O'Neal's wife had related to Deputy Powell. That was all

INVERNESS, A SUNFLOWER COUNTY TOWN, EARLY 1900S. *(from Fevers, Floods and Faith)*

they had, Jane O'Neal's story. The two companions would have discussed the merits of the woman's vehement accusations, scrutinizing details that might reveal their truth or falsity. Though neither George nor Joor had been at the store the night of March 4, 1873, no one was more intimately familiar with the physical arrangement of the building than George, and no one knew better the disposition of the human remains after the fire than Joor. Moreover, the sheriff would have passed along the few facts he had been able to learn about Jane O'Neal's curious personal history. George himself may have recalled seeing the woman in his store.[4]

Joor concluded that there was only one way to make an end of the matter. He told Deputy Powell to bring the men in.

> Mr. O'Neal was arrested and lodged in jail on last Friday, and Mr. Marsh on last Saturday. The two men upon being arrested seemed to be overwhelmed with astonishment, and the public generally known the two gentlemen so long and favorably are awfully surprised, and inclined to believe that they are the victims of a terrible mistake. The investigation was to take place to-day, Monday, at 10 o'clock, at Rolling Fork, where all the evidence will be produced by the prosecution.[5]

George was still there in Rolling Fork when the deputy made the arrests.[6] Then later that Saturday, when the *Sunflower* pulled away from Rolling Fork Landing, George was on board. Consequently, when the steamer pulled into Vicksburg early Monday morning, he and his fellow passengers were able to relate the latest news to the *Vicksburg Daily Herald.*

"Col. W. D. Brown has been engaged for the defense."[7]

George would have known Marsh and O'Neal, at least on sight. He would have encountered them between November of 1872 and February of 1873—if not before—when he was working almost continuously at Rolling Fork Landing to get the new co-partnership of Ring & Co. off the ground. The two rafters had brought their families into the Delta from Alabama about 1870, settling some four miles from the landing. Marsh's wife Harriet and O'Neal's wife Jane were sisters.[8]

The account that ran in the *Vicksburg Daily Herald* on Wednesday, August 22, 1883, made it clear that it was Jane O'Neal who resurrected the wan ghost of "the Rolling Fork tragedy:"

DEAD MEN TELL NO TALES, BUT A LIVE WOMAN DOES.
Revival of the Rolling Fork Horror—A Mystery Buried Ten Years in the Ashes of Impenetrable Darkness Dragged Into the Light—Marsh and O'Neal Accused of Murder By the Wife of the Latter.

A short news article appeared in our local columns yesterday morning, which no doubt startled this community from centre to circumference, and sent the light of many a man's memory backward with the celerity of a flash of lightening through the dim, dismal vista of ten long years, to a cold, rainy night in March, 1873, when the store of George F. Ring & Co., on Rolling Fork, in Sharkey county, was swept away by a horrible conflagration in which perished the lives of five human beings, who were either asleep or murdered.[9]

The newspaper man was not going to let pass this once-in-a-lifetime opportunity to showcase his literary dexterity.

This leap backward of mental vision was caused by the news . . . that Deputy Sheriff Judge Powell, of Sharkey county, had arrested George Marsh and M. C. O'Neal for the arson of Ring's store and the fiendish murder of its sleeping inmates. The arrest of both men created intense interest, both here and in river circles, where they are known, and among the people of Lower Sunflower, Little and Big Deer Creek, and Steele's Bayou, where they are well known and have been for many years, sometimes farming and sometimes engaged in rafting. George Marsh . . . is often in Vicksburg, and is well known to travelers up and down Sunflower river.

The other man, O'Neal, is not known to the writer. . . . The matter of the arrest was a surprise to everybody who knew them, as both seem to bear the reputation of peaceable law-abiding men. . . .[10]

Finally the reporter turned to the "live woman:"

> From Mr. George F. Ring, who was in the city day-before-yesterday, it was learned that the arrests of the two men had been made on the testimony of O'Neal's wife, who divulged that her husband and Marsh, robbed the store and then set fire to it on the night of March 4th, 1873. Mrs. O'Neal, several years ago, it is said, made revelations of a similar horrible character, accusing the same parties of the crime, but she was, on some evidence or other, adjudged a lunatic and locked up in the asylum, from which she has but recently been released. On recovering her liberty, she made the same statements, and their reiteration led to the arrest of the two men as above stated.[11]

(The *Greenville Times* reported it this way: "Mrs. O'Neal was placed in the Lunatic Asylum some years ago and recently released; since which time she has not lived with her husband."[12])

The Vicksburg reporter then summarized the facts of "the horrible tragedy" of March 4, 1873, and closed with this moralistic flourish:

> Whoever were the perpetrators of the foul and fiendish deed, they were hellians in human shape, and it is the ardent wish of every good citizen that their sin may find them out, and that they may be dragged out of the tomb of years and oblivion into the light of a dreadful expiation and retribution.[13]

Having concluded his business in the city, George left Vicksburg later this Wednesday, once again aboard the *Sunflower*, which pulled out promptly at 4 p.m.[14] Reaching Rolling Fork Landing on Friday, he proceeded directly up the creek to Joor's office at "the Point."[15]

It was over, the sheriff told him. The investigation had lasted two days, Monday and Tuesday. The outcome that Joor related to his long-time friend would appear in a final article in the *Vicksburg Daily Herald* of Saturday, August 25, 1883:

THE ROLLING FORK HORROR.
Marsh and O'Neal Tried and Discharged.

. . . When put to the test of a judicial investigation, [Jane O'Neal's] pretty story melted away like snow in the sun. . . .

It appears that a disagreement between O'Neal . . . and his wife, about two years ago, led to a separation and a suit for divorce. The woman told Powell that after she left O'Neal he continued to persecute her, and in order to rid herself of his malevolence, she was compelled to make the disclosures which she did, in which she declared that her husband and his brother-in-law, Marsh had burned Ring's store and murdered Mr. and Mrs. Moore, Willie Jeans, Joe Ring and Goudchat, ten years ago, and that their object was robbery.

Her relation of the affair was that the men had come to O'Neal's house, about four miles from the scene of the tragedy on the night of the occurrence, muddy, bloody and laden with bolts of dry goods. She said she had still some of the goods, which they then brought home in her possession, and showed Mr. Powell a dress which she said was made up from a bolt of calico taken from the burned store. Pursuing her story Mrs. O'Neal told how her husband, while laboring under excitement, had related to her the particulars of the murder and arson.[16]

Now, for the first and only time, the criminal accusations that the estranged wife had been broadcasting to the neighborhood appeared in durable and immutable newsprint for all the world and future generations to read:

According to her account the two men entered the store, which was a two story building, by clambering into one of the upper windows, the fastenings of which had been neglected. They first entered the room occupied by Moore and his wife and dispatched them in their bed, the instrument of death used being a woodsman's ax.[17]

An ax. No one had ever suggested that—not in written sources, at any rate. Not Noah Parker or Johnny Joor, not even Doc Chaney or the sexton J. Q. Arnold—professional men who examined the remains expressly to determine the cause of death—ventured that the weapon might have been an ax.

> The room of Willie Jeans was next entered. The little fellow had been kept awake by the pain of his arm, which he had broken a few days before by a fall from a tree, and pleaded piteously for his life. The crash of the ax through his skull stilled his cries forever. Gouchat, the clerk, was the next victim of the vengeful ax, and the murderers were proceeding down stairs to rob the store, when they heard a door open, and rushing out found that it was Joe Ring, who had been awakened by the noise they made and was running toward the woods for safety. He was pursued and overtaken on the brink of Sunflower river. One death dealing blow from the ax in the hands of O'Neal ended his life, and the two men then threw his body into the river, and returned to the store and completed their work of robbery and arson. This, according to Mrs. O'Neal, accounted for the fact that the remains of Joe Ring were not discovered amid the ruins after the burning when the other bodies were discovered.[18]

That was Jane O'Neal's story. But it did not hold.

> . . . The woman's statements were incoherent and disjointed, and the men succeeded in proving that on the night in question both of them were far away from the scene of the murder.[19]

The newsman then relished the chance to vindicate his tall, rustic river friend:

> To those who knew George Marsh especially, his arrest was a matter of great surprise, for he has borne the reputation with those who knew him of being one of the most harmless, good natured and inoffensive men in existence.[20]

(The *Greenville Times* reported more dispassionately: "O'Neal and Marsh . . . upon preliminary investigation were released."[21])

The outcome probably came as no surprise to George, familiar as he was with Jane O'Neal's history. Perhaps, after 10 years, it did not even matter to him any more how the disaster happened. It is easy to imagine George and his former cabinmate sitting in silence, their eyes fixed on the worn cypress floorboards of the sheriff's office. What more was there to say? Nevertheless, the *Herald* man, with flagrant disregard for the accuracy of his statements, composed a bombastic finale to his florid reportage:

> And so ends in nothingness another alleged clue to one of the darkest and bloodiest mysteries that ever occured to torture the curiosity of mankind. Here was one of the largest country stores in the state, located at one of the most important landing's on Deer Creek [in fact, it was on the Sunflower River], in easy access of some of the most populous plantations in Sharkey county (then Washington) [in fact, it was Issaquena County then], entered, plundered, its sleeping inmates murdered in their beds, and then set on fire and burned to the ground—and not a trace of the perpetrators, after ten long and weary years, yet discovered! It is not known whether any reward was offered at the time it occurred for the detection of those who committed the fearful deed. Addlepate Ames was Governor of the State at the time [in fact, R. C. Powers, the lieutenant governor, held the office at the time, and Adlebert Ames (derisively dubbed "Addlepate") was appointed after the fire], and it is safe to say, on general principles, that he never bestirred himself about the matter or offered a reward for the discovery and arrest of the assassins.
>
> The detective who will work up this case and unravel the dense mystery surrounding the Rolling Fork Horror, is a better one than Allen Pinkerton ever had in his employ, and will rank as the peer of Hawkshaw and the famous Monsieur Lecoq.[22]

Yes, already too much had been said. Too many rumors, too much speculation. The planter and the sheriff would have chatted about things of more immediate consequence.

Tracks were being laid along the high ground of Deer Creek. A line of the Louisiana, New Orleans and Texas Railway was fast approaching Rolling Fork. In just two months, on October 27, 1883, the first train would chug into town.[23] There would be hyperbolic declamations by local politicians, plenty of exhuberant flag-waving, and a band to blast out patriotic marches. As seat of justice and rail stop, the dusty village was destined to grow and thrive. Indeed, plans were already being made to incorporate just as soon as that train arrived.[24]

At last George left his friend and returned to Rolling Fork Landing to catch a north-bound packet. A sizeable pile of debris still marked the site where the enormous store had once loomed against the wilderness.[25] No one resided here any more. Rolling Fork Landing's "heyday" as a post office had lasted only two-and-a-half years, from 1871 to 1873.[26] As soon as the LNO&T began stopping at "the Point," passenger and freight business on the Sunflower River would drop off to nothing. There was no reason for George to rebuild here now. No longer would local residents need to refer to the town as "the Point" to distinguish it from the landing of the same name, because the place five miles down Rolling Fork Creek where the landing once was would no longer have any name at all.

Steaming up the bends of the Sunflower River, George stands out on deck to smoke a cigar, gaze at the familiar landscape, and repuzzle Mrs. O'Neal's story. Even at a distance of 125 years, and lacking the "Execution Docket" of Sheriff Joor—long ago vanished—and minus any other public record of the inquest of August 21–22, 1883, which the Sharkey County Courthouse might have held at one time, it is obvious that Jane O'Neal's testimony was full of holes.

She claimed that Jesse Moore and little Willie Jeans were axed to death in their respective beds. However, the position of their remains in the ruins seemed to indicate that the two of them died, *not* in their rooms, but rather at the door to the office.[27]

She claimed that "the murderers were proceeding down stairs to rob the store, when they heard a door open, and rushing out" saw Joe Ring. But the store was on the same level as the living quarters, *not* "down stairs."[28] And even if Mrs. O'Neal meant to say that the murderers were proceeding downstairs to rob the *warehouse*, both staircases—the wide stairs to the front gallery and the narrow stairs running down the rear

GINNED AND BALED COTTON BEING TRANSPORTED DOWN THE MAIN STREET OF INDIANOLA, PROBABLY TO THE RAILROAD STATION FOR SHIPMENT, 1890s. (*Courtesy Mississippi Department of Archives and History*)

of the building—were *outdoors*.[29] So the murderers would *not* be "rush-ing out," they would already *be* out. Besides, what could they have thought to rob from the warehouse, a few 500-pound bales of cotton? It made no sense.

Mrs. O'Neal claimed that the murderers saw "Joe Ring running toward the woods for safety." The woods were *behind* the store, to the *west*,[30] and indeed Joe could not swim,[31] so this would have been his only overland escape. But then she said that the murderers overtook him "on the brink of Sunflower River," which was in *front* of the store, to the *east*. No one fleeing for his life would have run *west* toward the woods, then veered around and run back *east* toward overflown creeks he could not swim across. Even if Joe had hoped to use as his vehicle of escape the one skiff that was tied up at the landing that night,[32] would he have turned from the potential safety of the woods and raced back into the arms of his pursuers? It just made no sense.

Mrs. O'Neal claimed that "the remains of Joe Ring were not dis-covered amid the ruins." Yet, in fact, Noah Parker's second inquest had found the few charred bones which the jurors agreed were the remains of Joe Ring.[33]

A few charred bones.

Surely that is not what George pictures when he thinks of his broth-er. He would see Joe as he knew him, dark brown hair toussled, gray-blue eyes playful. Perhaps, though, the successful immigrant on his way home is not pondering "A Dreadful Mystery" at all. The business-man is not given to ruminating. More likely, observing the rank upon rank of burst-open cotton bolls filing past the steamer thrills George with anticipation. Wide-brimmed straw hats on hunched shoulders poke out above the plants like a flock of ducks strewn across a sun-scorched marsh. Each day's pick must be weighed and tallied and ginned and baled and transported to market. There is so much to attend to at Saints Rest! There is so much yet to do in the Delta! So much yet to teach Nicholas![34]

GRANDMA RING

Here I am. I step out of the maroon Sundance rented from Alamo and peer up and down the tangle of cypress, willows and sycamores bordering Little Sunflower River. Pivoting, I survey the vast plain that ripples to the western horizon in an endless repetition of long straight furrows. It is a late afternoon in April 1993, and the fiery disk suspended in the sky is low, yet warm. Its oblique rays gild the successive ridges of topsoil, then splatter against the trees and underbrush along the river.

I close my bloodshot eyes and massage them. My fingers are tired. My arms are heavy. I have spent the entire day pouring through dusty, crumbling, worm-eatten packets in the courthouses of Sharkey and Issaquena Counties . . . for the second time. And for the second time I have found no public record of the arrest and interrogation of Dr. Parberry, Uncle Jimmy and the three other suspects in 1873. For the second time I have found no legal evidence of the arrest and interrogation of Marsh and O'Neal ten years later. A lot of the old records, one court clerk has informed me, were discarded when the new courthouse was built.[1]

Opening my eyes, I spy, about a hundred yards downstream, the chain link fence that marks the boundary of the Delta National Forest. From the map I picked up in the office of the Department of

Agriculture in Rolling Fork, I know that the forest includes the southern half of section 29.[2] So the fence confirms that I am standing in the
northeast quarter section George F. Ring purchased from George W.
Faison in 1866.

Glancing upriver I see the enormous equipment shed of corrugated
steel that the gas station attendant in Rolling Fork told me I would see.
Just beyond it sprawls the modern brick rambler he said I would come
to where the asphalt road ends and the dirt lane begins. Both buildings
are vaguely discernible through the gritty brown fog my Sundance has
raised. It hangs in the torpid air like Spanish moss.

I venture a few steps along the turnrow and spy the point where the
Little Sunflower receives Rolling Fork Creek. No current ripples the
water. Scarcely is there a trickle! The system of levees, irrigation canals
and drainage ditches fashioned by the U.S. Army Corps of Engineers
has reduced the Delta's arteries to shallow, near-stagnant brooks. My
imagination is taxed to picture steamboats like the *Lizzie* and the *B. H.
Hurt* and the *Sunflower* paddling up and down *these* waters.

Yet here, right here on this plowed earth my dusty loafers are
crunching now, was the landing where George F. Ring and Willie Jeans
erected their grand enterprise that winter of 1867/68. Through this
place passed thousands of people busily living their lives. I feel the sun
at my back, though it is drooping toward the edge of the world. My
shadow stretches deep into the mass of green and brown vines choking
the riverbank.

I tramp into the underbrush. The banks of the Little Sunflower are
steep and laced with prickly wild blackberry vines. Here, too, lie the
decomposing leaves of 120 autumns, the rotting branches and twigs and
scabs of bark of 120 winters. If I could reach the water I could leap
across it.—And this is springtime, *after* the rain! But the wild growth is
too dense and thorny. I turn around and high-step back to the turnrow.

Not far off I notice a stand of four, maybe five, pecan trees. Obviously
they have not been tended in many years. But they indicate that a grove
was planted here once, which means that somebody's house stood close
by. So I am able to situate more confidently now the precise site where
the huge two-and-a-half-story cypress building loomed up out of the
clearing. I am standing on the spot.

I am here. But there is nothing here. My eyes keep shifting from the pitiful vestige of a once-vital waterway to the expanse of ever-fertile, ever-fecund Delta soil, back and forth, because that is all there is. The landing is gone. The store is gone. The cypress cabins are gone. The hardwood forests are gone. The swamps are gone. The past has not left the tiniest physical trace of the entrepreneurial success George molded here. Even the natural world he knew no longer exists. It is the commonplace of the Ring brothers' story: no tangible remnant of their lives and deeds—other than one up-ended and collapsing commissary building—remains. They might never have been.

I start walking, slowly, with my eyes searching the ground, up and down the furrows. There must be *something* here, *something* to show that one of the largest country stores in the Delta, with an $11,000 stock of merchandise, stood here once. A whitish glint catches my eye. I stoop and pick it out of the dirt. A shard, a chunk of pottery. Part of the lip of a jug?

My pulse quickens.

A few more steps, and here is another one. And another! Lots of tiny potsherds, lodged in the furrows that have been turned over and over for 120 springs. They sparkle in the low late afternoon sunbeams.

I am excited now.

Up and back I pace, my eyes scanning eagerly every square inch of turned earth. I pick up something slender and weighty and hard, about four inches long, covered with dirt. I scrape at it with the car key and thumb it vigorously and cannot believe what I see. An iron spike, caked with rust. One of the "wrought nails" George testified using to build his store![3]

My back tingles with goosebumps.

My gait is faster now, my strides less measured. My eyes dart left and right, left and right. What else lies under these furrows gaping hungrily for cotton seed? How much of the gigantic heap of charred timbers and blackened bricks and burned merchandise lies buried here still?

Something else glitters. I grab it and rub it with my thumbs.—A thick disk of green glass. The bottom of a bottle.—The bottom of a *nineteenth-century* bottle, I know, because the glass is swirled!

I am here! At last. Thirty years of searching have brought me to the

NINETEENTH-CENTURY BOTTLE AND STONEWARE PLATE FOUND IN THE RIVERBED WHERE
ROLLING FORK CREEK EMPTIES INTO THE SUNFLOWER RIVER.
*(Gift to the author from Ron Bussey of Rolling Fork, who has salvaged hundreds of
bottles as well as pottery and china from the site, 1993; photograph by the author)*

ARTIFACTS UNEARTHED BY THE AUTHOR AT THE SITE WHERE THE
RING & CO. STORE STOOD, 1993.
(Photograph by the author)

place of the dreadful family story. How much of Joe Ring—and Jesse, Martha, little Willie and Goudchat—is folded into this fruitful and forgiving patch of earth?

In 1963, when I was a boy, my grandmother came to our house in a suburb of Buffalo. Smoothing out a length of cotton fabric on our dining room table—I think it was a floral print in soft yellows and greens—she told me while she cut out a dress that my great great grandfather had been murdered. And I did not believe her. Since that distant summer afternoon, 30 years of searching in thousands of historical sources have vindicated my youthful skepticism. Grandma was wrong.

Joe Ring was not murdered at all.

Something out of the ordinary certainly did happen, that I never doubted. The fact that Grandma had a tale to tell was evidence enough of that—regardless of how sketchy and garbled it had become over generations of retelling (shifting in time to *before* the Civil War), regardless of how many versions of it had evolved in different branches of the family (at least two). For if there had been nothing extraordinary about Joe's death and Barbara's voyage home, no story would ever have gotten started in the first place. Family lore always contains a kernel of truth. Or it would not be.

Unpuzzling what *really* happened that summer of 1873, and why, *that* was the quest I undertook. I set out to find any document that might help clarify the sketchiness and untangle the garble of Grandma's incredible tale. But to evaluate the documents I found, I had to familiarize myself with the cultural context in which they had been created: the Yazoo-Mississippi Delta during Reconstruction. As I did that, gradually, over three decades, I came to recognize that the oral tradition I had heard in my youth originated in the same context as the written materials I was ferreting out and studying. Grandma's conviction—"It was the darkies!"[4]—simply echoed the earliest conviction of the white residents of the neighborhood: "It is supposed that it was done by a band of armed negroes."[5] The supposition was one and the same, rooted in the unique society of Rolling Fork Landing in the spring of 1873, and consequently reflecting the mindset of that particular place and time.

And it was entirely wrong.

Every one of the 12 theories that circulated after the fire—they are summarized in Chapter 25—can be rebutted. No explanation is unassailable, because they all suffer from the same defect: Joe Ring, Jesse and Martha Moore, little Willie Jeans and Alphonse Goudchat Israel defy classification *as a group*. Only two of them were immigrants, the others were not. One of them was Catholic, three were Protestant, and one was a Jew. Three were men, but one was a woman of 19, and one a boy of 8. Three were from out of state, but the woman and child were native Mississippians. Therefore, any motive targeting a particular group—immigrants, Catholics, Jews, foreigners, Yankees, carpetbaggers or merchants—simply cannot apply to *all five*.

The only thing shared by *all five* was their race: all were Caucasian. And given the vehement emotions rampant in the Delta during the Reconstruction era, *this* was the common ground seized upon by the white populace to explain "the Rolling Fork tragedy." Race alone was deemed sufficient motive. That facile explanation, however, has never been supported by the evidence, not then and not now.

But there is one hypothesis among the 12 that does not *need* a motive, because it postulates no mortal perpetrator: "Act of God!"

It was an accident.

The five victims *did* have something in common besides their race after all: they were there. They just happened to be the ones fate had gathered into the store that night.

The fire was an accident.

That is why the two inquiries, one in 1873 and one in 1883, failed to indict any culprit. There *was* no culprit. Which is precisely the unbearable void that allowed for Chamberlin's conviction that it had to be George himself who did it. Who could prove otherwise?

It happened this way:

When Dr. Parberry and Uncle Jimmy the Irishman knocked on the door of Ring & Co. at about 11 or 12 o'clock, wanting to buy a bottle of whiskey, they found the building dark and the five inhabitants asleep. "They waked him up to get the whiskey," they said, meaning Goudchat.[6] To fetch it for them, the clerk had to light a lamp, likely a kerosene lamp, but maybe a lamp filled with whale oil.[7] He was half-asleep. He was fuzzy-headed. He made his way into the storeroom, retrieved a bottle of whiskey, and handed it over to the veterinarian and his buddy, most likely accepting a silver ten-cent piece in return.[8] Then he shuffled back to his cot in the office.

In his sleepy state, the young clerk neglected to extinguish the lamp, setting it down askew perhaps, or perhaps dropping it altogether. Or maybe the lamp had a hairline crack in it, or a tiny hole. One way or another the kerosene or whale oil seeped out across the floor and started dripping into the warehouse below. "The flooring was double," George explained, "out of inch cypress plank, not tongue and grooved, rough, nailed and spiked down."[9] Five years old, unfinished, unsealed, the cypress planks had dried out and shrunk.[10] Cracks had opened up between them, and just a few feet below those cracks stood several massive bales of cotton.

"When you speak of the destruction of a gin-house by fire," the senator from Washington addressed W. D. Brown in 1876, "let me ask you, in the first place, if a single match is applied to a gin-house is there any possibility of saving it?

"There is no possibility, sir. If it is seed-cotton, and you merely apply a match, if you have an adequate supply of water to apply to the fire instantly, you might save it; but if it is lint-cotton, it just burns instantly, like powder almost." [11]

The cotton stored in the Ring & Co. warehouse was ginned and baled. That is, it was *lint* cotton.

"Is there any possibility of saving a gin-house that is fired?

"But very little possibility.

"In these isolated houses, do the people have any means of extinguishing a conflagration when it is once started?

"We have nothing to depend upon. That mode of revenge is regarded as the surest."[12]

But if the five inmates were not already dead when the inferno erupted, why did none of them escape?

Smoke.

Smoke would have spread very quickly throughout the living quarters. "Inside of second story were 84 feet of partitions eleven feet high, of rough one-and-a-half-inch plank, cutting off six rooms," George said. "Also 80 feet of partition fourteen feet long, rough plank upright, separating the storeroom."[13] So much unfinished, unsealed cypress planking! The flooring, the walls, the doors, all were full of long slits between the boards. Very quickly the slumbering inhabitants were overcome by smoke.

But all five were not overcome at once. "[A]ll the bodies were found after the fire where they would have slept, except Jesse Moore's and Willie Jeans's," Joor reported. "Both appeared to lie where the door was leading into Goudchat's office."[14] The generally-held deduction, expressed by one newspaper reporter, was: "They must have heard the assassins in the office dispatching Mr. Goudchat."[15]

Indeed, Moore and little Willie were drawn to the office by Goudchat's cries. But maybe Joe's cries, too. Because Joe would have been there with the young Jewish clerk. Joe would have been sleeping on the second cot in the office, which was available because Johnny Joor happened to be away from the store that night. Furthermore, it was here, on this second cot in the office, that Joe customarily slept whenever he stayed at the store, and "all the bodies were found . . . where they *would have slept.*"

Only Goudchat and Joe were not shouting because assassins were "dispatching" them. They were shouting to warn the others of the fire. Or perhaps Moore and little Willie did not hear any cries at all, but simply headed straight for the origin of the smoke. Either way, it was not *entering* the office that they were struck down. They were *leaving* it.

Having found Goudchat and Joe already unconscious, maybe already wrapped in flames, the ambitious Pennsylvanian and the Delta orphan, choking and coughing, eyes stinging and tearing, were struggling to exit the office, struggling to get back to Martha and wake her and get out of the building, when they, too, succumbed to the thickening smoke.

Likely the spry lad reached the office first, since Moore had been immobilized for three-and-a-half weeks by "rheumatism." Indeed, little Willie may already have passed out by the time his weak and ailing foster-father got there. It may well have been Moore's attempt to save the boy, to carry the boy away from the smoke and the blaze, that distracted him, detained him, from returning to his bed to rouse his wife and flee.

"Death by violence" was the verdict returned by Noah Parker's jury of inquest.[16] "The skull of the one we took for Moore's appeared to have a scar as if a lick had mashed in one side of the skull," Joor said.[17] "Goudchat's head was very nearly severed from his body," George reported.[18] However, such mutilations could easily have resulted from a falling beam, a collapsing door post or lintel, bricks hurtling down. . . . The enormous two-and-a-half-story, 53-by-58-foot, all-cypress building was crumbling in flames upon the corpses. No "death-dealing blow from the vengeful ax"[19] (as one newsman dramatized it) was needed to gash Moore's skull or decapitate Goudchat. Or reduce Joe Ring to "only a few bones."[20]

"The body of Joseph Ring was not found right away," Noah Parker wrote, "as the large brick chimney had fallen in the direction where his bed had stood."[21]

Originating in the office off the storeroom, or perhaps in the storeroom itself, the fire ate rapidly into the rest of the building, reaching the five-foot-square double chimney of unorthodox construction that stood roughly in the middle. Therefore, when the "frame"[22] on which the brick chimney rested gave way, it gave way on the side where the fire was, the side toward the storeroom and office, causing the huge tower of bricks to come tumbling down in the direction of Joe's bed. Then, as the conflagration grew and intensified, the pile of bricks glowed red-hot and reduced Joe's body to far fewer remains than the charred bodies of the four other unfortunates.

"Oh, it was terrible!"

Grandma Ring reacted just as Joe Ring's contemporaries did, just as I myself still do. Only Grandma never knew, as I know now, how truly terrible it was. Grandma had never heard of the younger brother George, and the horrible accusations leveled against him—and Joe, too—following the calamity. She could not have imagined the anguish that the Rings suffered, and the disrepute brought upon their name, by criminal accusations that were absurd.

Had "George F. Ring, and his brother Joseph Ring, . . . faudulently burned and destroyed [the store] by fire," as William Chamberlin insisted,[23] to collect the insurance money, they could easily have devised any number of strategies to accomplish that end *without* slaughtering the entire household. They certainly knew where the cash was kept, and

who lived in the building, and where they slept. No evidence supports the contention that George or Joe had their friends and partners butchered. What is more, quite simply, they had no need.

As his store burned and his business family expired, George was at home in Vicksburg, sleeping beside Catherine.

And Joe? The allegation that Joe did not perish in the fire contradicts his character and personality. For he never did resurface, never did rejoin his wife and sons, and *this* the contented family man most assuredly would have done, had he survived. Moreover, there were the bones discovered in the ruins by Noah Parker's second jury of inquest.

Is it not possible, though, that the bones were not the remains of a human at all, but those of a dog, or maybe a cat? No. The intensity of the inferno would have reduced the skeleton of a dog or cat to ashes. Only the larger bones of someone the size of an adult person—the pelvis and femurs, probably, or skull or jawbone—could have survived the total destruction of the Ring & Co. building.[24]

It *was* terrible!

Grandma Ring was right about that, at least, though she had no idea how many coincidences had coalesced to make Joe's death a *real* tragedy. For Joe could have escaped dying that night; he could have left the landing on the *Bluella*.

"Joseph Ring," wrote Noah Parker, "was seen there at 10 o'clock, for the purpose of taking a boat for Vicksburg."[25] Indeed, the *B. H. Hurt* was advertised to leave Rolling Fork Landing for Vicksburg every Tuesday morning at 10 o'clock. But she failed to show up that March 4th.[26] Lucy Coker last saw Joe "standing on the gallery of the store about 9 o'clock of the night, talking to Mr. Moore. . . . Captain John King of the steamer *Bluella* left then with his boat, about 9 o'clock, and saw him when leaving."[27]

The sternwheeler *Bluella* arrived in Vicksburg a day-and-a-half later on Thursday morning, March 6th, "from Steel's Bayou . . . with 86 bales of cotton."[28] This means that after leaving Rolling Fork Landing, Captain King must have proceeded directly up Rolling Fork Creek to Deer Creek, down Deer Creek to Steele Bayou, down Steele Bayou to the Yazoo, to the Mississippi, to Vicksburg. Otherwise, he could not have gotten there in a day and a half. The *Bluella* pulled out again on Tuesday morning, March 11th, "for Deer Creek."[29]

In other words, King normally navigated Steele Bayou and Deer Creek, *not* the Sunflower River. Only two packets offered scheduled service up the Sunflower, the *Lizzie* and the *B. H. Hurt.*[30] Other steamers, such as the *Blanche*[31] and, evidently, King's *Bluella*, plied the Sunflower only occasionally as business warranted. It would have been rare, therefore, for Captain King to call at Rolling Fork Landing. So why did Joe Ring, wanting to go home and ready to leave, not seize this lucky chance and take the *Bluella*?

Perhaps King simply could not accommodate any more freight, and Joe, returning from business trips, would have had cotton. Eighty-six bales may have been the maximum trip for a small packet in the local trade, such as the *Bluella*.[32] Lingering out on the gallery of the store with Jesse Moore, Joe would have had no choice but to say "So long!" to John King, watch the *Bluella* pull away, and continue waiting for the late-running *B. H. Hurt.*

At that decisive moment, Barbara was in her new house on The Vicksburg Place, slumbering, she and her boys, peacefully.

In 1966, three years after I first questioned Grandma Ring about my ancestors, the two of us stood side-by-side in the shade, gazing at the headstone on Barbara's grave.

"I met her once," Grandma said. "It was 1912. Ha! When I think of it. 1912!"

Grandma had been a young bride in that long-ago year, and Grandpa had taken her to meet his grandmother. Barbara was 72 at the time.

"She was a big woman in her later years," Grandma recalled as we contemplated the lichen-laced monument, "pleasant and easy going."[33]

Pleasant and easy-going. Once again, Grandma's simple words left me nonplused. Wouldn't my great great grandmother have been a bitter woman, an angry woman? But now I realize, Barbara managed to carry on by accepting the sudden demise of her husband as the unfathomable will of God—just like the tragic drowning of little Peter Paul—*not* the wanton act of murderers. She believed it was an accident, a catastrophic fire. Which was a natural misfortune not at all unlike riverboat disasters, and far from unusual in the world of the bricklayer's daughter.

And Barbara was right.

GEORGE JOHN RING (SON OF GEORGE F. RING, JR.) AND FRANCES JOSEPHINE NOETH,
THE AUTHOR'S GRANDPARENTS, SEATED IN FRONT OF THE TWO WITNESSES
ON THEIR WEDDING DAY, BUFFALO, AUGUST 21, 1912.
(Photograph from the author's collection)

Now here I stand, right on the spot where Joe Ring drew his final breath on the night of March 4, 1873. I examine the contents of my soiled hands. A few shards of cheap everyday pottery. A rusty spike. The swirled bottom of a green glass bottle. Meager harvest of three decades of gathering!

My tired eyes look up. The disk has turned to orange and touched the earth and lost its fire. Dusk is spreading across the rippled fields that never end. I walk to the still-open door of the Sundance, which looks brown now, and lay my archaeological treasures on the passenger seat.

One last look: the tangled wall of black vegetation hugging the river, the ground, this dry, crumbly, readied ground, where they died, three men, a woman and a boy, that terrible night. Finally I have heard the shrieks. Finally I have seen the human forms rushing about in search of survival. But it was not murder. And in that I take solace. Possessed for a major portion of my life by "the Rolling Fork tragedy," I now accept the truth with relief and gratitude. Indeed, my 30 years of tormented toiling in the fields has yielded much more than the handful of artifacts on the passenger seat. The obsession is satisfied.

Heavily I fall into the driver's seat, pull the door, turn on the ignition, the headlights, and negotiate a dusty about-face in the turnrow. The small car jostles along the dirt path, slowly, through the abject blackness of the Delta. Looking up through the windshield I see a billion distant burning white jewels. The vast sky is aflame!

Reaching the paved road, I click on the high beams and press down on the accelerator. The level blacktop unravels endlessly before my blood-shot eyes. I glance in the rearview mirror. Nothing. The place where Rolling Fork Landing once was has long since disappeared. Yet I can see it, as though I were standing there, right in front of the monstrous funeral pyre, amid the fierce heat and smoke and roar, blackness all around and drizzle dribbling down the back of my neck. I can see it still.

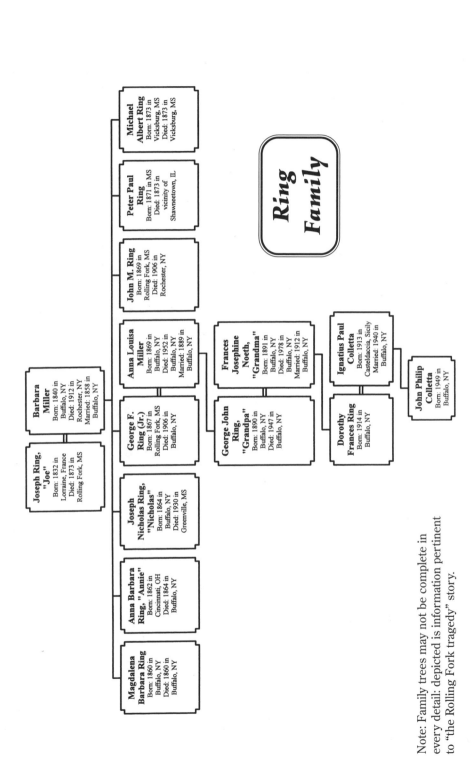

Ring Family

Joseph Ring, "Joe"
Born: 1832 in Lorraine, France
Died: 1873 in Rolling Fork, MS

Barbara Miller
Born: 1840 in Buffalo, NY
Died: 1912 in Rochester, NY
Married: 1858 in Buffalo, NY

Magdalena Barbara Ring
Born: 1860 in Buffalo, NY
Died: 1860 in Buffalo, NY

Anna Barbara Ring, "Annie"
Born: 1862 in Cincinnati, OH
Died: 1864 in Buffalo, NY

Joseph Nicholas Ring, "Nicholas"
Born: 1864 in Buffalo, NY
Died: 1930 in Greenville, MS

George F. Ring (Jr.)
Born: 1867 in Rolling Fork, MS
Died: 1906 in Buffalo, NY

Anna Louisa Miller
Born: 1869 in Buffalo, NY
Died: 1952 in Buffalo, NY
Married: 1889 in Buffalo, NY

John M. Ring
Born: 1869 in Rolling Fork, MS
Died: 1906 in Rochester, NY

Peter Paul Ring
Born: 1871 in MS
Died: 1873 in vicinity of Shawneetown, IL

Michael Albert Ring
Born: 1873 in Vicksburg, MS
Died: 1873 in Vicksburg, MS

George John Ring, "Grandpa"
Born: 1890 in Buffalo, NY
Died: 1947 in Buffalo, NY

Frances Josephine Noeth, "Grandma"
Born: 1891 in Buffalo, NY
Died: 1978 in Buffalo, NY
Married: 1912 in Buffalo, NY

Dorothy Frances Ring
Born: 1914 in Buffalo, NY

Ignatius Paul Colletta
Born: 1913 in Casteldaccia, Sicily
Married: 1940 in Buffalo, NY

John Philip Colletta
Born: 1949 in Buffalo, NY

Note: Family trees may not be complete in every detail: depicted is information pertinent to "the Rolling Fork tragedy" story.

Morris Family

Jacob Morris
Born: 1815 in Belgium
Died: 1866 in Vicksburg, MS
Married: 1849 in Vicksburg, MS

Catherine Hill
Born: 1828 in Ohmes, Hesse
Died: 1912 in Vicksburg, MS

George F. Ring
Born: 1834 in Lorraine, France
Died: 1902 in Vicksburg, MS
Married: 1868 in Vicksburg, MS

Herman Leppich
Born: 1845 in Germany
Died: 1881 in ?
Married: 1871 in ?

Elizabeth Morris, "Lizzie"
Born: 1852 in Vicksburg, MS
Died: 1923 in Vicksburg, MS

Richard C. Hallgren
Born: 1848 in Sweden
Died: 1889 in Vicksburg, MS
Married: 1887 in Vicksburg, MS?

Jacob Morris
Born: 1855 in Vicksburg, MS
Died: 1859 in Vicksburg, MS

Phillip Morris
Born: 1857 in Vicksburg, MS
Died: 1858 in Vicksburg, MS

William Morris
Born: 1859 in Vicksburg, MS
Died: 1859 in Vicksburg, MS

George Morris
Born: 1860 in Vicksburg, MS
Died: 1866 in Vicksburg, MS

Male Child Morris
Born: 1866 in Vicksburg, MS
Died: 1866 in Vicksburg, MS

Weber Family

Henry Nicholas Weber, "Hank"
Born: 1842 in Buffalo, NY
Died: 1903 in Buffalo, NY

Mary Magdalena Miller, "Lena"
Born: 1842 in Buffalo, NY
Died: 1919 in Buffalo, NY
Married: Abt. 1862 in ?

Edward Joseph Weber
Born: 1863 in Cincinnati, OH
Died: 1919 in Buffalo, NY

Helena Weber
Born: 1867 in Buffalo, NY
Died: 1871 in Cincinnati, OH

Theresa Elizabeth Weber, "Libbie"
Born: 1870 in Cincinnati, OH
Died: 1963 in Los Angeles, CA

George Hilberg
Married: 1888 in Cincinnati, OH

Mary Magdalena Weber
Born: 1874 in Vicksburg, MS

Matilda Weber
Born: 1878 in Cincinnati, OH

Henry Weber
Born: 1881 in Cincinnati, OH

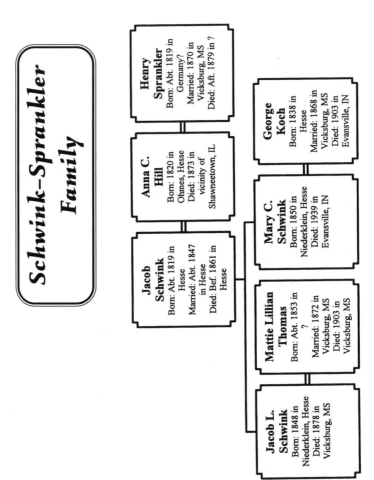

Schwink–Sprankler Family

Henry Sprankler
Born: Abt. 1819 in Germany?
Married: 1870 in Vicksburg, MS
Died: Aft. 1879 in ?

Anna C. Hill
Born: 1820 in Ohmes, Hesse
Died: 1873 in vicinity of Shawneetown, IL

Jacob Schwink
Born: Abt. 1819 in Hesse
Married: Abt. 1847 in Hesse
Died: Bef. 1861 in Hesse

George Koch
Born: 1838 in Hesse
Married: 1868 in Vicksburg, MS
Died: 1903 in Evansville, IN

Mary C. Schwink
Born: 1850 in Niederklein, Hesse
Died: 1939 in Evansville, IN

Mattie Lillian Thomas
Born: Abt. 1853 in ?
Married: 1872 in Vicksburg, MS
Died: 1903 in Vicksburg, MS

Jacob L. Schwink
Born: 1848 in Niederklein, Hesse
Died: 1878 in Vicksburg, MS

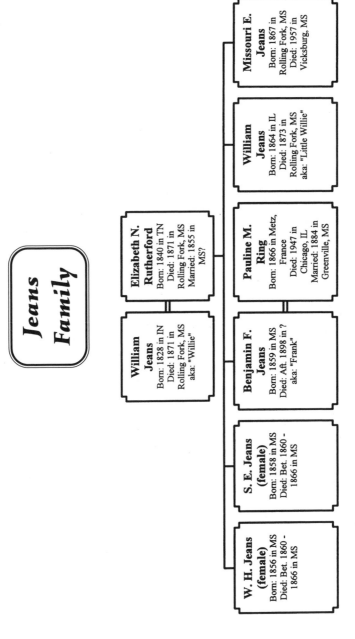

Jeans Family

William Jeans
Born: 1828 in IN
Died: 1871 in
Rolling Fork, MS
aka: "Willie"

Elizabeth N. Rutherford
Born: 1840 in TN
Died: 1871 in
Rolling Fork, MS
Married: 1855 in MS?

W. H. Jeans (female)
Born: 1856 in MS
Died: Bet. 1860 - 1866 in MS

S. E. Jeans (female)
Born: 1858 in MS
Died: Bet. 1860 - 1866 in MS

Benjamin F. Jeans
Born: 1859 in MS
Died: Aft. 1898 in ?
aka: "Frank"

Pauline M. Ring
Born: 1866 in Metz, France
Died: 1947 in Chicago, IL
Married: 1884 in Greenville, MS

William Jeans
Born: 1864 in IL
Died: 1873 in
Rolling Fork, MS
aka: "Little Willie"

Missouri E. Jeans
Born: 1867 in
Rolling Fork, MS
Died: 1957 in
Vicksburg, MS

Mott–O'Neal–Marsh Family

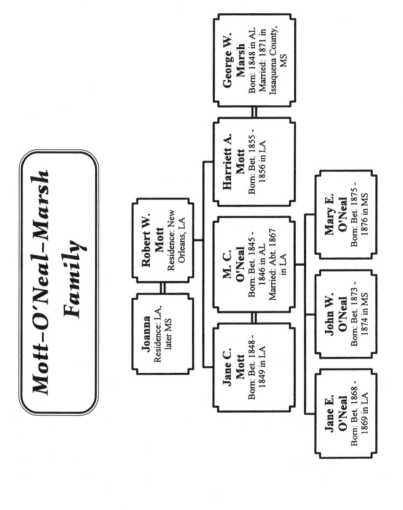

Robert W. Mott
Residence: New Orleans, LA

Joanna
Residence: LA, later MS

Harriett A. Mott
Born: Bet. 1855 - 1856 in LA

George W. Marsh
Born: 1848 in AL
Married: 1871 in Issaquena County, MS

M. C. O'Neal
Born: Bet. 1845 - 1846 in AL
Married: Abt. 1867 in LA

Jane C. Mott
Born: Bet. 1848 - 1849 in LA

Mary E. O'Neal
Born: Bet. 1875 - 1876 in MS

John W. O'Neal
Born: Bet. 1873 - 1874 in MS

Jane E. O'Neal
Born: Bet. 1868 - 1869 in LA

ACKNOWLEDGMENTS

What you see—a sweetly-blossoming lilac bush—would not exist if it were not for the extensive root system hidden underground. The plant derives its constitution and its shape from a complex mixture of ever-changing elements and influences from soil and air, sun and rain. So it is with a book such as this. The text you read is the final synthesis, the ultimate flowering, of a network of research that would itself fill another two or three comparable volumes, were it to be exposed to view. Unseen are the many hunches and hypotheses that were explored, but resulted in no relevant information; the far-reaching investigations that were conducted simply to understand the full significance of the discoveries that proved pertinent; the chain of drafts that were written and rewritten to assemble the multifarious materials into a single logical and comprehensible whole. *Only a Few Bones* owes its composition and its form to the contributions made over three decades by more people in more places than I could possibly thank—even remember—by name. Perhaps the surest way to acknowledge those individuals who helped most substantially is geographically, North and South. First, however, I wish to remember those who, sadly, have not lived to see the mature plant they helped to nourish.

GARDENERS WHOSE WORK IS DONE

My grandmother, Frances Noeth Ring, instigated the whole thing by firing my imagination with her stories. Ever willing to share, she responded patiently throughout the 1960s and 1970s to my incessant questions about her deceased husband's people, about what life was like when she was young in turn-of-the-century Buffalo. Many of the family photographs reproduced in this book were given to me by Grandma Ring.

Then in 1985, through correspondence, I had the good fortune to meet a southern gentleman "of the old school," an avid genealogist and local historian and former president of the Washington County Historical Society, Joseph T. Reilly. Joe was 76 at the time, still residing with his elder sister Katherine in the house on Main Street in Greenville in which they had been born. (Katherine, now 96, resides there still.) Intense and serious in his research, but quick to relate an amusing historical anecdote, Joe took a personal interest in my research, as the Reillys and the Rings had been neighbors and friends since his and Katherine's parents' day. Joe placed at my service his intimate knowledge of old Greenville, tapped into his wide circle of acquaintances on my behalf, and performed a good amount of legwork for me over the following 14 years.

Joe Reilly put me in touch with Louis Caffall Ring. Caffall (as he was known to family and friends) was a distant cousin of mine, 79 years old then, and living in Germantown, Tennessee. Fascinated to learn things about his father's family he had never heard before, he invited me to visit with him at this daughter's house in Greenville, saying he would show me the Delta, "God's country." Which he did in the spring of 1986. Our excursion through the world of his boyhood—Washington, Sharkey, Sunflower and Bolivar counties—constituted my proper and eye-opening introduction to the Delta. Easy-going, articulate, keen and cheerful, Caffall drove at a leisurely pace from one site to the next, reminiscing aloud. It is a cherished memory of mine.

It was on that same trip that I first heard about Joseph N. Kellas. I was in the library of the Old Court House Museum in Vicksburg, when a long-time employee there happened to walk by as I mentioned the surname "Ring." She stopped and said a man in West Seneca, New York, was also researching the Rings. In a moment she was on the telephone with the local genealogist employed by the man, and through this connection I met Joe Kellas—who turned out to be another distant cousin. Sixty-three years old, a detective to the core, with limitless patience and unflagging determination, Joe reveled in the web of family connections he uncovered in the old records of his native Buffalo. His discoveries far exceeded the information I had assembled as a boy, and over the following 13 years his help with portions of this book dealing with our mutual ancestors—especially the Millers and the Webers—was invaluable. The tie between us blossomed from kinship to friendship.

As my efforts expanded, I called upon Ruth Land Hatten for assistance. Ruth, an outstanding genealogist and author, was living at the time in Vicksburg, though later she moved to Jackson. Gracious in manner and perspicacious in research analysis—and always great fun—Ruth pursued between 1992 and 1999 many leads for me in Mississippi records. Though some of the paths she traveled turned into dead ends, even that exploration was essential if "our" final product was to be thoroughly researched.

Grandma Ring, Joe Reilly, Caffall Ring, Joe Kellas and Ruth Hatten are all deceased now. How much their knowledge and skills and eagerness to help contributed to this book. How much knowing them enhanced my life!

NORTH

Over the past 30 years I have never stopped turning to my mother, Dorothy Ring Colletta, to talk about relatives she knew as a girl growing up in Buffalo in the 1920s. She has always shared with me forthrightly and thoughtfully whatever she could recall of family customs and practices, nor has she ever declined to make a phonecall on my behalf, or go tramping downtown to search in Buffalo's repositories for information I sought. Without Mom's full support and active assistance, this book would be much less than it is.

Much of the information about Buffalo that appears in *Only a Few Bones* was learned when I was a young man, with the assistance of pastors, secretaries, librarians, archivists and court clerks who must, unfortunately, remain nameless here. For research in Cincinnati, I benefited from the help of Adele Blanton, an experienced researcher. During the final editing of the manuscript, Ellie Tritchler, a professional genealogist of Buffalo, made last-minute searches, double-checked facts, and supplied missing bibliographic data. I thank them all.

SOUTH

From the very start, I was welcomed warmly by Deltans who took this ignorant yet eager-to-learn Yankee under their wing. It was Joe Reilly who introduced me to Clinton I. Bagley, a fellow native of Greenville (and a member of my own generation). Architectural historian, librarian, archivist and Mississippi riverboat lecturer, Clint is an engaging expert on the life and lore of old Mississippi. He has never been shy about entertaining me, shocking me, and enlightening me, with the many juicy tales he knows about his state's old families. Clint provided pithy insights regarding Delta folk and Delta ways.

In short order Clinton Bagley introduced me to two friends of his, native sisters of Rolling Fork and life-long genealogists and local historians, Alice Clements Wade and Katherine Clements Branton. Alice and Kat have authored several volumes of abstracted public records pertaining to Washington, Sharkey, Issaquena, Sunflower and Bolivar counties. They opened to me their hearts, their homes, and their fathomless knowledge of the Delta, past and present. Never hesitant to go digging into the dank and dusty corners of courthouses, and dirty their hands with crumbling and cumbersome old tomes, Alice and Kat have fun-loving dispositions that turn grueling labor into an exciting treasure hunt. Our friendship has deepened beyond this book.

While Alice and Kat instructed me in the Delta, Eudora Hill, the genealogist whom Joe Kellas had employed, conducted substantial searches for me in Vicksburg records, particularly land deeds and probate files. The many hours she spent doggedly finding and photocopying documents provided me with a clear perspective on old Vicksburg's populace and industry.

Many others lent a hand. Anne Lipscomb Webster, head librarian at the Mississippi Department of Archives and History in Jackson—composed and methodical—and Mary Lois Ragland, genealogist in Vicksburg—snappy and energetic—searched many a record and wrote many a report to me. Their assistance never ended where professional requirements ended; rather, as native-born Mississippians, Anne and Mary Lois cheerfully offered valuable observations regarding our findings or lack of findings, along with insightful suggestions for further research. By this time it was the 1990s, and historical investigation had been facilitated by computers and e-mail.

Correspondence both electronic and old-fashioned with Linda Kious in Ocean Springs, Mississippi, a descendant of Johann Hill, elder brother of Catherine Morris Ring and Anna Schwink Sprankler, provided the Hessian origins of that family. Linda has been enthusiastic and generous in sharing information about her grandmother's temperament and activities in Sunflower County. Through Mary Lois Ragland I met John Davis of Bellevue, Nebraska, descendant of a brother of William Jeans. Mr. Davis furnished a variety of materials about the Jeans family that enhanced the saga of the Ring brothers with some important and fascinating detail.

In 1992 Dennis Kirchner of Union County, Kentucky, a young man much enamored of local history, escorted me to key sites associated with the sinking of the *Jennie Howell* and burial of Anna Sprankler. The following spring, Ben Lamensdorf, a planter of Cary, Mississippi, helped me locate and explore the site where the Ring & Co. store once stood. That same year Ron Bussey, a resident of Rolling Fork, showed me the collection of several hundred clear, cobalt and amber bottles he had retrieved from the riverbed where Rolling Fork Creek flows into the Sunflower River. Before I left his house, Ron had insisted that I take with me a bottle and an oval plate which may have come from the doomed Ring & Co. store or one of the many steamers that called at Rolling Fork Landing.

James C. Robertson, who owned Saints Rest until he retired and passed the business on to the next generation, escorted me around the plantation in 1994 and again in 1999. Mr. Robertson's love of the place clearly matches that once felt by George F. Ring. In Vicksburg, Evelyn C. White, secretary at St. Paul's R. C. Church, and Ann Gerache, secretary at Anshe Chesed Congregation, both responded beyond the call of duty to my requests for information from their record books.

READERS

I am indebted to 10 people for reading the manuscript and offering criticism and advice for improving it. John Willis, professor of history at the University of the South in Sewanee, Tennessee, is a Deltan by birth who wrote his doctoral dissertation on the economy of the Delta between 1865 and 1920. In 1990 John read and critiqued an early version of my chapters dealing with the Delta. His explanations helped me make them more accurate. Robert Connelly, a brilliant "idea man" and art director in the advertising industry, was honest enough and friend enough to tell me in 1991 that the opening chapters of my initial draft were lifeless and boring. The essential of good story-telling, Robert reminded me, is to entertain. Those pages were scrapped, and I opened the next draft—as Robert suggested—with the book's central incident, the fire. Three years later, Alice Wade and Katherine Branton read and commented on this book in what would be its longest and most novelistic version.

It was Craig W. Gill, senior editor, University Press of Mississippi, who convinced me of the wisdom of cutting the length of the work by 50 percent, rearranging several chapters to iron out the time line of the narrative, and paring back the fictional elaboration of scenes to root the work more solidly in non-fictional ground. This latest version was then read in its entirety and critiqued by Helen Hinchliff, a certified genealogist and Ph.D. with many admirable articles to her credit; Elsie Freeman Finch, former archivist at the National Archives in Washington, D.C., a dynamo of ideas and energy and erudition, who continues to edit books and advise on projects dealing with American history and archivism; Gordon Cotton, director of the Old Court House Museum-Eva W. Davis Memorial—a bearded, soft-hearted ol' country boy and beloved raconteur—who has been writing a local history column in Vicksburg's newspaper for many years, besides producing many volumes on the region's history; and Regina Hines Ellison, genealogist and newspaper columnist and long-time resident of Mississippi. Each reader brought to the editing process a different point of view, different skills and knowledge, and together their recommendations helped me produce a work I could never have produced by myself.

Throughout the editing and rewriting of the last few years, the astute and carefully-reasoned observations of Terrence E. Barr, Physician Assistant, allowed me to reach the satisfying conclusion that had been eluding me for so many years. At last, the quest was over. In addition, Terry's liberal assistance with indexing and proofreading sustained me through the final stages of producing this book. For this, and all the rest of Terry's support and encouragement and thoughtful discussion, I am forever grateful.

Finally, the artistic insight and professional skills of Ann Silberlicht transformed the entire text into a physical volume that could not better reflect the spirit of "the Rolling Fork tragedy." Brava, Ann!

What we see—the lilac in fragrant bloom—looks right, as though it could look, should look, no other way. If *Only a Few Bones* seems to read right, I must admit that it could have grown in many another shape, and well might have, and perhaps even should have. I alone know what my initial grandiose vision was, and how far short of it the present volume falls. Therefore, to all those kind individuals who assisted me, those named here and the others, I give my full thanks and deep gratitude, while reserving to myself alone the responsibility for the many flowers this lilac bush lacks.

NOTES

PROLOGUE: MARCH 4, 1873, 11:30 P.M.

1   To establish the social, political, economic, cultural and geographic setting of "the Rolling Fork tragedy," many particular studies have been consulted and these are cited in footnotes where the specific topic enters into the narrative. The historical framework relies primarily on: (1) William C. Harris, *The Day of the Carpetbagger: Republican Reconstruction in Mississippi* (Baton Rouge: Louisiana State University Press, 1979); (2) James Wilford Garner, *Reconstruction in Mississippi* (Baton Rouge: Louisiana State University Press, 1901); and (3) Eric Foner, *Reconstruction 1863–1877: America's Unfinished Revolution* (New York: Harper & Row, 1988). An excellent popular history for an introductory overview of the Yazoo-Mississippi Delta is: Frank E. Smith, *The Yazoo River* (New York: Rinehart & Co., Inc., 1954).

2   Deposition of William Muller, dated May 11, 1881, contained in the packet of *Katharina Ring et al. v. Barbara Ring et al.*, Case 299 (Equity), U.S. Circuit Court, Southern District of Mississippi; Records of District Courts of the United States, 1685–1991, RG 21; National Archives–Southeast Region, East Point, Georgia. Throughout the present work, all direct quotations, both in text and footnotes, are verbatim in every detail, including the nineteenth century's ubiquitous mis-spellings, idiosyncratic punctuation, and erratic capitalization. The editorial "[sic]," therefore, is never used. Furthermore, all dates are ordered "month-day-year" rather than today's standard "day-month-year" because that is how dates appear in all of the historical materials used by the author. For this same reason, the form "March 2nd," for example, or "October 3rd," is used rather than today's "March 2" and "October 3." Dates from European sources, however, are rendered as they appear in those sources: "day-month-year." In telling this nineteenth-century story, the author has endeavored to retain as authentic a nineteenth-century texture as possible.

3   Land deed, Mar. 14, 1871, Warren County Deed Book JJ: 41 (lot 15 of the old Barefield Plantation); Warren County Courthouse, Vicksburg. Also: map attached to agreement signed by Joseph Nicholas Ring, Aug. 12, 1899, to sell part of lot 15 to the United States; U.S. Department of the Interior, National Park Service, Vicksburg National Military Park, Vicksburg (photocopied for the author in 1997). One structure is indicated as a black square on the one road traversing the tract. This is the house.

4   Internet website for the Astronomical Applications Department, U.S. Naval Observatory, Washington, D.C.: http://aa.usno.navy.mil/AA/.

5   "Dead Men Tell No Tales," *Vicksburg Daily Herald*, Aug. 22, 1883: "On the night of Tuesday, March 4, 1873, while the steamer Lizzie . . . was lying at Choctaw land-ing, it being a cold, drizzly, rainey night, flames were seen rising above the cypress tree tops to the west of the river." This article, along with a related article that preceded it on Aug. 21st ("Resurrection of a Dreadful Mystery") and another that followed it on Aug. 25th ("The Rolling Fork Horror") were photocopied from the original newspapers in Vicksburg in 1986. Since then, the originals have disap-peared, and the author could locate no other copies of these issues to secure the precise page numbers for these three sources.

6   *Vicksburg Daily Times*, Mar. 5, 1873, p. 3.

7   George's testimony, contained in the packet of *George F. Ring v. Franklin Fire*

Insurance Co., Case 2573, Circuit Court of Warren County, in the attic of the courthouse in Vicksburg (hereafter "George's testimony, 2573"), p. 1.

8   See Chap. 22, p. 177 and n. 39. The house numbering system in Vicksburg was changed ca. 1890 (see Lee V. Richardson, Jr., and Thomas D. Godman, *In and About Vicksburg* (Vicksburg: The Gibraltar Publishing Co., 1890), 98), so the 1860s, 1870s and 1880s addresses given in this book are different from what they are today.

9   "To the Editor of the Daily Times," *Vicksburg Daily Times*, Mar. 19, 1873, p. 3.

10   Ibid.: ". . . Joseph Ring, who slept there that night, and was seen there at 10 o'clock, for the purpose of taking a boat for Vicksburg." The *B. H. Hurt* left Vicksburg two days late on Sunday evening, Mar. 2, 1873 (*Vicksburg Daily Times*, Mar. 3, 1873, p. 3), and returned almost two full days behind schedule on Friday afternoon, Mar. 7, 1873 (*Vicksburg Daily Times*, Mar. 8, 1873, p. 3). This would have brought the *B. H. Hurt* into Rolling Fork Landing on her return trip on Thursday, Mar. 6, 1873, rather than the usual scheduled time of 10 o'clock on Tuesday morning, Mar. 4, 1873. See Chap. 23, p. 183 and nn. 47 and 48.

1. MARCH 6, 1873

1   "River Intelligence," *Vicksburg Daily Times*, Mar. 7, 1873, p. 3: "Arrived: Tom Jasper, from St. Louis . . . The Tom Jasper passed down yesterday evening. She discharged for Vicksburg, 149 bales hay . . . ." The *Tom Jasper* is entry 5417 in: Frederick Way, Jr., *Way's Packet Directory, 1848–1983: Passenger Steamboats of the Mississippi River System Since the Advent of Photography in Mid-Continent America* (Athens, Ohio: Ohio University Press, 1983), 457.

2   "Geo. F. Ring & Co., Cotton Factors, and General Commission Merchants," advertisement in *The Daily Vicksburger*, 1874, passim: ". . . No. 5, Levee Street, (Near Clay Street,) . . . ." Quoted fully in Chap. 37, p. 274.

3   History and description of Vicksburg rely primarily on: (1) Lee V. Richardson, Jr., and Thomas D. Godman, *In and About Vicksburg* (Vicksburg: The Gibraltar Publishing Co., 1890); (2) H. P. Chapman and J. F. Battaile, *Picturesque Vicksburg and the Yazoo Delta* (Vicksburg: Vicksburg Printing and Publishing Co., 1895); and (3) Peter F. Walker, *Vicksburg, A People at War, 1860–1865* (Chapel Hill: University of North Carolina Press, 1960).

4   See n. 2 above.

5   *Vicksburg Daily Times*, Mar. 7, 1873, p. 3: "The weather was clear and pleasant throughout the day yesterday." It was the fifth day in a row of dry weather.

6   Claiming shipments of merchandise and storing them temporarily on a wharfboat were routine in George's business. See George's "Original Statement," dated Mar. 11, 1873, contained in the packet of *George F. Ring v. Franklin Fire Insurance Co.*, Case 2573, Circuit Court of Warren County, in the attic of the courthouse in Vicksburg (hereafter "George's statement"), p. 4.

7   See works cited in n. 3 above for descriptions of life on Vicksburg's landing.

8   "An Atrocious Murder," *Vicksburg Daily Times*, Mar. 7, 1873, p. 3: "Mr. Jaynes . . . arrived here yesterday evening, having come down in a skiff, and brought this distressing news . . . ." Quoted fully in Chap. 2, p. 15.

9   Ibid. The dramatization of this event is the author's.

10   The clerk's name appears variously in the sources: Goodchat, Gouchat, A. Godcheaux, A. Godshaw, Goodchaw, Alphonse Goutchot Israel, Goodshaw, John

Gouchatt, A. Goodhue and A. Goodchaud. To avoid confusion, "Goudchat" will be used consistently throughout this book.

11   "City Directory," *Vicksburg Daily Times*, Jan. 1, 1873, p. 5.

12   The main hot meal of the day was "dinner," served at noon; the evening meal was "supper," a much lighter repast taken rather late.

13   Character traits attributed to George are inferred from the documented deeds of his life, as well as the stories about him that his nephew, Joseph Nicholas Ring, related to his son, Louis Caffall Ring, who shared them with the author in personal interviews, 1985–86.

14   Most direct route to Joe's home, "The Vicksburg Place." See: "Map of the Barefield Plantation," dated July 1868, Warren County Deed Book FF: 650–651; Warren County Courthouse, Vicksburg; also, "Map of the Seige of Vicksburg," dated Aug. 20, 1863; Geography and Map Division, Library of Congress, Washington.

15   See n. 5 above.

16   Joseph Ring entry, Issaquena County 1868 Personal Tax Roll; Record Group 29, microcopy roll 230, Mississippi Department of Archives and History, Jackson: "On dogs of every name and species, 40 cents," Joe paid 40 cents. It is assumed that this dog, or a successor, was still with Joe in 1873, and that it was a hunting dog such as a retriever. The author thanks Anne Lipscomb Webster, Head Librarian of the Mississippi Department of Archives and History, for her enthusiastic assistance with the researching of this book, 1987–1999.

17   For Barbara's age, see Chap. 8, n. 43.

18   She would give birth 24 days later. See Chap. 17, n. 21.

19   See n. 5 above for weather, and Prologue, n. 4, for phase of the moon.

20   Fictitious name.

2. MARCH 7, 1873

1   George's testimony, 2573, pp. 1–2.

2   Ibid.

3   Testimony of W. D. Brown, June 22, 1876, *Mississippi in 1875. Report of the Select Committee to Inquire into the Mississippi Election of 1875, with the Testimony and Documentary Evidence*, 2 vols. (Washington: Government Printing Office, 1876), I: 702: "The Deer Creek country is somewhat isolated from the exterior world, and is distant from the Mississippi River on an average from twelve to fifteen miles, with an intervening miserable swamp, which, in some seasons of the year, is impassable. We have access to Vicksburgh at certain seasons of the year, but for six months of the year . . . it is inaccessible except by a tedious land-route to Vicksburgh, or a tedious drive to the Mississippi River across the miserable swamp." This is Senate Report 527, 44th Congress, 1st Session (hereafter "Boutwell Report").

4   The principle trail for reaching Rolling Fork Landing from Vicksburg was along the high ground that followed the many twists and turns of Deer Creek. There was regular packet service at this time (see Chap. 23, p. 183), but horseback was swifter. No bridge spanned the lower Yazoo before the twentieth century.

5   *Vicksburg Daily Times*, Mar. 8, 1873, p. 3: "The weather yesterday morning was clear and pleasant, but in the evening it clouded up and a heavy rain set in about dark."

6   Regarding George's character traits, see Chap. 1, n. 13. Regarding his age, see Chap. 8, n. 5.

7   Physical traits attributed to George are based on those of his three nephews: (1) Joseph Nicholas Ring, from five photographs, ca. 1882–ca. 1916, copies in author's possession, and descriptions in letters from his son, Louis Caffall Ring, to the author, 1985–86; (2) George F. Ring, from four photographs, ca. 1876, 1882 and 1904, originals in author's possession; and (3) John M. Ring, from physical descriptions in *Registers of Enlistments in the United States Army, 1798–1914*, vol. 105, "1900, R–Z," p. 17; National Archives micropublication M233, roll 54; and the pension file of his widow, Mary Emma Ring, Certificate 861,644, Philippine Insurrection, Veterans Administration.

8   *Vicksburg Daily Times*, February and March 1873, *passim*. Weather reports indicate that although March was dry except for the first, February had brought more rain than usual.

9   George's statement, p. 2.

10 "An Atrocious Murder," *Vicksburg Daily Times*, Mar. 7, 1873, p. 3.

11 The head of Rolling Fork Creek was in Deer Creek, its mouth (where Rolling Fork Landing was located) was in the Little Sunflower River. Jesse and Martha Moore, married three years, had no children of their own. Jesse Moore's father-in-law was John F. Coker, Martha's father.

12 The city's Democratic newspaper was the *Daily Vicksburger*, but it was published from December 1873 through January 1875 only.

13 See sources cited in Chap. 1, n. 3.

14 Baptismal records of "Anna Catharina Hill," born 15 Oct. 1820, and "Catharina Hill," born 12 Feb. 1828, daughters of Konrad Hill and Anna Catherina Pfeffer; Catholic church registers of Ohmes, Hesse, Germany; Katholisches Pfarramt, Ruhlkirchen, Germany. The author thanks Linda N. Kious of Ocean Springs, Mississippi—a great granddaughter of Rosa Hill Schawbloski, the daughter of Anna and Catherine's elder brother, Johann Hill—for sharing her extensive genealogical research on the origins of the Hill family (correspondence, 1993–1999). Physical traits and character traits attributed to Catherine and Anna are inferred from those of their niece, Rosa Hill Schawbloski (photograph and descriptive texts supplied by Linda N. Kious), as well as their Hessian heritage and social milieu as wives of German-speaking immigrant businessmen of Vicksburg.

15 Regarding the spirit of lawlessness in Mississippi during Reconstruction, and how much it appalled newcomers and visitors, see: Harris, *The Day of the Carpetbagger*, 8–9, 26–30, 251–252, 371, 377–388, 687–688, 707–708 and 714–715.

16 See works about the Delta cited in Chap. 11, n. 1. See also: Harris, *The Day of the Carpetbagger*, 377; and Marie Hemphill, *Fevers, Floods and Faith* (Indianola, Mississippi: Sunflower County Historical Society, 1980), 37–39.

17 Testimony of W. D. Brown, June 22, 1876, "Boutwell Report," I: 702: "If the colored people were disposed to do that thing [injure the whites], and had the capacity for organization, and could keep their own counsel, they could annihilate the white people in a very short while, there is such disparity between their numbers. . . ."

18 Garner, *Reconstruction in Mississippi*, 115. Law quoted in: Anthony Walton, *Mississippi, An American Journey* (New York: Alfred A. Knopf, 1996), 180.

19 John C. Willis, *On the New South Frontier: Life in the Yazoo-Mississippi Delta,*

1865–1920 (doctoral dissertation, College of William and Mary, Williamsburg, Virginia, 1991), 57.

20 Garner, *Reconstruction in Mississippi*, 285.

21 Testimony of W. D. Brown, June 22, 1876, "Boutwell Report," I: 706: "I think that the people generally had them [side-arms], for every man in the country was careful to have arms, and to have them where he could readily put his hands on them." See also: Harris, *The Day of the Carpetbagger*, 379; Willis, *On the New South Frontier*, 94; Garner, *Reconstruction in Mississippi*, 288; and Hemphill, *Fevers, Floods and Faith*, 141.

22 Henry P. Scott was sheriff of Issaquena County. See: Eric Foner, *Freedom's Lawmakers, A Directory of Black Officeholders During Reconstruction*, rev. ed. (Baton Rouge: Louisiana State University Press, 1996), 190.

23 Charles E. Furlong was sheriff of Warren County. See: *Vicksburg Daily Times*, 1872 and 1873, passim.

24 See Harris, *The Day of the Carpetbagger*, 430–480. Ridgley Ceylon Powers, Ohioan and Lieutenant Governor under James L. Alcorn, became acting governor on Dec. 1, 1871, when Alcorn resigned to run for the U.S. Senate, and served until Jan. 21, 1874, when Adelbert Ames was elected to the office.

25 The next meeting of the mayor, carpetbagger Benjamin A. Lee, and the eight aldermen, [Mr.] Beck, Samuel Fischel, I. Reinhardt and Jacob A. Klein (white immigrants) and A. W. Dorsey, Weldon W. Edwards, [Mr.] Johnson and J. H. Coates (blacks), was held in city hall on Mar. 10, 1873; see: "Board of Aldermen," "Official Proceedings," *Vicksburg Daily Times*, Mar. 20, 1873, p. 2. The next meeting of the sheriff, carpetbagger Charles E. Furlong, and the six supervisors, Albert Johnson and William Thornton Montgomery (blacks) and William McGee, George W. Rogers, A. C. Fisk and W. S. Jones (whites), was held in the courthouse on Mar. 28, 1873; see: "The City," "Board of Supervisors," *Vicksburg Daily Times*, Mar. 29, 1873, p. 3.

26 Sources make frequent reference to "rumors" regarding "the Rolling Fork tragedy," yet only four different explanations for the disaster are stated explicitly. Other possibilities will be inferred from the social, political and economic conditions existing at Rolling Fork Landing in 1873, and these will be evaluated in turn as those issues enter into the narrative. The full array of 12 hypotheses will then be recapitulated in Chap. 25.

27 It is likely that George assigned a few hands to guard the house.

28 See works about the Delta cited in Chap. 11, n. 1.

29 "To the Editor of the Daily Times," *Vicksburg Daily Times*, Mar. 19, 1873, p. 3: "Joseph Ring had no watch with him, having left the same at home in Vicksburg. . . ."

30 "River Intelligence," *Vicksburg Daily Times*, Mar. 8, 1873, p. 3. The *B. H. Hurt* is listed in: Harry P. Owens, *Steamboats and the Cotton Economy: River Trade in the Yazoo-Mississippi Delta* (Jackson: University Press of Mississippi, 1990), 168.

31 "Dead Men Tell No Tales," *Vicksburg Daily Herald*, Aug. 22, 1883.

32 Ibid.

33 "City Directory," *Vicksburg Daily Times*, Jan. 1, 1873, p. 5.

34 "Sexton's Report," *Vicksburg Daily Times*, Mar. 11, 1873, p. 3.

35 "The City," *Vicksburg Daily Times*, Mar. 8, 1873, p. 3.

36 Ibid., and burial record of "A. Godcheaux," Mar. 7, 1873; *Chevra Kadisha,*

Strangers Graves Section, pp. 108–109, line 91; Anshe Chesed Congregation, Vicksburg: "Residence, Rolling Fork; Age, 21; Cause of Death, Murdered & burnt."

3. MARCH 8, 1873

1   See Chap. 2, n. 4.

2   *Vicksburg Daily Times*, Mar. 8, 1873, p. 3. Quoted fully in Chap. 2, n. 5.

3   Map constructed by the author from Jas. M. Seales & David Stratton, surveyors, *Issaquena County Land Ownership Maps* (New Orleans: Hugh Lewis, 1873); Geography and Map Division, Library of Congress, Washington.

4   George's statement, p. 1.

5   Description of the store is based on George's statement, pp. 14-16. The author has come across no reference to any other building in the Delta (or elsewhere) that comes even close to resembling the store George built. The design was evidently his own, functional yet highly individualistic. Barns housing livestock sometimes had long horizontal expanses of latticework on the ground level for ventilation. It is conceivable that a mule or two, as well as Jesse Moore's oxen, were stabled on the ground level of Ring & Co., though no record states as much.

6   See works about the Delta cited in Chap. 11, n. 1.

7   George's statement, p. 14.

8   Ibid., 15: "There were four outside doors, two of them folding 6x8 feet, the other two 3x7 feet."

9   Ibid., 14.

10   Ibid., 15.

11   Ibid.

12   Ibid.

13   George's statement, p. 15, says only, "50 feet counter;" dividing that length into two counters is based on typical post-Civil War store design. See Thomas D. Clark, *Pills, Petticoats, & Plows: The Southern Country Store* (Norman, Oklahoma: University of Oklahoma Press, 1964), 22.

14   Inventory of store is based on George's "Proofs of Loss," contained in the packet of *George F. Ring v. Franklin Fire Insurance Co.*, Case 2573, as well as typical post-Civil War country store inventories as described in Clark, *Pills, Petticoats, & Plows*, 17–34 especially, and Hemphill, *Fevers, Floods and Faith*, 55–56, 99, 602–603. See also Willis, *On the New South Frontier*, 169. Country merchants in more populous areas would often carry coffins, too, and the necessary materials for draping them: fabrics, coffin fringe and coffin tacks.

15   George's statement, p. 16.

16   See Clark, *Pills, Petticoats, & Plows*, 19, 29–30; and Ruth F. Walker, *800-Sharkey County-General Information and Points of Interest* (10-page typescript of notes for a WPA history that was evidently never written, vertical file, Rolling Fork-Sharkey County Library, Rolling Fork, Mississippi, 1937), bearing hand-written annotations of Alice Wade, 7.

17   George's statement, p. 15.

18   Ibid., 15–16.

19   See n. 14 above.

20   Arrangement of rooms is interpolated from George's statement, which does not articulate the precise position of every room.

21   George's statement, p. 15.

22   George's statement, p. 6: "I left Rolling Fork Landing on the 20th February last. . . ."

23   Joor's "Original Statement," contained in the packet of *George F. Ring v. Franklin Fire Insurance Co.*, Case 2573 (hereafter "Joor's statement"), p. 4.

24   Jeans & Ring entry, Issaquena County 1868 Personal Tax Roll; Record Group 29, microcopy roll 230, Mississippi Department of Archives and History, Jackson: "On each rifle, shot gun, or army gun, 50 cents," Jeans & Ring paid 50 cents.

25   See Chap. 2, n. 21.

26   Jesse Moore-Martha Coker marriage record, Feb. 22, 1870, Warren County Marriage Book H: 234; County Clerk's Office, Vicksburg.

27   Joor's statement, p. 4.

28   "Dead Men Tell No Tales," *Vicksburg Daily Herald*, Aug. 22, 1883.

29   An iron safe was as common a country store fixture as a pot-belly stove. See Clark, *Pills, Petticoats, & Plows*, 80–81, and Helen Dick Davis, ed., *Trials of the Earth, The Autobiography of Mary Hamilton* (Jackson: University Press of Mississippi, 1992), 42.

30   George's statement does not describe who slept where, except that the clerks slept in the office. However, since Joor referred to "Mr. Moore's room," it is assumed that little Willie Jeans slept in a room of his own.

31   George's statement, p. 15.

32   George would have obtained his furniture from Vicksburg.

33   George's statement, p. 15.

34   *George F. Ring v. Charles E. Wright*, Case 337, *Minutes of the Circuit Court of Issaquena County*, Nov. Term 1865, Book B: 282, in the courthouse in Mayersville.

35   George's testimony, 2573, p. 2.

4. MARCH 8, 1873, EVENING

1   George's statement, p. 8.

2   John F. Coker-Lucy Cons [?] marriage record, June 29, 1868, Warren County Marriage Book H: 143; County Clerk's Office, Vicksburg. Given the ages of John Coker's three children (see George's statement, pp. 9, 13), it is obvious that they were the offspring of an earlier marriage, and that Lucy was most likely his second wife.

3   George's statement, p. 13: "She [Martha] has a father, brother & sister living at Rolling Fork Landing—Mr. John Coker is her father."

4   Claim of John F. Coker "for Work" against the estate of Jesse Moore, filed Aug. 20, 1873, Issaquena County probate file no. 26, County Clerk's Office, Mayersville.

5   Age estimated, based on birthyear—ca. 1854—of his eldest child, Martha. See Jesse Moore household, 1870 U.S. Census, Issaquena County (Schola Precinct), Mississippi, p. 287; National Archives micropublication M593, roll 731: "[Martha Moore], 16."

6   "To the Editor of the Daily Times," *Vicksburg Daily Times*, Mar. 19, 1873, p. 3.

7   Ibid., and George's statement, p. 9.

8   "Dead Men Tell No Tales," *Vicksburg Daily Herald*, Aug. 22, 1883.

9   George's statement, p. 8. The *Bluella* is listed in: Owens, *Steamboats and the Cotton Economy*, 168.

10   "To the Editor of the Daily Times," *Vicksburg Daily Times*, Mar. 19, 1873, p. 3.

11   Claim of John F. Coker "for funeral Expences . . . $20.00" against the estate of

Jesse Moore, filed Aug. 20, 1873, Issaquena County probate file no. 26, County Clerk's Office, Mayersville.

12   The *B. H. Hurt* carrying Goudchat's remains arrived in Vicksburg on Friday afternoon, Mar. 7, 1873; a typical run from Rolling Fork Landing to Vicksburg took about one-and-one-half days; therefore, the remains would have been placed on the *B. H. Hurt* on Thursday morning, Mar. 6, 1873.

13   Inventory of the estate of Jesse Moore, filed Oct. 7, 1873, Issaquena County probate file no. 26, County Clerk's Office, Mayersville.

14   George's statement, p. 8.

15   Ibid.

16   Inventory of the estate of Jesse Moore.

17   George's statement, p. 8.

18   Ibid.

19   Ibid., 9.

20   "Local Intelligence," *Vicksburg Daily Times*, Apr. 9, 1873, p. 3.

21   George's statement, p. 9.

22   Ibid.

23   Joor's statement, p. 1.

24   Ibid., 3.

25   Ibid.

26   Ibid., 4.

27   "An Atrocious Murder," *Vicksburg Daily Times*, Mar. 19, 1873, p. 3.

28   See, for example, Hemphill, *Fevers, Floods and Faith*, 90–91, and Harris, *The Day of the Carpetbagger*, 251–252.

29   Rumors of armed blacks roaming the Delta appear to have been rampant during Reconstruction. They were incited more by the whites' sense of vulnerability, and the general social upheaval and vehement sentiments of the age, than by the few violent actions of blacks—such as the ones cited in n. 28 above—that actually occurred.

30   See Chap. 2, n. 26.

31   George's statement, p. 16.

32   Precisely when George spoke with Parker is not recorded. It could have been Sunday morning.

33   Age based on Noah Parker household, 1870 U.S. Census, Issaquena County (Schola Precinct), Mississippi, p. 274; National Archives micropublication M593, roll 731: "Parker Noah, 24."

34   Assumption based on his race and probability.

35   Magistrate's Certificate, dated Apr. 5, 1873, contained in the packet of *George F. Ring v. Franklin Fire Insurance Co.*, Case 2573: ". . . I am the Magistrate most contiguous to the place of the fire. . . ."

36   Noah Parker household, 1870 U.S. Census, and Foner, *Freedom's Lawmakers*, 167.

37   George's testimony, contained in the packet of *George F. Ring v. Franklin Fire Insurance Co.*, Case 2572, Circuit Court of Warren County, in the attic of the courthouse in Vicksburg (hereafter "George's testimony, 2572"), p. 3.

38   For history of blacks entering the Delta, see Chap. 13, pp. 101–102.

39   Noah Parker household, 1870 U.S. Census: "Attended school within the year" column is checked; "Cannot read" and "Cannot write" columns are not checked.

40   Character traits attributed to Parker are based on the documented deeds of his life

and his own published words.

41 Foner, *Freedom's Lawmakers*, 167.

42 Ibid.

43 Testimony of W. D. Brown, June 22, 1876, "Boutwell Report," I: 708.

44 Ibid., 701, quoted in Chap. 37, p. 277.

45 Magistrate's Certificate, dated Apr. 5, 1873, contained in the packet of *George F. Ring v. Franklin Fire Insurance Co.*, Case 2573: ". . . I am acquainted with the character and circumstances of the parties insured [i.e., George, Joe and Martha]. . . ."

46 "To the Editor of the Daily Times," *Vicksburg Daily Times*, Mar. 19, 1873, p. 3.

47 Ibid.

48 Ibid.

49 For advertised schedule of the *B. H. Hurt*, see Chap. 23, p. 183, and nn. 47 and 48; for actual schedule, see Prologue, p. 8 and n. 10.

50 Joor's statement, p. 2.

51 Ibid.

52 George's statement, p. 7, supported by Joor's statement, p. 2.

53 Joor's statement, p. 2.

54 *Biographical and Historical Memoirs of Mississippi*, 2 vols. (Chicago: The Goodspeed Publishing Co., 1891), I: 538-540. Physical traits are fictitious.

55 Joor's statement, p. 2.

56 Ibid., 3.

57 Ibid., 2.

58 "To the Editor of the Daily Times," *Vicksburg Daily Times*, Mar. 19, 1873, p. 3.

59 Joor's statement, pp. 2–3.

60 George's statement, p. 7.

61 Joor's statement, p. 4.

62 "Dead Men Tell No Tales," *Vicksburg Daily Herald*, Aug. 22, 1883.

63 Ibid.

64 Testimony of W. D. Brown, June 22, 1876, "Boutwell Report," I: 718: "Q. When you speak of the destruction of a gin-house by fire, let me ask you, in the first place, if a single match is applied to a gin-house is there any possibility of saving it?—A. There is no possibility, sir. If it is seed-cotton [not yet ginned], and you merely apply a match, if you have an adequate supply of water to apply to the fire instantly, you might save it; but if it is lint-cotton [ginned], it just burns instantly, like powder almost. [The cotton stored at Ring & Co. would have been ginned and baled—lint cotton.] Q. Is there any possibility of saving a gin-house that is fired?—A. But very little possibility. Q. In these isolated houses, do the people have any means of extinguishing a conflagration when it is once started?—A. We have nothing to depend upon. That mode of revenge is regarded as the surest."

65 See Chap. 2, n. 26.

66 Fires also devastated Delta towns; see Hemphill, *Fevers, Floods and Faith*, 362, and "Fire in Greenville, Almost the Entire Business Portion of the Town Destroyed, Fifty Business Houses Burned," *Greenville Times*, Sept. 2, 1874, p. 2.

67 "To the Editor of the Daily Times," *Vicksburg Daily Times*, Mar. 19, 1873, p. 3.

68 For statutory jurisdictions of Noah Parker and Sheriff Scott, see Chaps. 18 and 19, especially Chap. 19, n. 24.

69 Regarding Sheriff Scott's reputation, see Chap. 18, pp. 148–150.

70 George Ring entry, Issaquena County 1868 Personal Tax Roll; Record Group 29,

microfilm roll 230, Mississippi Department of Archives and History, Jackson: "On dogs of every name and species, 40 cents," George paid 80 cents. When George left the landing it is likely that his two dogs remained there for his occasional hunts. Even if they did not, it is highly unlikely that Moore and Joor did not have a hunting dog or two. Regarding the value of keeping dogs, see Davis, *Trials of the Earth*, 166.

71   "To the Editor of the Daily Times," *Vicksburg Daily Times*, Mar. 19, 1873, p. 3, final paragraph quoted in Chap. 7, p. 46.

5. March 10, 1873

1   Leaving Rolling Fork Landing on Sunday morning, the typical ride of one-and-one-half days would put George in Vicksburg late on Monday. That he was in Chamberlin's office on Tuesday is documented (see Chap. 6, n. 1).

2   Knowing that Barbara is waiting to hear whether her husband is alive or dead, it is inconceivable that George would delay reporting to her.

3   Character traits attributed to Barbara are inferred from the documented deeds of her life, as well as the cultural heritage of her childhood home. See also Chap. 15, nn. 31, 32, and Chap. 13, n. 22.

4   Physical traits attributed to Barbara are based on: (1) those of her father and brother Nicholas, taken from a photograph, ca. 1874, copy in author's possession; and (2) traits typical of Lorrainians which have reappeared among Barbara's descendants, such as olive complexion and faint freckles across the nose.

5   *Vicksburg Daily Times*, Mar. 11, 1873, p. 3.

6   "Mr. Joseph Ring, In a/c with Geo. F. Ring," Feb. 18, 1874, a financial statement prepared by George for Barbara, listing expenditures and credits, Oct. 15, 1868–July 25, 1873, marked "Copy" and not in George's hand. Passed from Joseph Nicholas Ring to his son Louis Caffall Ring, who photocopied it for the author in 1985.

7   Conjecture based on the practices of the Catholic Church and Barbara's religiosity. It is more likely that Father Leray's assistant, Father F. C. Bohmert, would make such a "house call," rather than the pastor himself.

6. March 11, 1873

1   George's testimony, 2572, p. 6: "The first statement was made on or about March 11th 1873. . . . I was in Chamberlin's office in Vicksburg when I made the first statement." "Original Statement" is dated Mar. 11, 1873.

2   "City Directory," *Vicksburg Daily Times*, Jan. 1, 1873, p. 5. Offices such as Chamberlin's were upstairs of shops. George's statement, p. 10: "I went *up* [emphasis added] to Mr. Chamberlin's office."

3   Joor's statement bears the same date as George's, Mar. 11, 1873.

4   George's testimony, 2572 and 2573, make continual references to "Mr. Love the adjuster," "Major Love the agent of the defendant," and "Major A. E. Love" as being present at this meeting.

5   George's statement, p. 7.

6   Household of "W. M. Chamblin,"1880 U.S. Census, Warren County (Vicksburg, Fourth Ward), Mississippi, p. 426; National Archives micropublication T9, roll 667.

7   Traits deduced from the documented deeds of his life.

8   Household of "W. M. Chamblin,"1880 U.S. Census: "Cannot read" and "Cannot write" columns are *not* checked.

9   Chamberlin could not have performed the functions of an insurance agent without being able to do arithmetic.

10 William M. Chamberlin-Sallie G. Fulkerson marriage record, June 29, 1871, Warren County Marriage Book H: 307; County Clerk's Office, Vicksburg. (The marriage was inadvertently recorded in the "white" volume rather than the "colored" volume.)

11 Chamberlin does not appear in the 1870 U.S. census of Vicksburg; however, his marriage and dealings with George F. Ring indicate that he was working in the city by 1871.

12 Household of "W. M. Chamblin,"1880 U.S. Census: "Wm . . . son . . . 8 . . . ."

13 George's statement, p. 10, and testimony, 2572, p. 2.

14 See illustrations in: Foner, *Reconstruction*, unnumbered pages following p. 386, and p. 540; Eric Foner and Olivia Mahoney, *America's Reconstruction: People and Politics after the Civil War* (New York: HarperCollins, 1995), 96, 98, 100, 102, 105; and Foner, *Freedom's Lawmakers*, passim.

15 George's statement, p. 13.

16 For example, see "Fire in Greenville, Almost the Entire Business Portion of the Town Destroyed, Fifty Business Houses Burned," *Greenville Times*, Sept. 2, 1874, p. 2. Of the 63 merchants listed as suffering a loss, 33 had insurance, but only two of those had sufficient insurance to cover their loss.

17 George's statement, p. 16, and Joor's statement, p. 4, are both co-signed "H. N. Martin, Notary Public."

18 George's statement, p. 1.

19 Ibid., 1–5.

20 Ibid., 6.

21 Ibid., 12.

22 Ibid.

23 Ibid., 6–7.

24 *Vicksburg Daily Times*, Mar. 12, 1873, p. 3: "The weather yesterday was very pleasant."

25 George's statement, pp. 10–11; and "Copies of Policies of Ring & Co. on Stock of Merchandise at Rolling Fork Landing . . . and on Building . . . ," 2-page addendum to George's statement.

26 Ibid., and George's testimony, 2573, pp. 2–3.

27 George's statement, p. 11; "Copies of Policies of Ring & Co. . . . ;" and George's testimony, 2573, pp. 3–4.

28 "Copies of Policies of Ring & Co. . . . ."

29 George's statement, p. 10; "Copies of Policies of Ring & Co. . . . ;" and George's testimony, 2572, pp. 1–4.

30 George's statement, p. 10; "Copies of Policies of Ring & Co. . . . ;" and George's declaration, contained in the packet of *George F. Ring, Guardian, v. Liverpool, London & Globe Insurance Co.*, Case 1768, U.S. Circuit Court, Southern District of Mississippi; National Archives—Southeast Region, East Point, Georgia (hereafter "George's declaration, 1768"), pp. 2–4.

31 "Copies of Policies of Ring & Co. . . . ."

32 George's statement, p. 8.

33 Ibid., 16.

34 Joor's statement, pp. 1–2.

35   Ibid., 3.

7. MARCH 14, 1873

1   "To the Editor of the Daily Times," *Vicksburg Daily Times*, Mar. 19, 1873, p. 3.
2   *Vicksburg Daily Times*, Mar. 15, 1873, p. 3: "The weather yesterday was clear and
      pleasant." It is possible that the weather at Rolling Fork Landing was different
      from Vicksburg's; the author, however, could find no "closer" source.
3   "To the Editor of the Daily Times," *Vicksburg Daily Times*, Mar. 19, 1873, p. 3.
4   All reports agree that the store was reduced to ashes.
5   "To the Editor of the Daily Times," *Vicksburg Daily Times*, Mar. 19, 1873, p. 3.
6   Ibid.
7   Joseph Ring entry, Mar. 19, 1873, *Ledger of Burials*, Fisher Funeral Home; in pos-
      session of Fisher-Riles Funeral Home, Vicksburg (photocopied for the author in
      1991): "Remains of Joseph Ring, 42 years . . . ." Transcribed with minor errors in
      Fisher Funeral Home Records, II: 121, a typescript in the Old Courthouse Museum,
      Vicksburg. A thorough search of the record books and loose papers in the
      Issaquena County Courthouse, Mayersville, failed to disclose the original report.
8   "To the Editor of the Daily Times," *Vicksburg Daily Times*, Mar. 19, 1873, p. 3.
9   Ibid.
10   The *Lizzie* left Vicksburg one day late on Wednesday, Mar. 12, 1873, at 5 p.m.
      (*Vicksburg Daily Times*, Mar. 13, 1873, p. 3), and returned on Tuesday, Mar. 18,
      1873, in the morning (*Vicksburg Daily Times*, Mar. 19, 1873, p. 3). This would have
      brought the *Lizzie* into Rolling Fork Landing on her return trip on Sunday,
      Mar. 16, 1873, two days after this second inquest. The *Lizzie* is entry 3527 in:
      Way, *Way's Packet Directory*, 290. She is also listed in: Owens, *Steamboats and the
      Cotton Economy*, 175.

8. JOE AND BARBARA

1   History and description of Buffalo rely primarily on: (1) H. Perry Smith, ed.,
      History of the City of Buffalo and Erie County, 2 vols. (Syracuse: D. Mason & Co.,
      1884); (2) Scott Eberle and Joseph A. Grande, *Second Looks, A Pictorial History of
      Buffalo and Erie County* (Norfolk: The Donning Company, 1987); (3) Richard C.
      Brown and Bob Watson, *Buffalo, Lake City in Niagara Land* (Buffalo: Windsor
      Publications, 1981); (4) Samuel M. Welch, *Recollections of Buffalo During the
      Decade from 1830 to 1840, or Fifty Years Since* (Buffalo: Peter Paul & Bro., 1891);
      and (5) William Ketchum, *Authentic and Comprehensive History of Buffalo, with
      Some Account of Its Early Inhabitants Both Savage and Civilized* (Buffalo: Rockwell,
      Baker & Hill, 1864). History and description of Buffalo's German-speaking trades-
      men's society in particular rely on the extensive genealogical research in primary
      source materials conducted by the author and his cousin, Joseph N. Kellas of West
      Seneca, New York, recently deceased, on their Lorrainian ancestors in Buffalo,
      1830s–1880s, as well as the published sources cited above.
2   Trades selected from 1850 U.S. Census, Erie County (Buffalo, Fourth Ward), New
      York, *passim*; National Archives micropublication M432, roll 502. Household of
      John Miller (Barbara's father), p. 416; households of Nicholas Miller (grandfather)
      and Nicholas Miller (uncle), p. 394. All are listed as "mason." Buffalo city directo-
      ries confirm this to mean "bricklayer," and not "stonemason."
3   Joseph Ring, Declaration of Intention, Mar. 28, 1856; *Erie County Alien*

Declarations II: 190; Circuit Clerk's Office, Buffalo; and George Ring, ditto.

4 Birth year deduced from records that sometimes provide conflicting information: (1) Joseph Ring entry, *Consolidated List, Class I (vol. II, L–R), Second District, Ohio*, p. 276; Records of Office Subdivisions, 1862–66, Enrollment Branch, General Records, Enrollment Lists and Reports, RG 110, National Archives, Washington: "30" (as of July 1, 1863); (2) Joseph Ring household, 1870 U.S. Census, Issaquena County (Schola Precinct), Mississippi, p. 285; National Archives micropublication M593, roll 731: "38;" (3) Policy No. 29541, July 21, 1871, Germania Life Insurance Company; in possession of successor company, The Guardian Life Insurance Company of America, New York, New York (photocopied for the author in 1995): "Name of Assured, Joseph Ring; Age at Issue, 39; [Birthdate?], 27 [month illegible] '32;" and (4) Joseph Ring entry, Mar. 19, 1873, *Ledger of Burials*, Fisher Funeral Home; in possession of Fisher-Riles Funeral Home, Vicksburg (photocopied for the author in 1991): "42."

5 Birth year deduced from records that sometimes provide conflicting information: (1) "Geo. Ring" entry, Ship *South America* Passenger List, May 21, 1853, p. 6; *Passenger Lists of Vessels Arriving at New York, NY, 1820–1897*; National Archives micropublication M237, roll 125: "18;" (2) J. S. Joor household, 1860 U.S. Census, Issaquena County, Mississippi, p. 873; National Archives micropublication M653, roll 582: "23;" (3) George F. Ring, Petition for Naturalization, Nov. 27, 1867; *Minutes of the Circuit Court of Issaquena County* B: 490, Circuit Clerk's Office, Mayersville: ". . . came to the United States of America in the year 1853 . . . he was under the age of eighteen years when he arrived . . . ;" (4) George F. Ring household, 1870 U.S. Census, Warren County (Vicksburg, First Ward), Mississippi, p. 215; National Archives micropublication M593, roll 751: "36;" (5) George's statement, Mar. 11, 1873, p. 1: "39;" (6) "George Ring" household, 1880 U.S. Census, Warren County (Vicksburg, Second Ward), Mississippi, p. 365; National Archives micropublication T9, roll 667: "46;" (7) George F. Ring household, 1900 U.S. Census, Sunflower County, Mississippi, Enumeration District 49, Sheet 7; National Archives micropublication T623, roll 828: "65;" (8) George F. Ring entry, Aug. 20, 1902, *Ledger of Burials*, Fisher Funeral Home; in possession of Fisher-Riles Funeral Home, Vicksburg (photocopied for the author in 1991): "68;" (9) "Death of Mr. G. F. Ring," *Vicksburg Daily Herald*, Aug. 20, 1902, p. 6: "aged 68 years;" and (10) George F. Ring tombstone, Division A, Square 157, Cedar Hill Cemetery, Vicksburg: "6 April 1833–20 Aug. 1902."

6 No record has been found stating that the brothers were born in Lorraine; the circumstantial evidence, however, is convincing. See especially the death record of Pauline M. (Ring) Jeanes (see n. 14 below), certificate no. 17100 (1947), Illinois Department of Public Health, Springfield: "Birthplace, Metz, France; birthplace of father, Metz, France; birthplace of mother, Metz, France." Many of the German-speaking immigrants to Buffalo were French citizens from Alsace and Lorraine. However, they blended so easily into the larger Germanic population that, for non-German government officials and record keepers, their separate identity was quickly lost. George and Joe are often recorded as "German."

7 Joseph Ring-Walburga Müller marriage record, Nov. 25, 1858; *Ehen*, 1851–1872, p. 48, St. Michael's R. C. Church, Buffalo; *Microfilmed Records of Buffalo Parishes*, roll 281, Buffalo and Erie County Public Library. (The surname spelled variously in the old records as "Müller," "Muller," "Mueller" and "Miller" eventually became

standardized as "Miller." "Walburga" appears to have been a variant of "Barbara.")

8   See literacy columns in U.S. censuses listed in nn. 4 and 5 above.

9   *Buffalo City Directory for 1857* (Buffalo: E. R. Jewett & Co., 1857), 258: "joiner;" *Buffalo City Directory for 1859* (Buffalo: E. R. Jewett, 1859), 257: "carp.;" *Buffalo City Directory for 1860* (Buffalo: E. R. Jewett, 1860), 336: "carp.;" Joseph Ring entry, *Consolidated List, Class I (vol. II, L–R), Second District, Ohio*, p. 276; Records of Office Subdivisions, 1862–66, Enrollment Branch, General Records, Enrollment Lists and Reports, RG 110, National Archives, Washington: "Carpenter."

10   "Geo. Ring" entry, Ship *South America* Passenger List, May 21, 1853, p. 6; *Passenger Lists of Vessels Arriving at New York, NY, 1820–1897*; National Archives micropublication M237, roll 125. See Chap. 13, n. 23.

11   "Marine Intelligence," *New York Daily Times*, May 21, 1853, p. 8.

12   Passenger lists of all ships arriving in New York from Le Havre, Jan. 1, 1852, through May 31, 1853, have been searched.

13   Joseph Ring, Petition for Naturalization, Apr. 16, 1858; *Erie County Naturalizations*, 17: 377; Circuit Clerk's Office, Buffalo: ". . . and it appearing to the satisfaction of this Court . . . that the said applicant has resided within the limits and under the jurisdiction of the United States, for five years . . . ." The author doubts the accuracy of this statement. Given the history of these two brothers, it is much more likely that George came first, and Joe followed, rather than the other way around. The lack of an arrival record for Joe, Jan. 1, 1852, through May 31, 1853, supports this suspicion. A search of arrival records for the remainder of 1853 would probably result in one for Joe.

14   Burial record of "Elisabeth Schlitzer, nata Ring," Aug. 12, 1852 (died Aug. 10, 1852); *Liber Sepultorum, 1851–1868*: 3, St. Michael's R. C. Church, Buffalo; *Microfilmed Records of Buffalo Parishes*, roll 281, Buffalo and Erie County Public Library; *Cincinnati City Directory for 1863* (Cincinnati: Williams & Co., 1863), 293: "Ring John, h. 233 W. 6th;" and Benjamin Franklin Jeans-Pauline Ring marriage record, Feb. 21, 1884, Washington County Marriage Book 7 (colored): 139; County Clerk's Office, Greenville, Mississippi (see n. 6 above).

15   Joseph Ring, Declaration of Intention, Mar. 28, 1856; *Erie County Alien Declarations* II: 190; Circuit Clerk's Office, Buffalo; and George Ring, ditto.

16   *Buffalo City Directory for 1857*, 302: "Waterman, Darius W. builder . . . ."

17   "Death of Darius W. Waterman," *Buffalo Commercial Advertiser*, July 24, 1885, p. 3.

18   *Buffalo City Directory for 1857*, 258.

19   Regarding character traits of Joe, see Chap. 9, n. 4; regarding character traits of George, see Chap. 1, n. 13.

20   George's statement, p. 1.

21   Physical description is based on a photograph of John Miller seated at a picnic table with his eldest son Nicholas and other family members, ca. 1874; copy in author's possession.

22   Character traits are based on the documented deeds of John Miller's life, as well as traits typical of the Lorrainian immigrants in Buffalo generally.

23   Baptismal record of "Jean Muller," 22 Aug. 1809 (born 21 Aug. 1809, "fils legitime de Nicolas Muller, mason d'Obergailbach, et de Anne Marie Grosse"); Catholic church registers of Obergailbach, Department of the Moselle, Province of

Lorraine, France; microfilm 1423280, Item 37, Family History Library, Salt Lake City, Utah. *Etat Nominatif des personnes qui ont obtenu les passeports pour l'Etranger pendant le mois*, Préfecture de la Moselle, 1 Mars 1830, ADMos 106 M 1; Archives, Département de la Moselle, Metz, France. John's father received a passport for his family to emigrate to America on Feb. 17, 1830.

24 Baptismal, marriage and burial registers of Obergailbach record occupations of males.

25 History of Lorrainian emigration drawn primarily from: (1) Camille Maire, *L'Emigration des Lorrains en Amérique, 1815–1870* (Metz: Presse Universitaire, 1980); (2) Norman Laybourn, *L'Emigration des Alsaciens et des Lorrains du xviiie au xxe Siècle*, 2 vols. (Strasbourg: Presse Universitaire, 1986); and (3) Jean Houpert, *Les Lorrains en Amérique du Nord* (Metz: Presse Universitaire, 1985).

26 Nicholas "Muller" entry, Ship *Nile* Passenger List, May 24, 1830, p. 2; *Passenger Lists of Vessels Arriving at New York, NY, 1820–1897*; National Archives micropublication M237, roll 14.

27 "Marine Journal," *New York American*, May 24, 1830, p. 2: "Ship Nile, [John] Rockett [captain], from Havre, sailed evening of the 4th of April . . . ." For an account of the extreme severity of the winter of 1829/30, with a specific reference to John Miller's family, see Maire, *L'Emigration des Lorrains en Amérique, 1815–1870*, 80.

28 No documentation exists to prove that the Miller party used the Erie Canal. However, as participants in a mass migration that followed the route described here, it is most likely that they did. See works cited in n. 25 above.

29 See works cited in n. 1 above.

30 Ibid.

31 Land deed, Aug. 13, 1831, Erie County Deed Book 16: 387; Erie County Courthouse, Buffalo. That this house was frame is based on typical houses in Buffalo's Fourth Ward at this time (see works cited in n. 1 above). See also n. 41 below.

32 Nicholas Miller, Declaration of Intention, Aug. 22, 1831; *Erie County Alien Declarations* I: 1; Circuit Clerk's Office, Buffalo.

33 Baptismal record of "Anne Marie Jaxs," 19 Nov. 1811 (born the same day, "fille legitime de Jean Jaxs, mason, et de Marie Elisabeth Rohr"); Catholic church registers of "Gros Redergen" [Gros Rederching], Department of the Moselle, Province of Lorraine, France; microfilm 1423010, Item 1, Family History Library, Salt Lake City, Utah. Anna Maria's family has been reconstructed by the author using standard genealogical sources. New York State Census, 1855, Buffalo, Wards 4, 5, 6 and 7, listing Anna Maria Jax's relatives, indicates that they have been in the city 24 years; microfilm 225, rolls 1 and 2, Buffalo and Erie County Public Library, Buffalo.

34 This is borne out by comparing the surnames that appear in the church registers of Obergailbach and Gros Rederching pertaining to the "Muller" and Jax families with the surnames appearing in the parish, land, census and probate records of Buffalo that involve the Millers and Jaxes.

35 John Miller-[Anna] Maria Jax marriage record, Sept. 26, 1833; *Liber Inthronizatorum et Baptizatorum, 1829–1836*, p. [32], St. Louis's R. C. Church, Buffalo; *Microfilmed Records of Buffalo Parishes*, roll 348 (vol. 2), Buffalo and Erie County Public Library.

36   Rev. Thomas Donohue, D.D., *History of the Diocese of Buffalo* (Buffalo: Buffalo Catholic Publication Co., 1929), 195–198.

37   Miller-Jax marriage, Sept. 26, 1833; and Donohue, *History of the Diocese of Buffalo*, 195.

38   This custom is borne out by the author's reconstruction of numerous Lorrainian families of Buffalo during the 1830s, '40s, and '50s.

39   Baptismal records of "Catharina Miller," Jan. 6, 1835 (born Jan. 3, 1835) and "Maria Miller," Jan. 10, 1836 (born the same day); *Baptismal Register, 1829–1836*: [79] and [143], St. Louis's R. C. Church, Buffalo; *Microfilmed Records of Buffalo Parishes*, roll 348 (vol. 1), Buffalo and Erie County Public Library.

40   Land deed, Sept. 24, 1839, Erie County Deed Book 56: 355; Erie County Courthouse, Buffalo. John Miller first appears in Buffalo city directories in 1838, living "Cherry Street below Michigan."

41   Early maps show this house as frame; Sanborn Fire Insurance Map of 1868 shows this house, as well as John's father's house on Washington Street, as brick.

42   Baptismal records of "Elisabetha Muller," July 23, 1837 (born July 21, 1837) and "Nicholas Muller," Nov. 25, 1838 (born Nov. 20, 1838); *Baptismal Register, 1835–1843*: [73] and [125], St. Louis's R. C. Church, Buffalo; *Microfilmed Records of Buffalo Parishes*, roll 348 (vol. 1), Buffalo and Erie County Public Library.

43   Baptismal record of "Barbara Muller," June 17, 1840 (born the same day); *Baptismal Register, 1835–1843*: [202], St. Louis's R. C. Church, Buffalo; *Microfilmed Records of Buffalo Parishes*, roll 348 (vol. 1), Buffalo and Erie County Public Library.

44   Ibid.

45   Ibid., and Donohue, *History of the Diocese of Buffalo*, 196.

46   Baptismal record of "Maria Magdalena Müller," Jan. 2, 1842 (born Jan. 1, 1842); *Baptismal Register, 1835–1843*: [274], St. Louis's R. C. Church, Buffalo; *Microfilmed Records of Buffalo Parishes*, roll 348 (vol. 1), Buffalo and Erie County Public Library.

47   Donohue, *History of the Diocese of Buffalo*, 197, and illustration, 37.

48   Ibid., 197–198. See also "Modernity in the Service of Tradition: Catholic Lay Trustees at Buffalo's St. Louis Church and the Transformation of European Communal Traditions, 1829–1855," *Journal of Social History*, vol. XV, no. 3 (summer 1982): 655–684.

49   Donohue, *History of the Diocese of Buffalo*, 200–202, and illustration, 37; *The Centenary of St. Mary's Church* (Buffalo: Saint Mary's Church, 1944), 17.

50   Baptismal records of "Maria Catharina Muller," Jan. 23, 1844 (born Jan. 22, 1844), John Henry Miller, Sept. 21, 1845 (born Sept. 17, 1845), and "Theresia Muller," Oct. 17, 1847 (born Oct. 14, 1847), *Baptismal Register* 1: 52 [1844 is out of sequence], 20 and 76, and "Paul Mueller," Sept. 18, 1849 (born Sept. 16, 1849); *Baptismal Register* 2: 37; St. Mary's R. C. Church, Buffalo; *Microfilmed Records of Buffalo Parishes*, roll 280, Buffalo and Erie County Public Library.

51   See works cited in n. 1 above.

52   Ibid.

53   Thomas E. Harney, *Canisius College, The First Nine Years, 1870–1879* (New York: Vantage Press, 1971), 69.

54   *Buffalo City Directory for 1851–52* (Buffalo: Jewett, Thomas & Co., 1851), 230: "Miller, Nicholas, sr. mason, 485 Washington" and "Miller, Nicholas, jr. mason, 487

Washington."

55 Harney, *Canisius College, The First Nine Years*, 69.

56 Marriage and burial registers, St. Michael's R. C. Church, Buffalo; *Microfilmed Records of Buffalo Parishes*, roll 281, Buffalo and Erie County Public Library.

57 Miller and Jax households, 1850 U.S. Census, Erie County (Buffalo, Fourth Ward), New York; National Archives micropublication M432, roll 502, passim.

58 John Miller household, 1850 U.S. Census, Erie County (Buffalo, Fourth Ward), New York, p. 416; National Archives micropublication M432, roll 502: "Persons over 20 yr's of age who cannot read and write" column is *not* checked for John.

59 Ibid.: "Persons over 20 yr's of age who cannot read and write" column *is* checked for Anna Maria.

60 John Miller household, 1850 U.S. Census: "Attended School within the year" column is checked for Nicholas, 11, Barbara, 9, Magdalena, 8, and Catherine, 7. John Miller household, 1860 U.S. Census, Erie County (Buffalo, Seventh Ward), New York, p. 262; National Archives micropublication M653, roll 747: "Attended School within the year" column is checked for Paul, 10, and Theresa, 8. The custom of using parochial rather than public schools was carried down to the author's generation of the family.

61 Donohue, *History of the Diocese of Buffalo*, 201; *The Centenary of St. Mary's Church*, 17.

62 Donohue, *History of the Diocese of Buffalo*, 378, 380.

63 For a long time, the nuns were all native-born German-speakers.

64 Based on "Attended School within the year" column, 1850 and 1860 U.S. Censuses, and when John Miller's sons start appearing in Buffalo city directories with an occupation.

65 "Sickness in the Fourth Ward," *Buffalo Commercial Advertiser*, Aug. 30, 1852, p. 2.

66 "Cholera," *Buffalo Commercial Advertiser*, Sept. 2, 1852, p. 2.

67 Burial record of "Maria Elizabetha Zahm, nata Müller," Aug. 17, 1852 (died Aug. 16, 1852); *Liber Sepultorum, 1851–1868*: 3, St. Michael's R. C. Church, Buffalo; *Microfilmed Records of Buffalo Parishes*, roll 281, Buffalo and Erie County Public Library.

68 Elizabeth had three children from a first marriage to John Hansgen, and one son by her second husband, Nicholas Zahm. Baptismal, marriage and burial registers of St. Louis's, St. Mary's and St. Michael's R. C. Churches, Buffalo.

69 Burial record of Nicholas Jax, Aug. 21, 1852 (died Aug. 20, 1852, "cholera"); *Liber Mortuorum, 1850–1865*: [19], St. Mary's R. C. Church, Buffalo; *Microfilmed Records of Buffalo Parishes*, roll 280, Buffalo and Erie County Public Library.

70 Burial record of Nicholas Zahm, Sept. 5, 1852 (died Sept. 3, 1852); *Liber Sepultorum, 1851–1868*, St. Michael's R. C. Church, Buffalo; *Microfilmed Records of Buffalo Parishes*, roll 281, Buffalo and Erie County Public Library.

71 [Anna] Maria Miller household, 1855 New York State Census, Buffalo (Fourth Ward), New York; microfilm 225, roll 2, item 110, Buffalo and Erie County Public Library.

72 Burial record of Anna Maria Miller, Sept. 5, 1852 (died Sept. 4, 1852, "cholera"); *Liber Mortuorum, 1850–1865*: [23], St. Mary's R. C. Church, Buffalo; *Microfilmed Records of Buffalo Parishes*, roll 280, Buffalo and Erie County Public Library.

73 Burial record of "Nicolaus Muller," Sept. 6, 1852 (died Sept. 5, 1852); *Liber Sepultorum, 1851–1868*: [5], St. Michael's R. C. Church, Buffalo; *Microfilmed*

Records of Buffalo Parishes, roll 281, Buffalo and Erie County Public Library.

74   Baptismal record of Ottilia Barbara Mosbach, Jan. 28, 1855 (born Jan. 15, 1855); *Register of Baptisms* 3: 121, St. Mary's R. C. Church, Buffalo; *Microfilmed Records of Buffalo Parishes*, roll 280, Buffalo and Erie County Public Library.

75   See, for examples, Erie County Deed Book 56: 341; 76: 263; 78: 387; 117: 407; Erie County Courthouse, Buffalo.

76   See works cited in n. 1 above.

77   Ibid.

78   Land Deed, May 19, 1857, Erie County Deed Book 182: 221, 223; Erie County Courthouse, Buffalo.

79   Thomas E. Harney, *AMDG: A History of Canisius College*, vol. III (New York: Vantage Press, 1988), 89–92. First two academic years, 1870–71 and 1871–72, were held in a house around the block at 434 Ellicott Street.

80   Conrad Kuhn household, 1850 U.S. Census, Erie County (Buffalo, Fourth Ward), New York, p. 416; National Archives micropublication M432, roll 502.

81   Ibid.

82   Ring-Müller marriage record, Nov. 25, 1858.

83   *Buffalo Commercial Advertiser*, Nov. 25, 1858, p. 3.

84   Ring-Müller marriage record, Nov. 25, 1858.

85   *Buffalo City Directory for 1859*, 257; *Buffalo City Directory for 1860*, 336.

86   Joseph Ring, Petition for Naturalization, Apr. 16, 1858.

9. The War, North

1   Baptismal record of Magdalena Barbara Ring, Feb. 5, 1860 (born Jan. 29, 1860); *Taufen*, 1851–1882: 114, St. Michael's R. C. Church, Buffalo; *Microfilmed Records of Buffalo Parishes*, roll 281, Buffalo and Erie County Public Library.

2   Physical traits attributed to Joe are based on those of his three sons: (1) Joseph Nicholas Ring, from five photographs, ca. 1882–ca. 1916, copies in author's possession, and descriptions in letters from his son, Louis Caffall Ring, to the author, 1985–86; (2) George F. Ring, from four photographs, ca. 1876, 1882 and 1904, originals in author's possession; and (3) John M. Ring, from physical descriptions in *Registers of Enlistments in the United States Army, 1798–1914*, vol. 105, "1900, R–Z," p. 17; National Archives micropublication M233, roll 54; and the pension file of his widow, Mary Emma Ring, Certificate 861,644, Philippine Insurrection, Veterans Administration.

3   Photograph of Joe's son George F. Ring, taken ca. 1904, shows him smoking a corn-cob pipe.

4   Character traits attributed to Joe are inferred from the documented deeds of his life, as well as the salient traits of his two elder sons: (1) Joseph Nicholas Ring, from letters and remembrances of his son, Louis Caffall Ring, shared with the author, 1985–86; and (2) George F. Ring, from recollections of the author's grandmother, Frances Noeth Ring, regarding what she had heard from her husband, George John Ring, who was George F. Ring's son.

5   Joe appears in the *Buffalo City Directory for 1860* (Buffalo: E. R. Jewett, 1860), 336, published probably in early spring; he does *not* appear in the 1860 U.S. Census, taken in June.

6   Research has not uncovered any relatives who left the Buffalo area before Barbara did.

7   See histories of Buffalo cited in Chap. 8, n. 1.

8   History and description of Cincinnati rely primarily on: (1) Lewis Alexander
    Leonard, *Greater Cincinnati and Its People: A History* (Cincinnati: Lewis Historical
    Publishing Co., Inc., 1927); (2) Marilyn Green and Michael Bennett, *Cincinnati, A
    Pictorial History* (Norfolk, Va.: Donning Co., 1986); and (3) *Cincinnati, A Guide to
    the Queen City and Its Neighbors* (Cincinnati: The Cincinnati Historical Society,
    1987) [reprint of the WPA Guide to Cincinnati].

9   See works cited in n. 8 above.

10 Supposition based on the fact that their next child was baptized at St. Augustine's,
    and that this was one of the neighborhoods peripheral to downtown Cincinnati
    being formed by German-speaking immigrants at this time. See Rev. John H.
    Lamott, S.T.D., *The History of the Archdiocese of Cincinnati, 1821–1921*
    (Cincinnati: Frederick Pustet Co., Inc., 1921).

11 Buffalo-to-Cincinnati was a common migration route for German immigrants at
    this time. See works cited in n. 8 above. See also n. 43 below.

12 *Record of Enrollment, Jennie Howell*, Aug. 16, 1869: ". . . said Ship or Vessel was
    built at Cincinnati in . . . 1869 . . . ;" Inland Rivers Library, Department of Rare
    Books & Special Collections, Public Library of Cincinnati & Hamilton County.

13 Roebling would surpass this achievement when he built the Brooklyn Bridge 20
    years later.

14 "The Visit of the President-Elect" and "To-day's Ceremonies," *Cincinnati Daily
    Commerical*, Feb. 12, 1861, p. 2, and "Telegraphic News," "Journey of the
    President-Elect," *Cincinnati Daily Commerical*, Feb. 12, 1861, p. 3.

15 "The President's Progress," "The Journey to Cincinnati," "Speeches and
    Incidents," "Great Enthusiasm," *Cincinnati Daily Commerical*, Feb. 13, 1861, p. 2.

16 "Reception in Cincinnati," *Cincinnati Daily Commerical*, Feb. 13, 1861, p. 2.

17 See works cited in n. 8 above.

18 "Local Matters," "Departure of Our Guests," *Cincinnati Daily Commercial*,
    Feb. 14, 1861, p. 2.

19 See works cited in n. 8 above.

20 Ibid.

21 Ibid.

22 Ibid. Cincinnati was a center for the hospitalization of wounded soldiers.

23 Shelby Foote, *The Civil War, A Narrative*, 3 vols. (New York: Random House,
    1958–1973), I: 260–263. Although the *Monitor* did not destroy, or even damage,
    the *Virginia* (*Merrimac*), this historic sea battle effectively neutralized the threat
    of the Confederate Navy for the remainder of the war.

24 Baptismal Record of "Anna Mar." Ring, Mar. 30, 1862 (born Mar. 22, 1862);
    Baptismal Register 1859–1862: n.p., St. Augustine's R. C. Church, Cincinnati;
    Historical Archives of the Chancery, Archdiocese of Cincinnati, Cincinnati. It
    appears from the sources cited in Ch. 10, nn. 4 and 5, that this infant was called
    "Anna Barbara" rather than her baptismal "Anna Maria."

25 Physical traits are based on full-length portrait photograph, ca. 1870s, copy in
    author's possession, and the fact that Hank Weber's parents were Lorrainian. His
    attire, including top hat and gloves, is extraordinarily dapper for a man of his
    social standing, and reflects his upbringing in the home of a tailor (see n. 27
    below).

26 Letter of Elizabeth Weber Hilberg to Joseph N. Kellas, Feb. 11, 1958, copy in

author's possession: "My Father and Mother went to Cincinnati when they was 20 years old and got married." That would be 1862. However, Henry N. Weber household, 1900 U.S. Census, Erie County (Buffalo), New York, Enumeration District 96, Sheet 14; National Archives micropublication T623, roll 1027, indicates: "Years married, 39." That would place their marriage between mid-1860 and mid-1861. A far-reaching search has uncovered no marriage record to resolve this conflict—which supports the notion that the couple eloped. Nevertheless, whether Lena and Henry were married in 1860, '61 or '62, it is unlikely that they appeared in Cincinnati prior to March of 1862, or they would have acted as godparents to their niece, Anna B. Ring.

27 Baptismal record of "Heinrich Nicolaus" Weber, Jan. 30, 1842 (born Jan. 9, 1842); *Baptismal Register*, German Evangelical Lutheran Church, Buffalo; *Microfilmed Records of Buffalo Parishes*, Buffalo and Erie County Public Library. See the biography of his father, Nicholas Weber, in: *Geschichte der Deutschen in Buffalo und Erie County, N.Y., mit Biographien und Illustrationen hervorragender Deutsch-Amerikaner, welche . . .* (Buffalo: Reinecke & Zesch, 1898), 31.

28 Nicholas Weber household, 1860 U.S. Census, Erie County (Buffalo, Twelfth Ward), New York, p. 136; National Archives micropublication M653, roll 749: "[son] Henry . . . painter;" Henry Weber household, 1870 U.S. Census, Hamilton County (Cincinnati, Twenty-Third Ward), Ohio, p. 749; National Archives micropublication M593, roll 1217: "Daily Laborer;" same, 1880 U.S. Census, Hamilton County (Cincinnati), Ohio, Enumeration District 148, Sheet 5; National Archives micropublication T9, roll 1026: "laborer;" same, 1900 U.S. Census, Erie County (Buffalo), New York, Enumeration District 96, Sheet 14; National Archives micropulication T623, roll 1027: "Janitor;" *Cincinnati City Directory for 1869*: "Finke & Weber, commission, forwarding & produce merchants;" *1870*: "Finke & Weber;" *1874*: "grocer;" *1876*: "bookkeeper;" *1884/5*: "watchman."

29 See works cited in n. 8 above.

30 Ibid.

31 Gerald McKinney Petty, comp., *Index of the Ohio Squirrel Hunters Roster* (Columbus, Ohio: Petty's Press, Printer, 1984), ii.

32 *The War of the Rebellion: A Compilation of the Official Records of the Union and Confederate Armies*, Series I, Vol. XVI, Part II–Correspondence, etc. (Washington: Government Printing Office, 1886), 476 (hereafter *Official Records, Army*).

33 Petty, *Index of the Ohio Squirrel Hunters Roster*, ii.

34 *Official Records, Army*, Series I, Vol. XVI, Part II–Correspondence, etc., 488.

35 See works cited in n. 8 above.

36 *Official Records, Army*, Series I, Vol. XVI, Part II–Correspondence, etc., 500.

37 Ibid., 504.

38 Ibid., 505.

39 Ibid., 511.

40 Ibid., 514.

41 Baptismal record of Edward Joseph Weber, Mar. 8, 1863 (born Feb. 26, 1863); *Baptismal Register* 1862–1863: 25, St. Francis Seraph R. C. Church, Cincinnati; Historical Archives of the Chancery, Archdiocese of Cincinnati, Cincinnati.

42 Foote, *The Civil War*, II: 635. The Confederate draft law preceded by a full year the U.S. draft law.

43 Joseph Ring entry, *Consolidated List, Class I (vol. II, L–R), Second District*, Ohio,

p. 276; Records of Office Subdivisions, 1862–66, Enrollment Branch, General Records, Enrollment Lists and Reports, RG 110, National Archives, Washington. A John Ring, relationship unknown, is residing at the same address. See *Cincinnati City Directory for 1863* (Cincinnati: Williams & Co., 1863), 293: "Ring John, h. 233 W. 6th."

44 "The Draft is a hard necessity . . ." and "The clamor raised soon after the passage of the Conscription Act . . . ," *Cincinnati Daily Commercial*, July 13, 1863, p. 2, and "The Draft—The New York Mob—The Inflammatory Newspapers," *Cincinnati Daily Commercial*, July 16, 1863, p. 2.

45 *Cincinnati Daily Commercial*, July 1863, *passim*.

46 Foote, *The Civil War*, II: 635.

47 Ibid., 635–637.

48 See Nancy Justus Morebeck, *Civil War Draft Records: An Index to the 38th Congressional Districts of 1863* (Vacaville, Calif.: the author, 1997), 1: "The draft , which was very unpopular, would *not* be applied in any locality that had already met its quota of recruits." The president would issue a "call" for a specified number of volunteers, with the proviso that, after a certain number of days, if that quota was not met, conscription would be implemented to make up the shortfall.

49 Eberle and Grande, *Second Looks*, 69, and Brown and Watson, *Buffalo*, 102. Men who accepted a cash bounty to enlist, then deserted at the first opportunity, were called "bounty jumpers." Some of these deserters would then re-enlist in a different enrollment district to collect another bounty, then desert a second time, and a third. The problem was rampant throughout the war.

50 See works cited in n. 8 above.

51 *Cincinnati, A Guide to the Queen City and Its Neighbors*, 185.

52 *Cincinnati City Directory for 1863* (Cincinnati: Williams & Co., 1863), 293: "Ring Joseph, watchman, wks. 133 Race."

53 Ibid., 369, "Architects;" p. 375, "Cabinet Ware Manufacturers & Dealers" and "Carpenters & Builders;" and p. 393, "Painters (house & sign)."

54 Ibid., 377, "Coffee and Spice Mills."

55 See works cited in n. 8 above.

56 Ibid.

57 Ibid.

58 Ibid.

59 *Official Records, Army*, Series I, Vol. XXIII, Part I–Reports, 634.

60 Ibid.

61 Ibid., 636.

62 See works cited in n. 8 above.

63 Time when Joe and Barbara left Cincinnati deduced from: burial record of Anna Barbara Ring, Apr. 28, 1864 (died the same day); *Records of the United German & French R. C. Cemetery*, Book 3, *United German & French R. C. Association*: 259 [map of Section D, Lot 7, with dates of burials]; and Book 34, *Register of Burials, 1859–1873*: [n.p.; burials are alphabetical, and thereunder chronological]; microfilm no. 1411807, Family History Library, Salt Lake City, Utah: "Late Residence: Cherry Street."

10. Buffalo

1 Eberle and Grande, *Second Looks*, 69, and other works cited in Chap. 8, n. 1.

2   The author was able to find no military record whatsoever for any member of the Miller, Jax, and related families. In addition, scanning Buffalo newspapers of the war years reveals a city occupied primarily with its daily commerce. For thousands of Buffalonians, it appears, the war was very distant.

3   Brown and Watson, *Buffalo*, 106–107, and other works cited in Chap. 8, n. 1.

4   Burial Record of Anna Barbara Ring, Apr. 29, 1864 (died Apr. 28, 1864); *Liber Sepultorum, 1851–1868*: 48, St. Michael's R. C. Church, Buffalo; *Microfilmed Records of Buffalo Parishes*, roll 281, Buffalo and Erie County Public Library. Also, Burial Record of Anna Barbara Ring, Apr. 28, 1864 (died the same day); *Records of the United German & French R. C. Cemetery*, Book 34, *Register of Burials, 1859–1873*: [n.p.; burials are alphabetical, and thereunder chronological]; microfilm no. 1411807, Family History Library, Salt Lake City, Utah: "Disease: Infl[uenza] of Lungs."

5   Anna B. Ring tombstone, Section D, lot 7, United German & French R. C. Cemetery, Cheektowaga, New York.

6   Baptismal Record of Joseph Nicholas Ring, July 3, 1864 (born July 1, 1864); *Taufen, 1851–1882*: 168, St. Michael's R. C. Church, Buffalo; *Microfilmed Records of Buffalo Parishes*, roll 281, Buffalo and Erie County Public Library. Throughout this book, to avoid confusion between father and son, Joseph Nicholas Ring is called simply "Nicholas."

7   Recollections of Louis Caffall Ring, son of Joseph Nicholas Ring, shared with the author in interviews, 1985–86.

8   Foote, *The Civil War*, III: 469–470.

9   "No Commutation," *Buffalo Commercial Advertiser*, June 30, 1864, p. 2; "By the President of the United States of America, A Proclamation" and "New Call for Troops," *Buffalo Commercial Advertiser*, July 19, 1864, pp. 1 and 2.

10   Brown and Watson, *Buffalo*, 102. See also Chap. 9, n. 48.

11   Ibid. See also Chap. 9, n. 49.

12   Nevertheless, it must be noted that one artillery battery was composed entirely—officers and enlisted men—of Buffalonians of German descent (Brown and Watson, *Buffalo*, 106).

13   "The Journey of the Dead," "Arrival & Reception of the Remains of President Lincoln," "Repose of the Body in St. James Hall," "The People taking their Last Look," "A Solemn Day in the City," *Buffalo Commercial Advertiser*, Apr. 28, 1865, p. 4.

14   Ibid.

15   Ibid.

16   Ibid.

11. GEORGE

1   History and description of the Delta rely primarily on: (1) John C. Willis, *On the New South Frontier: Life in the Yazoo-Mississippi Delta, 1865–1920* (doctoral dissertation, College of William and Mary, Williamsburg, Virginia, August 1991); (2) Dunbar Rowland, *History of Mississippi, The Heart of the South*, 4 vols. (Chicago: The S. J. Clarke Publishing Co., 1925), especially II, Chaps. XLIV–XLVIII, "The Counties of Mississippi;" (3) *Biographical and Historical Memoirs of Mississippi*, 2 vols. (Chicago: The Goodspeed Publishing Co., 1891), I, Chap. X, "Counties of the Second Choctaw Cession, or New Purchase of 1820;" and (4) interviews and cor-

respondence with Alice Clements Wade and Katherine Clements Branton, native sisters of Rolling Fork, 1988–1998. The author thanks these two splendid local historians for the valuable research assistance, patient and unflagging encouragement, and generous hospitality they provided that Yankee as he endeavored to learn the unique history and distinctive ways of the Delta.

2   See Chap. 8, nn. 5 and 20.

3   See Chap. 8, n. 10.

4   See works cited in n. 1 above; also, Michael Wayne, *The Reshaping of Plantation Society, The Natchez District, 1860–1880* (Baton Rouge: Louisiana State University Press, 1983).

5   See works cited in n. 1 above; also, Hemphill, *Fevers, Floods and Faith*, 141.

6   Ibid.

7   Ibid.

8   Ibid. Regarding the levees, see: Harris, *The Day of the Carpetbagger*, 42–43, 486–489.

9   *Biographical and Historical Memoirs of Mississippi*, I: 204–205, 538.

10   Ibid.; also, see works cited in n. 1 above.

11   Ibid., 205, 538–539.

12   Hemphill, *Fevers, Floods and Faith*, 5, 54.

13   *Biographical and Historical Memoirs of Mississippi*, I: 205, 538–539.

14   Ibid., 711–712.

15   Ibid.; also, Land Deed, May 3, 1860, Issaquena County Deed Book D: 108; Issaquena County Courthouse, Mayersville.

16   Testimony of W. D. Brown, June 22, 1876, "Boutwell Report," I: 704: "To explain myself, there are two places known as Rolling Fork; one is the mouth of the Rolling Fork, and the other is a point six miles above where it receives Deer Creek. The point above is named as 'The Point' or 'Rolling Fork,' indiscriminately; and the point below is always called 'Rolling Fork.'"

17   Personal interviews and observation of the author on research trips to Rolling Fork, 1971–1994.

18   Willis, *On the New South Frontier*, 167–169.

19   *Biographical and Historical Memoirs of Mississippi*, I: 538–540.

20   Ibid.; also, William I. Chaney household, 1860 U.S. Census, Issaquena County, Mississippi, p. 872; National Archives micropublication M653, roll 582; also, roll 598, Slave Schedules, p. 68.

21   Testimony of W. D. Brown, June 22, 1876, "Boutwell Report," I: 695: "The ratio of the aggregate population a few years ago, I think, was about twelve or thirteen [blacks] to one [white]; that is my recollection. That proportion has decreased within the last two or three years on account of the immigration of the whites to the bottom district;" see also Willis, *On the New South Frontier*, 17–18.

22   See works cited in n. 1 above.

23   Testimony of W. D. Brown, June 22, 1876, "Boutwell Report," I: 702: "As I said a while ago, the white population is now much larger than several years ago. Take my neighborhood, for instance, as a sample: there, within a radius of two miles, I could include five or six families, perhaps six or seven families. Along farther down [Deer Creek] remote from the town, or the village [Rolling Fork], the plantations are larger and the whites much more sparse; sometimes one or two white people on a plantation, while there are perhaps from 100 to 150 colored people of

all sizes and sexes; sometimes two or three [whites] on a plantation where there are 40 or 50 negroes;" see also Willis, *On the New South Frontier*, 56–57.

24   J. S. Joor household, 1860 U.S. Census, Issaquena County, Mississippi, p. 873; National Archives micropublication M653, roll 582.

25   John S. Joor, born ca. 1846, was the son of George Joor and Catherine P. Shelby; both parents were dead by 1850. See Evan W. Shelby household, 1850 U.S. Census, Issaquena County, Mississippi, p. 297; National Archives micropublication M432, roll 373: "John S. Joor . . . [age] 5 . . . [born] Mississippi;" also, George Joor probate file, no. 248, County Clerk's Office, Issaquena County Courthouse, Mayersville.

26   See Chap. 8, p. 47.

27   Charles E. Wright, for example, was another planter who employed George. See: *George F. Ring v. Charles E. Wright*, Cases 337 and 339, *Minutes of the Circuit Court of Issaquena County*, Nov. Term 1865, Book B: 282, and May Term 1866, Book B: 333–335, in the courthouse in Mayersville.

28   Ibid.

29   George Ring entry, Issaquena County 1860 Personal Tax Roll; Record Group 29, microcopy roll 230, Mississippi Department of Archives and History, Jackson.

12. THE WAR, SOUTH

1   Foote, *The Civil War*, II: 206–207.

2   Geoffrey C. Ward, with Ric Burns and Ken Burns, *The Civil War: An Illustrated History* (New York: Alfred A. Knopf, Inc., 1990), 199, details vividly the ineffectiveness of the blockade. The most famous "blockade runner" of them all, of course, was Margaret Mitchell's dashing Rhett Butler.

3   Foote, *The Civil War*, I: 394. In October of 1862 the age limit was extended to 18–45 (Foote, *The Civil War*, I: 780).

4   Although no document dated between the 1860 census (taken in June) and an 1865 Issaquena County Circuit Court case (brought in spring term) has been found to prove that George remained in the Rolling Fork neighborhood for the duration of the war, the circumstantial evidence narrated in Chaps. 11, 12 and 13 supports that conclusion. A thorough search of military records, both Union and Confederate, at the National Archives and the Mississippi Department of Archives and History, failed to uncover any record that could be George's. Regarding the significant number of men who succeeded in evading military service, see: Garner, *Reconstruction in Mississippi*, 23–24.

5   Provisions of the Confederate draft law have been gathered from several sources, including Foote, *The Civil War*, Ward, *The Civil War*, and Rowland, *History of Mississippi*.

6   George had declared his intention to become a citizen (see Chap. 8, p. 48), but he had not yet petitioned for naturalization.

7   Testimony of W. D. Brown, June 22, 1876, "Boutwell Report," I: 708.

8   Ibid., 693, 703; also, W. D. Brown household, 1860 U.S. Census, Issaquena County, Mississippi, p. 872; National Archives micropublication M653, roll 582; also, roll 598, Slave Schedules, pp. 68–69.

9   Testimony of W. D. Brown, June 22, 1876, "Boutwell Report," I: 702.

10   Household of W. D. Brown, 1870 U.S. Census, Issaquena County (Schola Precinct), Mississippi, p. 266; National Archives micropublication M593, roll 731;

also, household of W. D. Brown, 1880 U.S. Census, Sharkey County (Beat 3), Mississippi, p. 139; National Archives micropublication T9, roll 664.

11 W. D. Brown household, 1860 U.S. Census; also roll 598, Slave Schedules, pp. 68–69.

12 Testimony of W. D. Brown, June 22, 1876, "Boutwell Report," I: 708.

13 Joor's statement, p. 1.

14 William B. "Macquillen" household, 1850 U.S. Census, Issaquena County, Mississippi, p. 298; National Archives micropublication M432, roll 373.

15 Ibid.

16 William B. "Macquillen" household, 1860 U.S. Census, Issaquena County, Mississippi, p. 871; National Archives micropublication M653, roll 582.

17 Ibid.; also roll 598, Slave Schedules, p. 68.

18 Testimony of W. D. Brown, June 22, 1876, "Boutwell Report," I: 708 (quoted in full on p. 94), makes clear that there were white men, especially "old citizens," residing on Deer Creek plantations in 1863.

19 *Biographical and Historical Memoirs of Mississippi*, I: 539.

20 Foote, *The Civil War*, II: 206. The "Steele's Bayou Expedition" is documented in *Official Records, Army*, Series I, Vol. XXIV, Part I–Reports, 430–467, and *Official Records of the Union and Confederate Navies in the War of the Rebellion* (Washington: Government Printing Office, 1911), Series I, Vol. 24, 474–501 (hereafter *Official Records, Navy*).

21 Foote, *The Civil War*, II: 207–208; also *Official Records, Army*, Series I, Vol. XXIV, Part I–Reports, 431, and *Official Records, Navy*, Series I, Vol. 24, 475.

22 Foote, *The Civil War*, II: 207–208; also *Official Records, Army*, Series I, Vol. XXIV, Part I–Reports, 432–434.

23 Ibid.

24 Foote, *The Civil War*, II: 208; also *Official Records, Navy*, Series I, Vol. 24, 475.

25 Quoted in Foote, *The Civil War*, II: 208–209; source not cited.

26 Foote, *The Civil War*, II: 209–210.

27 *Official Records, Army*, Series I, Vol. XXIV, Part I–Reports, 465–466.

28 *Biographical and Historical Memoirs of Mississippi*, I: 539.

29 *Official Records, Army*, Series I, Vol. XXIV, Part I–Reports, 466.

30 Quoted in Foote, *The Civil War*, II: 210; source not cited.

31 *Official Records, Army*, Series I, Vol. XXIV, Part I–Reports, 458–459; also *Biographical and Historical Memoirs of Mississippi*, I: 539.

32 *Official Records, Army*, Series I, Vol. XXIV, Part I–Reports, 434, 459, and *Official Records, Navy*, Series I, Vol. 24, 495.

33 *Official Records, Navy*, Series I, Vol. 24, 491.

34 *Official Records, Army*, Series I, Vol. XXIV, Part I–Reports, 434–435, 459, and *Official Records, Navy*, Series I, Vol. 24, 495.

35 *Official Records, Army*, Series I, Vol. XXIV, Part I–Reports, 435, 460.

36 Ibid., 435.

37 Foote, *The Civil War*, II: 211.

38 *Official Records, Army*, Series I, vol. XXIV, Part I–Reports, 436.

39 Ibid.

40 *Biographical and Historical Memoirs of Mississippi*, I: 712: "[George W. Faison, Jr.] was born in Issaquena County, Miss., February 23, 1861, and in 1863 was brought by his parents to Sunflower county. . . ." On Sunflower County as a safe haven dur-

ing the war, see Hemphill, *Fevers, Floods and Faith*, 60. See also n. 61 below.

41 Hemphill, *Fevers, Floods and Faith*, 115. The "shantyboat experience" was not peculiar to the Faisons; see Hemphill, 43, 321, and Davis, *Trials of the Earth*, 162.

42 *Official Records, Army*, Series I, vol. XXIV, Part I–Reports, 505.

43 Bern Keating, *A History of Washington County, Mississippi* (Greenville: The Greenville Junior Auxiliary, 1976), 41–42.

44 *Biographical and Historical Memoirs of Mississippi*, I: 213–215.

45 *Official Records, Army*, Series I, vol. XXIV, Part I–Reports, 501–503, 507–508.

46 Ibid., 508.

47 Keating, *A History of Washington County*, 42.

48 *Official Records, Army*, Series I, vol. XXIV, Part I–Reports, 509.

49 Ibid., 502.

50 Ibid., 505–506.

51 Rowland, *History of Mississippi*, I: 809. The Indian mound and the remnants of a rebuilt Mount Helena are still there.

52 *Official Records, Army*, Series I, vol. XXIV, Part I–Reports, 505.

53 Testimony of W. D. Brown, June 22, 1876, "Boutwell Report," I: 708–709. Brown gives a slightly more detailed account in the work sited in n. 54 below.

54 J. S. McNeily, *From Organization to Overthrow of Mississippi's Provisional Government, 1865–1868* (Jackson: Mississippi Historical Society, 1916), 49.

55 *Official Records, Army*, Series I, vol. XXIV, Part I–Reports, 709.

56 Promulgated Jan. 1, 1863, and read by Union officers to blacks residing in territory under Union control. See Rowland, *History of Mississippi*, I: 805–810.

57 *Official Records, Army*, Series I, vol. XXIV, Part I–Reports, 505.

58 Rowland, *History of Mississippi*, I: 817 and 824.

59 McNeily, *From Organization to Overthrow of Mississippi's Provisional Government*, 50. Quotation is from a letter from W. D. Brown to J. S. McNeily.

60 Rowland, *History of Mississippi*, I: 883.

61 Ibid., 816, includes Issaquena in a list of Delta counties held by Union forces for the remainder of the war. However, it is clear from the *Official Records* that Federal control extended only to the territory along the Mississippi River, and did not reach very far into the less-accessible interior. (Rowland also includes Washington and Sunflower in his list, but there, too, Federal occupation was limited to the more easily accessible regions of the counties.) See also n. 68 below.

62 Foote, *The Civil War*, III: 125–126, 172.

63 Garner, *Reconstruction in Mississippi*, 27.

64 Ibid.

65 Ibid., 22-24.

66 *Official Records, Army*, Series I, vol. XXIV, Part I–Reports, 568, 572. Bolivar was assigned September; Washington, October; Issaquena, November.

67 Keating, *A History of Washington County*, 43.

68 *Official Records, Army*, Series I, vol. XXIV, Part I–Reports, 568, 572. Rowland, *History of Mississippi*, I: 810, 818–819, 830, 867, and Garner, *Reconstruction in Mississippi*, 29–32, discuss the brisk illegal commerce that transpired during the second half of the war between some residents of the Delta and the Union men living among them. "The source of the problem was the phenomenal rise in the price of cotton" (Garner, 31). It was a mortifying aggravation for officials both North and South that so many men engaged in the lucrative trafficking of cotton.

Whether or not George F. Ring ever "traded with the Yankees" is impossible even to speculate. Nevertheless, a supply of greenbacks amassed during the war would certainly have helped George establish himself in business afterwards, when all Confederate dollars, bonds and scrip suddenly became worthless paper.

69   Ibid., 567, 571.

70   Ibid., 568, 571.

71   Ibid., 568, 571-572.

72   Ibid., 571.

73   Ibid., 572.

74   Apr. 9, 1865. Foote, *The Civil War*, III: 939–956, narrates the events of this day in moving detail.

13. COTTON

1   No record provides the route Joe and Barbara took to reach the Deer Creek neighborhood, or the date of their arrival. However, given the state of the South's railways in 1865, it is most likely that the Rings traveled by river. Arriving in Vicksburg and then going up Deer Creek would have been much easier than stopping at Greenville (burned out by the Yankees) or Tallula and journeying overland. The time would most probably have been the spring of 1865.

2   Gordon A. Cotton and Ralph C. Mason, *With Malice Toward Some, The Military Occupation of Vicksburg, 1864–1865* (Vicksburg: Vicksburg and Warren County Historical Society, 1991), 7–8; also, Hemphill, *Fevers, Floods and Faith*, 86–87.

3   The date when the Webers arrived in Mississippi is not documented. However, it is likely that they traveled with the Rings.

4   "River Intelligence" and steamer advertisements, *Vicksburg Daily Herald*, May and June 1865, indicate that there was regularly-scheduled (though not daily) steamer service up the Yazoo River at this time. Although no mention appears about service on Deer Creek, given the number of plantations along that waterway, it is presumed that some of the "Yazoo steamers" serviced Deer Creek.

5   Cotton and Mason, *With Malice Toward Some*, contains numerous anecdotal (and documented) stories that illustrate vividly the contempt felt by the "defeated" Vicksburgers for their occupying "victors."

6   Ibid.

7   Testimony of W. D. Brown, June 22, 1876, "Boutwell Report," I: 702: "The plantations many of them are large, and the whites are, as compared with the colored people, sparse and scattered; not so much so now as they were a few years ago, as the white element is increasing largely in that country. Q: Is the country divided into large plantations? A: Yes, sir; although not so much so as once, for they are being somewhat cut up;" also, Willis, *On the New South Frontier*, 5: "Thousands of immigrants came to the Delta . . . between 1865 and 1900."

8   Garner, *Reconstruction in Mississippi*, 135–136, 260; Willis, *On the New South Frontier*, 9; Harris, *The Day of the Carpetbagger*, 91–92; and Davis, *Trials of the Earth*, 83–84.

9   Willis, *On the New South Frontier*, 5–6, and Harris, *The Day of the Carpetbagger*, 277–280, 508–509, 574–575.

10   Willis, *On the New South Frontier*, 8–9.

11   Harris, *The Day of the Carpetbagger*, 482.

12   Willis, *On the New South Frontier*, 8–9.

13   Ibid.
14   Ibid., 108–109, and Harris, *The Day of the Carpetbagger*, 278–280.
15   Willis, *On the New South Frontier*, 149–151.
16   Ibid., 9-12, and Harris, *The Day of the Carpetbagger*, 509–510.
17   Willis, *On the New South Frontier*, 9–12.
18   Ibid., 27, n. 3; p. 95.
19   Ibid., 4.
20   Chapman and Battaile, *Picturesque Vicksburg and the Yazoo Delta*, 45.
21   Ibid., 38.
22   Joseph Nicholas Ring told his son Louis Caffall Ring that George used "earthy and profane language." That was one of the reasons why Joseph Nicholas Ring's wife, Lena Caffall, did not want to live "under Uncle George's roof" at Saints Rest plantation. (Interviews with Louis Caffall Ring, 1985–1986.) Lena Caffall, like Barbara, was the daughter of an immigrant tradesman and, like Barbara, grew up with many siblings in an urban Germanic Catholic household. Barbara's sensibilities would have been much akin to those of Lena Caffall.
23   "Geo. Ring" entry, Ship *South America* Passenger List, May 21, 1853, p. 6; *Passenger Lists of Vessels Arriving at New York, NY, 1820–1897*; National Archives micropublication M237, roll 125: "OCCUPATION" column contains ditto marks carrying down "Farmer" from two lines above. The author dismisses this as an error, as every adult male on the ship is so labeled. The laxity of the compilers of ships' passenger lists in recording such information, and the frequency of errors, is well known to users of U.S. passenger arrival records. It would have been most unusual for one brother (Joseph) to be a tradesman (carpenter), while the other brother (George) was a farmer—as Chapter 8 hopefully demonstrates. "The Country to which they severally belong" column contains a squiggly line the length of the page, carrying down "Germany" from the top line. This, too, is blatantly wrong for George. The compiler of the list simply repeated this device on every page, making every passenger on board the ship a native of Germany. George himself swore in the Issaquena County courthouse in 1867 that he was a native of France. (Nevertheless, in spite of these two errors, the author is convinced that the "Geo. Ring" appearing in the passenger list of the Ship *South America* is indeed Joseph Ring's younger brother, because the year of his arrival in America (1853), and his age at arrival (18), are correct, besides which Le Havre was the port of departure used by the vast majority of Alsatians and Lorrainians emigrating at that time, and thorough searching has uncovered no other passenger arrival record listing any George Ring at all—the name being extremely rare.)
24   Willis, *On the New South Frontier*, 57.
25   Ibid., 90.
26   Chapman and Battaile, *Picturesque Vicksburg and the Yazoo Delta*, photographs on pp. 41, 43 and 69; also, Richardson and Godman, *In and About Vicksburg*, photograph on p. 229.
27   Interviews with Alice Wade and Katherine Branton, 1988–1998. These sisters have spent their entire adult lives on cotton plantations in Sharkey County.
28   Ibid.
29   Ibid., and Davis, *Trials of the Earth*, 174.
30   Chapman and Battaile, *Picturesque Vicksburg and the Yazoo Delta*, 38.
31   Ibid.

32   Interviews with Alice Wade and Katherine Branton, 1988–1998.

33   Ibid.; also, Chapman and Battaile, *Picturesque Vicksburg and the Yazoo Delta*, 38.

34   Ibid.

35   George F. Ring entry, Issaquena County 1866 Personal Tax Roll; Record Group 29, microcopy roll 230, Mississippi Department of Archives and History, Jackson: "On each bale of Cotton grown or produced the year next preceeding the assessment—One dollar: . . . $15.00."

36   Assumption; precisely what arrangement George, Joe and Hank agreed upon— one jointly-owned crop or three individually-owned crops—is not known. Certainly by 1871 Joe was raising his own cotton (see Chap. 15, n. 84), but he was probably raising his own cotton for some years before then.

14. THE STORE

1   Land deed, Jan. 1, 1866, Issaquena County Deed Book D: 223; Issaquena County Courthouse, Mayersville.

2   *Biographical and Historical Memoirs of Mississippi*, I: 711–712; also Hemphill, *Fevers, Floods and Faith*, 772.

3   Ibid.; also Hemphill, *Fevers, Floods and Faith*, 115–116; also Willis, *On the New South Frontier*, 175.

4   George's statement, p. 1, and land deed, undated, but recorded Oct. 24, 1867, Issaquena County Deed Book D: 388; Issaquena County Courthouse, Mayersville.

5   William Jeans household, 1860 U.S. Census, Issaquena County, Mississippi, p. 871; National Archives micropublication M653, roll 582.

6   Ibid. (3 children, all born Mississippi; household also includes William's two younger brothers); also, William "Jeanes" household, 1870 U.S. Census, Issaquena County (Rolling Fork Precinct), Mississippi, p. 269; National Archives micropublication M593, roll 731 (2 elder children no longer listed; 2 children born Mississippi, 1 born Illinois; 2 brothers enumerated separately with their own families). John Davis of Bellevue, Nebraska, a descendant of one of William Jeans's brothers, has conducted extensive genealogical research on the Jeans family, and the author thanks him for information (letters to the author, 1993–1994).

7   Ibid.

8   William Jeans farm, 1860 U.S. Census, Agricultural Schedule, Issaquena County, Mississippi, p. 5; microcopy roll 178, Mississippi Department of Archives and History, Jackson.

9   William "Jeanes" household, 1870 U.S. Census: "Wm, 5, born Illinois."

10   George's statement, p. 4.

11   Land deed, Jan. 1, 1866, Issaquena County Deed Book D: 223: ". . . To have and to hold said tract or parcel of land *with all the appurtenances* [emphasis added] and privileges thereunto belonging . . . ."

12   Garner, *Reconstruction in Mississippi*, 249–253.

13   Ibid., 254.

14   Ibid., 261.

15   Ibid., 261, 267; also Willis, *On the New South Frontier*, 57–58.

16   Garner, *Reconstruction in Mississippi*, 249, 256.

17   Willis, *On the New South Frontier*, 58–59.

18   Ibid., 32–33.

19   Ibid., 85–88.

20   Ibid., 53–54.

21   Ibid., 58.

22   See Chap. 2, n. 26.

23   Resentment felt by some blacks toward their former masters may have worked in George's favor. See Willis, *On the New South Frontier,* 57: "In December 1865, Foster reported that ex-slaves in Issaquena County's plantation belt 'refuse to enter into contracts with native planters for the ensuing year, but express entire willingness to do so with northerners. . . .'"

24   Garner, *Reconstruction in Mississippi,* 133: ". . . they [ex-slaves] soon returned to the plantations and begged for employment." However, see also 256–257: ". . . it became necessary in some instances to order them [ex-slaves] back to the plantations by military force."

25   On the disastrous cotton harvests of 1866 and 1867, see: Garner, *Reconstruction in Mississippi,* 126, 132, 137; also, Wayne, *The Reshaping of Plantation Society,* 63–66.

26   Ibid.

27   Ibid., 64, and Harris, *The Day of the Carpetbagger,* 69–70.

28   Jeans & Ring entry, Issaquena County 1866 Personal Tax Roll; Record Group 29, micocopy roll 230, Mississippi Department of Archives and History, Jackson.

29   George F. Ring entry, Issaquena County 1866 Personal Tax Roll; Record Group 29, microcopy roll 230, Mississippi Department of Archives and History, Jackson.

30   Lewis C. Gray, "Local Market Organization and Methods," in Henry C. Dethloff and C. Joseph Pusateri, eds., *American Business History: Case Studies* (Arlington Heights, Illinois: Harlan Davidson, Inc., 1987), Table 4-1, 115.

31   *George F. Ring v. Charles E. Wright,* Cases 337 and 339, *Minutes of the Circuit Court of Issaquena County,* Nov. Term 1865, Book B: 282, and May Term 1866, Book B: 333–335, in the courthouse in Mayersville.

32   William Jeans entry, Issaquena County 1866 Personal Tax Roll; Record Group 29, microcopy roll 230, Mississippi Department of Archives and History, Jackson.

33   Jeans & Ring entry, Issaquena County 1868 Personal Tax Roll; Record Group 29, microcopy roll 230, Mississippi Department of Archives and History, Jackson.

34   Mississippi State Census of 1866 (enumerated Nov. 20th), Issaquena County; Record Group 28, microcopy roll 547, Mississippi Department of Archives and History, Jackson, shows the Rings and Webers are there: "H. 'Webber,' 26," followed by "Geo Ring, 30," followed by "Joe Ring, 33," and farther down the same page, "'S.' Webber, 25 (female)," followed by "'S.' Ring, 28 (female)," and lastly "Joe Ring, 2," would be Lena and Barbara and Joseph Nicholas.

35   See n. 25 above.

36   Ibid.

37   Wayne, *The Reshaping of Plantation Society,* 68, and Harris, *The Day of the Carpetbagger,* 110–112.

38   By Oct. 19, 1867, the Webers were back North, where Lena had a daughter in Buffalo. Baptismal Record of "Helena Weber," Oct. 27, 1867 (born Oct. 19, 1867); *Taufen, 1851–1882*: 225, St. Michael's R. C. Church, Buffalo; *Microfilmed Records of Buffalo Parishes,* roll 281, Buffalo and Erie County Public Library.

39   George's statement, p. 1.

40   Ibid., 2.

41   Ibid., 16.

42   Ibid., 14.

43   Ibid., 14–15.
44   Ibid., 15.
45   "To the Editor of the Daily Times," *Vicksburg Daily Times*, Mar. 19, 1873, p. 3.
46   George's statement, p. 14.
47   Ibid.
48   Ibid.
49   Ibid., 15.
50   Ibid.
51   Ibid., 14.
52   Ibid.
53   Ibid., 15.
54   Ibid.
55   Ibid.
56   Ibid.

15. The Delta

1   Land deed, Dec. 11, 1867, Issaquena County Deed Book D: 391; Issaquena County
     Courthouse, Mayersville.
2   Regarding Joe's character traits, see Chap. 9, n. 4; regarding Barbara's character
     traits, see Chap. 5, n. 3.
3   Description of daily life in the Delta relies primarily on: (1) Marie M. Hemphill,
     Fevers, Floods and Faith, A History of Sunflower County, Mississippi, 1844–1976
     (Indianola, Miss.: Sunflower County Historical Society, 1980); (2) Helen Dick
     Davis, ed., *Trials of the Earth, The Autobiography of Mary Hamilton* (Jackson:
     University Press of Mississippi, 1992); (3) William Alexander Percy, *Lanterns on
     the Levee, Recollections of a Planter's Son* (New York: Alfred A. Knopf, 1941); and
     (4) interviews and correspondence with Alice Wade and Katherine Branton,
     1988–1998.
4   Davis, *Trials of the Earth*, 113, 191, 205–206.
5   Baptismal record of George F. Ring, Apr. 30, 1867 (born Jan. 15, 1867); *Baptismal
     Register* 1: 194, St. Paul's R. C. Church, Vicksburg.
6   See Chap. 8, nn. 39, 42, 43, 46 and 50.
7   See Chap. 9, p. 60, and Chap. 10, p. 72.
8   Baptismal record of George F. Ring, Apr. 30, 1867: "Sp[onsor]. Rosalia Contella."
     The housekeeper's name appears in other baptismal records as well, evidently
     whenever a godparent was needed in a pinch. For her position, see: "Leray, F. X."
     household, 1870 U.S. Census, Warren County (Vicksburg, Ward 5), Mississippi,
     p. 273; National Archives micropublication M593, roll 751: "Cantella, R., 28,
     Servant." For "George F. Ring, Jr.," see *Katharina Ring et al. v. Barbara Ring
     et al.*, cited in Prologue, n. 2.
9   See Chap. 14, p. 116.
10   Typical household chores taken from works cited in n. 3 above.
11   Hemphill, *Fevers, Floods and Faith*, 293, 465; Davis, *Trials of the Earth*, 65, 99.
12   Davis, *Trials of the Earth*, 57, 203, 222.
13   Conversations with Alice Wade and Katherine Branton, 1988–1998.
14   Davis, *Trials of the Earth*, 215.
15   Conversations with Alice Wade and Katherine Branton, 1988–1998.
16   Ibid.

17   Assumption; it is unlikely that an urban craftsman such as Joe would know much about hunting.

18   See Chap. 4, n. 70.

19   See Chap. 1, n. 16.

20   Hemphill, *Fevers, Floods and Faith*, 35, 37; Davis, *Trials of the Earth*, 57, 222.

21   See n. 17 above.

22   Davis, *Trials of the Earth*, 154.

23   Conversations with Alice Wade and Katherine Branton, 1988–1998.

24   Davis, *Trials of the Earth*, 40.

25   Ibid.

26   Ibid., 121.

27   Conversations with Alice Wade and Katherine Branton, 1988–1998.

28   Photographs reveal that George's nephew, Joseph Nicholas Ring, was a cigar smoker, as was his grandnephew, George John Ring. The practice was common among German Americans. On the popularity of whittling, see Clark, *Pills, Petticoats, & Plows*, 30.

29   On the popularity of playing poker, see Hemphill, *Fevers, Floods and Faith*, 35.

30   Regarding the consumption of alcoholic beverages, see Harris, *The Day of the Carpetbagger*, 579–580: "The Delta especially was reputed to be 'a veritable Sodom' where 'whiskey drinking, gambling and Sabbath-breaking were the common and prevailing sins of the country.'"

31   Joseph Nicholas Ring told his son Louis Caffall Ring that George "drank liberally." That was one of the reasons why Joseph Nicholas Ring's wife, Lena Caffall, did not want to live "under Uncle George's roof" at Saints Rest plantation. (Interviews with Louis Caffall Ring, 1985–1986.) Also, claims of liquor dealers for several cases of liquor against the estate of George F. Ring, filed Aug. 25, 1902, Warren County probate file no. 4350, County Clerk's Office, Vicksburg. Also, reports of dinner parties given at George's residences appearing in the society columns of Sunflower and Warren County newspapers.

32   Lena Caffall, like Barbara, was the daughter of an immigrant tradesman and, like Barbara, grew up with many siblings in an urban Germanic Catholic household. Barbara's sensibilities would have been much akin to those of Lena Caffall.

33   See Chap. 13, n. 22.

34   In July of 1873, when Barbara—whose parents had been living in the United States for 10 years already when she was born—purchased a headstone for her deceased son, it was inscribed not in English, but in German. See Chap. 33.

35   George's statement, pp. 1, 6.

36   Jesse Moore household, 1870 U.S. Census, Issaquena County (Schola Precinct), Mississippi, p. 287; National Archives micropublication M593, roll 731.

37   "J. More, 24" entry, Mississippi State Census of 1866 (enumerated Nov. 20th), Issaquena County; Record Group 28, microcopy roll 547, Mississippi Department of Archives and History, Jackson. This listing comes immediately after the household of "Wm Janes, 38," which is obviously—given the composition of the family—Willie Jeans.

38   Land deed, Mar. 27, 1869, Issaquena County Deed Book E: 384; Issaquena County Courthouse, Mayersville.

39   Inventory of the estate of Jesse Moore, filed Oct. 7, 1873, Issaquena County probate file no. 26, County Clerk's Office, Mayersville.

40 Ibid.

41 The Cokers do not appear among the residents of Rolling Fork Landing in the federal census enumerated in August of 1870. However, John F. Coker's claim "for Work" against the estate of Jesse Moore, filed Aug. 20, 1873, lists "March 1, 1870," as the earliest date when funds were due him for four months' work. Therefore, Coker was already in Moore's employ by November of 1869.

42 See Chap. 4, nn. 2–5.

43 Parberry and "Uncle Jimmy" do not appear among the residents of Rolling Fork Landing in the federal census enumerated in August of 1870. However, given the veterinarian's notoriety in the neighborhood by 1873, it is presumed that he and his friend arrived within a short time after the census was taken.

44 Willis, *On the New South Frontier*, 9–10, and the author's own research indicate that four classes may be distinguished in the post-war Delta: 1) planters, 2) whites with some education, craft or trade, 3) poor whites, and 4) blacks. Percy, *Lanterns on the Levy*, 19, posits only three classes—planters, poor whites and blacks—although he does acknowledge at least a small fourth class as well: "Forming a small intermediate white class were the managers and slave-drivers and bosses, men of some ability and force, mostly illiterate." (p. 20).

45 Jesse Moore-Martha Coker marriage record, Feb. 22, 1870, Warren County Marriage Book H: 234; County Clerk's Office, Vicksburg.

46 Regarding the term "carpetbagger," its proper use, and its popular misuse, see Garner, *Reconstruction in Mississippi*, 135–136, and Foner, *Reconstruction*, 294–297.

47 The "Place of Birth" column of the 1870 federal census reveals that only a very small minority of Delta residents was born in Mississippi.

48 See Testimony of W. D. Brown, June 22, 1876, "Boutwell Report," I: 716.

49 Ibid., 701.

50 See Chap. 2, n. 26.

51 Garner, *Reconstruction in Mississippi*, 228–232.

52 Harris, *The Day of the Carpetbagger*, 375.

53 Ibid., 382, 388–389, and Percy, *Lanterns on the Levee*, 225–241.

54 Special Order No. 79, Apr. 20, 1869; *Special Orders*, Vol. 604-B; Fourth Military District (Department of Mississippi); Records of the Adjutant General's Office, 1780s–1917, RG 94, National Archives, Washington. See also: Letter dated Apr. 21, 1869; *Letters and Telegrams Sent, Apr. 1867–Mar. 1870*; Fourth Military District (Department of Mississippi), Office of Civil Affairs; Records of United States Army Continental Commands, 1821–1920, RG 393, National Archives, Washington.

55 *The Revised Code of the Statute Laws of the State of Mississippi* (Jackson: E. Barksdale, State Printer, 1857), Chap. LIX, Sec. IV, "Of the Jurisdiction and Powers of the Boards of Police," pp. 416–417.

56 Oath of Office, May 7, 1869; *Registers of Letters Received, Mar. 1867–Feb. 1870*; Fourth Military District (Department of Mississippi), Office of Civil Affairs; Records of United States Army Continental Commands, 1821–1920, RG 393, National Archives, Washington.

57 *Minutes of the Board of Police*, May Regular Term 1869 (17th May), pp. 115, 123, 127, 131; Issaquena County Courthouse, Mayersville.

58 Ibid., Special July Term 1869, p. 134.

59 *The Revised Code of the Statute Laws of the State of Mississippi* (1857), Chap. LIX, Sec. II, "Of the meetings of the Boards of Police," p. 415.

60   Regarding the spirit of lawlessness in Mississippi during Reconstruction, see
      Chap. 2, n. 15.

61   Willis, *On the New South Frontier*, 166–167.

62   Testimony of W. D. Brown, June 22, 1876, "Boutwell Report," I: 714.

63   "Dead Men Tell No Tales," *Vicksburg Daily Herald*, Aug. 22, 1883.

64   See Chap. 2, n. 26.

65   *The Revised Code of the Statute Laws of the State of Mississippi* (1857), Chap. LIX,
      Sec. II, "Of the meetings of the Boards of Police," p. 415.

66   *Minutes of the Board of Police*, May Regular Term 1869 (17th May), p. 131; Special
      July Term 1869, p. 143; Issaquena County Courthouse, Mayersville.

67   Ibid., Special Term 1870, p. 191.

68   Pension File of John's widow, Mary Emma Ring, Certificate 861,644, Philippine
      Insurrection; Veterans Administration: "birthday, June 17, 1869, birthplace, Rolling
      Fork, Miss." This birthdate and this birthplace are both confirmed in: John Ring,
      death certificate no. 41588 (1906), New York State Department of Health—Bureau
      of Vital Statistics, Albany. No baptismal record for John Ring has been found.

69   Joseph Ring household, 1870 U.S. Census, Issaquena County (Schola Precinct),
      Mississippi, p. 285; National Archives micropublication M593, roll 731.

70   Joseph Ring entry, Issaquena County 1871 Personal Tax Roll; Record Group 29,
      microcopy roll 230, Mississippi Department of Archives and History, Jackson.

71   Land deed, Mar. 10, 1869, Issaquena County Deed Book E: 389; Issaquena County
      Courthouse, Mayersville.

72   Age estimated from: William Jeans household, 1860 U.S. Census, Issaquena
      County, Mississippi, p. 871; National Archives micropublication M653, roll 582;
      also William "Jeanes" household, 1870 U.S. Census, Issaquena County (Rolling
      Fork Precinct), Mississippi, p. 269; National Archives micropublication M593, roll
      731.

73   George's statement, p. 2.

74   Ibid. For age, see n. 72 above.

75   George's statement, p. 13.

76   Yellow fever and malaria (often called "swamp fever" in the Delta) were diseases
      of late summer—July through October—carried by mosquitoes. They did not
      occur in the spring. Cholera, however, a water-borne disease, was known to erupt
      in springtime, although it, too, was most prevalent in late summer. It is also possi-
      ble that the Jeanses succumbed to typhus—borne by fleas, lice or mites—or an
      infectious disease as common as rheumatic fever (also called scarlet fever, and
      known today as strep throat). The author thanks Terrence E. Barr, Physician
      Assistant at Walter Reed Army Medical Center, Washington, D.C., for his help in
      researching questions regarding human anatomy, health and medicine.

77   Land deed, Mar. 14, 1871, Warren County Deed Book JJ: 41; Warren County
      Courthouse, Vicksburg.

78   Ibid.

79   Peter P. Ring tombstone, Section 8, lot 483, St. Joseph's Roman Catholic Cemetery,
      Evansville (Vanderburgh County), Indiana: "Peter P., Sohn von J. u. B. Ring, geb. 5
      Mai 1871, gest. 26 Juli 1873." No baptismal record for Peter Paul Ring has been
      found.

80   *General Probate Docket* I: 2, and *Register of Claims*, "Estate of William Jeans," p. 74;
      Issaquena County Clerk's Office, Mayersville.

81 George's statement, p. 13. See also: Estate of William Jeans, probate packet 243, Issaquena County Courthouse, Mayersville.

82 Policy No. 29541, July 21, 1871, Germania Life Insurance Company; in possession of successor company, The Guardian Life Insurance Company of America, New York, New York (photocopied for the author in 1995).

83 Ibid.: "Terminated in . . . 1873; Cause of Death . . . [blank]."

84 "Mr. Joseph Ring, In a/c with Geo. F. Ring," Feb. 18, 1874, a financial statement prepared by George for Barbara, listing expenditures and credits, Oct. 15, 1868-July 25, 1873, marked "Copy" and not in George's hand. Passed from Joseph Nicholas Ring to his son Louis Caffall Ring, who photocopied it for the author in 1985. ($3,307.86 for 40 bales of about 450 pounds each = $82.69 per bale = roughly $.18 per pound.)

85 Ibid.

86 Ibid.

87 Ibid.: "Sept. 1, 1871, Cash paid Meyer for hauling lumber, $3.00; Cash paid Ben Leas for hauling lumber, $50.00; Dec. 28, 1871, Drayage 8 loads to house, $16.00; Jan. 13, 1872, Meyer for Drayage, $7.00."

16. The "Vicksburg Place"

1 Gordon A. Cotton, *The Old Court House* (Raymond, Miss.: Keith Printing Co., Inc., 1982), and personal inspection by the author on research trips, 1986–99.

2 *Vicksburg Daily Whig*, June 17, 1858, quoted in Cotton, *The Old Court House*, 11.

3 The author thanks Gordon A. Cotton, director of the Old Court House Museum-Eva W. Davis Memorial, for his spirited support and assistance in the researching of this book.

4 All engravings of Vicksburg as viewed from the Mississippi River show prominently the spire of St. Paul's. See, for example, *Harper's Weekly, A Journal of Civilization*, Aug. 2, 1862, p. 484.

5 Richardson and Godman, *In and About Vicksburg*, 148, 150.

6 See *Vicksburg Evening Post*, Dec. 7, 1953, p. 10.

7 The author is indebted to the Rev. John P. Egan, former pastor of St. Paul's, now deceased, and his secretary, Evelyn C. White, for graciously opening the sacramental registers of their parish to his research.

8 The closest schools would have been in Greenville, one public (see Keating, *A History of Washington County*, 47), and one parochial (see Joseph Thomas Reilly, *St. Joseph's Roman Catholic Church* (Greenville: St. Joseph's R. C. Church, 1990), 3).

9 Richardson and Godman, *In and About Vicksburg*, 112. See also Sister Mary Emmanuel Harper, R.S.M., "Early History and First Graduates of St. Francis Xavier Academy," *Mississippi River Routes*, The Vicksburg Genealogical Society Quarterly Journal, Vol. 6 (fall 1998), No. 1: 1–7.

10 Garner, *Reconstruction in Mississippi*, 273–278: "The troops were withdrawn from the state, with the exception of small detachments at two or three of the larger towns, and the civil authorities were left to perform their duties uninterfered with." The last contingents of Union soldiers were removed by Rutherford B. Hayes.

11 Also, in 1871 half of Vicksburg's police force was comprised of blacks (see Foner, *Reconstruction*, 362).

12 "City Directory," *Vicksburg Daily Times*, Jan. 1, 1873, p. 5: "Commission Merchants . . . Muller, William, Clay, cor. Front Levee; Grocers . . . Muller, William, Clay, cor. Front Levee." Also: *Vicksburg Daily Times*, Apr. 24, 1874, p. 4: "The high water having commenced to flood Mr. William Muller's store on the corner of Clay and Levee streets, he is busy removing his stock of goods." That Muller's store was located *under* The Sunflower Exchange is established by the sources cited in n. 13 below, in conjunction with those cited in n. 15 of Chap. 21.

13 Anna "Swink" household, 1870 U.S. Census, Warren County (Vicksburg, First Ward), Mississippi, p. 215; National Archives microcopy M593, roll 751: "[Swink] Jacob, 21, Bartender." Also: "City Directory," *Vicksburg Daily Times*, Jan. 1, 1873, p. 5: "Saloons . . . Schwink, J L, Levee sw cor. Clay." Also: Claims of George F. Ring "for rent of property on South West Corner of Clay and Levee Streets . . ." against the estate of Jacob Schwink, filed Dec. 1878 and Jan. 1879, Warren County probate file no. 3079, County Clerk's Office, Vicksburg. For the name of the saloon, see: "The Knife, Probable Fatal Affray, The Prisoner Released on $100 Bail," *Vicksburg Daily Times*, Feb. 26, 1874, p. 4: ". . . the Sunflower exchange . . . saloon . . . on the corner of Clay and Levee Streets . . . Mr. Schwink . . . one of the proprietors . . . ." Also: *Vicksburg City Directory of 1877* (Vicksburg: A. C. Tuttle, 1877), 165: "Schwink, Jacob L., prop. Sunflower Exchange, cor. Clay and Levee, res. Same." Because of the steep incline of Clay Street running down to the river, the entrance to The Sunflower Exchange would have been at ground level on Levee Street, while the entrance to the grocery store underneath would have been at ground level on Clay Street.

14 "City Directory," *Vicksburg Daily Times*, Jan. 1, 1873, p. 5.

15 United States Department of Commerce, Bureau of the Census, *Sixteenth Census of the United States: 1940; Population* (Washington: U.S. Government Printing Office, 1942), I: 568: "Table 2.—Population of Cities of 10,000 or More from Earliest Census to 1940" shows Vicksburg's population in 1870 at 12,443.

16 Richardson and Godman, *In and About Vicksburg*, 126–128, and Chapman and Battaile, *Picturesque Vicksburg*, 37–44.

17 "Map of the Siege of Vicksburg," dated Aug. 20, 1863; Geography and Map Division, Library of Congress, Washington.

18 Warren County Deed Book FF: 650–651: "Map of the Barefield Plantation."

19 Land deed, Mar. 14, 1871, Warren County Deed Book JJ: 41; Warren County Courthouse, Vicksburg.

20 Land deed, Oct. 31, 1870, Warren County Deed Book II: 69–71; Warren County Courthouse, Vicksburg.

21 Land deed, Mar. 14, 1871, Warren County Deed Book JJ: 41.

22 Land deeds, Nov. 11, 1899–July 16, 1900, Warren County Deed Book 92: 183, 187, 199, 238 (Nov. 21, 1899, Joseph Nicholas Ring *et al.*, grantors), 239, 256, 261, 491; also 118: 556–557 (Jan. 2, 1911, Joseph Nicholas Ring *et al.*, grantors).

23 Map attached to agreement signed by Joseph Nicholas Ring, Aug. 12, 1899, to sell part of lot 15 to the United States; U.S. Department of the Interior, National Park Service, Vicksburg National Military Park, Vicksburg (photocopied for the author in 1997). Also: telephone conversation with Mr. W. T. McHann, who lives in Vicksburg, Sept. 15, 1999. Mr. McHann was 11 years old in 1927 when his father purchased the 15-acre tract on which the Ring house had stood. He remembers vividly that there was no house on the land when his father bought it, as his father

had to raise a new frame house before the family could move out to the property.

24 "Mr. Joseph Ring, In a/c with Geo. F. Ring," Feb. 18, 1874, a financial statement prepared by George for Barbara, listing expenditures and credits, Oct. 15, 1868–July 25, 1873, marked "Copy" and not in George's hand. Passed from Joseph Nicholas Ring to his son Louis Caffall Ring, who photocopied it for the author in 1985. ("Dec. 28, 1871, 2 Sacks Grass Seek from Jeans, $1.00.")

25 Warren County Deed Book FF: 650–651: "Map of the Barefield Plantation."

26 Correspondence of Joseph Nicholas Ring with the heirs of Joseph Ring living in New York and Ohio, September-October 1925, to arrange the sale of the last piece of "the Vicksburg Place." These letters were passed from Joseph Nicholas Ring to his son Louis Caffall Ring, who photocopied them for the author in 1985.

17. MARCH 19, 1873

1 "Funeral Notice," *Vicksburg Daily Times*, Mar. 19, 1873, p. 3. The house is described in Chap. 22, pp. 177–178.

2 Joseph Ring entry, Mar. 19, 1873, *Ledger of Burials*, Fisher Funeral Home; in possession of Fisher-Riles Funeral Home, Vicksburg (photocopied for the author in 1991): ". . . one Rose Wood Finished Coffin . . . ."

3 Ibid.

4 "Funeral Notice," *Vicksburg Daily Times*, Mar. 19, 1873, p. 3 (third column).

5 "To the Editor of the Daily Times," *Vicksburg Daily Times*, Mar. 19, 1873, p. 3 (fourth column).

6 *Vicksburg Daily Times*, Mar. 20, 1873, p. 3.

7 Regarding the Jeans orphans, see Chap. 23, p. 180.

8 That Joseph Nicholas Ring was intelligent and perceptive is clear from the author's correspondence and conversations with his son, Louis Caffall Ring, 1985–1986, as well as Joseph Nicholas Ring's later educational achievements and professional and personal accomplishments. See Chaps. 38 and 39.

9 Letters from Louis Caffall Ring to the author, Nov. 22 and 25, 1985.

10 Letter from Elizabeth Weber Hilberg to Joseph N. Kellas, Feb. 11, 1958. Photocopy in author's possession.

11 Ibid.

12 "Funeral Notice," *Vicksburg Daily Times*, Mar. 19, 1873, p. 3. Also: Joseph Ring entry, Mar. 19, 1873, *Ledger of Burials*, Fisher Funeral Home; in possession of Fisher-Riles Funeral Home, Vicksburg (photocopied for the author in 1991): ". . . use of Hearse & Servises . . . use of 2 Hack . . . ."

13 For a picture of the hearse, see the advertisement for "Frank J. Fisher, Embalmer and Funeral Director" in Chapman and Battaile, *Picturesque Vicksburg*, 155.

14 Presumption based on prevailing social convention.

15 For flowers and trees typical of Vicksburg, see Chapman and Battaile, *Picturesque Vicksburg*, 12, and Richardson and Godman, *In and About Vicksburg*, 97–98.

16 St. Paul's earliest register of burials, including the year 1873, has disappeared. It is inconceivable, however, given George and Barbara's cultural heritage, that Joe would not have been given a Catholic Mass.

17 Richardson and Godman, *In and About Vicksburg*, picture on p. 150.

18 The pastor, or his assistant, Father Bohmert, would have accompanied the casket to the grave to perform the final rites.

19 Description of Cedar Hill is based on author's personal observation.

20   The author has examined the "Morris-Ring" family plot. Among the marked graves are several grave-size places without headstones.

21   Baptismal record of Michael Albert Ring, May 4, 1873 (born "Feb. 30, 1873"); *Baptismal Register* 2: 82, St. Paul's R. C. Church, Vicksburg. "*Feb.* 30" was probably a slip on the part of the priest for "*Mar.* 30;" see Chap. 25, n. 3.

18. APRIL 9, 1873

1   "Local Intelligence," *Vicksburg Daily Times*, Apr. 9, 1873, p. 3.

2   See Chap. 19, especially n. 19.

3   See Chap. 2, n. 26.

4   Regarding the Mississippi State Lunatic Asylum in Jackson during Reconstruction, see Harris, *The Day of the Carpetbagger*, 39–40, 66, 152, 361–365.

5   See Chap. 2, n. 26.

6   Character traits attributed to Scott are based on the documented deeds of his life and his own published words.

7   *The Revised Code of the Statute Laws of the State of Mississippi* (Jackson: Alcorn & Fisher, State Printers, 1871), Chap. 3, Art. XII, "Duties of Sheriffs," pp. 61–62.

8   Testimony of H. P. Scott, June 10, 1876, "Boutwell Report," I: 589.

9   Foner, *Freedom's Lawmakers*, 190.

10   Ibid.

11   Testimony of H. P. Scott, June 10, 1876, "Boutwell Report," I: 589.

12   "Stife[?], Chas" household, 1870 U.S. Census, Issaquena County (Tallula Precinct), Mississippi, p. 319; National Archives micropublication M593, roll 731: ". . . W[hite], 22, Depy. Sheriff, [born] Ohio . . . ."

13   "Joor, J S" household, 1870 U.S. Census, Issaquena County (Tallula Precinct), Mississippi, p. 319; National Archives micropublication M593, roll 731: ". . . W[hite], 24, Depy. Sheriff, [born] Mississippi . . . ."

14   *Minutes of the Board of Police*, December Special Term 1870 (Dec. 5th), p. 192; Issaquena County Courthouse, Mayersville.

15   Testimony of W. D. Brown, June 22, 1876, "Boutwell Report," I: 716.

16   Terms on the Board of Police lasted two years (*Revised Code*, 1857, Chap. LIX, Sec. I, Art. 1, p. 414). Joe's name appears in the *Minutes of the Board of Police* as a member from May 1869 to December 1870 only. His term would have expired in May of 1871.

17   Testimony of W. D. Brown, June 22, 1876, "Boutwell Report," I: 716.

18   *The Revised Code of the Statute Laws of the State of Mississippi* (1871), Chap. 3, Art. XII, "Duties of Sheriffs," p. 57.

19   Testimony of H. P. Scott, June 10, 1876, "Boutwell Report," I: 596.

20   Had John S. Joor still been a deputy sheriff at the time of "the Rolling Fork tragedy," the copious paperwork and testimony of the consequent insurance trials, or the newspaper articles, would surely have mentioned this fact.

21   Testimony of H. P. Scott, June 10, 1876, "Boutwell Report," I: 591–592.

22   Ibid., 596.

23   Foner, *Freedom's Lawmakers*, 190 (quotation not attributed, but probably taken from the "Boutwell Report").

24   H. P. Scott entry, *Indexes to Deposit Ledgers in Branches of the Freedman's Savings and Trust Company, 1865–1874*; Records of the Freedman's Savings and Trust Company; Records of the Office of the Comptroller of the Currency, RG 101;

National Archives micropublication M817, roll 3, Vicksburg, Miss.: "Scott, H. P. . . . 6561, 6663." (*Registers of Signatures of Depositors in Branches of the Freedman's Savings and Trust Company, 1865–1874*, roll 15, Vicksburg, Miss., is missing many pages, including those containing accounts 6561 and 6663.)

25   *Biographical and Historical Memoirs of Mississippi*, I: 203.

26   Testimony of W. D. Brown, June 22, 1876, "Boutwell Report," I: 702, 717.

27   *The Revised Code of the Statute Laws of the State of Mississippi* (1871), Chap. 10, Art. I, "Election and Qualification," p. 257.

28   Ibid., Chap. 10, Art. II, "Their Civil Jurisdiction," p. 259, and Art. III, "Their Criminal Jurisdiction," p. 259.

29   The 1870 U.S. Census of Issaquena County, for instance, lists three justices of the peace, seven short of the statutory quota.

30   *The Revised Code of the Statute Laws of the State of Mississippi* (1871), Chap. 3, Art. XVI, "Duties of Constables," pp. 71–73.

31   Garner, *Reconstruction in Mississippi*, 305–307.

32   Harris, *The Day of the Carpetbagger*, 298.

33   A thorough search of the record books and loose papers in the Issaquena County Courthouse, Mayersville, failed to uncover any execution docket or minute book kept by H. P. Scott, any docket or minute book of Noah Parker's, or any coroner's record book for the year 1873. Alice Wade and Katherine Branton wrote to the author in 1988: "This whole case gives [us] a feeling of one big cover-up. . . . And still there is not ONE BONA FIDE CLUE that the event ["the Rolling Fork tragedy"] even took place as far as the records of Sharkey and Issaquena Counties are concerned. . . . We scanned the Circuit Docket books, and Minute book, thinking if a cover-up job was performed, perhaps they missed something, but it is as though those people [J. W. Parberry *et al.*] never existed in the context for which we were searching. . . ."

19. APRIL 10, 1873

1   *Vicksburg Daily Times*, Apr. 11, 1873, p. 3.

2   George's declaration, 1768, p. 5.

3   Replication of The Franklin Fire Insurance Co. to George's claims, contained in the packet of *George F. Ring v. Franklin Fire Insurance Co.*, Case 2573.

4   George's testimony, 2573, pp. 3–4.

5   Chamberlin's testimony, contained in the packet of *George F. Ring v. Franklin Fire Insurance Co.*, Case 2573 (hereafter "Chamberlin's testimony, 2573"), p. 1.

6   Chamberlin's testimony, contained in the packet of *George F. Ring v. Franklin Fire Insurance Co.*, Case 2572 (hereafter "Chamberlin's testimony, 2572"), p. 1.

7   George's testimony, 2572, pp. 2–9.

8   Ibid., 2.

9   Ibid., 1–2, 4.

10   Chamberlin's testimony, 2572, p. 5.

11   Ibid., 2.

12   Replications of The Franklin Fire Insurance Co. to George's claims, contained in the packets of *George F. Ring v. Franklin Fire Insurance Co.*, Case 2573, and *George F. Ring v. Franklin Fire Insurance Co.*, Case 2572.

13   See Chap. 2, n. 26.

14   George's declaration, 1768, p. 5.

15   Ibid.

16   Ibid.

17   Certificate of Insurance, Liverpool, London & Globe, dated Feb. 26, 1873, labeled Exhibit A in the packet of *George F. Ring, Guardian, v. Liverpool, London & Globe*, Case 1768, U.S. Circuit Court, Southern District of Mississippi; Records of District Courts of the United States, 1685–1991, RG 21; National Archives—Southeast Region, East Point, Georgia.

18   Liverpool, London & Globe's instructions to the jury, contained in the packet of *George F. Ring, Guardian, v. Liverpool, London & Globe*, Case 1768, U.S. Circuit Court, Southern District of Mississippi; Records of District Courts of the United States, 1685–1991, RG 21; National Archives—Southeast Region, East Point, Georgia.

19   George's declaration, contained in the packet of *George F. Ring v. Franklin Fire Insurance Co.*, Case 3006, Circuit Court of Warren County, in the attic of the courthouse in Vicksburg, p. 5: ". . . [the Franklin Fire Insurance Co.] did moreover, by and through its duly authorized agents and officers [agent Chamberlin and adjuster Love], falsely, wickedly and deceitfully represent unto the said 'Mechanics & Traders Insurance Company' and the said 'Great Western Mutual Insurance Company,' that the said plaintiff [George] had himself wickedly and feloneously burned or caused to be burned the said property [Ring & Co.] so insured by them, and thereby persuaded, influenced and induced the said last named Insurance Companies, also, to refuse to pay the said plaintiff said sums of money. . . ."

20   Ibid.

21   "Passion Week Services in Christ Church," *Vicksburg Daily Times*, Apr. 9, 1873, p. 3: "Service every morning (except Friday) at 6 o'clock. Service every evening at 5:30 o'clock. Next Friday being Good Friday, there will be full morning service, a sermon appropriate to the day, at 11 o'clock. Easter services . . . ."

22   "Local Intelligence," *Vicksburg Daily Times*, Apr. 11, 1873, p. 3.

23   See Chap. 18, n. 33.

24   Civil and/or criminal action taken in a case as serious as "the Rolling Fork tragedy" fell within the jurisdiction of the Circuit Court. It was the duty of Sheriff Scott to arrest any suspects and hold them for trial in the jail in Tallula. Justices of the Peace could adjudicate only civil cases "where the principal of the debt, the amount of the demand, or the value of the property sought to be recovered, shall not exceed one hundred and fifty dollars," and criminal cases "where the punishment prescribed does not extend beyond a fine and imprisonment in the county jail." Parker, therefore, had no authority to *try* any persons suspected of perpetrating "the Rolling Fork tragedy." (*The Revised Code of the Statute Laws of the State of Mississippi*, 1871, Chap. 3, Art. XII, pp. 61–62, and Chap. 10, Arts. II and III, p. 259.)

25   "Local Intelligence," *Vicksburg Daily Times*, Apr. 23, 1873, p. 3.

26   Summons dated Nov. 2, 1874, contained in the packet of *George F. Ring v. Franklin Fire Insurance Co.*, Case 2572: "The within named . . . J W Parberry . . . after diligent search cannot be found in my County, nor could I find any place of [his] usual abode in my County by which I could serve his process by Posting copy on door &c. [signed] H P Scott Sheriff By I H Mobley D. Shff."

20. April 14, 1873

1 George's testimony, 2572, p. 6. The date George provided from memory, "17th day of April 1873," is incorrect; the second statement was sworn to and signed on April 14, 1873, as all other documents in the packet corroborate. For address of the law firm: "City Directory," *Vicksburg Daily Times*, Jan. 1, 1873, p. 5.

2 This is a successful law firm of the "Gilded Age," thriving in a rich and important city. See William Seale, *Tasteful Interlude: American Interiors Through the Camera's Eye, 1860–1917* (Nashville: American Association for State and Local History, 1988).

3 P. H. Reaney and R. M. Wilson, *A Dictionary of English Surnames*, 3rd ed. (London: Routledge, 1991), 70, and Augustus Wilfrid Dellquest, *These Names of Ours: A Book of Surnames* (New York: Thomas Y. Crowell Co., 1938), 55, as well as other English surname dictionaries concur that Buck is an old English surname.

4 At 40 Buck would still have a full head of hair and mustache.

5 "Buck, R. L." household, 1860 U.S. Census, Warren County (Vicksburg), Mississippi, p. 970; National Archives micropublication M653, roll 592: "27;" "Buck, R. S." household, 1870 U.S. Census, Warren County (Vicksburg, Seventh Ward), Mississippi, p. 305; National Archives micropublication M593, roll 751: "37;" and "R. S. Buck" household, 1880 U.S. Census, Warren County (Vicksburg, Fourth Ward), Mississippi, p. 445; National Archives micropublication T9, roll 667: "45."

6 "Buck, R. S." household, 1870 U.S. Census: "Real Estate . . . $12,000; Personal Estate . . . $2,000."

7 U.S. Censuses of 1850, 1860, 1870 and 1880 provide Kentucky as Buck's place of birth; 1850 Census gives Virginia as the place of birth of his father and mother, and lists his father's occupation as "Merchant." See also Buck's obituary in: *Vicksburg Evening Post*, Sept. 19, 1892, p. 4.

8 Richard S. Buck-Juliana S. Randolph marriage record, Feb. 3, 1859, Warren County Marriage Book G: 482; County Clerk's Office, Vicksburg. U.S. Censuses of 1860, 1870 and 1880 give her place of birth as Mississippi; 1880 Census gives Mississippi as the place of birth of her father and mother.

9 "Buck, R. S." household, 1870 U.S. Census: "[Buck], B[ertha], 10; W[error for Richard S., Jr.], 5; R[andolph], 4/12." U.S. Census of 1880 shows no younger children. See also Buck's obituary.

10 *Vicksburg City Directory for 1877* (Vicksburg: A. C. Tuttle, 1877), p. 80: "Buck & Clark (R. S. Buck and E. D. Clark) attorneys sw cor. Clay and Washington." See Clark's obituary in: *Vicksburg Evening Post*, Mar. 28, 1885, p. 2.

11 George's "Second Statement," contained in the packet of *George F. Ring v. Franklin Fire Insurance Co.*, Case 2573 (hereafter "George's second statement"), p. 5: "[signed] Geo. F. Ring [and] J[acob] Adler, Justice of the Peace."

12 Ibid., 3.

13 Ibid., 2.

14 Ibid., 3.

15 Magistrate's Certificate, dated Apr. 5, 1873, appended to George's second statement.

16 Exhibit B, appended to George's second statement.

17 A. E. Love's Receipt, dated Apr. 15, 1873, contained in the packet of *George F. Ring*

v. Franklin Fire Insurance Co., Case 2573.

18   Hemphill, *Fevers, Floods and Faith*, 370: " . . . George Ring. Described by old set-
     tlers . . . as a 'Dutchman' . . . ." In nineteenth-century America, "Dutchman" was a
     common corruption of "Deutschman." George's popular identity derived evidently
     from his German accent.

21. CATHERINE

1   George's statement, pp. 1, 6.
2   History and description of Vicksburg's German-speaking mercantile society rely
     primarily on the author's original-source research on families associated with his
     Ring ancestors, 1850s–1880s, and to a lesser, supportive extent, on the published
     sources cited in Chap. 1, n. 3.
3   Native places and occupations of German-surnamed residents are taken from the
     1850, 1860 and 1870 U.S. Censuses, Warren County (Vicksburg), Mississippi, *pas-
     sim*; National Archives micropublications M432, roll 382, M653, roll 592, and
     M593, roll 751. Also: Vicksburg city directories, advertisements in newspapers,
     Warren County naturalization records and land deeds, as well as the published
     sources cited in Chap. 1, n. 3. Various religions come from church, synagogue and
     cemetery records, as well as oral family tradition and published sources.
4   See n. 2 above. The history of the note George held that was secured by his inter-
     est in Rolling Fork Landing (see Chap. 19, p. 154, and Chap. 23, pp. 179 and 182)
     provides one case in point.
5   George's statement, p. 6.
6   William Muller household, 1870 U.S. Census, Warren County (Vicksburg, Fourth
     Ward), Mississippi, p. 249; National Archives micropublication M593, roll 751:
     "Muller, Wm . . . Grocer . . . [born] Prussia . . . ."
7   George's statement, p. 6.
8   *Vicksburg Daily Herald*, Sept. 19–Dec. 18, 1869, p. varies with each issue.
9   Conclusion based on the order of surnames in "Ring & Muller."
10   William Muller household, 1870 U.S. Census: "Muller, Wm . . . 35." That would
     make Muller about 33–34 in 1868, and George, 34–35.
11   Ibid. William and his wife Odelia were both born in Prussia; both of their children
     were born in Mississippi: "Frederick . . . 4" and "Alice [error for Claire Elizabeth]
     . . . 2." See n. 12 below.
12   Baptismal records of Fritz Muller, June 4, 1866 (born May 23, 1866) and Claire
     Elizabeth Muller, August 27, 1868 (born July 4, 1868); *Baptismal Register* 1: 179
     and 215, St. Paul's R. C. Church, Vicksburg.
13   See Chap. 16, n. 12.
14   See Chap. 16, n. 13.
15   *Vicksburg Business Directory of 1858* (New Orleans: A. Mygatt & Co., 1858), 3:
     "Just, George, Levee cor. Clay [under Coffee House]; *Vicksburg City Directory of
     1860* (Vicksburg: H. C. Clarke, 1860), 25: "Just George, coffee house cor. Levee
     and Clay sts;" and 29: "Morris Jacob, coffee-house, cor. Levee and Clay sts." It
     appears that George Just, a relative of Catherine's, was a partner of Jacob
     Morris's. Also: *Vicksburg City Directory of 1861* (original not available; reprinted in
     the *Vicksburg Evening Post* in 1961 under the rubric, "100 Years Ago;" photocopy
     in the library of the Old Court House Museum, Vicksburg): "Just George, coffee
     house, cor. Levee and Clay Sts;" and "Morris Jacob, coffee house cor. Levee and

Clay sts."

16   Ibid., and n. 30 below.

17   Jacob Morris, Petition for Naturalization, Dec. 10, 1852; *Warren County Natur-alizations*, R: 348; Circuit Clerk's Office, Vicksburg: ". . . native of Belgium . . . ."

18   *Herald Directory of the City of Vicksburg* (Vicksburg: H. H. Bein & Co., 1866), 46: "Morris Jacob Family Grocer S.E. cor. Clay st. and Front Row, res. same."

19   See 1850, 1860, 1870 and 1880 U.S. censuses, and city directories for 1858, (none found for 1859), 1860, 1861, (none found for 1862–65), 1866, (none found for 1867–76), 1877, (none found for 1878–85), 1886, (none found for 1887–94), 1895, 1896 and 1897.

20   See Chap. 2, n. 14.

21   Jacob Morris household, 1850 U.S. Census, Warren County (Vicksburg), Mississippi, p. 174; National Archives micropublication M432, roll 382: "Persons over 20 Yr's of age who cannot read and write" column is *not* checked for Catherine. Jacob Morris household, 1860 U.S. Census, Warren County (Vicksburg), Mississippi, p. 941; National Archives micropublication M653, roll 592: "Persons over 20 Yr's of age who cannot read and write" column is *not* checked for Catherine. George F. Ring household, 1870 U.S. Census, Warren County (Vicksburg, First Ward), Mississippi, p. 215; National Archives micropubli-cation M593, roll 751: "Cannot read" and "Cannot write" columns are *not* checked for Catherine. "George Ring" household, 1880 U.S. Census, Warren County (Vicksburg, Second Ward), Mississippi, p. 365; National Archives micropublica-tion T9, roll 667: "Cannot read" and "Cannot write" columns are *not* checked for Catherine. Nevertheless, Catherine's formal education was probably minimal. Her signature is invariably written in deliberate and unpracticed German script.

22   Jacob Morris household, 1860 U.S. Census: "[Morris] Elizabeth . . . 8, [born] Mississippi." Also: George F. Ring household, 1870 U.S. Census: "Elizabeth Morris . . . 18, [born] Mississippi."

23   Jacob Morris Probate File, no. 2230, Warren County Clerk's Office, Vicksburg.

24   See n. 36 below.

25   Age deduced from records that sometimes provide conflicting information: (1) Jacob Morris household, 1850 U.S. Census: "33;" (2) Jacob Morris household, 1860 U.S. Census: "46;" (3) Mary Lois S. Ragland, comp., *Fisher Funeral Home Records, Vicksburg, Mississippi, 1854–1867* (Vicksburg: Heritage Books, 1992), 281: "Morris, Jacob, 20 Sept 1866, 58;" and (4) Jacob Morris tombstone, Division A, Square 157, Cedar Hill Cemetery, Vicksburg: "May 1815–Sept. 20, 1866."

26   Jacob Morris household, 1850 U.S. Census.

27   Jacob Morris entry, Warren County 1851 Personal Tax Roll; Record Group 29, microcopy roll 512, Mississippi Department of Archives and History, Jackson.

28   Character traits attributed to Jacob Morris are based on the documented facts of his life.

29   Jacob Morris, Petition for Naturalization, Dec. 12, 1854; *Warren County Naturalizations*, R: 348, Circuit Clerk's Office, Vicksburg.

30   Land deed, June 21, 1854, Warren County Deed Book Y: 555–556 (lots 10 and 11, square I); Warren County Courthouse, Vicksburg.

31   Land deed, Feb. 7, 1855, Warren County Deed Book Z: 96–97 (lots 12 and 13, square I); Warren County Courthouse, Vicksburg.

32   Since Morris's grocery store and residence stood on lot 13, and his coffee house

stood on lots 10 and 11, his boarding house must have stood on lot 12.

33   *Herald Directory of the City of Vicksburg* (Vicksburg: H. H. Bein & Co., 1866), 46: "Morris Jacob Family Grocer S.E. cor. Clay st. and Front Row, res. same."

34   Land deed, Jan. 9, 1860, Warren County Deed Book BB: 615 (lot 9, square I); Warren County Courthouse, Vicksburg. The author thanks Eudora Hill of Delta, Louisiana, for the knowledgeable and diligent assistance she rendered, 1986–1990, securing and photocopying many records pertaining to Jacob Morris and his kin.

35   Jacob Morris household, 1860 U.S. Census.

36   Jacob Morris-Catherine Hill marriage record, Apr. 9, 1849, Warren County Marriage Book G: 30; County Clerk's Office, Vicksburg.

37   That Jacob Morris was Jewish is assumed from his name, his close association with Jacob Steiner (see p. 169), his absence from St. Paul's records as godfather or marriage witness, and the fact that only four of his six children were baptized at St. Paul's, three of whom were several months or years old (see n. 38 below). That Catherine was Roman Catholic is known from the fact that her marriage record to George F. Ring, a Roman Catholic, does not indicate "*vicatae Religionis*" (see n. 76 below), and the fact that her sister, Anna, was Roman Catholic (see n. 86 below).

38   Baptismal records of Elizabeth "Maurice," Mar. 27, 1853 (born July 2, 1852), Jacob "Maurice," June 2, 1859 (born Apr. 16, 1855), William "Maurice," Aug. 1, 1859 (born July 29, 1859), and George Morris, Apr. 18, 1861 (born Dec. 22, 1860), St. Paul's R. C. Church, Vicksburg. For births of the other two children (baptismal records not found), see Ragland, *Fisher Funeral Home Records*, 64: "Morris, Phillip, 12 Aug 1858, 19 months;" and 280: "Morris, _____ (Mr.)," 9 Sept 1866, infant child."

39   Ragland, *Fisher Funeral Home Records*, 64: "Morris, Jacob, 5 June 1859, 4 years;" and "Morris, Phillip, 12 Aug 1858, 19 months;" and "Morris, Jacob [error for William, as confirmed by the 1860 U.S. Census, Mortality Schedule, Warren County (Vicksburg), p. 2], Aug 1859, infant child."

40   Anna does not appear in the 1860 census of Vicksburg; however, she is in the city with her children by the spring of 1861: see n. 41 below.

41   Baptismal record of George Morris, Apr. 18, 1861 (born Dec. 22, 1860); *Baptismal Register* 1: 79, St. Paul's R. C. Church, Vicksburg: ". . . GodFather was Jacob Shwink . . . ." For his age, see: Anna "Swink" household, 1870 U.S. Census, Warren County (Vicksburg, First Ward), Mississippi, p. 215; National Archives micropublication M593, roll 751: [Swink], Jacob, 21."

42   See Chap. 16, n. 13.

43   Martha Lois Koch Long, *The Johann Philipp Koch Family* (no place: no publisher, 1971), 107: "Mary Catherine Schwink (born) 13 Sept. 1850, Niederklein, Alsford, Germany."

44   Baptismal record of Elizabeth "Maurice," Mar. 27, 1853 (born July 2, 1852); *Baptismal Register* 1: 3, St. Paul's R. C. Church, Vicksburg.

45   George Koch-Mary "Swink" marriage record, Aug. 25, 1868; *Register of Marriages* 1, p. 69, St. Paul's R. C. Church, Vicksburg.

46   See n. 2 above.

47   Walker, *Vicksburg, A People at War*, 25–26.

48   Biographical files in the library of the Old Court House Museum, Vicksburg, as well as published lists, such as H. Grady Howell, Jr., comp., *For Dixie Land I'll*

Take My Stand: A Muster Listing of All Known Mississippi Confederate Soldiers, Sailors, and Marines, 2 vols. (Madison, Miss.: Chickasaw Bayou Press, 1998), reveal that a number of Vicksburg's Germanic residents did serve in the Confederate armed forces during the war, while many others evidently avoided military service.

49 Regarding the siege, see Walker, *Vicksburg, A People at War,* 157–200; also, Gordon Cotton, *Yankee Bullets, Rebel Rations* (Raymond, Mississippi: Keith Printing Co., Inc., 1984).

50 See Walker, *Vicksburg, A People at War,* especially pp. 145, 173, 185–186.

51 Ibid., especially pp. 201–224; Garner, *Reconstruction in Mississippi,* 29–38; and Cotton, *With Malice Toward Some,* passim.

52 See Chap. 12, pp. 96–97.

53 Cotton, *With Malice Toward Some,* 157–159, transcribes this document.

54 Ibid., p. 158, reads, "Moses, Jacob," by mistake. The original reads, "Mores, Jacob."

55 *Herald Directory of the City of Vicksburg* (Vicksburg: H. H. Bein & Co., 1866), 46: "Morris Jacob Family Grocer S.E. cor. Clay st. and Front Row, res. same."

56 Willis, *On the New South Frontier,* 171–173.

57 "Morris, Jacob & Co." entry, *Internal Revenue Assessment Lists for Mississippi, 1865–1866,* District 2, Division 21, Monthly Assessment, Jan. 1866; National Archives micropublication M775, roll 2.

58 "Morris, Jacob" entry, *Internal Revenue Assessment Lists for Mississippi, 1865–1866,* District 2, Division 21, Annual Assessment, 1866; National Archives micropublication M775, roll 2.

59 See Cotton, *With Malice Toward Some,* 19: "Among many people alcohol was enjoyed with less restraint than most of us would find acceptable today."

60 Harris, *The Day of the Carpetbagger,* 591.

61 Ragland, *Fisher Funeral Home Records,* 280: "Morris, _____ (Mr.), 9 Sept 1866, infant child;" and "Moris, George, 13 Sept 1866, 5 years, 9 months, Cholera."

62 "Local News," *Vicksburg Daily Herald,* Sept. 21, 1866, p. 3.

63 Jacob Morris tombstone, Division A, Square 157, Cedar Hill Cemetery, Vicksburg.

64 Ragland, *Fisher Funeral Home Records,* 281: "Morris, Jacob, 20 Sept 1866 . . . use of hearse . . . use of 5 hacks."

65 This practice was not uncommon. It dated back to the Married Women's Separate Property Act passed by the Mississippi legislature in 1839. See *Mississippi Code of Statute Laws,* 1839, Ch. 46, p. 72.

66 Once again, Catherine is being depicted as typical. See Chap. 2, n. 14.

67 Land deed, Oct. 22, 1866, Warren County Deed Book EE: 3; Warren County Courthouse, Vicksburg: "cash."

68 See works cited in Chap. 1, n. 3.

69 Turnbull Spring Bayou must have been very small, as it does not appear on the old maps of Vicksburg, and it seems to have disappeared completely by the early part of the twentieth century. That it existed once is known from descriptions in the city's old land deeds; see, for example, Warren County Deed Book KK: 408–409, dated Sept. 13, 1871, whereby George F. Ring sells Joseph Ring a triangular parcel of land bordered by Turnbull Spring Bayou (forming the southwest side), Glass Bayou (the northwest side), and Farmer Street (the eastern side). On a research trip in 1987 the author spoke with an elderly resident of this neighbor-

hood who said that he remembered the bayou. It wasn't much of a stream, and if it had a name, he never heard it. He said that it was "put underground in conduits" running down to Glass Bayou when he was a small boy, perhaps around 1920. Three thousand acres in this vicinity had been purchased in 1817 by Robert James Turnbull (Warren County Deed Book B: 50–53).

70   Sanborn Fire Insurance Map of Vicksburg, dated Apr. 12, 1886 (New York: Sanborn Map & Publishing Co., 1886); Geography and Map Division, Library of Congress, Washington.

71   Anna "Swink" household, 1870 U.S. Census.

72   See Chap. 29.

73   Jacob Morris Probate File, no. 2230, Warren County Clerk's Office, Vicksburg.

74   Ibid. George Just, a relative of Catherine's and business partner of Jacob Morris's, and E. W. Wallin acted as sureties for her $3,000 bond. The name of Jacob Steiner, a relative of Catherine's by his marriage to Mary Elizabeth Hill, also appears (see n. 96 below).

75   Land Deed, June 29, 1867, Warren County Deed Book EE: 263 (lot 8, square I); Warren County Courthouse, Vicksburg.

76   George F. Ring-"Catharine" Morris marriage record, Aug. 25, 1868; *Register of Marriages* 1, p. 69, St. Paul's R. C. Church, Vicksburg.

77   Presumption based on custom.

78   George Koch-Mary "Swink" marriage record, Aug. 25, 1868; *Register of Marriages* 1, p. 69, St. Paul's R. C. Church, Vicksburg: ". . . Dispensation (*vicatae Religionis*) was granted to the parties." For his age, see: Long, *The Johann Philipp Koch Family*, 107.

79   Long, *The Johann Philipp Koch Family*, 46–50. Also: Anna "Swink" household, 1870 U.S. Census: "Cook, George . . . Tinner . . . ." Also: *Evansville City Directory for 1874* (Evansville: Brandis & Meadows, 1874), 184: "Koch George, Manufacturer of Tin, Copper and Sheet Iron Ware; also, Dealer in Stoves, &c, 1012 W. Pennsylvania."

80   Long, *The Johann Philipp Koch Family*, 46–50.

81   Ibid., 48. Also: *Evansville City Directory for 1874*, 184: "Koch Henry, Manufacturer of Tin, Copper and Sheet Iron Ware; also, Dealer in Stoves, &c, 411 3d Av, Residence, 409 3d Av."

82   Long, *The Johann Philip Koch Family*, 56.

83   Ibid., 51.

84   *The Vicksburg Evening Post* of Dec. 12, 1992, contains a brief history of the city's Lutheran congregation and the founding of its church building. (See vertical file in the Search Room of the Vicksburg and Warren County Public Library, Vicksburg.)

85   See *Registers of Marriages*, St. Paul's R. C. Church, Vicksburg.

86   Henry "Sprinkle"-Anna Schwink marriage record, June 9, 1870; *Register of Marriages* 1, p. 80, St. Paul's R. C. Church, Vicksburg: ". . . Dispensation (*vicatae Religionis*) was granted to the parties."

87   Samuel Fischel household, 1870 U.S. Census, Warren County (Vicksburg, Third Ward), Mississippi, p. 244; National Archives micropublication M593, roll 751: "Samuel Fischel . . . 42 . . . merchant . . . [born] Bavaria." However, Leo E. Turitz and Evelyn Turitz, *Jews in Early Mississippi* (Jackson: University Press of Mississippi, 1983), 48, state that Samuel "came from Alsace-Lorraine."

88   Ibid.

89   Samuel Fischel household, 1870 U.S. Census: "[Fischel] A., 11, female, [born] Louisiana; [Fischel] A., 10, male, [born] Louisiana."

90   Turitz, *Jews in Early Mississippi*, 48.

91   Samuel Fischel household, 1870 U.S. Census: "[Fischel], [blank], 4, male, [born] Mississippi."

92   Turitz, *Jews in Early Mississippi*, 43.

93   See Chap. 36, and especially George's testimony, 2572, passim.

94   See advertisements and social items in the Vicksburg newspapers, and Turitz, *Jews in Early Mississippi*, 43–56.

95   Turitz, *Jews in Early Mississippi*, vi, xi, xiv–xvi.

96   Betty Couch Wiltshire, *Marriages and Deaths from Mississippi Newspapers, Vol. 4: 1850–1861* (Bowie, Md.: Heritage Books, Inc., 1989), 266.

97   See n. 74 above.

98   The Herman Leppich-Elizabeth Morris marriage record cannot be found. Other sources, however, prove the union. See the monument inscriptions in the Morris/Ring family plot at Cedar Hill Cemetery, Division A, Square 157, Lot 2: "Elizabeth Morris Leppich Hallgren, b. 1851, d. 1923;" "Herman Leppich, b. 1845, d. 1881;" "Richard Hallgren, b. 1848, d. 1889." See also the probate file of Elizabeth Morris Leppich Hallgren, Probate file no. 6747, Warren County Courthouse, Vicksburg, as well as her obituary, *Vicksburg Evening Post*, June 9, 1923, p. 5. That Herman Leppich was Jewish is known from oral family lore related to the author by Linda N. Kious, great granddaughter of Rosa Hill Schawbloski, the daughter of Catherine and Anna's elder brother, Johann Hill (correspondence, 1993-1999).

99   Advertisement in the *Vicksburg Times & Republican*, 1873, passim: "Lager Beer Saloon of Leppich & Hibou/ 128 Washington St./ Keep on hand the best St. Louis lager beer." Also advertisement in the *Vicksburg Daily Commercial*, 1878, passim: "Leppich is selling Weber's Cincinnati Beer at $2.75 per keg/ Which is superior in quality and taste to any other kind in market/ Soda Water 50 Cents Per Box. If you want to save money, patronize the pioneer of the Beer Trade. H. Leppich/ 128 Washington St."

100 George F. Ring-"Catharine" Morris and George Koch-Mary "Swink" marriage records.

22. LAND

1   Deed of trust, June 15, 1869, Warren County Deed Book GG: 150–151; Warren County Courthouse, Vicksburg.

2   Gray, "Local Market Organization and Methods," Table 4-1, 114–115; see also: Harris, *The Day of the Carpetbagger*, 274–276.

3   Regarding this "boom psychology" among Vicksburg merchants as well as the cotton planters, see Harris, *The Day of the Carpetbagger*, 276–277, 280–281.

4   Deed of trust, June 15, 1869, Warren County Deed Book GG: 150–151.

5   Ibid., recorded June 17, 1869.

6   Garner, *Reconstruction in Mississippi*, 312–313, and Willis, *On the New South Frontier*, 99–105.

7   Land deed, Nov. 15, 1869, certified in Warren County, Nov. 17, 1869, recorded Nov. 22, 1869, Washington County Deed Book X: 141–142; Washington County Courthouse, Greenville. In 1871 this property fell within the redrawn boundaries

of Sunflower County (see Chap. 37, p. 274).

8   Ibid.

9   For details about the courthouse, see Cotton, *The Old Court House*, 29.

10   Description of auction is based on typical land auctions of the day.

11   "River News," "Business, Weather, etc.," *Vicksburg Daily Herald*, Nov. 16, 1869, p. 3: "The weather has been disagreeable since out last, rain having prevailed."

12   Land deed, Nov. 15, 1869, certified in Warren County, Nov. 17, 1869, recorded Nov. 22, 1869, Washington County Deed Book X: 141–142.

13   The relative was George Just, trustee of Eliza Goetz, the New York City owner of the plantation. George Just had been a partner of Jacob Morris's. He also owned considerable acreage adjoining the western boundary of "the Vicksburg Place" (see Chap. 16, p. 138, map).

14   Hemphill, *Fevers, Floods and Faith*, 115, 122–123.

15   Garner, *Reconstruction in Mississippi*, 267.

16   Willis, *On the New South Frontier*, 26–43, and Harris, *The Day of the Carpetbagger*, 353–361.

17   Willis, *On the New South Frontier*, 49–53, and Harris, *The Day of the Carpetbagger*, 501–503.

18   Willis, *On the New South Frontier*, 53.

19   Ibid., 67–78.

20   Ibid., 68; also interviews with Alice Wade and Katherine Branton, 1988–1998.

21   See, for example, n. 24 below.

22   Hemphill, *Fevers, Floods and Faith*, 29 (map), 91–92 and 371.

23   Township 20, Range 6 West: lots 9 and 15 in Section 22 (80 acres); lots 1, 2, 3, 6 and 7 in Section 26 (202 acres); west half of southwest quarter of Section 23 (80 acres); and lots 52 and 59 of Block "K" in Shaw (1 acre). See Bolivar County deeds in the courthouse in Cleveland.

24   Land deed, Mar. 11, 1870, Warren County Deed Book HH: 247–248; Warren County Courthouse, Vicksburg.

25   Willis, *On the New South Frontier*, 167–173. See also "The Cotton Factor," Section 4 in Henry C. Dethloff and C. Joseph Pusateri, eds., *American Business History: Case Studies* (Arlington Heights, Illinois: Harlan Davidson, Inc., 1987), 95–116.

26   Regarding the "crop lien" or "cotton mortgage" system, see Harris, *The Day of the Carpetbagger*, 481–483.

27   For examples see land deeds, Apr. 11, 1872, Sunflower County Deed Book A: 76 and 77, and Mar. 9, 1874, Sunflower County Book B: 174–186; Sunflower County Courthouse, Indianola.

28   "Local News," *Vicksburg Herald*, July 22, 1869, p. 4. The editor was William R. Spears. See Harris, *The Day of the Carpetbagger*, 282–283.

29   Note, for example, the make-up of Vicksburg's city council in 1873, Chap. 2, n. 25.

30   Letter dated Mar. 2, 1869; *Registers of Letters Received, Mar. 1867–Feb. 1870*; Fourth Military District (Department of Mississippi), Office of Civil Affairs; Records of United States Army Continental Commands, 1821–1920, RG 393, National Archives, Washington.

31   George F. Ring, Petition for Naturalization, Nov. 27, 1867; *Minutes of the Circuit Court of Issaquena County* B: 490, Circuit Clerk's Office, Mayersville.

32   Special Order No. 79, Apr. 20, 1869; *Special Orders*, Vol. 604-B; Fourth Military District (Department of Mississippi); Records of the Adjutant General's Office,

1780s–1917, RG 94, National Archives, Washington.

33 Regarding George's probable business dealings with Confederate commissaries, see Chap. 12, p. 91.

34 See Chap. 39, p. 296.

35 George F. Ring household, 1870 U.S. Census, Warren County (Vicksburg, First Ward), Mississippi, p. 215; National Archives micropublication M593, roll 751.

36 Land deed, Oct. 22, 1866, Warren County Deed Book EE: 3; Warren County Courthouse, Vicksburg.

37 Description of the grounds is based on the author's inspection of the site in 1989, as well as trees and flowers typical of Vicksburg (see Chap. 17, n. 15).

38 Sanborn Fire Insurance Map of Vicksburg, dated May 1907 (New York: Sanborn Map Company, 1907), sheet 2. Earlier Sanborn maps of Vicksburg (1886, 1892, 1897 and 1902) do not show the Adams Street house, as they depict only the center city. By 1907 the city had grown up around the house.

39 Disposition of the rooms is based on typical floor plans of Victorian houses. See William Seale, *Tasteful Interlude: American Interiors Through the Camera's Eye, 1860–1917.*

40 See Chap. 39, p. 305.

41 George F. Ring household, 1870 U.S. Census: "Value of Real Estate, $60,000; Value of Personal Estate, $20,000;" William "Jeanes" household, 1870 U.S. Census, Issaquena County (Rolling Fork Precinct), Mississippi, p. 269; National Archives micropublication M593, roll 731: "Value of Real Estate, $10,000; Value of Personal Estate, $3,000."

23. RING & CO.

1 Land deed, Mar. 27, 1869, Issaquena County Deed Book 5: 544; Issaquena County Courthouse, Mayersville. Typescript copy in Sharkey County Courthouse, Rolling Fork.

2 George's statement, p. 4: "No part of the $1,500 was ever paid. I never have taken any deed or writing back from Jeans & Moore. I never commenced any suit to enforce my lien for the purchase money." Also George's testimony, 2572, p. 2: "I was the owner of that note when the policy sued on was taken out [Feb. 1, 1873]. I still own it and it is unpaid [Nov. 17, 1874]."

3 *General Probate Docket* I: 2; Issaquena County Clerk's Office, Mayersville.

4 Ibid., 3.

5 Ibid., 2–3: "Date of Application for Letters, Mar. 27, 1871; Date of Granting of Letters, Mar. 30, 1871."

6 Entry for "Estate of William Jeans, Deceased," *Administrator's Bond and Letters*; Issaquena County Chancery Court, Mayersville, Mississippi.

7 "Alexander S. B." household, 1870 U.S. Census, Issaquena County (Rolling Fork Precinct), Mississippi, p. 265; National Archives micropublication M593, roll 731: ". . . Farmer . . . Value of Real Estate, $7,000; Value of Personal Estate, $400." (Jeans household is enumerated on p. 269.) See also: "Samuel B. Alexander" entry, Mississippi State Census of 1866, Issaquena County; Record Group 28, microcopy roll 547, Mississippi Department of Archives and History, Jackson.

8 "Watson L. C." household, 1870 U.S. Census, Issaquena County (Schola Precinct), Mississippi, p. 279; National Archives micropublication M593, roll 731: ". . . 55, male, white, Farmer . . . Value of Real Estate, [blank]; Value of Personal Estate,

$1,750."

9   *General Probate Docket* I: 2; Issaquena County Clerk's Office, Mayersville.
10 George's statement, p. 2.
11 Ibid., 1–2.
12 "Mrs. W. R. Hackett, Dies Here Friday/ Long-Time Citizen," *Vicksburg Evening Post*, June 1, 1957, p. 1: "Mrs. Missouri Elizabeth Jeanes Hackett, one of Vicksburg's oldest residents, died . . . Born in Rolling Fork on February 5, 1867 . . . Mrs. Hackett came to Vicksburg at the age of four and lived with her guardian and family of George F. Ring . . . ." It is assumed that Benjamin Franklin Jeans came with her, since he did not remain with his younger brother, "Little Willie," in the Delta.
13 George's statement, p. 2.
14 George would end up recovering a portion of the debt. See Chap. 37, p. 275.
15 George's statement, p. 3.
16 Ibid.
17 Ibid.
18 "Alexander S. B." household, 1870 U.S. Census, Issaquena County (Rolling Fork Precinct), Mississippi, p. 265; National Archives micropublication M593, roll 731: "Lloyd S. A., 21, Dry Goods Merchant."
19 George's statement, p. 3.
20 Ibid.
21 Ibid., 4.
22 Ibid., 13.
23 Ibid., 3; also the "report to accompany inventory" of Jesse Moore's estate, dated September 24, 1873, Issaquena County probate file no. 26, County Clerk's Office, Mayersville.
24 Ibid.
25 Claim of John F. Coker "for Work" against the estate of Jesse Moore, filed Aug. 20, 1873, Issaquena County probate file no. 26, County Clerk's Office, Mayersville.
26 Jesse Moore household, 1870 U.S. Census, Issaquena County (Schola Precinct), Mississippi, p. 287; National Archives micropublication M593, roll 731: "Moore [Martha], 16."
27 For Joe's increasingly broad interests in cotton, see n. 49 below.
28 George's statement, p. 4.
29 Ibid., 3.
30 Ibid., 8.
31 Ibid., 9.
32 "Joor, J. S." household, 1870 U.S. Census, Issaquena County (Tallula Precinct), Mississippi, p. 319; National Archives micropublication M593, roll 731: "24, single . . . ." It would be a few years yet before Joor married; see John S. Joor-Kate E. Waddell marriage record, June 27, 1878, Sharkey County Clerk's Office, Rolling Fork.
33 "Joor, J. S." household, 1870 U.S. Census: "Depy. Sheriff."
34 George's statement, p. 11, and Joor's statement, p. 1.
35 Joor's statement, p. 1.
36 George's statement, p. 12.
37 Ibid., 4–5.
38 Ibid., 5.

39 George's testimony, 2572, passim.

40 George's statement, p. 4.

41 Ibid., 4–5.

42 Ibid., 5.

43 Ibid., 5–6.

44 Family tradition (see Prologue, p. 3, and quotation from Elizabeth Weber Hilberg letter, Chap. 17, p. 142) supported by circumstantial evidence. See also n. 45 below.

45 George stated in his testimony: "I was the managing partner in the concern" (p. 6), and "he [Joe] spent most [not all] of his time here [Vicksburg]" (p. 9).

46 Advertisements appearing near "River Intelligence" column, *Vicksburg Daily Times*, 1873, passim.

47 Calculations by author based on arrival and departure information, "River Intelligence" column, *Vicksburg Daily Times*, 1873, passim.

48 Ibid. See also Owens, *Steamboats and the Cotton Economy*, 132–133.

49 For examples see land deeds, Sept. 13, 1871, and June 4, 1872, Warren County Deed Books KK: 408 and UU: 339; Warren County Courthouse, Vicksburg; also, land deed, Nov. 20, 1872, Sunflower County Deed Book A: 56; Sunflower County Courthouse, Indianola.

50 George's statement, p. 11. Regarding "bouts of rheumatism," see also Davis, *Trials of the Earth*, 4, 9, 12, 21. The term "rheumatism," used popularly in the nineteenth century, may refer to Scarlet Fever, since Moore was only 30. (Terrence E. Barr, P.A., Walter Reed Army Medical Center, Washington, D.C.)

51 "The City," *Vicksburg Daily Times*, Mar. 8, 1873, p. 3.

52 "An Atrocious Murder," *Vicksburg Daily Times*, Mar. 7, 1873, p. 3.

53 Willis, *On the New South Frontier*, 178–179. See also Clark, *Pills, Petticoats, & Plows*, 275–276. Regarding Poles from Prussia, see Ch. 24, nn. 34–36.

54 Hemphill, *Fevers, Floods and Faith*, 198–199; Percy, *Lanterns on the Levee*, 17; and James C. Cobb, ed., *The Mississippi Delta and the World: The Memoirs of David L. Cohn* (Baton Rouge: Louisiana State University Press, 1995), 89–91.

55 Hemphill, *Fevers, Floods and Faith*, 198–199; Clark, *Pills, Petticoats, & Plows*, 6–8; and Turitz, *Jews in Early Mississippi*, xii–xiii.

56 Willis, *On the New South Frontier*, 181.

57 Ibid.

58 Ibid., 180.

59 See Clark, *Pills, Petticoats, & Plows*, 279, and Davis, *Trials of the Earth*, 83, 103. Also personal interview with Ben Lamensdorf, Jewish planter and life-time resident of Sharkey County, May 1993.

60 Louis Fischel household, 1870 U.S. Census, Issaquena County (Tallula Precinct), Mississippi, p. 325; National Archives micropublication M593, roll 731: "Ret[ail] Grocer."

61 Turitz, *Jews in Early Mississippi*, 48.

62 Turitz, *Jews in Early Mississippi*, 57–78; Willis, *On the New South Frontier*, 182–183; Cobb, *The Mississippi Delta and the World*, 3; and Davis, *Trials of the Earth*, 83. Nevertheless, at least one outside observer, Mark Twain, in his *Life on the Mississippi* (New York: NAL Penguin (a Signet Classic edition), 1960), originally published in 1883, painted a negative and unkind portrait of the "Israelite" merchant of the Delta (pp. 210–211).

63   Willis, *On the New South Frontier*, 173–183.
64   Although the *Vicksburg Daily Times* (Mar. 8, 1873, p. 3) reported that Goudchat "was a native of the city of Paris," the author wonders whether this French Jew might not have been—in reality—a German-speaker from Alsace.
65   It has already been noted, however, that the Ku Klux Klan never gained a foothold in the black counties of western Mississippi. See Chap. 15, p. 129 and n. 53.
66   See Chap. 2, n. 26.
67   "The City," *Vicksburg Daily Times*, Jan. 3, 1873, p. 3.
68   Ibid., Jan. 17, 1873, p. 3.
69   Joor's statement, p. 1.
70   George's statement, p. 11.

24. ROLLING FORK LANDING

1   George's statement, p. 6.
2   See Chap. 2, n. 21.
3   Hemphill, *Fevers, Floods and Faith*, 194–195, describes one "journey" to buy staples which, although it occurred in a somewhat earlier period, shows what a rare and vital "event" shopping was for residents of the Delta's backcountry. See also Davis, *Trials of the Earth*.
4   For the popular use of chewing tobacco, see Clark, *Pills, Petticoats, & Plows*, 29–30, 118–119. The dramatization of this initial encounter is the author's.
5   "Dead Men Tell No Tales," *Vicksburg Daily Herald*, Aug. 22, 1883.
6   Attire of river folk is based on conversations with Alice Wade and Katherine Branton, 1989–1998.
7   "Marsh, G. W." household, 1870 U.S. Census, Issaquena County (Schola Precinct), Mississippi, p. 275; National Archives micropublication M593, roll 731: "22." This would make him about 25 in January 1873.
8   "Oneal, C. M." household, 1880 U.S. Census, Sharkey County (Enumeration District 115, Beat 4), Mississippi, p. 155; National Archives micropublication T9, roll 664: "24." However, other data in this record and other primary sources indicate that this is an error for "34." This would make him about 27 in January 1873. (The 1880 census taker of Beat 4, Enumeration District 115, Sharkey County, was extraordinarily negligent and sloppy. Among numerous errors, omissions and ideosyncracies, he reversed the first and second given names, or first and second initials, of every resident in his beat. See Alice Wade and Katherine Branton, eds., *Early Mississippi Records*, vol. V, *Records of Issaquena County and Sharkey County* (Greenville: the editors, 1986), 123.)
9   Ibid.: "[Oneal], C. Jane, wife, 31." This would make her about 24 in January 1873. Also: "Marsh, W. G." household, 1880 U.S. Census, Sharkey County (Enumeration District 115, Beat 4), Mississippi, p. 155; National Archives micropublication T9, roll 664: "[Marsh], J. Anna, wife, 24." However, other primary sources indicate that "J. Anna" is an error for "Harriet." This would make her about 17 in January 1873.
10   See n. 6 above.
11   "Oneal, C. M." household, 1880 U.S. Census: "[Oneal], E. Jane, daughter, 11." This would make her about 4 in January 1873.
12   The author is indebted to Ruth Land Hatten, C.G.R.S., of Jackson, recently deceased, for her professional and thoughtful research assistance on the Mott,

Marsh and O'Neal families. Ruth died suddenly as she was about to read and cri-
tique the finished manuscript of this book. She was a beloved colleague of the
author's.

13   George W. Marsh-Harriett A. Mott marriage record, Apr. 10, 1871, Issaquena
County Marriage Book 2: 74; County Clerk's Office, Mayersville.

14   See n. 8 above. No document has been found revealing what the "M" and "C"
stand for.

15   Censuses show that Marsh and O'Neal both came from Alabama: "Marsh, G. W."
household, 1870 U.S. Census, Issaquena County (Schola Precinct), Mississippi,
p. 275; National Archives micropublication M593, roll 731: "22, born Alabama;"
and "Oneal, C. M." household, 1880 U.S. Census: "24, born Alabama." However, it
appears that they did not arrive in the Rolling Fork neighborhood together.
George Marsh appears in the census of Issaquena County enumerated in August
1870, while the O'Neals do not. But the George Marsh-Hariett A. Mott marriage
record places Harriett there by April 1871. Given the persistent close ties among
these family members, it is logical to presume that when the 15- or 16-year-old
Harriett married in Issaquena County, her elder sister's family was there with her.
That would mean that the O'Neals (with younger sister Harriett) came into
Issaquena County between August 1870 and April 1871.

16   "The Rolling Fork Horror," *Vicksburg Daily Herald*, Aug. 25, 1883.

17   The "Value of Real Estate" and "Value of Personal Estate" columns of the 1870 and
1880 U.S. Censuses cited above are both blank for the Marshes and O'Neals; the
"Cannot Read" and "Cannot Write" columns are both checked; and the
"Occupation" column is marked "farmer" for both heads of household.

18   For descriptions of this poor white class, see Willis, *On the New South Frontier*,
66–67; Percy, *Lanterns on the Levee*, 19–20; and Davis, *Trials of the Earth*, 162–163.

19   See Willis, *On the New South Frontier*, 165–167, and Clark, *Pills, Petticoats, &
Plows*, passim.

20   Ibid. See also Hemphill, *Fevers, Floods and Faith*, 293–294, and Walker, *800-
Sharkey County—General Information and Points of Interest*, 6–7.

21   See George's statement, p. 5, and Clark, *Pills, Petticoats, & Plows*, 3, 84–97.

22   Calculation by the author using the 1870 census of Issaquena County. See also
Chap. 11, n. 21.

23   Ibid.

24   George's statement, p. 5.

25   Joor's statement, p. 3.

26   Willis, *On the New South Frontier*, 172–173; Harris, *The Day of the Carpetbagger*,
483–484; and Clark, *Pills, Petticoats, & Plows*, 271–280.

27   Regarding the operations of George's *other* partnership, Ring & Muller, George
said: "We did a heavy credit business, and necessarily will lose a large amount."
(George's statement, p. 6). Although scholars have written much about the evils of
the credit system that developed after the Civil War, about the "rapacious merchants" who grew rich by enslaving both laborer and landowner to perpetual debt
peonage (see works cited in n. 26 above, as well as Twain, *Life on the Mississippi*,
210–211), George Ring's experience illustrates that merchants took enormous
risks, and thereby suffered frequent and severe financial losses. The author has
found no published work that addresses what the economic and social effects on a
community might have been of a "cash only" policy, such as Ring & Co.'s, so out

of the ordinary was it.
28 See Chap. 2, n. 26.
29 Joor's statement, p. 4.
30 For discussions of the increased importance of country merchants after the Civil War, see Willis, *On the New South Frontier*, 165–173, and Clark, *Pills, Petticoats, & Plows*, 3–16.
31 Regarding the "haphazard" bookkeeping practices of country merchants, and the distrust it aroused in customers, see Clark, *Pills, Petticoats, & Plows*, 285–287.
32 See Chap. 2, n. 26.
33 George's statement, pp. 6–7.
34 "Jonas" Paradise household, 1870 U.S. Census, Issaquena County (Schola Precinct), Mississippi, p. 275; National Archives micropublication M593, roll 731: "Ret[ail] Merchant." Next door lives "Marsh, G. W." (see n. 7 above).
35 Ibid.: ". . . [born] Poland . . . ."
36 Many immigrants from East Prussia were German-speaking Poles. See Cobb, *The Mississippi Delta and the World*, 3: "[David Cohn's] . . . parents had come . . . from a village lying in a twilight zone between Germany and Poland." Also, Catherine Ring's niece, Rosa Hill, who immigrated to Vicksburg in 1873, married in 1875 a Vincent Schawbloski, very likely a native of East Prussia. Different sources record his place of birth as Prussia, Germany, Poland and "Poland, Germany" (see correspondence with Linda N. Kious, 1993–1999). (Cohn was Jewish; Schawbloski was Catholic.)
37 Based on large build typical of slavic men. See description of David Cohn's father in Cobb, *The Mississippi Delta and the World*, 4.
38 Summons for John Paradise (and others) contained in the packet of *George F. Ring v. Franklin Fire Insurance Co.*, Case 2572, Circuit Court of Warren County, in the attic of the courthouse in Vicksburg.
39 Joor's statement, p. 3.
40 See Chap. 4, n. 64.
41 George's statement, p. 7.
42 Joor's statement, p. 3.
43 Willis, *On the New South Frontier*, 66–67.
44 Ibid., 61 ("In the plantation districts, freedmen and the scrupulous whites who dealt with them as equals faced opposition ranging from fraud to execution.") and 88 ("Those whites who attempted to deal fairly with ex-slaves were subject to physical violence and destruction of their property.").
45 See Chap. 2, n. 26.
46 George's statement, p. 6, and "River Intelligence," *Vicksburg Daily Times*, Feb. 25, 1873, p. 3.
47 "River Intelligence," *Vicksburg Daily Times*, Feb. 25, 1873, p. 3.
48 Ibid.
49 No document states precisely when Joe left Vicksburg. He was definitely at Rolling Fork Landing by Sunday, Mar. 2, 1873 (Joor's statement, p. 3). It is not likely, however, that he had been there continuously since the previous week, when George was there, as George makes no mention in any statement or testimony of *leaving* his brother at the store. Moreover, Joe would have had no reason to spend two weeks at the landing; his business trips would have been much shorter than that. Therefore, it is most likely that Joe left Vicksburg *after* George

had returned, and the only boat that could have gotten him to Rolling Fork
Landing by Mar. 2nd was the *Lizzie,* leaving Feb. 25th, because the *B. H. Hurt* was
up the Sunflower River at the time.

50   "The City," *Vicksburg Daily Times,* Feb. 25, 1873, p. 3: "The Lenton season begins
tomorrow. It will be appropriately observed by all good Catholics, of both the
Roman and Episcopal persuasion in this city." The distribution of ashes on Ash
Wednesday would have been an annual observance in the cyclical Roman Catholic
liturgy celebrated at St. Paul's.

25. MAY 4, 1873

1   The baptismal record of Michael Albert Ring, May 4, 1873 (born "Feb. 30, 1873");
Baptismal Register 2: 82, St. Paul's R. C. Church, Vicksburg, contains marginalia
indicating that the sacrament was administered "*privatim,*" meaning "in private" or
"at home." "*Feb.* 30" was probably a slip on the part of the priest for *Mar.* 30; see
n. 3 below.

2   *Vicksburg Daily Times,* May 4, 1873, p. 3: "The weather was clear and pleasant."

3   Ring, "Mike A.," entry, May 5, 1873, *Ledger of Burials,* Fisher Funeral Home; in
possession of Fisher-Riles Funeral Home, Vicksburg; typescript in Old Court
House Museum, Vicksburg: ". . . 6 weeks; Spasms . . . ." The burial was billed to
"Mr. Ring," and it was most likely George who provided the information, saying
the infant was "6 weeks" old. In reality, if the baby was born Mar. 30, 1873, he
would have been five weeks and one day old.

4   "Mr. Joseph Ring, In a/c with Geo. F. Ring," Feb. 18, 1874, a financial statement
prepared by George for Barbara, listing expenditures and credits, Oct. 15,
1868–July 25, 1873, marked "Copy" and not in George's hand. Passed from Joseph
Nicholas Ring to his son Louis Caffall Ring, who photocopied it for the author in
1985.

5   Ibid. For Whitehead's and O'Leary's professions, which are not specified in the
financial statement, see: "City Directory," *Vicksburg Daily Times,* Jan. 1, 1873, p. 5.
Dr. Richard O'Leary would be elected mayor of Vicksburg in 1874 (see Chap. 35,
p. 251).

6   See n. 4 above: "Dec. 28, 1871, 2 Sacks Grass Seed from Jeans, $1.00."

7   Ibid.: ". . . 1 Cow . . . [$]75.00 . . . ."

8   Ibid.: ". . . Gray Mare & Colt . . . [$]125.00 . . . ."

9   See Chap. 4, p. 30.

10   See Chap. 4, p. 32–33.

11   See Chap. 14, p. 114.

12   See Chap. 15, p. 128.

13   See Chap. 15, p. 131.

14   See Chap. 18, p. 148.

15   John S. Joor-Kate E. Waddell marriage record, June 27, 1878, Sharkey County
Clerk's Office, Rolling Fork.

16   See Chap. 18, p. 148.

17   See Chap. 19, p. 155.

18   See Chap. 23, p. 185.

19   Assumption based on their origins.

20   See Chap. 24, p. 191.

21   Ibid.

22   See Chap. 24, p. 193.

23   The baptismal record of Michael Albert Ring, May 4, 1873, is signed "T. C. Bohmert." "*Patrini fuerunt*" ("Godparents were") has been amended to read "*Patrinus fuit*" ("Godfather was"), and the name "*Georgas Rich*" has been written on the line.

24   See n. 1 above.

25   See n. 3 above. It is assumption that the infant was buried in his baptismal gown. Penny Colman, *Corpses, Coffins, and Crypts: A History of Burial* (New York: Henry Holt and Co., 1997), 131, cites one example of a young girl who in 1942 was buried "wearing her white first communion dress."

26. JULY 15, 1873

1   Power of Attorney, July 15, 1873, Warren County Deed Book NN: 690–691; Warren County Courthouse, Vicksburg.

2   See histories cited in Ch. 8, n. 1.

3   Deposition of William Muller, dated May 11, 1881, contained in the packet of *Katharina Ring et al. v. Barbara Ring et al.*, Case 299 (Equity), U.S. Circuit Court, Southern District of Mississippi; Records of District Courts of the United States, 1685-1991, RG 21; National Archives—Southeast Region, East Point, Georgia.

4   Ibid.

5   See "Mr. Joseph Ring, In a/c with Geo. F. Ring," Feb. 18, 1874, a financial statement prepared by George for Barbara, listing expenditures and credits, Oct. 15, 1868–July 25, 1873, marked "Copy" and not in George's hand. Passed from Joseph Nicholas Ring to his son Louis Caffall Ring, who photocopied it for the author in 1985.

6   "Notice to the Public," *Vicksburg Daily Times*, July 27, 29 and 30, 1873, p. 2.

7   Ibid.

8   *Barbara Ring v. The Germania Life Insurance Company*, Case 26, *Minutes of the Circuit Court of Issaquena County*, May Term 1873, Book C: 364–365; Issaquena County Courthouse, Mayersville.

9   *Vicksburg Daily Times*, July 16, 1873, p. 3.

10   "Notice to the Public," *Vicksburg Daily Times*, July 27, 29 and 30, 1873, p. 2.

27. JULY 20, 1873

1   "River Intelligence," *Vicksburg Daily Times*, July 20, 1873, p. 3: "Arrivals . . . Jennie Howell from New Orleans . . . Departures . . . Jennie Howell for Cincinnati . . . ." For a departure to be reported in the morning newspaper, the steamboat had to have left very early.

2   *Vicksburg Daily Times*, July 22, 1873, p. 3.

3   "Floating palace" and "floating sepulchre" were common terms in the steamboat age. All description of riverboats and riverboat life, unless otherwise indicated, relies primarily on: (1) Mark Twain, *Life on the Mississippi* (New York: NAL Penguin (a Signet Classic edition), 1960) (originally published in 1883); and (2) Louis C. Hunter and Beatrice Jones Hunter, *Steamboats on the Western Rivers: An Economic and Technological History*, 2nd ed. (New York: Octagon Books, 1969).

4   *Record of Enrollment, Jennie Howell*, Aug. 16, 1869; Inland Rivers Library, Department of Rare Books & Special Collections, Public Library of Cincinnati & Hamilton County. This is a photocopy of the original enrollment certificate in

Certificates of Enrollment, Headquarters Records of the Bureau of Navigation, Records of the Bureau of Marine Inspection and Navigation, 1774–1973, RG 41, National Archives, Washington.

5   "Steamer Jennie Howell Snagged and Sunk—Loss of Life," *Cincinnati Commercial*, July 27, 1873, p. 1: 'Special Telegram to the Commercial' . . . Shawneetown, Ill., July 26 . . . ."

6   *Report of the Supervising Inspector-General* (Washington, D.C.: Steamboat Inspection Service, 1874) 234: "Memphis, Tenn. . . . Steamers inspected during the year ending December 31, 1872 . . . Jennie Howell . . . 552.24 tons . . . ." Also "River Intelligence," *Evansville Daily Journal*, July 28, 1873, p. 7.

7   Way, *Way's Packet Directory*, "Preface," (n.p.). The *Jennie Howell* is entry 2990, p. 245.

8   "River Intelligence," *Vicksburg Daily Times*, July 20, 1873, p. 3.

9   See Prologue, p. 3.

10 Letter of Elizabeth Weber Hilberg to Joseph N. Kellas, Feb. 11, 1958, copy in author's possession.

11 "The Jennie Howell Disaster," *Evansville Daily Journal*, July 28, 1873, p. 5.

12 "The City," *Vicksburg Daily Times*, Aug. 3, 1873, p. 4: "Mr. George F. Ring departed for Detroit, Michigan, yesterday, to join his family . . . ."

13 "Local News," *Vicksburg Daily Times*, Oct. 3, 1873, p. 4: "Mr. George F. Ring has returned with his family from Michigan, where they have been spending the summer . . . ."

14 "Steamer Jennie Howell Snagged and Sunk—Loss of Life," *Cincinnati Commercial*, July 27, 1873, p. 1: "'Special Telegram to the Commercial' . . . Cairo, July 26 . . . ."

15 Long, *The Johann Philipp Koch Family*, 50.

16 "*Jennie Howell*," dated January 1873, Photograph No. 2990; Frederick Way Collection, Inland Rivers Library, Department of Rare Books & Special Collections, Public Library of Cincinnati & Hamilton County, Cincinnati, Ohio.

17 "A Sad Calamity," *Vicksburg Daily Times*, July 27, 1873, p. 3: ". . . ill-fated steamer . . . ;" "River News," *Memphis Daily Avalanche*, Aug. 2, 1873, p. 4: "'Miscellaneous' . . . ill-fated steamer . . . ;" "The Jennie Howell Disaster," *Evansville Daily Journal*, July 28, 1873, p. 5: ". . . ill-fated vessel . . . ."

28. July 25, 1873

1   "River and Steamboat News," *Cincinnati Commercial*, July 26, 1873, p. 7: "'Our Special River Telegrams' . . . Cairo, July 25.–Arrived . . . Jennie Howell from New Orleans, 6 AM."

2   "River and Steamboat News," *Cincinnati Commercial*, July 20-27, 1873. Weather conditions in the port cities on the Mississippi and Ohio are reported daily.

3   See Chap. 27, n. 3.

4   Calculated by the author using "River Intelligence" columns, May, June and July, 1873.

5   Ibid.

6   "River Intelligence," *Evansville Daily Journal*, July 28, 1873, p. 7: "'Miscellaneous'. . . ."

7   See Chap. 21, p. 167 and nn. 78–83.

8   "River and Steamboat News," *Cincinnati Commercial*, July 26, 1873, p. 7: "'Our

Special River Correspondence' . . . Cairo, July 26 . . . ."

9   Ibid.

10   "River Intelligence," *Evansville Daily Journal*, July 28, 1873, p. 7: "'Miscellaneous' . . .
     She [*Jennie Howell*] . . . had, upon leaving Memphis . . . 49 cabin passengers . . . ."
     After leaving Cairo, however, when the *Jennie Howell* sank, the number of cabin pas-
     sengers on board had been reduced by 14. See "Steamer Jennie Howell Snagged
     and Sunk—Loss of Life," *Cincinnati Commercial*, July 27, 1873, p. 1: "'Special
     Telegram to the Commercial' . . . Cairo, July 26 — . . . There were 35 passengers
     aboard at the time."

11   "River and Steamboat News," *Cincinnati Commercial*, July 27, 1873, p. 7: "'Our
     Special River Corresondence' . . . Cairo, July 25 . . . ."

12   Character traits attributed to Frank Buskirk are based on mentions of him in
     "River and Steamboat News," *Cincinnati Commercial*, July 26-31, 1873, as well as
     traits typical of riverboat clerks as described in the sources cited in Chap. 27, n. 3.

13   "River Intelligence," *Evansville Daily Journal*, July 28, 1873, p. 7: "'Miscella-
     neous' . . . . "

14   Way, *Way's Packet Directory*, 46. Entry 0541 is the *Belle Vernon*, on which Billy
     Shaw served after his rather traumatic apprenticeship on the *Jennie Howell*.

15   "River and Steamboat News," *Cincinnati Commercial*, July 28, 1873, p. 7: "'Our
     Special River Correspondence' . . . Cairo, July 26 . . . ."

16   Ibid.

17   "Steamer Jennie Howell Snagged and Sunk—Loss of Life," *Cincinnati
     Commercial*, July 27, 1873, p. 1: "'Special Telegram to the Commercial' . . . Cairo,
     July 26 . . . . " Also "River and Steamboat News," *Cincinnati Commercial*, July 28,
     1873, p. 7: "'Our Special River Correspondence' . . . Cairo, July 26 . . . ."

18   "The Jennie Howell Disaster," *Evansville Daily Journal*, July 28, 1873, p. 5.

19   "River and Steamboat News," *Cincinnati Commercial*, July 26, 1873, p. 7: "'Our
     Special River Telegrams' . . . Cairo, July 25 . . . ."

20   "*Jennie Howell*," dated January 1873, Photograph No. 2990, Frederick Way
     Collection, Inland Rivers Library, Department of Rare Books & Special
     Collections, Public Library of Cincinnati & Hamilton County, Cincinnati, Ohio.

21   "The Jennie Howell Disaster," *Evansville Daily Journal*, July 28, 1873, p. 5.

22   Ibid.

23   "River Intelligence," *Evansville Daily Journal*, July 29, 1873, p. 7: "'Miscella-
     neous' . . . ."

24   Ibid.

25   Long, *The Johann Philipp Koch Family*, 50.

26   "The Jennie Howell Disaster," *Evansville Daily Journal*, July 28, 1873, p. 5.

27   Ibid. The name appears variously as "Clouser" and "Chouser."

28   Assumption based on custom and the number of berths per stateroom (two). See
     also n. 29 below.

29   Deduction based on newspaper accounts of the sinking.

30   "The Jennie Howell Disaster," *Evansville Daily Journal*, July 28, 1873, p. 5.

31   Ibid.: ". . . their state-room being upon the larboard side of the boat . . . ."

32   Ibid.: ". . . while the son was in another state-room. . . ." Descriptions of the sink-
     ing seem to place this room next to that of his parents.

33   "River and Steamboat News," *Cincinnati Commercial*, July 30, 1873, p. 7:
     "'Miscellaneous' . . . ."

34   Deduction based on two berths—one upper, one lower—per stateroom.
35   "Mr. Joseph Ring, In a/c with Geo. F. Ring," Feb. 18, 1874, a financial statement
     prepared by George for Barbara, listing expenditures and credits, Oct. 15,
     1868–July 25, 1873, marked "Copy" and not in George's hand. Passed from Joseph
     Nicholas Ring to his son Louis Caffall Ring, who photocopied it for the author in
     1985.
36   Richard Elwell Banta, *The Ohio* (New York: Rinehart & Co., Inc., 1949), 14–15.
37   See Twain, *Life on the Mississippi*, 51, 59 and 69.
38   "River and Steamboat News," *Cincinnati Commercial*, July 27, 1873, p. 7: "'Our
     Special River Correspondence' . . . Cairo, July 25 . . . ."
39   Internet website for the Astronomical Applications Department, U.S. Naval
     Observatory, Washington, D.C.: http://aa.usno.navy.mil/AA/.
40   "River and Steamboat News," *Cincinnati Commercial*, July 31, 1873, p. 7: "'Our
     Special River Correspondence' . . . Cairo, July 28 . . . Mr. John Moldridge, who
     was at the wheel . . . ."
41   Pilots on the Ohio would certainly have spread the word about a snag so bad that
     it had already sunk a ship. See "River Intelligence," *Evansville Daily Journal*,
     July 28, 1873, p. 7: "Captain Jack Grammar, about a week ago, advised Colonel
     Merrill of the location of this dangerous snag, and requested its removal."
42   Banta, *The Ohio*, 14, 292, 298–299, and Owens, *Steamboats and the Cotton
     Economy*, 133.
43   "Steamer Jennie Howell Snagged and Sunk—Loss of Life," *Cincinnati
     Commercial*, July 27, 1873, p. 1: "'Special Telegram to the Commercial' . . .
     Evansville, Ind., July 26 . . . ."
44   Ibid.: "'Western Associated Press Telegram' . . . Cairo, July 26 . . . ."
45   "River and Steamboat News," *Cincinnati Commercial*, July 20–27, 1873. Whether
     the river is rising or falling, and the current depth of the water in the channel, is
     communicated daily among the port cities on the Mississippi and Ohio.
46   "River Intelligence," *Evansville Daily Journal*, July 28, 1873, p. 7: ". . . packets have
     been running between it [the snag] and the Kentucky shore . . . ."

29. July 26, 1873, About 2–4 A.M.

1   "River and Steamboat News," *Cincinnati Commercial*, July 31, 1873, p. 7: "'Our
     Special River Correspondence' . . . Cairo, July 28 . . . ."
2   Regarding piloting steamboats in the dark, see Twain, *Life on the Mississippi*,
     46–50.
3   "River and Steamboat News," *Cincinnati Commercial*, July 31, 1873, p. 7: "'Our
     Special River Correspondence' . . . Cairo, July 28 . . . ."
4   "The Jennie Howell Disaster," *Evansville Daily Journal*, July 28, 1873, p. 5.
5   Halliday's stateroom in the officer's cabin was one deck below the hurricane roof.
6   "River and Steamboat News," *Cincinnati Commercial*, July 31, 1873, p. 7: "'Our
     Special River Correspondence' . . . Cairo, July 28 . . . ."
7   Ibid.
8   "The Jennie Howell Disaster, *Evansville Daily Journal*, July 28, 1873, p. 5.
9   Ibid.
10   Ibid.
11   Ibid.: ". . . when the boat careened most of her freight on deck slipped over-
     board. . . ." For cargo on board at the time, see Chap. 28, p. 212.

12   "River and Steamboat News," *Cincinnati Commercial*, July 31, 1873, p. 7: "'Our Special River Correspondence' . . . Cairo, July 28.—In less than three minutes the boat had careened, until her state-rooms on one side were in the water. . . .'"

13   Regarding the most probable position of the staterooms occupied by the Ring party, see Chap. 28, p. 218. The fact that the only cabin passengers to drown were all in the Ring party supports the conjecture that their staterooms were farthest to stern, which part of the ship sank first and fastest and deepest.

14   Regarding which berths Barbara and her boys probably used, see Chap. 28, pp. 219–220.

15   "The Jennie Howell Disaster," *Evansville Daily Journal*, July 28, 1873, p. 5: "The snag . . . created a terrific noise, which awoke almost all on board, which probably accounts for the small loss of life."

16   "River and Steamboat News," *Cincinnati Commercial*, July 31, 1873, p. 7: "'Our Special River Correspondence' . . . Cairo, July 28 . . . . '"

17   "Steamer Jennie Howell Snagged and Sunk—Loss of Life," *Cincinnati Commercial*, July 27, 1873, p. 1: "'Special Telegram to the Commercial' . . . Cairo, July 26 . . . The passengers ran forward and crawled up on the edge of the guard. . . .'"

18   Knowing how to swim was not common among nineteenth-century urbanites of the tradesman's class, especially the women. See Chap. 4, p. 27.

19   Assumption based on the fact that John apparently never left his mattress.

20   "The Jennie Howell Disaster, *Evansville Daily Journal*, July 28, 1873, p. 5.

21   "River and Steamboat News," *Cincinnati Commercial*, July 31, 1873, p. 7: "'Our Special River Correspondence' . . . Cairo, July 28 . . . .'"

22   "River Intelligence," *Evansville Daily Journal*, July 29, 1873, p. 7: "'Miscellaneous' . . . Buskirk . . . escaped in his drawers . . . .'"

23   Ibid.: "A young lady arrayed in a single garment . . . in that meager attire. . . .'"

24   "River and Steamboat News," *Cincinnati Commercial*, July 31, 1873, p. 7: "'Our Special River Correspondence' . . . Cairo, July 28 . . . .'"

25   Ibid.

26   "The Jennie Howell Disaster," *Evansville Daily Journal*, July 28, 1873, p. 5.

27   Ibid.

28   Letter of Elizabeth Weber Hilberg to Joseph N. Kellas, Feb. 11, 1958, copy in author's possession.

29   See Prologue, p. 3.

30   "The Jennie Howell Disaster," *Evansville Daily Journal*, July 28, 1873, p. 5: ". . . in five minutes her cabin was full of water." Also "Steamer Jennie Howell Snagged and Sunk—Loss of Life," *Cincinnati Commercial*, July 27, 1873, p. 1: "'Special Telegram to the Commercial' . . . Cairo, July 26 . . . the boat now lies edgeways, with her bow fast on the snag and stern in deep water. . . .'"

31   "The Jennie Howell Disaster, *Evansville Daily Journal*, July 28, 1873, p. 5.

32   "River and Steamboat News," *Cincinnati Commercial*, July 30, 1873, p. 7: "'Our Special River Correspondence' . . . Cairo, July 28 . . . .'"

33   Deck crew = ca. 30, cabin crew = ca. 22, officers = ca. 8 (see Chap. 28, pp. 212, 217 and 219); cabin passengers = 35, deck passenger = 1 (see Chap. 28, p. 213).

34   "Steamer Jennie Howell Snagged and Sunk—Loss of Life," *Cincinnati Commercial*, July 27, 1873, p. 1: "'Special Telegram to the Commercial' . . . Evansville, Ind., July 26 . . . The Quickstep arrived at the wreck twenty minutes after the disaster."

35 "The Jennie Howell Disaster," *Evansville Daily Journal*, July 28, 1873, p. 5. The *Quickstep* is entry 4621 in Way, *Way's Packet Directory*, 382.

36 "River Intelligence" columns indicate that the *Quickstep* ran up and down the Ohio River between Evansville and Cairo, stopping in Shawneetown (and perhaps other smaller intermediate ports) as business required. See also Way, *Way's Packet Directory*, 382.

37 "The Jennie Howell Disaster," *Evansville Daily Journal*, July 28, 1873, p. 5.

38 "Steamer Jennie Howell Snagged and Sunk—Loss of Life," *Cincinnati Commercial*, July 27, 1873, p. 1: "'Special Telegram to the Commercial' . . . Evansville, Ind., July 26 . . . The Quickstep arrived at the wreck twenty minutes after the disaster."

39 "River and Steamboat News," *Cincinnati Commercial*, July 31, 1873, p. 7: "'Our Special River Correspondence' . . . Cairo, July 28 . . . .'"

40 "The Jennie Howell Disaster," *Evansville Daily Journal*, July 28, 1873, p. 5.

41 "River Intelligence," *Evansville Daily Journal*, July 29, 1873, p. 7: "'Miscellaneous' . . . Buskirk and the passengers express the warmest thanks and most heartfelt gratitude to the officers and crew of the Quickstep . . . for their large hearted kindness and benevolence extended to those shipwrecked on the Howell."

42 "Steamer Jennie Howell Snagged and Sunk—Loss of Life," *Cincinnati Commercial*, July 27, 1873, p. 1: "'Special Telegram to the Commercial' . . . Evansville, Ind., July 26.—A dispatch from Walter B. Pennington, clerk of the Quickstep . . . ."

43 Assumption based on custom. See sources cited in Chap. 27, n. 3.

44 "River Intelligence," *Evansville Daily Journal*, July 28, 1873, p. 7: "The Storm that opened about midnight Friday, with a flurry of wind and a few drops of rain, soon passed away, but new clouds gathered, and near morning another violent storm of wind with a heavier rain set in."

45 "River and Steamboat News," *Cincinnati Commercial*, July 31, 1873, p. 7: "'Our Special River Correspondence' . . . Cairo, July 28 . . . .'"

46 "River Intelligence," *Evansville Daily Journal*, July 29, 1873, p. 7: "'Miscellaneous' . . . .'"

47 Ibid.

48 "Steamer Jennie Howell Snagged and Sunk—Loss of Life," *Cincinnati Commercial*, July 27, 1873, p. 1: "'Special Telegram to the Commercial' . . . Cairo, July 26 . . . .'"

49 Ibid.: "'Special Telegram to the Commercial' . . . Shawneetown, Ill., July 26 . . . Mr. Buskirk . . . returned to the wreck this morning . . . ." Obviously, then, Buskirk was among those who had arrived in Shawneetown on board the *Quickstep*.

50 "The Jennie Howell Disaster," *Evansville Daily Journal*, July 28, 1873, p. 5.

51 Assumption based on custom. See works cited in Chap. 27, n. 3.

52 "Steamer Jennie Howell Snagged and Sunk—Loss of Life," *Cincinnati Commercial*, July 27, 1873, p. 1: "'Special Telegram to the Commercial' . . . Shawneetown, Ill., July 26 . . . ."

53 See wire dispatches quoted and cited in Chap. 30, p. 230.

30. JULY 26, 1873, DAYTIME

1 "River Intelligence," *Evansville Daily Journal*, July 28, 1873, p. 7. The weather in Shawneetown would have been similar to that in neighboring Evansville.

2   In river towns the church bell served as an alarm in times of emergency. See
    sources about life along the inland rivers cited in Chap. 27, n. 3. For location of the
    First Methodist Church, see n. 14 below.
3   "The Jennie Howell Disaster," *Evansville Daily Journal*, July 28, 1873, p. 5.
4   "Steamer Jennie Howell Snagged and Sunk—Loss of Life," *Cincinnati
    Commercial*, July 27, 1873, p. 1: "'Special Telegram to the Commercial' . . .
    Shawneetown, Ill., July 26 . . . ."
5   Ibid.: ". . . Mr. Buskirk . . . returned to the wreck this morning . . . ." Obviously,
    then, Buskirk was among those who had arrived in Shawneetown on board the
    Quickstep.
6   "The Jennie Howell Disaster," *Evansville Daily Journal*, July 28, 1873, p. 5.
7   See sources about life along the inland rivers cited in Chap. 27, n. 3.
8   "River Intelligence," *Evansville Daily Journal*, July 28, 1873, p. 7: "'Miscellaneous' . . .
    Shawneetown, July 26 . . . ."
9   "Steamer Jennie Howell Snagged and Sunk—Loss of Life," *Cincinnati
    Commercial*, July 27, 1873, p. 1: "'Special Telegram to the Commercial' . . .
    Shawneetown, Ill., July 26 . . . ."
10 Unless otherwise noted, travel times are estimates derived from averaging arrival
    and departure data appearing in "River Intelligence" during the summer of 1873.
11 "Steamer Jennie Howell Snagged and Sunk—Loss of Life," *Cincinnati
    Commercial*, July 27, 1873, p. 1: "'Special Telegram to the Commercial' . . . Cairo,
    July 26 . . . ."
12 "River and Steamboat News," *Cincinnati Commercial*, July 27, 1873, p. 7:
    "'Miscellaneous' . . . ."
13 Ibid., July 30, 1873, p. 7: "'Our Special River Correspondence' . . . ."
14 History and description of Shawneetown rely primarily on: (1) *Illinois, A
    Descriptive and Historical Guide* (Chicago: A. C. McClurg & Co. (for the Work
    Projects Administration), 1946), 435–437; (2) Sanborn Fire Insurance Map of
    Shawneetown, dated May 1885 (New York: Sanborn Map & Publishing Co., 1885)
    (this is the earliest Sanborn map of Shawneetown available); Geography and Map
    Division, Library of Congress, Washington; and (3) "A Walking Tour of Historic
    Old Shawneetown" (Springfield, Ill.: Division of Tourism, Department of Business
    and Economic Development, n.d.).
15 There was one other hotel in town, the Lafayette, but it was 50 years older and
    very much smaller.
16 See works cited in n. 14 above.
17 "Steamer Jennie Howell Snagged and Sunk—Loss of Life," *Cincinnati
    Commercial*, July 27, 1873, p. 1: "'Special Telegram to the Commercial' . . .
    Shawneetown, Ill., July 26 . . . ."
18 "The Jennie Howell Disaster," *Evansville Daily Journal*, July 28, 1873, p. 5.
19 "A Sad Calamity," *Vicksburg Daily Times*, July 27, 1873, p. 3.
20 "River Intelligence," *Evansville Daily Journal*, July 28, 1873, p. 7. The weather in
    Shawneetown would have been similar to that in neighboring Evansville.
21 "River and Steamboat News," *Cincinnati Commercial*, July 27, 1873, p. 7: "'Our
    Special River Telegrams' . . . Cairo, July 26 . . . The T.F. Eckert went to her assis-
    tance at noon." Also "'Miscellaneous' . . . The wrecking steamer Eckert has gone
    to her [*Jennie Howell*'s] assistance." The *T. F. Eckert* is entry 5272 in: Way, *Way's
    Packet Directory*, 440–441.

22 "Steamer Jennie Howell Snagged and Sunk—Loss of Life," *Cincinnati Commercial*, July 27, 1873, p. 1: "'Special Telegram to the Commercial' . . . Shawneetown, Ill., July 26 . . . ."

23 Deduction, since it will be the *Arkansas Belle* that will bring Halliday and his crew and the salvaged freight back to Shawneetown later this day (see n. 30 below). The *Arkansas Belle* is entry 0349 in Way, *Way's Packet Directory*, 30.

24 "Steamer Jennie Howell Snagged and Sunk—Loss of Life," *Cincinnati Commercial*, July 27, 1873, p. 1: "'Special Telegram to the Commercial' . . . Shawneetown, Ill., July 26 . . . ."

25 "The Jennie Howell Disaster," *Evansville Daily Journal*, July 28, 1873, p. 5

26 "Steamer Jennie Howell Snagged and Sunk—Loss of Life," *Cincinnati Commercial*, July 27, 1873, p. 1: "'Special Telegram to the Commercial' . . . Shawneetown, Ill., July 26 . . . ."

27 "River Intelligence," *Evansville Daily Journal*, July 28, 1873, p. 7. The weather in Shawneetown would have been similar to that in neighboring Evansville.

28 "River and Steamboat News, *Cincinnati Commercial*, July 27, 1873, p. 7: "'Our Special River Telegrams' . . . Cairo, July 26 . . . Arrived . . . Quickstep, from Evansville, 7 P.M." Steaming down the Ohio from Evansville, and arriving in Cairo at 7:00 p.m., the *Quickstep* would have passed the wreck of the *Jennie Howell* sometime that afternoon.

29 "River and Steamboat News," *Cincinnati Commercial*, July 29, 1873, p. 7: "'Our Special River Telegrams' . . . Shawneetown, July 28 . . . ."

30 Ibid. See also "The Jennie Howell Disaster," *Evansville Daily Journal*, July 28, 1873, p. 5: "Another child of Mrs. Ring was missing immediately after the disaster, but was found in the morning asleep upon a mattress, floating in the state-room."

31 Letter of Elizabeth Weber Hilberg to Joseph N. Kellas, Feb. 11, 1958, copy in author's possession.

32 See Prologue, p. 3.

33 Letter of Louis Caffall Ring to the author, July 14, 1986.

34 "Casualties," *Cincinnati Commercial*, July 28, 1873, p. 1: "Cairo, Ill., July 27 . . . ."

35 "River and Steamboat News," *Cincinnati Commercial*, July 30, 1873, p. 7: "'Our Special River Correspondence' . . . Cairo, July 28 . . . ."

36 "River Intelligence," *Vicksburg Daily Times*, July 29, 1873, p. 3.

37 "The Jennie Howell Disaster," *Evansville Daily Journal*, July 28, 1873, p. 5.

31. July 27, 1873

1 "River Intelligence," *Evansville Daily Journal*, July 28, 1873, p. 7: "'Miscellaneous' . . . The Arkansas Belle arrived early yesterday morning." To arrive in Evansville by early morning, the steamer must have left Shawneetown around dawn. See Chap. 30, n. 10.

2 "The Jennie Howell Disaster," *Evansville Daily Journal*, July 28, 1873, p. 5.

3 "River Intelligence," *Evansville Daily Journal*, July 28, 1873, p. 7: "'Miscellaneous' . . . ."

4 "The Jennie Howell Disaster," *Evansville Daily Journal*, July 28, 1873, p. 5.

5 Similar to the *Quickstep*, the *Arkansas Belle* was a sidewheeler on the Cairo-Evansville route. She left Evansville at 4:00 p.m. three days a week. See the "*Arkansas Belle*" advertisement printed regularly in the *Evansville Daily Journal* on the same page as "River Intelligence." See also Way, *Way's Packet Directory*, 30.

6 "The Jennie Howell Disaster," *Evansville Daily Journal*, July 28, 1873, p. 5.

7   See Chap. 30, n. 10.

8   "River Intelligence," *Evansville Daily Journal*, July 28, 1873, p. 7: "'Miscellaneous' . . . ."

9   History and description of Evansville rely primarily on: (1) Frank M. Gilbert, *History of the City of Evansville and Vanderburg* [sic] *County Indiana*, 2 vols. (Chicago: The Pioneer Publishing Co., 1910); (2) Robert P. Patry, *City of the Four Freedoms: A History of Evansville, Indiana* (Evansville: Friends of Willard Library, 1996); (3) Sanborn Fire Insurance Map of Evansville, dated 1884 (New York: Sanborn Map & Publishing Co., 1884) (this is the earliest Sanborn map of Evansville available); Geography and Map Division, Library of Congress, Washington; (4) *Evansville City Directory for 1872–73* (Evansville: Brandis & Meadows, 1872); *Evansville City Directory for 1874* (Evansville: Brandis & Meadows, 1874). No directory was published in 1873.

10   "River Intelligence," *Evansville Daily Journal*, July 28, 1873, p. 7: "'Miscellaneous' . . . ."

11   Physical description of George Koch is based on his photograph (Long, *The Johann Philipp Koch Family*, 104) and the descriptions of two of his brothers contained in their military records (Ibid., 48).

12   "Ring, Peter Paul" entry, July 29, 1873, *Record of Burials*, St. Joseph's Catholic Cemetery, Evansville, Indiana: ". . . Mortuary, Reising." These records have been published in typescript: Karen A. Schoenbachler, *St. Joseph's Catholic Cemetery* (Evansville: the author, 1987); however, the entries are not always complete and they sometimes contain errors of transcription. Also *Evansville City Directory for 1872–73*, 232.

13   "River Intelligence," *Evansville Daily Journal*, July 28, 1873, p. 7.

14   See sources cited in n. 9 above.

15   Sanborn Fire Insurance Map of Evansville, dated 1884, sheet 18, and Long, *The Johann Philipp Koch Family*, 50. See also Chap. 27, p. 208.

16   *Evansville City Directory for 1874*, 184.

17   Physical description of Mary Schwink Koch is based on her photograph (Long, *The Johann Philipp Koch Family*, 104).

18   Letter of Elizabeth Weber Hilberg to Joseph N. Kellas, Feb. 11, 1958, copy in author's possession.

19   "Steamer Jennie Howell Snagged and Sunk—Loss of Life," *Cincinnati Commercial*, July 27, 1873, p. 1.

20   *Cincinnati City Directory for 1873* (Cincinnati: Williams & Co., 1873), 862: "Weber Henry, h. Highland Av., Corryville." For Corryville's hilly location, see Chap. 9, p. 62, and n. 8.

21   "River Intelligence," *Evansville Daily Journal*, July 29, 1873, p. 7: "'Miscellaneous' . . . The Eckert came up to her [the *Jennie Howell*] Sunday morning."

22   "The Jennie Howell Disaster," *Evansville Daily Journal*, July 28, 1873, p. 5. The *Umpire* is entry 5492 in Way, *Way's Packet Directory*, 462.

23   "River and Steamboat News," *Cincinnati Commercial*, July 31, 1873, p. 7: "'Our Special River Correspondence' . . . Cairo, July 28 . . . ."

24   "River Intelligence," *Evansville Daily Journal*, July 28, 1873, p. 7: "'Miscellaneous' . . . ."

25   Ibid.

26   "River and Steamboat News," *Cincinnati Commercial*, July 31, 1873, p. 7: "'Our Special River Correspondence' . . . Cairo, July 28 . . . ."

27   "River Intelligence," *Evansville Daily Journal*, July 29, 1873, p. 7: "'Miscellaneous' . . . ."

28 "River and Steamboat News," *Cincinnati Commercial*, July 31, 1873, p. 7: "'Our Special River Correspondence' . . . Cairo, July 28 . . . .'"

29 Ibid.

30 "River and Steamboat News," *Cincinnati Commercial*, July 29, 1873, p. 7: "'Our Special River Telegrams' . . . Shawneetown, July 28 . . . Buskirk, the clerk, also left on the Lawrence."

31 "River and Steamboat News," *Cincinnati Commercial*, July 31, 1873, p. 7: "'Our Special River Correspondence' . . . Cairo, July 28 . . . The T.F. Eckert returned from the wreck of the Jennie Howell, yesterday, and brought down Captain Halliday and his brother." Evidently, Lewis Halliday stayed only briefly in Evansville (where he arrived early Sunday morning on the *Arkansas Belle*), for he was back in Shawneetown in time to join his brother on the *T. F. Eckert* on Sunday evening or Monday morning.

32 "River and Steamboat News," *Cincinnati Commercial*, July 29, 1873, p. 7: "'Our Special River Telegrams' . . . Shawneetown, July 28 . . . The Eckert was at the wreck yesterday, but could do nothing, and left for Cairo;" and July 31, 1873, p. 7: "'Our Special River Correspondence' . . . Cairo, July 28 . . . The Eckert has again begun the work of drawing up that railroad iron."

33 "River and Steamboat News," *Cincinnati Commercial*, Aug. 1, 1873, p. 7: "'Our Special River Correspondence' . . . Cairo, July 30 . . . .'"

34 Ibid.: "'Miscellaneous' . . . ."

35 "Coroner's Inquest, A. K. Sprengall, held 27 July 1873, filed 30 August 1873," Union County Courthouse, Morganfield, Kentucky. This document, along with five related receipts, and many other loose papers, was included in a supervised destruction of old records deemed unimportant by the state archivist during the winter of 1992–93. It was retrieved by Dennis A. Kirchner, local historian and historical records saver of Union County, who gave it to the author. The author thanks Mr. Kirchner not only for this document, but for all of the valuable assistance he rendered as the author's guide during a research visit to Union County in 1992. Also "River and Steamboat News," *Cincinnati Commercial*, July 29, 1873, p. 7: "'Our Special River Telegrams' . . . Shawneetown, July 28 . . . The body of Mrs. Springle was recovered at Caseyville yesterday evening."

36 "River and Steamboat News," *Cincinnati Commercial*, July 31, 1873, p. 7: "'Our Special River Correspondence' . . . Cairo, July 28 . . . .'"

37 "Coroner's Inquest, A. K. Sprengall."

38 Receipt for payment for services, signed by Burrel Johnson [his mark], original document in author's possession. See n. 35 above.

39 Receipt for payment for services, signed by A. J. Brown, original document in author's possession. See n. 35 above.

40 Receipt for payment for services, signed by L. B. Steel, original document in author's possession. See n. 35 above.

41 "Coroner's Inquest, A. K. Sprengall."

42 "River Intelligence," *Evansville Daily Journal*, July 28, 1873, p. 7: "Yesterday was cloudy and warm, with a light rain nearly all day, at times becoming quite copious;" and "River and Steamboat News," *Cincinnati Commercial*, July 28, 1873, p. 7: "'Our special River Telegrams' . . . Cairo, July 27 . . . Cloudy, with a heavy rain last night, and this morning cool;" and "River and Steamboat News," *Cincinnati Commercial*, July 29, 1873, p. 7: "'Our special River Telegrams' . . . Cairo, July 28 . . . Rain last

night. Clear . . . ." Caseyville, located between Cairo and Evansville, would have experienced similar weather on Sunday.

43   Terrence E. Barr, P.A., Walter Reed Army Medical Center, Washington, D.C.

44   "Coroner's Inquest, A. K. Sprengall."

45   Ibid.

46   Ibid.

47   Description based on author's on-site inspection, research trip of 1992.

48   "River Intelligence," *Evansville Daily Journal*, July 29, 1873, p. 7: "'Miscellaneous' . . . The body of Mrs. Sprangler was found and decently buried at Caseyville."

49   Although Pierson may have waited until Monday morning before wiring Evansville, it seems reasonable to assume that—a river town resident himself and intimately familiar with the trials peculiar to river life—he would have been sensitive enough to inform the family *immediately*.

50   See nn. 38, 39 and 40 above. Also Receipt for payment for services, signed by H. A. Pierson, and receipt for payment for coffin, signed "Jones & Dyer," original documents in author's possession. See n. 35 above.

32. JULY 28, 1873

1   It is also possible that only Barbara accompanied Koch, or even that Koch handled their affairs by himself.

2   "River Intelligence," *Evansville Daily Journal*, July 29, 1873, p. 7.

3   *Evansville City Directory for 1872–73* (Evansville: Brandis & Meadows, 1872), 232.

4   "Springler, Anna K." entry, July 31, 1873, *Record of Burials*, St. Joseph's Catholic Cemetery, Evansville, Indiana.

5   Patry, *City of the Four Freedoms*, 61 (text and photograph).

6   *Evansville City Directory for 1872–73*, 17, and Sanborn Fire Insurance Map of Evansville, dated 1884 (New York: Sanborn Map & Publishing Co, 1884), sheet 4; Geography and Map Division, Library of Congress, Washington.

7   See Chap. 21, n. 83.

8   "The Jennie Howell Disaster," *Evansville Daily Journal*, July 28, 1873, p. 5.

9   "River Intelligence," *Evansville Daily Journal*, July 29, 1873, p. 7: "'Miscellaneous' . . . ." The *Morning Star* is entry 4039 in Way, *Way's Packet Directory*, 331.

10   Ibid., and "The Jennie Howell Disaster," *Evansville Daily Journal*, July 28, 1873, p. 5.

11   "The Jennie Howell Disaster," *Evansville Daily Journal*, July 28, 1873, p. 5.

12   "River Intelligence," *Evansville Daily Journal*, July 29, 1873, p. 7: "'Miscellaneous' . . . ."

13   Ibid. The *Lawrence* is entry 3390 in Way, *Way's Packet Directory*, 280.

14   Ibid.

15   "River and Steamboat News," *Cincinnati Commercial*, July 30, 1873, p. 7: "'Our Special River Correspondence' . . . ."

33. JULY 29, 1873

1   Burial record of Peter Paul Ring, July 29, 1873 (died July 26, 1873); *Register of Burials, 1849–1886*: 223, Holy Trinity R. C. Church, Evansville, Indiana; *Microfilmed Records of Holy Trinity Roman Catholic Church*, reel 2, Willard Library, Evansville. That the three boys attended the funeral with Barbara is assumption.

2   Gilbert, *History of the City of Evansville and Vanderburg* [sic] *County Indiana*, I:

321–322.

3   Burial record of Peter Paul Ring, July 29, 1873: "... per Carolam Loescher."
4   "River and Steamboat News," *Cincinnati Commercial*, July 30, 1873, p. 7: "'Our Special River Telegrams' ... Evansville, July 29 ...."
5   *Evansville City Directory for 1872–73* (Evansville: Brandis & Meadows, 1872), 25: "St. Joseph's Catholic Cemetery Association.—office 86 Main; Grounds, Cynthiana Road, three miles from Court House."
6   "Ring, Peter Paul" entry, July 29, 1873, *Record of Burials*, St. Joseph's Catholic Cemetery, Evansville, Indiana: "Interment no. 306, section 8, lot 483." Also Schoenbachler, *St. Joseph's Catholic Cemetery*, "Preface."
7   Description of cemetery is based on author's on-site inspection, research trip of 1992, and Schoenbachler, *St. Joseph's Catholic Cemetery*, "Preface."
8   Ibid. They were carved and put in place the previous year, 1872.
9   It is very likely that the monument was set in place by the time of the funeral. It is a standard child's tombstone, pre-carved and ready to be inscribed when ordered—which would have been the previous morning, or perhaps even the day before that—Sunday—when Barbara first arrived in Evansville with the body.
10   Peter P. Ring tombstone, Section 8, lot 483, St. Joseph's Catholic Cemetery, Evansville, Indiana. Evidently George Koch selected a mortuary—John G. Reising—of the Germanic community. Whether it was he or Barbara who requested that the monument be inscribed in German, however, no one will ever know.
11   See n. 1 above.

34. JULY 31, 1873

1   "Springler, Anna K" entry, July 31, 1873, *Record of Burials*, St. Joseph's Catholic Cemetery, Evansville, Indiana: "Interment no. 310, section 8, lot 62."
2   Ibid.
3   Letter of Elizabeth Weber Hilberg to Joseph N. Kellas, Feb. 11, 1958, photocopy in author's possession.
4   "The City," *Vicksburg Daily Times*, Aug. 3, 1873, p. 4.
5   Long, *The Johann Philipp Koch Family*, 50. Almost every member of the family is buried, *not* in Evansville's Catholic cemetery, but rather in its non-denominational Locust Hill Cemetery (Long, 107–109).
6   There was no passenger rail service between Evansville and Cincinnati in 1873 (see histories cited in Chap. 31, n. 9). Barbara would have taken a riverboat or, if she could not bring herself to get on another boat, stagecoach.
7   *Cincinnati Directory for 1873* (Cincinnati: Williams & Co., 1873), 862.
8   Baptismal record of Edward Joseph Weber, Mar. 8, 1863 (born Feb. 26, 1863); *Baptismal Register 1862–1863*: 25, St. Francis Seraph R. C. Church, Cincinnati; Historical Archives of the Chancery, Archdiocese of Cincinnati, Cincinnati.
9   Baptismal record of "Theresa Elizabeth" Weber, May 3, 1870 (born Apr. 26, 1870); *Baptismal Register 1868–1874*: 10, St. George's R. C. Church, Cincinnati; Historical Archives of the Chancery, Archdiocese of Cincinnati, Cincinnati.
10   "Local News," *Vicksburg Daily Times*, Oct. 3, 1873, p. 4: "Mr. George F. Ring has returned with his family from Michigan, where they have been spending the summer."

35. VICKSBURG

1   "Local News," *Vicksburg Daily Times*, Oct. 3, 1873, p. 4.
2   See Chap. 36.
3   *Vicksburgh* [sic] *Troubles. Report of the Select Committee to Visit Vicksburgh.* (Washington: Government Printing Office, 1875). This is House Report 265, 43rd Congress, 2nd Session (hereafter "Vicksburgh Troubles"). The account given here is derived from Garner, *Reconstruction in Mississippi*, 328–337; Harris, *The Day of the Carpetbagger*, 634–649; Foner, *Reconstruction*, 558; and testimony of Judge George F. Brown, Dec. 31, 1874, "Vicksburgh Troubles," 494–519.
4   Garner, *Reconstruction in Mississippi*, 292.
5   Ibid., 277.
6   Ibid., 274–277.
7   Ibid., 292–293.
8   Paragraph based on Garner, *Reconstruction in Mississippi*, 328, and testimony of Judge George F. Brown, Dec. 31, 1874, "Vicksburgh Troubles."
9   See biographical sketch of Peter Crosby in Foner, *Freedom's Lawmakers*, 54.
10 Paragraph based on Garner, *Reconstruction in Mississippi*, 328, 331, and testimony of Judge George F. Brown, Dec. 31, 1874, "Vicksburgh Troubles."
11 Paragraph based on Garner, *Reconstruction in Mississippi*, 328, and Foner, *Freedom's Lawmakers*, 54.
12 Samuel Fischel was elected alderman in Nov. 1871 (see Chap. 2, n. 25), and re-elected in Nov. 1873 (see "Official," "Board of Mayor and Aldermen," *Vicksburg Daily Times*, Nov. 27, 1873, p. 3).
13 Paragraph based on Garner, *Reconstruction in Mississippi*, 329, Harris, *The Day of the Carpetbagger*, 634–635, and Foner, *Reconstruction*, 558.
14 Paragraph based on Garner, *Reconstruction in Mississippi*, 329–330, and Harris, *The Day of the Carpetbagger*, 635–636.
15 Paragraph based on Garner, *Reconstruction in Mississippi*, 331, and Foner, *Reconstruction*, 558.
16 Unattributed quotation from Foner, *Reconstruction*, 558.
17 Garner, *Reconstruction in Mississippi*, 332, and "The Taxpayers' Meeting," *Vicksburg Daily Times*, Dec. 2, 1874, p. 4.
18 Garner, *Reconstruction in Mississippi*, 332, and Foner, *Reconstruction*, 558.
19 "The Taxpayers' Meeting," *Vicksburg Daily Times*, Dec. 2, 1874, p. 4.
20 Paragraph based on Garner, *Reconstruction in Mississippi*, 332, and Harris, *The Day of the Carpetbagger*, 646.
21 Foner, *Freedom's Lawmakers*, 54.
22 Paragraph based on Garner, *Reconstruction in Mississippi*, 332, and testimony of Judge George F. Brown, Dec. 31, 1874, "Vicksburgh Troubles."
23 Garner, *Reconstruction in Mississippi*, 283, n. 4, and testimony of Judge George F. Brown, Dec. 31, 1874, "Vicksburgh Troubles."
24 See Chap. 36.
25 *Vicksburg Daily Times*, Dec. 2, 1874, p. 4.
26 Garner, *Reconstruction in Mississippi*, 332, and testimony of Judge George F. Brown, Dec. 31, 1874, "Vicksburgh Troubles."
27 Ibid., and *Vicksburg Daily Times*, Dec. 3, 1874, p. 4.
28 Paragraph based on Garner, *Reconstruction in Mississippi*, 332–333, Harris, *The Day of the Carpetbagger*, 646–647, and Foner, *Reconstruction*, 558.
29 Paragraph based on Garner, *Reconstruction in Mississippi*, 333.

30   Regarding the Jeans orphans, see Chap. 23, p. 180.

31   "Geo. F. Ring, Cotton Factor and General Commission Merchant," advertisement in *The Daily Vicksburger*, 1874, passim. Quoted in full in Chap. 37, p. 274.

32   See Chap. 22, p. 177.

33   Paragraph based on Garner, *Reconstruction in Mississippi*, 333.

34   Paragraph based on "War of Races!" *Vicksburg Daily Times*, Dec. 7, 1874, p. 4, Garner, *Reconstruction in Mississippi*, 333, and Harris, *The Day of the Carpetbagger*, 647. Also Foner, *Reconstruction*, 558, quotes testimony in "Vicksburgh Troubles:" "(The 'battle,' one participant related, 'didn't require any valor,' for it pitted whites armed with long-range rifles against blacks who possessed only shotguns and pistols.)."

35   Ibid.

36   "War of Races!" *Vicksburg Daily Times*, Dec. 7, 1874, p. 4; and Garner, *Reconstruction in Mississippi*, 333–334.

37   Paragraph based on "War of Races!" *Vicksburg Daily Times*, Dec. 7, 1874, p. 4; and Garner, *Reconstruction in Mississippi*, 334.

38   Ibid., and Harris, *The Day of the Carpetbagger*, 647.

39   Ibid.

40   Ibid.

41   Paragraph based on "War of Races!" *Vicksburg Daily Times*, Dec. 7, 1874, p. 4.

42   Ibid.

43   Harris, *The Day of the Carpetbagger*, 648, and Foner, *Reconstruction*, 558: "In the days that followed, armed bands roamed the countryside, murdering perhaps 300 blacks."

44   *Vicksburg Daily Times*, Dec. 9, 1874, p. 4.

45   Testimony of Judge George F. Brown, Dec. 31, 1874, "Vicksburgh Troubles."

46   *Vicksburg Daily Times*, Dec. 10, 1874, p. 4.

47   Ibid.

48   Garner, *Reconstruction in Mississippi*, 335.

49   Ibid., 334–335, and Harris, *The Day of the Carpetbagger*, 648.

50   Garner, *Reconstruction in Mississippi*, 334.

51   Ibid., 335.

52   Ibid., 336, and Foner, *Reconstruction*, 558.

53   "A Card to the Editor," *Vicksburg Daily Times*, Dec. 14, 1874, p. 4.

54   See Chap 36.

55   See n. 3 above.

56   Garner, *Reconstruction in Mississippi*, 337, and "Vicksburgh Troubles," pp. I–XXXVI.

57   "Local News," *Vicksburg Daily Times*, Nov. 11, 1874, p. 4.

58   Burial Records of Holy Trinity R. C. Church in Evansville, Indiana, contain no record of a funeral for Anna.

59   "Sprankle, Ann K. (Mrs.)" entry, Nov. 11, 1874, *Ledger of Burials*, Fisher Funeral Home; in possession of Fisher-Riles Funeral Home, Vicksburg; typescript in Old Court House Museum, Vicksburg: ". . . Removed from Evansville, Indiana . . . ." Also Anna C. Sprankler tombstone, Division C, Square 142, Cedar Hill Cemetery, Vicksburg. Also *Vicksburg Daily Times*, Nov. 11, 1874, p. 4: "It sprinkled a little this morning."

60   The account of the "Redemption" given here is derived from Garner,

Reconstruction in Mississippi, 372–396; Harris, *The Day of the Carpetbagger*, 649–686; and Foner, *Reconstruction*, 559–562.

61   Paragraph based on Garner, *Reconstruction in Mississippi*, 372, Harris, *The Day of the Carpetbagger*, 650–660, and Foner, *Reconstruction*, 559.

62   Paragraph based on Garner, *Reconstruction in Mississippi*, 373–375, and Harris, *The Day of the Carpetbagger*, 649.

63   Paragraph based on Garner, *Reconstruction in Mississippi*, 375, and Harris, *The Day of the Carpetbagger*, 649.

64   Paragraph based on Garner, *Reconstruction in Mississippi*, 375, Harris, *The Day of the Carpetbagger*, 661–662, and Foner, *Reconstruction*, 559.

65   Paragraph based on Garner, *Reconstruction in Mississippi*, 378–379, Harris, *The Day of the Carpetbagger*, 660–661, and Foner, *Reconstruction*, 559–560.

66   Paragraph based on Garner, *Reconstruction in Mississippi*, 376–377, Harris, *The Day of the Carpetbagger*, 671–672, and Foner, *Reconstruction*, 560.

67   Paragraph based on Garner, *Reconstruction in Mississippi*, 379–381, Harris, *The Day of the Carpetbagger*, 663–668, and Foner, *Reconstruction*, 560–561.

68   Paragraph based on Garner, *Reconstruction in Mississippi*, 382–383, and Harris, *The Day of the Carpetbagger*, 670–671.

69   Paragraph based on Garner, *Reconstruction in Mississippi*, 387–388, Harris, *The Day of the Carpetbagger*, 672–673, and Foner, *Reconstruction*, 561.

70   Paragraph based on Garner, *Reconstruction in Mississippi*, 392–396, Harris, *The Day of the Carpetbagger*, 684–686, and Foner, *Reconstruction*, 561–562.

36. THE TRIALS

1   "Circuit Court, Assignments for Tomorrow," *Vicksburg Daily Times*, Nov. 12, 1874, p. 4: "2573—Geo. F. Ring survivor vs. Franklin Insurance Co.; 2572—Geo. F. Ring vs. Franklin Insurance Co."

2   Summons dated Nov. 2, 1874, contained in the packet of *George F. Ring v. Franklin Fire Insurance Co.*, Case 2572: "The within named . . . J W Parberry . . . after diligent search cannot be found in my County, nor could I find any place of [his] usual abode in my County by which I could serve his process by Posting copy on door &c. [signed] H P Scott Sheriff By I H Mobley D. Shff."

3   Cotton, *The Old Court House*, 29.

4   *Vicksburg Daily Times*, Nov. 13, 1874, p. 4. Evidence in the text of the *Vicksburg Daily Times* indicates that during this period it was an *evening* newspaper, although previously it was a *morning* newspaper.

5   When court was in session, it always brought a special animation to the courthouse town. It was very good for local buinesses.

6   See Chap. 35.

7   Minutes of the Circuit Court of Warren County for Nov. 13, 1874, show that George's cases were not the first to be heard.

8   It was probably at this time that Judge George F. Brown combined into a single suit the three actions regarding Ring & Co.'s merchandise. See n. 25 below. Regarding the postponement of trials, and the hardship that this placed on detained witnesses, see Davis, *Trials of the Earth*, 173–174, as well as the letter George wrote to the editor of the *Sunflower Tocsin*, quoted in Chap. 39, pp. 296–297.

9   *Vicksburg Daily Times*, Nov. 16, 1874, p. 4: "Weather cloudy today, with a slight fall

of rain."

10 *Vicksburg Daily Times*, Nov. 17, 1874, p. 4.

11 Description of the interior of the courthouse is based on Cotton, *The Old Court House*, passim, and inspections made by the author during research trips, 1986–1999. The courtroom today is substantially the same as it was in 1874.

12 Garner, *Reconstruction in Mississippi*, 234, 285.

13 The author's extensive research on nineteenth-century families indicates that the era was astoundingly litigious, although the same may also be said for the seventeenth and eighteenth centuries as well.

14 *George F. Ring v. Charles E. Wright*, Cases 337 and 339, *Minutes of the Circuit Court of Issaquena County*, Nov. Term 1865, Book B: 282, and May Term 1866, Book B: 333–335, in the courthouse in Mayersville.

15 "C. E. Wright" entry, 1860 U.S. Census, Slave Schedules, Issaquena County, Mississippi, p. 75; National Archives micropublication M653, roll 598.

16 *George F. Ring and Catherine Ring, his wife, v. Steamer R. E. Lee*, Case 934, June Term 1870, U.S. District Court, Southern District of Mississippi; Records of the District Courts of the United States, RG 21; National Archives—Southeast Region, East Point, Georgia.

17 This decision was reported. See *Federal Cases* (St. Paul: West Publishing Co., 1895), Book 20, Case No. 11,690, pp. 519–520. The *Robert E. Lee* is entry 4777 in Way, *Way's Packet Directory*, 395–397. This was the very time—June 30–July 4, 1870—when the *Robert E. Lee* raced the *Natchez* up the Mississippi River from New Orleans to St. Louis, and won (see Twain, *Life on the Mississippi*, 117–118).

18 See, for example: *Ring & Muller v. Jesse Palmer*, Case 529, Circuit Court of Issaquena County (Dec. Term 1872); *Frederick Glass v. Ring & Muller*, Case 2565, Circuit Court of Warren County (Spring Term 1874); *Ring & Muller v. Donahoe & Byrnes*, Case 991, Circuit Court of Warren County (Spring Term 1874); *Martin S. Carpenter v. Roach & Ring*, Case 2549, Circuit Court of Warren County (Spring Term 1874); and *George F. Ring v. Alfred Williams, E. F. Williams, and Leigh Clark*, Case 84, Chancery Court of Sharkey County, Rolling Fork (Dec. 1883); in the courthouse in Rolling Fork.

19 Based on author's inspection of numerous nineteenth-century Mississippi circuit court docket books and newspapers.

20 *Geo. F. Ring, Guardian, v. Liverpool, London & Globe Insurance Co.*, Case 1768, U.S. Circuit Court, Southern District of Mississippi; Records of the District Courts of the United States, RG 21; National Archives—Southeast Region, East Point, Georgia.

21 *Geo. F. Ring, Surviving Partner, v. Franklin Fire Insurance Co.*, Case 2573, Circuit Court of Warren County, Vicksburg; in the attic of the courthouse in Vicksburg.

22 *Geo. F. Ring, Surviving Partner, v. Great Western Mutual Insurance Co.*, Case 2645, Circuit Court of Warren County, Vicksburg; no separate packet for this case has been found. See n. 25 below.

23 *Geo. F. Ring, Surviving Partner, v. Mechanics & Traders Insurance Co.*, Case 2644, Circuit Court of Warren County, Vicksburg; no separate packet for this case has been found. See n. 25 below.

24 *Geo. F. Ring, Surviving Partner, v. Franklin Fire Insurance Co.*, Case 2572, Circuit Court of Warren County, Vicksburg; in the attic of the courthouse in Vicksburg.

25 The suits against Great Western Mutual and Mechanics & Traders, which were

originally filed as two distinct cases, were combined (probably on Nov. 13, 1874) into the Franklin suit, Case 2573. All three actions sued on policies on the same merchandise, and the documents contained in the packet for Case 2573—including George's original statement, copies of the policies, and penciled courtroom testimony—include repeated reference to all three policies. Combining the three actions into a single trial makes sense, as they would have required the same witnesses, evidence, etc.; the issues were intimately intertwined. Therefore, only *two* Ring & Co. trials were heard in the Circuit Court of Warren County on Nov. 17–18, 1874, one regarding the merchandise, the other regarding the building. In this chapter, for clarity and brevity, these two trials are recounted as a single event, and all description of the proceedings, unless otherwise noted, is based on the contents of the two Franklin packets, Cases 2572 and 2573.

26 See Chap. 19.

27 *Geo. F. Ring, Guardian, v. Liverpool, London & Globe Insurance Co.*, Case 1768, U.S. Circuit Court, Southern District of Mississippi.

28 *Vicksburg Daily Times*, Nov. 17, 1874, p. 4.

29 The packets of Cases 2572 and 2573 contain transcriptions in pencil of the testimony of George and Chamberlin, but no transcriptions of the testimony of the 18 witnesses. The identities of the witnesses are based on the executed subpeonas and pay vouchers in the packets.

30 No biographical facts have been found for Hosey McMurray. This obscurity suggests that he may have been a member of the poor and transient white class.

31 "Eatman, E. C." household, 1870 U.S. Census, Issaquena County (Schola Precinct), Mississippi, p. 286; National Archives micropublication M593, roll 731: "25, male, white, Farmer, [no real estate], $1000 [personal estate], [born] Mississippi, [cannot read, cannot write columns are *not* checked];" lives alone.

32 Assumption based on their race and probability.

33 "Williams, Alfred" household, 1870 U.S. Census, Issaquena County (Rolling Fork Precinct), Mississippi, p. 256; National Archives micropublication M593, roll 731: "47, male, black, farm laborer, [no real or personal property], [born] Mississippi, [cannot read, cannot write columns *are* checked];" with wife and children. (There is another Alfred Williams listed in Skipwith Precinct, p. 317—"35, male, black, farm laborer, [no real or personal property], [born] Mississippi, [cannot read, cannot write columns *are* checked];" with wife and children in the home of "Aunt Jastha," a 70-year-old black woman—but his distance from Rolling Fork Landing makes this Alfred Williams much less likely to be the one summoned to George's trials.)

34 There is no Joseph Robertson listed in Issaquena County in the 1870 Census. He must have come into the county between the enumeration and the disaster of Mar. 4, 1873.

35 "Marshal, Bob" household, 1870 U.S. Census, Issaquena County (Schola Precinct), Mississippi, p. 286; National Archives micropublication M593, roll 731: "60, male, black, farm laborer, [no real or personal estate], [born] South Carolina, [cannot read, cannot write columns *are* checked];" with wife.

36 "Rushing, Bryant" household, 1870 U.S. Census, Issaquena County (Schola Precinct), Mississippi, p. 286; National Archives micropublication M593, roll 731: "63, male, black, farm laborer, [no real or personal estate], [born] North Carolina, [cannot read, cannot write columns *are* checked];" with wife.

37 "Tubberville, Joe" household, 1870 U.S. Census, Issaquena County (Schola Precinct), Mississippi, p. 287; National Archives micropublication M593, roll 731: "30, male, black, farm laborer, [no real or personal estate], [born] Mississippi, [cannot read, cannot write columns *are* checked];" with wife and children.

38 Assumption based on the 1870 census: Bryant Rushing is listed five lines below W. I. Chaney (p. 286), and Joe Tubberville is listed two lines below Wm. B. McQuillen (p. 287).

39 Summons in the packet of Case 2573: ". . . Bob Marshall, on Dr. Moore's place . . . ."

40 Also summoned from Isssaquena County but not found by Sheriff Henry P. Scott: J. W. Parberry, John Paradise, R. Y. Alexander and Henry Brown.

41 *Vicksburg Daily Times*, Nov. 18, 1874, p. 4.

42 No biographical facts have been found for Dr. Henry S. Fischel.

43 Gordon Cotton, *Asbury: A History* (Vicksburg: the author, 1994), Chapter X, "The Nailers," 136–146.

44 Charles Riles, *Through Open Gates: History, Symbolisms, and Legends of Vicksburg's Cedar Hill Cemetery* (Jackson: Hederman Brothers, 1989), 84; and Mary Lois Ragland, transcriber, *R. V. Booth, Private Memoranda*, a typescript in the Old Court House Museum, Vicksburg, I: 1; and Dunbar Rowland, Mississippi, III: 63.

45 No biographical facts have been found for this Wesley D. Night.

46 Also summoned from Warren County but not found by Sheriff Peter Crosby: Ceb Smith of the Steamer *Lizzie*, with books for trip no. 26—Nov. 1872.

47 Minutes of the Circuit Court of Warren County for Nov. 18, 1874, show that George's cases were not the last to be heard.

48 *Vicksburg Daily Times*, Nov. 19, 1874, p. 4.

49 Ibid.

50 *George F. Ring v. The Franklin Fire Insurance Co.*, Case 3005, Circuit Court of Warren County, Vicksburg (Spring 1875); in the attic of the courthouse in Vicksburg.

51 *George F. Ring v. The Franklin Fire Insurance Co.*, Case 3006, Circuit Court of Warren County, Vicksburg (Spring 1875); in the attic of the courthouse in Vicksburg.

52 All description of the proceedings of these two suits, unless otherwise noted, is based on the contents of the two packets, Cases 3005 and 3006.

53 Minute Book of the Supreme Court of Mississippi, Oct. Term 1876, p. 21; Supreme Court Clerk, Jackson: "Wednesday, November 22nd 1876 . . . #1653, Franklin Fire Ins Co vs George W. Ring . . . ." The cases had been assigned the docket numbers of 1653 and 1654. For the Supreme Court's dismissal of #1654, see p. 20 of the Minute Book. The reader is reminded that, for clarity and brevity, the two suits are recounted in this chapter as a single event. The Mississippi Department of Archives and History, Jackson, has a microfilm copy of the Minute Book.

54 There is no further record of them.

55 See, for example: *Fannie E. Gaunt & William Gaunt (her husband) & Ellen E. Hinman & B. B. Hinman (her husband) v. George Ring*, Case 2245, U.S. Circuit Court, Southern District of Mississippi (Fall Term 1875), and *Katharina Ring et al. v. Barbara Ring et al.*, Case 299, U.S. Circuit Court, Southern District of Mississippi (Spring Term 1881), and *August, Bernheim & Bauer v. George F. Ring*, Case 3184, U.S. Circiut Court, Southern District of Mississippi (Fall Term 1884); Records of the District Courts of the United States, RG 21; National Archives—

Southeast Region, East Point, Georgia.

56　"W. M. Chamblin" household, 1880 U.S. Census, Warren County (Vicksburg, Fourth Ward), Mississippi, p. 426; National Archives micropublication T9, roll 667: "Insurance Agt." See also n. 57 below.

57　*Vicksburg City Directory for 1877* (Vicksburg: A. C. Tuttle, 1877), 82: "Chamberlin, Wm M., Ins. Agt., 167 Washington, res. es. Locust, bet. Jackson and Open Woods." Also *Vicksburg Daily Commercial*, 1881, passim: "1868. Established 1868./ W.M.CHAMBERLIN,/ General Insurance Agent,/ Fire, River and Marine./ Represents the/ [five insurers with assets listed]/All kinds of desirable risks, in city or country, solicited. Gin Houses, Saw Mills, Country/ Stores and Dwellings written,/ [three more lines of text]/ Office over Baum & Co's. VICKSBURG, MISS." and *Vicksburg Evening Post*, 1883, passim: "W. M. Chamberlin / General Insurance Agent / FIRE, MARINE, ACCIDENT AND LIFE./ Office—Up-stairs, cor. Washington and Crawford Sts., Vicksburg."

37. BUSINESS

1　That the Webers traveled with the Rings is assumption. Hank appears in the *Cincinnati City Directory for 1874* (Cincinnati: Williams & Co., 1874), 926, published probably in early spring: "Weber, Henry, grocer, Highland Av., Corryville." (This is identical to the entry in the 1873 directory.) He does *not* appear in the *Cincinnati City Directory for 1875*. The earliest documentation of Hank's return to Vicksburg dates from when he signed as witness the original copy of "Mr. Joseph Ring, In a/c with Geo. F. Ring," Feb. 18, 1874, a financial statement prepared by George for Barbara, listing expenditures and credits, Oct. 15, 1868–July 25, 1873, marked "Copy" and not in George's hand. Passed from Joseph Nicholas Ring to his son Louis Caffall Ring, who photocopied it for the author in 1985. Four months after Hank signed this statement, a daughter of his and Lena's was baptized in Vicksburg: Baptismal record of Mary Magdalena Weber, June 17, 1874 (born May 9, 1874); *Baptismal Register* 2: 109, St. Paul's R. C. Church. Finally, five months later, on Nov. 18, 1874, Hank endorsed two pay vouchers for witnesses at George's trials who could only make their mark; see packets of Cases 2572 and 2573, Circuit Court of Warren County, Vicksburg.

2　For the importance of family members to business enterprises in the post-war Delta, see Willis, *On the New South Frontier*, 176–177.

3　All description of the Panic of 1873 in this chapter, unless otherwise noted, is based on Foner, *Reconstruction*, 512–524.

4　"The Cotton Factor," in Dethloff and Pusateri, eds., *American Business History*, 115.

5　See Willis, *On the New South Frontier*, 97–98.

6　Ibid., 98.

7　Ibid., 99–104. See also the many notices of bankruptcy in the *Vicksburg Daily Times* and *The Daily Vicksburger*, 1874, passim.

8　*The Daily Vicksburger*, 1874, passim.

9　See Willis, *On the New South Frontier*, 73–74.

10　Hemphill, *Fevers, Floods and Faith*, 29 (map) and 91–92.

11　Ibid., 371. See deed books and plat maps of Sunflower County, Township 19, Range 5 West, in the courthouse in Indianola.

12　Township 20, Range 6 West: lots 9 and 15 in Section 22 (80 acres); lots 1, 2, 3, 6 and 7 in Section 26 (202 acres); west half of southwest quarter of Section 23 (80 acres); and lots 52 and 59 of Block "K" in Shaw (1 acre). See deed books and plat maps of Bolivar County in the courthouse in Cleveland.

13   "Mrs. Barbara Ring, in a/c with Geo. F. Ring, For the settlement of the Estate of the late Jos. Ring Deceased," dated Buffalo, Oct. 9, 1893, a statement of "Interest 10% per Annum, a/c from Aug 1st 1873 to Aug 1st 1893," and other related financial papers and promissory notes made out to Barbara from George to terminate his obligations to her. Passed from Joseph Nicholas Ring to his son Louis Caffall Ring, who photocopied them for the author in 1985.

14   See Chap. 39, p. 299 and nn. 31 and 36.

15   Estate of Jesse Moore, Issaquena County probate file no. 26, County Clerk's Office, Mayersville.

16   See n. 13 above. George collected 10 percent of the value of Joe's estate every year that he handled it.

17   George's statement, p. 13: "I administered on the estate of William Jeans. Sold some little personal property. His plantation was under mortgage and sold by the mortgagor. The sale paid the debt, and I collected about $5,000 of that sale."

18   Letter from Elizabeth Weber Hilberg to Joseph N. Kellas, Feb. 11, 1958; photocopy in author's possession.

19   Testimony of Thomas Marshall Miller (Parker's attorney), June 19, 1876, "Boutwell Report," I: 669.

20   Testimony of W. D. Brown, June 22, 1876, "Boutwell Report," I: 717.

21   Ibid., 708 and 716.

22   Testimony of Thomas Marshall Miller, June 19, 1876, "Boutwell Report," I: 669.

23   "Boutwell Report." All description of the events narrated in this chapter, unless noted otherwise, is based on this report.

24   Testimony of H. P. Scott, June 10, 1876, "Boutwell Report," I: 591–592.

25   Ibid., 589, and testimony of W. D. Brown, p. 718, and testimony of Bowie Foreman, p. 601.

26   Testimony of Thomas Marshall Miller, June 19, 1876, "Boutwell Report," I: 668.

27   Testimony of H. P. Scott, June 10, 1876, "Boutwell Report," I: 598.

28   Ibid., 590. See also Foner, *Reconstruction*, 562.

29   Testimony of W. D. Brown, June 22, 1876, "Boutwell Report," I: 695.

30   Ibid., 696.

31   That Parker was among those arrested and detained is evident from the later statement that he was among those who escaped.

32   Testimony of W. D. Brown, June 22, 1876, "Boutwell Report," I: 696.

33   Ibid., 701. See also Harris, *The Day of the Carpetbagger*, 375–378.

34   Testimony of Bowie Foreman, June 16, 1876, "Boutwell Report," I: 600.

35   Two months earlier, Ames had indeed ordered 1,000 Springfield breechloaders to arm the state militia he was forming to ensure a fair and peaceful election on Nov. 2nd. These are the arms he later locked in storage. Perhaps this public action gave credence to the rumor that the blacks of Issaquena County were receiving arms in secret from the governor, and that those arms were coming from the North.

36   For the scant biographical facts known about Colonel Ball, see testimony of Thomas Marshall Miller (Parker's attorney), June 19, 1876, "Boutwell Report," I: 671, 679.

37   Testimony of W. D. Brown, June 22, 1876, "Boutwell Report," I: 712.

38   Ibid., 698.

39   Foner, *Freedom's Lawmakers*, 190.

40   *Cincinnati City Directory for 1876* (Cincinnati: Williams & Co., 1876), 988: "Weber
      Henry, b.k. [bookkeeper] 13 W. 7th, h. 1080 Vine." This *may* be Hank. *Cincinnati
      City Directory for 1877* (Cincinnati: Williams & Co., 1877), 1021: "Weber Henry,
      lab. [laborer], h. 1084 Vine, Corryville." This is *definitely* Hank, as it is repeated
      verbatim in the 1878 directory, and compares perfectly with: "Weber, Henry"
      household, 1880 U.S. Census, Hamilton County (Cincinnati, 12th Ward), Ohio,
      Enumeration District 148, Sheet 5; National Archives micropublication T9, roll
      1026.

41   In 1893 the Webers moved back to Buffalo, where they stayed. See Buffalo city
      directories and the 1900 U.S. Census for Buffalo.

42   George's statement, p. 4. See deed books of Sharkey County in the courthouse in
      Rolling Fork.

43   *Biographical and Historical Memoirs of Mississippi*, I: 203–204; also Walker, *800-
      Sharkey County-General Information and Points of Interest*, 5.

44   *Biographical and Historical Memoirs of Mississippi*, I: 203.

45   Chapman and Battaile, *Picturesque Vicksburg*, 29–30. See references to this in
      Twain, *Life on the Mississippi*, 14 and 214.

46   Rowland, *History of Mississippi*, I: 214–217.

47   Jacob L. Schwink tombstone, Division C, Square 142, Lot 2, Cedar Hill Cemetery,
      Vicksburg: "Died of yellow fever Aug. 23, 1878."

48   Probate file of Jacob Schwink, Warren County Probate file no. 3079, County
      Clerk's office, Vicksburg.

38. NICHOLAS

1   John Miller household, 1875 New York State Census, Erie County (Buffalo,
      Seventh Ward), New York, p. 121; microfilm at the Buffalo and Erie County Public
      Library. John Miller was living at this time in his house at 15, not 11, Cherry. Also
      Buffalo City Directory for 1875 (Buffalo: The Courier Co., 1875), 559: "Ring,
      Barbara, wid. h. r. [house rear] 15 Cherry."

2   The 1875 New York State Census, 1880 U.S. Census, and Buffalo city directories
      continue to list John Miller as mason or bricklayer, never retired, until he died in
      1885.

3   Photograph in author's possession.

4   Censuses and city directories show the appearance and disappearance of John
      Miller's children and grandchildren in his three houses at 11, 13 and 15 Cherry
      Street.

5   See n. 1 above.

6   Photograph of George F. Ring with his class at St. Michael's, taken about 1876;
      also Barbara Ring household, 1880 U.S. Census, Erie County (Buffalo, Seventh
      Ward, 11 Cherry Street), New York, Enumeration District 148, p. 273; National
      Archives micropublication T9, roll 830: "Attended school within the Census year"
      checked for George (aged 13) and John (10). It is assumed that Nicholas had
      attended the same parish school.

7   Thomas E. Harney, *Canisius College, The First Nine Years, 1870–1879* (New York:
      Vantage Press, 1971), 255: "Ring, Joseph, Buffalo, N.Y., 77–78." The reader is

reminded that Nicholas's full name was Joseph Nicholas Ring. His middle name is used in this work to avoid confusing him with his father, also named Joseph.

8   Barbara Ring household, 1880 U.S. Census: "Ring Joseph [Nicholas] . . . 15 . . . cabinet maker." Also Buffalo city directories: 1881, "Ring Joseph [aged 16], finisher, b. [boards] 11 Cherry;" 1882, "Ring George F. [aged 15], h. 11 Cherry;" 1884, "Ring, George F. [aged 17], wks. 92 Pearl, b. 11 Cherry" and "Egloff, Peter [varnisher and cabinet maker, Barbara's brother-in-law], wks. 92 Pearl, h. 19 Cherry;" 1887, "Ring, George F., finisher, w. A. Cutler & Son, h. 11 Cherry."

9   *Buffalo City Directory for 1886* (Buffalo: The Courier Co., 1886), 780: "Ring John [aged 16], upholsterer, wks. 13 Front ave. b. 11 Cherry;" and *Buffalo City Directory for 1890* (Buffalo: The Courier Co., 1890), 819: "Ring, John M., upholsterer, wrks. 42 Eagle, h. 11 Cherry."

10 "Mr. Joseph Ring, In a/c with Geo. F. Ring," February 18, 1874, a financial statement prepared by George for Barbara, listing expenditures and credits, Oct. 15, 1868–July 25, 1873, marked "Copy" and not in George's hand. Passed from Joseph Nicholas Ring to his son Louis Caffall Ring, who photocopied it for the author in 1985.

11 Miscellaneous financial papers of Barbara's, dated 1890 and 1893, passed from Joseph Nicholas Ring to his son Louis Caffall Ring, who photocopied them for the author in 1985.

12 See nn. 8 and 9 above.

13 Buffalo city directories, 1875–77: "Ring, Barbara, wid., h. r. 15 Cherry;" and 1878–92: "Ring, Barbara, wid., h. 11 Cherry."

14 Baptismal record of Joseph Alexander Egloff, December 22, 1878 (born December 13, 1878); *Taufen, 1851–1882*: 360, St. Michael's R. C. Church, Buffalo, New York; *Microfilmed Records of Buffalo Parishes*, roll 281, Buffalo and Erie County Public Library.

15 See works cited in Chap. 8, n. 1.

16 "Local Matters," "Our Jubilee. The Semi-Centennial of Buffalo. Exercises at St. James Hall on Monday Evening. Historical Address by the Hon. E. Carlton Sprague. Remarks by Mayor Cleveland—Letters of Regret from Prominent Citizens, &c., &c., &c.," *Buffalo Commercial Advertiser*, July 5, 1882, p. 4.

17 Ibid.

18 Ibid.

19 See works cited in Chap. 8, n. 1.

20 Ibid.

21 Louis Caffall Ring to the author, November 25, 1985.

22 Physical traits of the Ring brothers are taken from: (1) Joseph Nicholas Ring: five photographs, ca. 1882–ca. 1916, copies in author's possession, and descriptions in letters from his son, Louis Caffall Ring, to the author, 1985–86; (2) George F. Ring: four photographs, ca. 1876, 1882 and 1904, originals in author's possession; and (3) John M. Ring: physical descriptions in *Registers of Enlistments in the United States Army*, 1798–1914, National Archives micropublication M233, roll 54, and in the pension file of his widow, Mary Emma Ring, Philippine Insurrection, Certificate 861,644, in custody of the Veterans Administration. Character traits of the Ring brothers are taken from: (1) Joseph Nicholas Ring: letters and remembrances of his son, Louis Caffall Ring, shared with the author, 1985–86; and (2) George F. Ring: recollection of the author's grandmother, Frances Noeth Ring,

regarding what she had heard from her husband, George John Ring, who was George F. Ring's son.

23 See Chap. 9, n. 3.

24 Louis Caffall Ring, letters and interviews with the author, 1985–86.

25 "Form for the Physical Examination of a Recruit," dated August 4, 1900, in the pension file of John Ring's widow, Mary Emma Ring, Philippine Insurrection, Certificate 861,644, in custody of the Veterans Administration.

26 Supposition, since trains were replacing steamboats by this time.

39. Saints Rest

1 Supposition, since trains were replacing steamboats by this time.

2 Photographs of Joseph Nicholas Ring, son of Joseph Ring, and George John Ring and Louis Caffall Ring, grandsons of Joseph Ring, show that the Ring men, by their fifties, were stout and graying.

3 It is unthinkable that a planter in Sunflower County in 1881 would *not* own at least one dog, and very likely several. That George's dog was a Labrador retriever, however, is supposition.

4 Letter from Louis Caffall Ring to the author, Nov. 22, 1985.

5 Ibid. Joseph Nicholas Ring spent his entire adult life in the Delta, dying in Greenville in 1930. See letter from Louis Caffall Ring to the author, Nov. 22, 1985.

6 For history and description of the Delta, see Chap. 11, n. 1, most particularly Willis, *On the New South Frontier.*

7 See Twain, *Life on the Mississippi*, 145–146.

8 See Davis, ed., *Trials of the Earth, The Autobiography of Mary Hamilton*, passim.

9 Hemphill, *Fevers, Floods and Faith*, 106, 118, 123, 647.

10 Ibid., 115–116; also *Biographical and Historical Memoirs of Mississippi*, I: 712.

11 Willis, *On the New South Frontier*, 185.

12 Joseph Nicholas Ring was 16 years old from July 1, 1880, through June 30, 1881, and he was received by George at Saints Rest. The federal census of 1880 records that on June 12th of that year George and Catherine were still residing in Vicksburg. Records of the Post Office (see n. 14 below) indicate that George was residing at Saints Rest by January of 1882. However, it appears from Sunflower County records (see n. 13 below) that George was spending substantial amounts of time at Saints Rest before he moved there with his wife.

13 Hemphill, *Fevers, Floods and Faith*, 370.

14 "Saints Rest," entry, *Record of Appointment of Postmasters, 1832–Sept. 30, 1971*; Records of the Post Office Department, RG 28; National Archives micropublication M841, roll 69, Sunflower County, Miss.: "George F. Ring, 13 Jan. '82."

15 Hemphill, *Fevers, Floods and Faith*, 118.

16 Ibid.

17 Ibid.

18 Ibid.

19 Ibid., 119.

20 Ibid., 370.

21 Ibid., 601.

22 Newspaper clipping marked "3/6/1891," scrapbooks of William Richardson French, Indianola Public Library.

23 Newspaper clipping marked "1894," scrapbooks of William Richardson French,

Indianola Public Library.

24 Hemphill, *Fevers, Floods and Faith*, 371.

25 Ibid.; also Mrs. James Holmes McWilliams, "Holly Ridge, Mississippi," a three-page typescript dated March 14, 1974; photocopied for the author in 1994 by James C. Robertson, then owner of Saints Rest Plantation. The author thanks Mr. Robertson for sharing his historical materials regarding Holly Ridge and Saints Rest, and for his gracious hospitality during the author's research trips of 1994 and 1999.

26 Hemphill, *Fevers, Floods and Faith*, 426.

27 See, for example, the deed books of Bolivar County in the courthouse in Cleveland.

28 "Personal," *Vicksburg Evening Post*, March 5, 1898, p. 4.

29 Hemphill, *Fevers, Floods and Faith*, 370; also McWilliams, "Holly Ridge, Mississippi," 1.

30 "Jeans, B. F." entry, 1880 U.S. census, Sunflower County ("All West Sunflower River"), Mississippi, p. 14; National Archives micropublication T9, roll 665: "21, single, Agent." The George W. Faison household appears on p. 18.

31 Ibid.

32 Besides the evidence discussed in this chapter, a holographic will written by George on August 24, 1887, was signed by B. F. Jeans as witness. See Warren County probate file no. 4350, filed Aug. 25, 1902, County Clerk's Office, Warren County, Mississippi.

33 "Jeans, B. F." entry (#626), Sunflower County 1885 Personal Tax Roll; Record Group 29, microcopy roll 464, Mississippi Department of Archives and History, Jackson: "Where did you reside last year?—Bolivar County. Where do you reside this year?—Geo. F. Ring's."

34 "Sunrise" entry, *Record of Appointment of Postmasters, 1832–Sept. 30, 1971*; Records of the Post Office Department, RG 28; National Archives micropublication M841, roll 67, Bolivar County, Mississippi: "Benj. F. Jeanes, 10 Jan. '84." Name changed to "Shawsburgh" by Mar. 9, 1886, and finally to "Shaw" by May 11, 1886.

35 B. F. Jeans-Pauline Ring marriage record, Feb. 21, 1884, Washington County Marriage Book 7 (colored): 139; County Clerk's Office, Greenville, Mississippi. Entering the record into the "colored" volume was obviously an oversight on the part of the county clerk. Regarding Pauline Ring see Chap. 8, nn. 6 and 14.

36 W. R. Hackett-"Elizabeth" Jeans marriage record, Aug. 12, 1884, Warren County Marriage Book I: 145; County Clerk's Office, Vicksburg, Mississippi. See also "Mr. and Mrs. W. R. Hackett Celebrate Golden Wedding Anniversary on Tomorrow," *Vicksburg Evening Post*, Aug. 11, 1934, p. 8: ". . . In the old Ring home in Springfield on the afternoon of August 12, 1884, Will R. Hackett, a young employee in the old Vicksburg Bank took for his bride Miss Elizabeth M. Jeanes, formerly of Rolling Fork . . . ."

37 Telephone interview with Missouri Jeans Hackett's daughter-in-law, Mrs. Chester Hackett, in 1993, by Mary Lois Ragland (on behalf of John Davis, a Jeans descendant), shared with the author by John Davis in a letter of April 24, 1994.

38 The description of Saints Rest given here is based on a map of the plantation dated August 1905 and evidently drawn for the new owner, Frank Binder, who called the place, "Prost Plantation." That name, however, seems never to have displaced

"Saints Rest." Today this map hangs in the dining room of James C. Robertson, former owner of Saints Rest, in Indianola, Mississippi.

39   Clinton I. Bagley, architectural historian, Jackson. The author thanks Clinton I. Bagley, a native of Greenville and a lecturer of many years on Mississippi history, for the many observations regarding Delta society, culture and architecture he shared eagerly with the curious Yankee author, 1986-1999. For an example of this type of Delta plantation house, see the description of George W. Faison's original residence in Hemphill, *Fevers, Floods and Faith*, 116.

40   "Ring, Geo. F." entry (#710), Sunflower County 1885 Personal Tax Roll; Record Group 29, microcopy roll 464, Mississippi Department of Archives and History, Jackson.

41   Ibid.

42   "Ring, Geo. F." entry, Sunflower County 1876 Personal Tax Roll; Record Group 29, microcopy roll 464, Mississippi Department of Archives and History, Jackson: ". . . 20 cattle . . . ;" also "Ring, Geo. F." entry, Sunflower County 1895 Personal Tax Roll; Record Group 29, microcopy roll 465, Mississippi Department of Archives and History, Jackson: ". . . 40 cattle . . . ."

43   "Ring, Geo. F." entry (#710), Sunflower County 1885 Personal Tax Roll; Record Group 29, microcopy roll 464, Mississippi Department of Archives and History, Jackson.

44   Ibid.

45   "Ring, Geo. F." entry (#710), Sunflower County 1885 Personal Tax Roll, enumerates 22 men residing on Saints Rest. Their families are not enumerated. Seven of these men reappear as residents of "St Rest" in: 1890 U.S. Census, "Special Schedule of Surviving Soldiers, Sailors, and Marines, and Widows, etc.," Sunflower County (Beats 2 & 3), Mississippi, pp. 2-4; National Archives micropublication M123, roll 26. All seven are listed as "Conf[ederate]" veterans. Also listed as "Conf." is George F. Ring. However, no military service record of any kind has been found for George.

46   See n. 38 above. The statistics are printed on the map.

47   Ibid.

48   On-site inspection by the author, and conversations with James C. Robertson on research trips, 1994 and 1999.

49   Ibid.

50   Catherine Ring died in Vicksburg on Feb. 21, 1912. See her obituary in the *Vicksburg Daily Herald*, Feb. 22, 1912, p. 6. See also her tombstone, Division A, Square 157, Cedar Hill Cemetery: "12 Feb. 1836–21 Feb. 1912." (Birthyear is wrong by eight years, as Catherine was born in 1828; see Chap. 2, n. 14.)

51   Letter of Louis Caffall Ring to the author, dated Nov. 22, 1985.

52   *Vicksburg Daily Commercial*, November 28, 1881, p. 4.

53   Hemphill, *Fevers, Floods & Faith*, 633–634.

54   The house alone would be spared once again during the catastrophic flood of 1927. Conversation with James C. Robertson during research trip of 1994.

55   Quoted in Hemphill, *Fevers, Floods and Faith*, 427.

56   See, for example, the quotation on p. 297.

57   See Chap. 15, n. 28.

58   See n. 33 above.

59   For character traits of Nicholas, see Chap. 38, n. 22.

60 "Josef Nicolaus Ring-Lena Caffall" marriage record, Apr. 20, 1892; *Register of Marriages, 1877–1912*: 11, St. Joseph's R. C. Church, Greenville, Mississippi.
61 "Bold Robbery," *Greenville Times*, Jan. 19, 1878, p. 1.

40. "A Dreadful Mystery"

1   "Resurrection of a Dreadful Mystery," *Vicksburg Daily Herald*, Aug. 21, 1883. The *Sunflower* is listed in Owens, *Steamboats and the Cotton Economy*, 181.
2   "Dead Men Tell No Tales," *Vicksburg Daily Herald*, Aug. 22, 1883.
3   "Joor, John S." entry, 1880 U.S. Census, Sharkey County (Enumeration District 115, Beat 3, Village of Rolling Fork), Mississippi, p. 138; National Archives micropublication T9, roll 664: "Sheriff." He was reelected in November 1881 for another two-year term.
4   See Chap. 24, pp. 187–189.
5   "Resurrection of a Dreadful Mystery," *Vicksburg Daily Herald*, Aug. 21, 1883.
6   Deduced from the chronology of the events reported in the *Vicksburg Daily Herald* in conjunction with the timetable of the steamer *Sunflower* as reported in the *Vicksburg Daily Commercial*, 1882, *passim*: "For Sunflower River. Steamer Sunflower leaves every Wednesday, at 4 p.m., going as high as navigation permits. Geo. W. Bookout, Master, E. C. Carroll, Supt., Geo. H. Smith, Clerk, W. S. Jones, Agent." No issues of the *Vicksburg Daily Herald* for 1883 could be found (see Prologue, n. 5). George used the steamer *Sunflower* regularly for travel between Saints Rest and Vicksburg; see for example: *Vicksburg Daily Commercial*, Feb. 6, 1882: "Arrived by the steamer Sunflower this morning: . . . Capt. Geo. F. Ring. . . ."
7   "Resurrection of a Dreadful Mystery," *Vicksburg Daily Herald*, Aug. 21, 1883.
8   For documentation on the Marsh and O'Neal families, see Ch. 24, nn. 7-18.
9   "Dead Men Tell No Tales," *Vicksburg Daily Herald*, Aug. 22, 1883.
10 Ibid.
11 Ibid.
12 "An Old Crime," *Greenville Times*, Aug. 25, 1883, p. 2. The author is indebted to Joseph T. Reilly, local historian *par excellence* of Greenville (recently deceased at the age of 89), for the invaluable research assistance he rendered with buoyant enthusiasm, and for his enlightening friendship, 1985–1999. Joseph Reilly, who resided for his entire life in the house where he was born (his sister Katherine, now 96, lives there still), knew the family of Joseph Nicholas Ring well, and was a life-long acquaintance of Louis Caffall Ring.
13 "Dead Men Tell No Tales," *Vicksburg Daily Herald*, Aug. 22, 1883.
14 See n. 6 above.
15 It is a logical assumption that George, eager to learn the outcome of Sheriff Joor's investigation, would have stopped in Rolling Fork on his way back up the Sunflower River to Saints Rest.
16 "The Rolling Fork Horror," *Vicksburg Daily Herald*, Aug. 25, 1883.
17 Ibid.
18 Ibid.
19 Ibid.
20 Ibid.
21 *Greenville Times*, Sept. 1, 1883, p. 3.
22 "The Rolling Fork Horror," *Vicksburg Daily Herald*, Aug. 25, 1883.
23 Walker, *800-Sharky County-General Information and Points of Interest*, 5.

24   Ibid.

25   Assumption; who would have taken the trouble to remove the ruins, and why?

26   "Rolling Fork Landing" entry, *Record of Appointment of Postmasters, 1832–Sept. 30, 1971*; Records of the Post Office Department, RG 28; National Archives micropublication M841, roll 67, Issaquena County, Mississippi: "A. Lloyd, 19 Jun. '71; discontinued 13 Nov. '73."

27   Joor's statement, p. 4.

28   See Chap. 3, pp. 20–22.

29   Ibid.

30   See Chap. 14, p. 118.

31   See Chap. 4, p. 27.

32   Ibid.

33   Joseph Ring entry, Mar. 19, 1873, *Ledger of Burials*, Fisher Funeral Home; in possession of Fisher-Riles Funeral Home, Vicksburg (photocopied for the author in 1991): "Remains of Joseph Ring, 42 years . . . ." Transcribed with minor errors in *Fisher Funeral Home Records*, II: 121, a typescript in the Old Court House Museum, Vicksburg. A thorough search of the record books and loose papers in the Issaquena County Courthouse, Mayersville, failed to disclose the original report.

34   George F. Ring died in Vicksburg on Aug. 20, 1902. See his obituary in the *Vicksburg Daily Herald*, Aug. 20, 1902, p. 6. See also his tombstone, Division A, Square 157, Cedar Hill Cemetery: "6 April 1833–20 Aug. 1902." (Birthyear is wrong by one year, as George was born in 1834; see Chap. 8, n. 5.)

EPILOGUE: GRANDMA RING

1   The current Sharkey County courthouse was built in 1902, and the current Issaquena County courthouse dates from about 1950.

2   *Delta and Homochitto National Forests* (U.S. Department of Agriculture, Forest Service, Southern Branch, 1983).

3   George's statement, p. 15.

4   See the Prologue, p. 3.

5   "An Atrocious Murder," *Vicksburg Daily Times*, Mar. 7, 1873, p. 3.

6   George's statement, p. 9.

7   See Davis, *Trials of the Earth*, 116.

8   Cost of a bottle of whiskey is estimated from historical currency conversion tables.

9   George's statement, p. 14.

10   This is a common characteristic of frame construction.

11   Testimony of W. D. Brown, June 22, 1876, "Boutwell Report," I: 718.

12   Ibid.

13   George's statement, p. 15.

14   Joor's statement, p. 4.

15   "Dead Men Tell No Tales," *Vicksburg Daily Herald*, Aug. 22, 1883.

16   Ibid.

17   Joor's statement, pp. 2–3.

18   George's statement, p. 7.

19   "The Rolling Fork Horror," *Vicksburg Daily Herald*, Aug. 25, 1883.

20   "To the Editor of the Daily Times," *Vicksburg Daily Times*, Mar. 19, 1873, p. 3.

21   Ibid.

22 George's statement, p. 15.

23 *George F. Ring v. The Franklin Fire Insurance Co.*, Case 3005, Circuit Court of Warren County, Vicksburg (Spring 1875); in the attic of the courthouse in Vicksburg.

24 Terrence E. Barr, P.A., Walter Reed Army Medical Center, Washington, D.C.

25 "To the Editor of the Daily Times," *Vicksburg Daily Times*, Mar. 19, 1873, p. 3.

26 See Chap. 23, p. 183.

27 George's statement, p. 8.

28 "River Intelligence," *Vicksburg Daily Times*, Mar. 7, 1873, p. 3.

29 Ibid., Mar. 11, 1873, p. 3.

30 See Chap. 23, p. 183.

31 George's statement, pp. 4–5.

32 See Owens, *Steamboats and the Cotton Economy*, 168: "Bluella . . . 74.75 [tons] . . . 86.2 [feet long] x 21.2 [feet wide] x 3.4 [feet deep]." The *B. H. Hurt* was comparable in size (p. 168); the *Lizzie* was twice as big (p. 175).

33 Barbara married a second time, a harness maker from Germany named Michael Forster who lived in her neighborhood in Buffalo, and they moved to Rochester, New York. See Michael Forster-Barbara Ring marriage record, May 31, 1891; *Marriage Register*, Saints Peter and Paul's R. C. Church, Rochester. Barbara died in Rochester in 1912, three months after the visit from her grandson and his bride. See her death notice in the *Rochester Union and Advertiser*, Nov. 25, 1912, p. 9. See also her tombstone, Section 13, Lot 118, Holy Sepulchre Cemetery: "Barbara Forster, 1841–1912." (Birth year is wrong by one year, as Barbara was born in 1840; see Chap. 8, n. 43.)

AUTHOR'S NOTE

Over the past 30 years, as the author made discoveries about Joe and George Ring and Barbara Miller, he published a number of short works narrating various parts of their story. Where information in this book differs from information contained in those earlier works, the present volume is to be considered the mature, more accurate version.